Phantom Tales
of the Night

CONTENTS

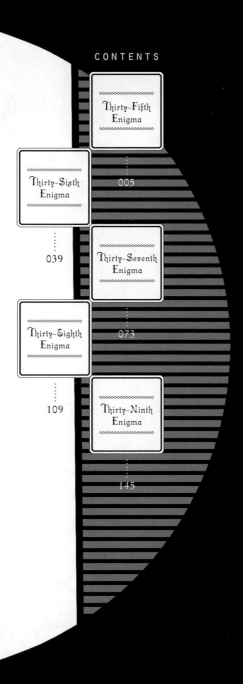

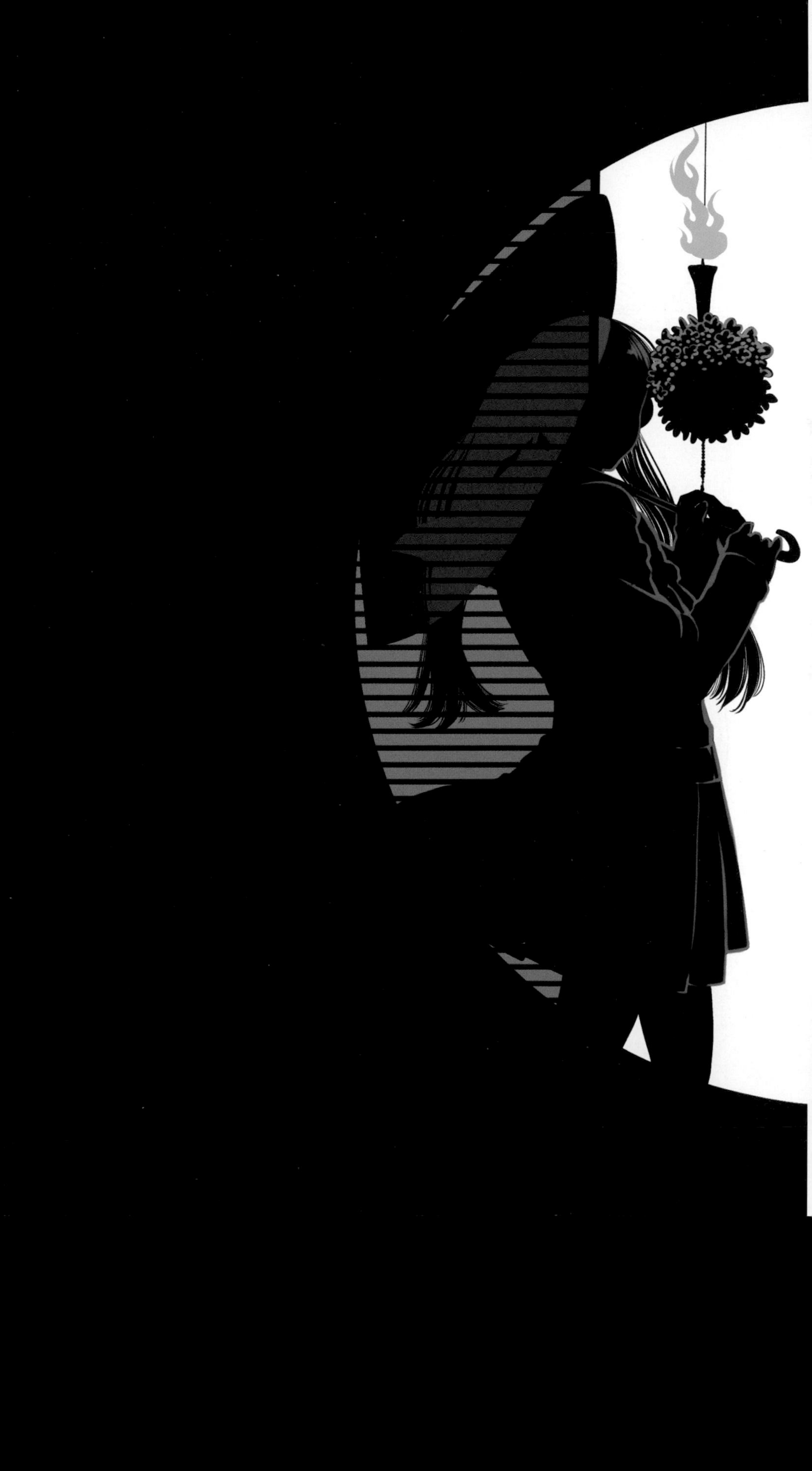

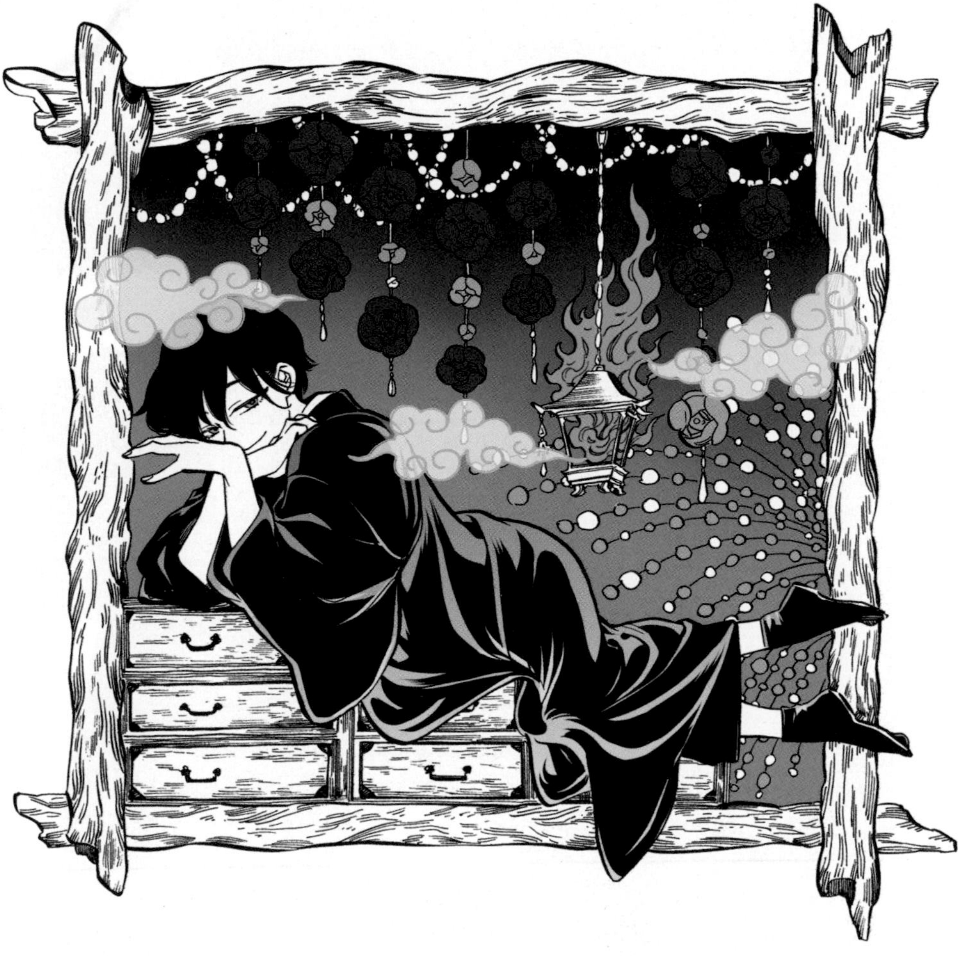

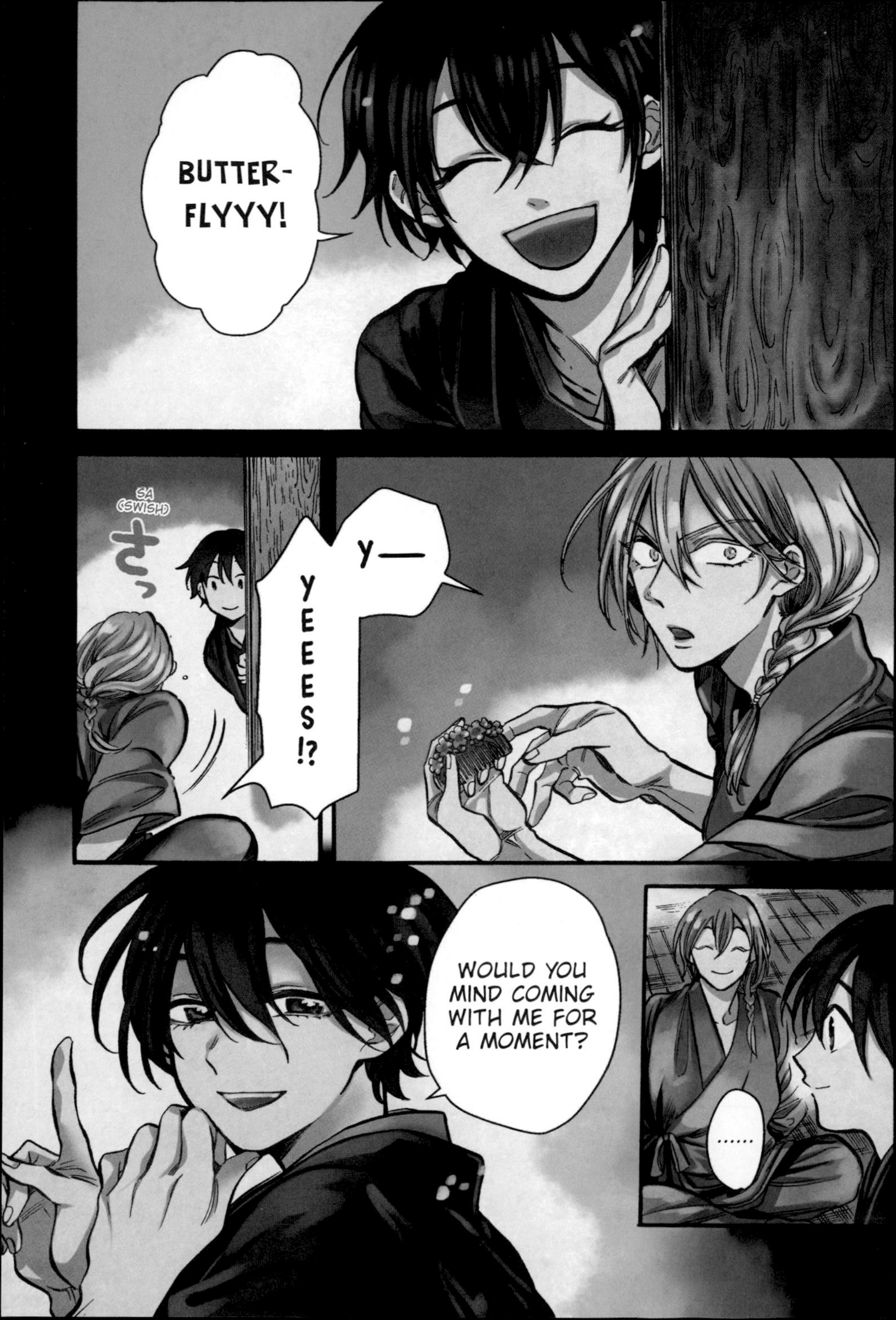
BUTTER-FLYYY!
Y—
YEEEES!?
SA (SWISH)
さっ
......
WOULD YOU MIND COMING WITH ME FOR A MOMENT?

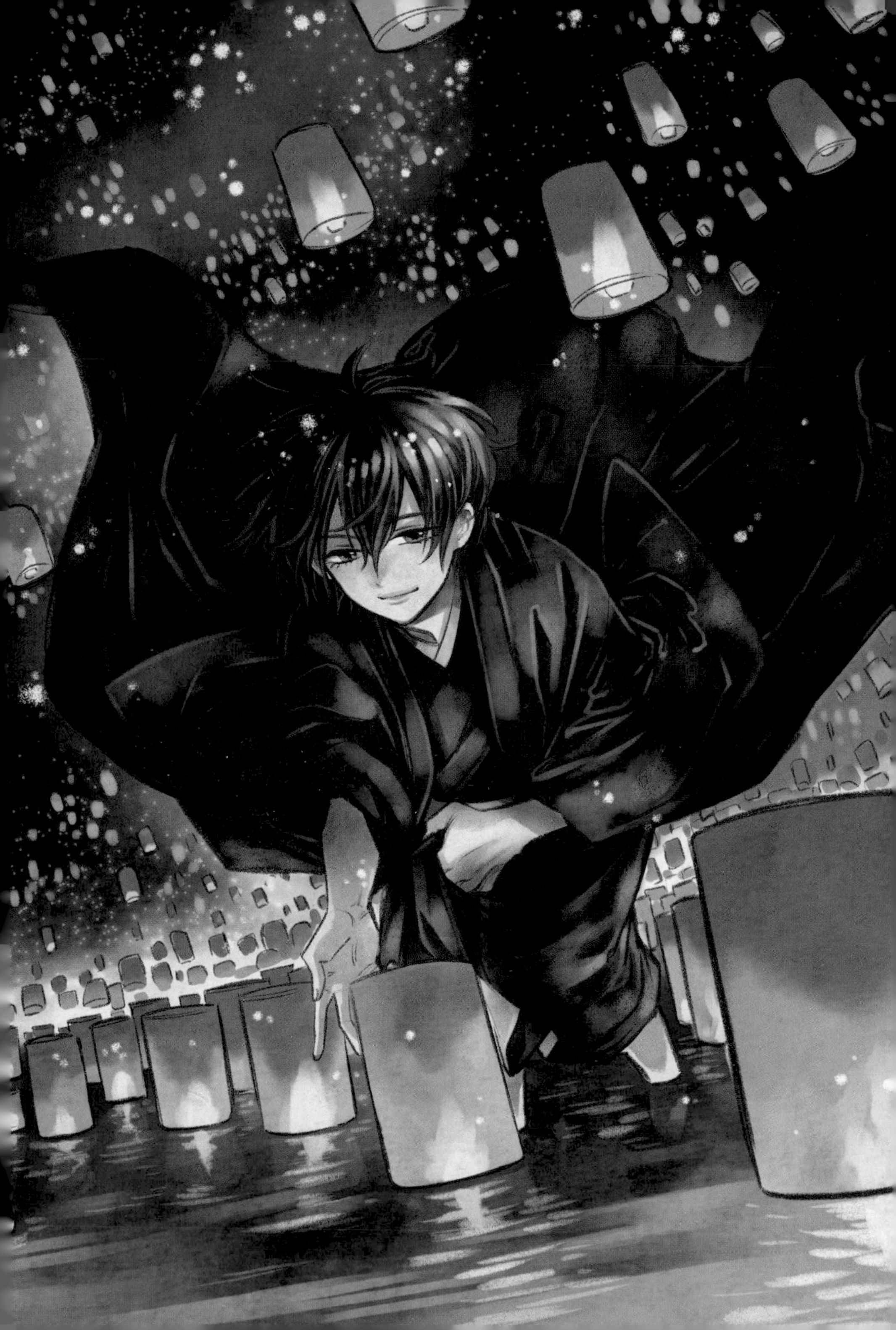

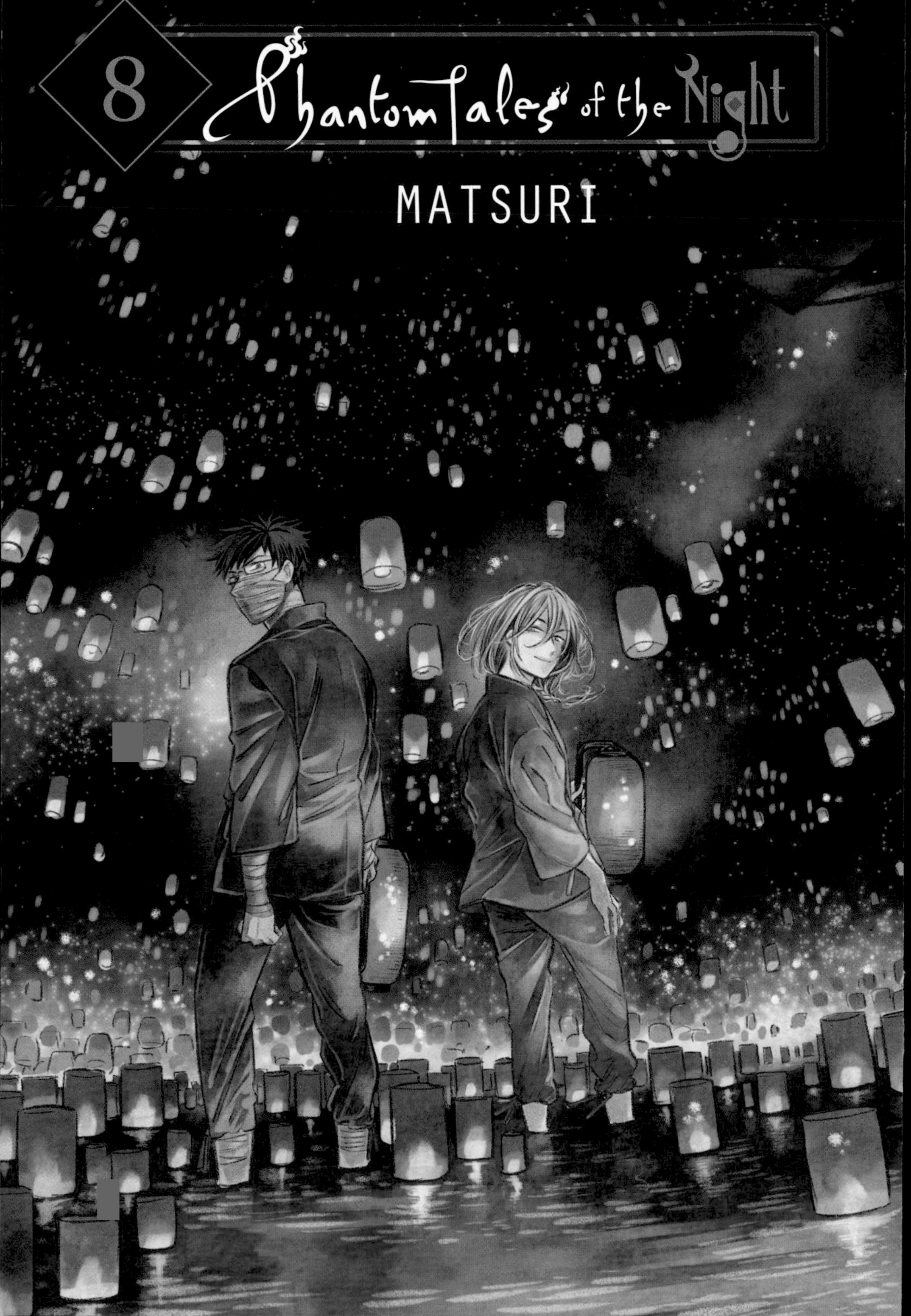
8
Phantom Tales of the Night
MATSURI

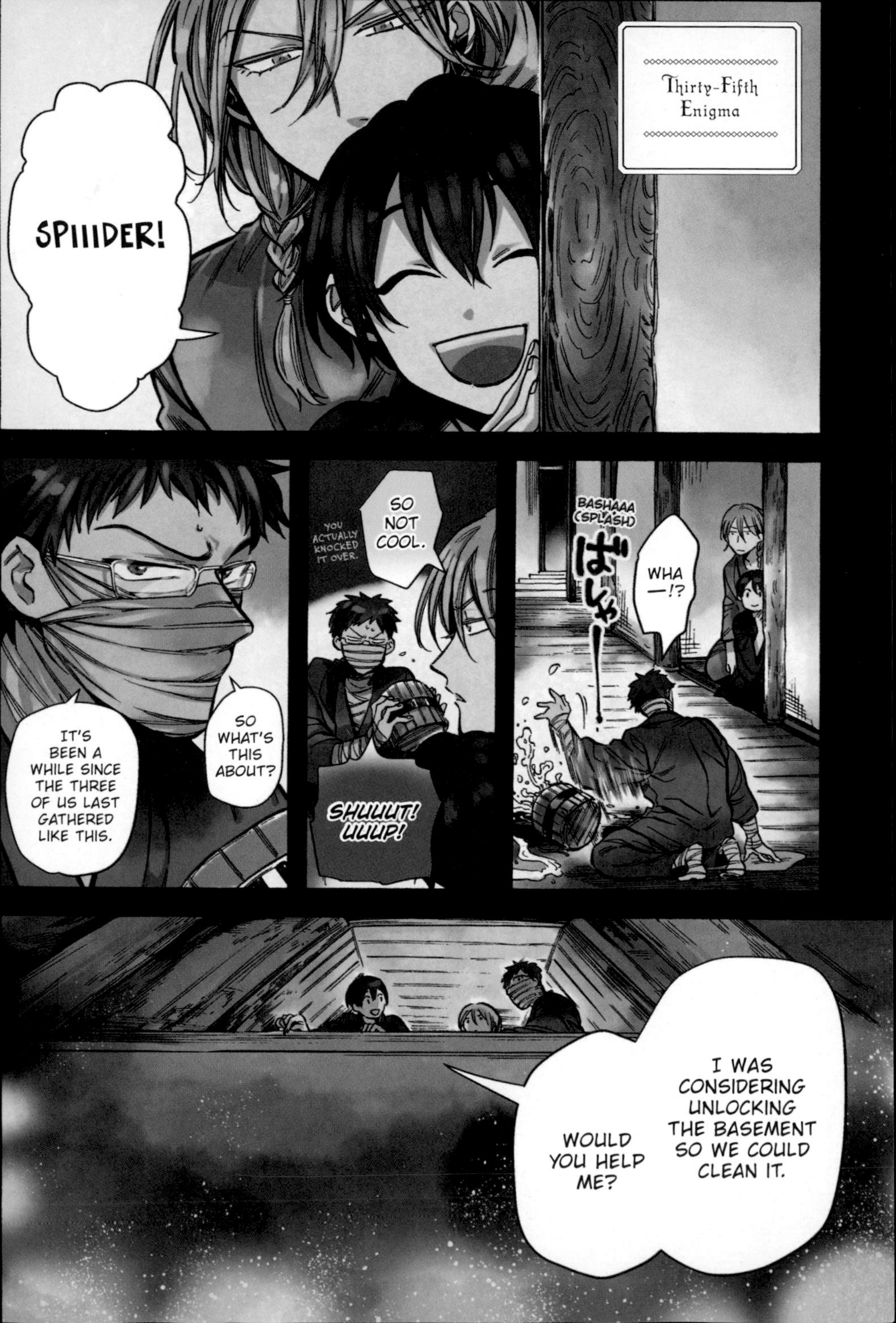
Thirty-Fifth Enigma
SPIIIDER!
BASHAAA (SPLASH) ばしゃ!
WHA—!?
SO NOT COOL.
YOU ACTUALLY KNOCKED IT OVER.
SHUUUT! UUUP!
SO WHAT'S THIS ABOUT?
IT'S BEEN A WHILE SINCE THE THREE OF US LAST GATHERED LIKE THIS.
I WAS CONSIDERING UNLOCKING THE BASEMENT SO WE COULD CLEAN IT.
WOULD YOU HELP ME?

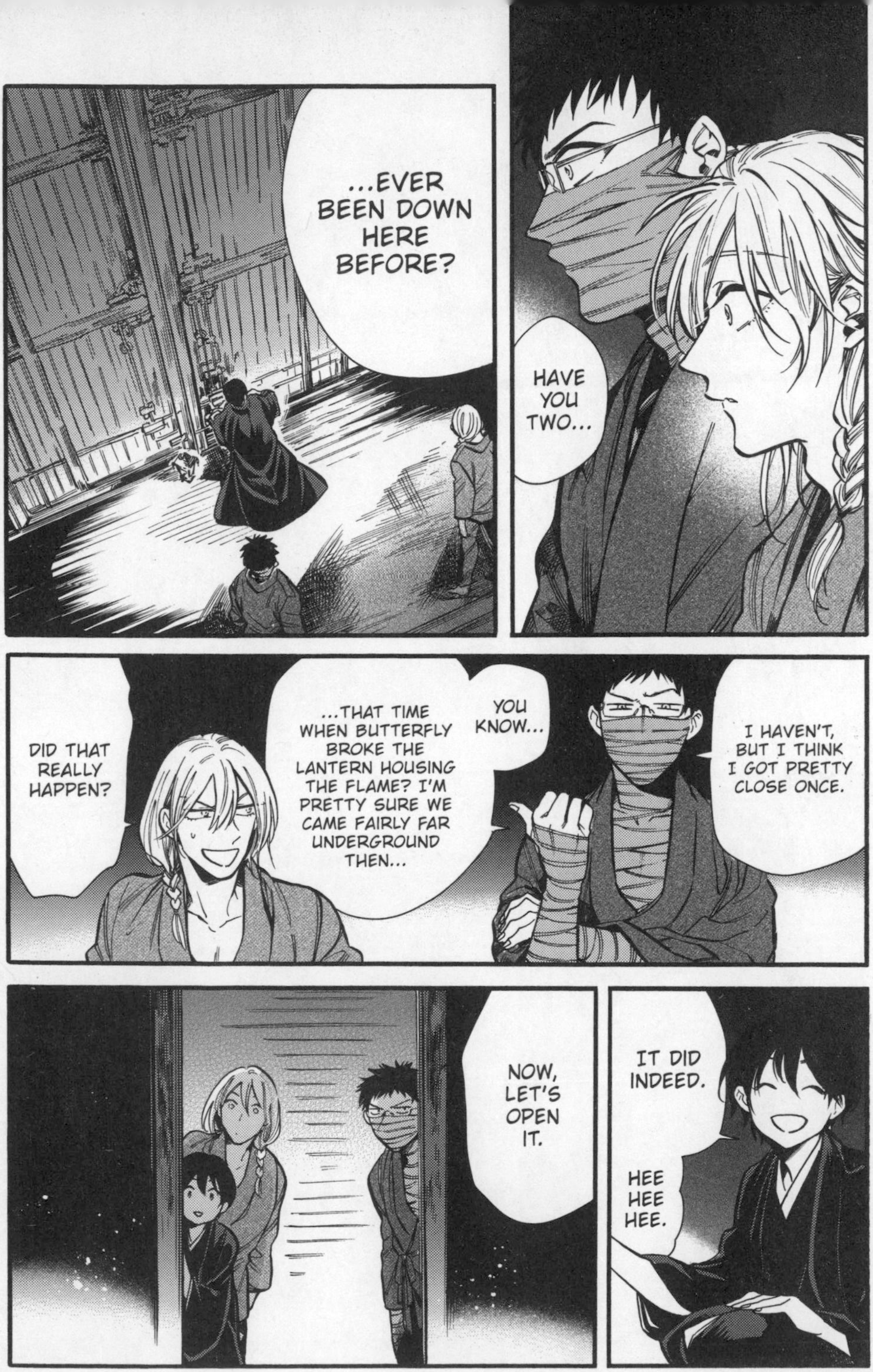
HAVE YOU TWO...
...EVER BEEN DOWN HERE BEFORE?
I HAVEN'T, BUT I THINK I GOT PRETTY CLOSE ONCE.
YOU KNOW...
...THAT TIME WHEN BUTTERFLY BROKE THE LANTERN HOUSING THE FLAME? I'M PRETTY SURE WE CAME FAIRLY FAR UNDERGROUND THEN...
DID THAT REALLY HAPPEN?
IT DID INDEED.
HEE HEE HEE.
NOW, LET'S OPEN IT.

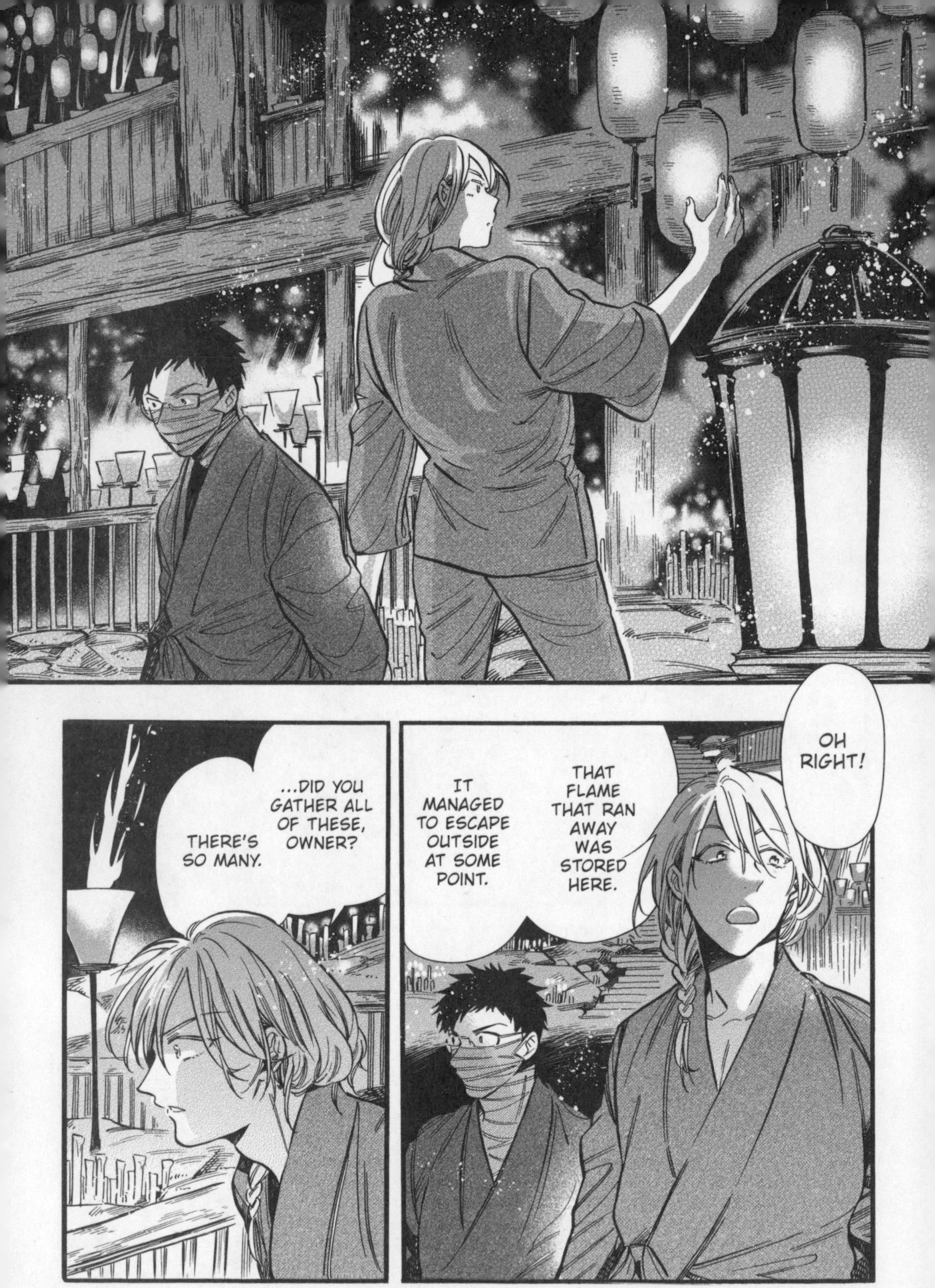
OH RIGHT!
THAT FLAME THAT RAN AWAY WAS STORED HERE.
IT MANAGED TO ESCAPE OUTSIDE AT SOME POINT.
...DID YOU GATHER ALL OF THESE, OWNER?
THERE'S SO MANY.

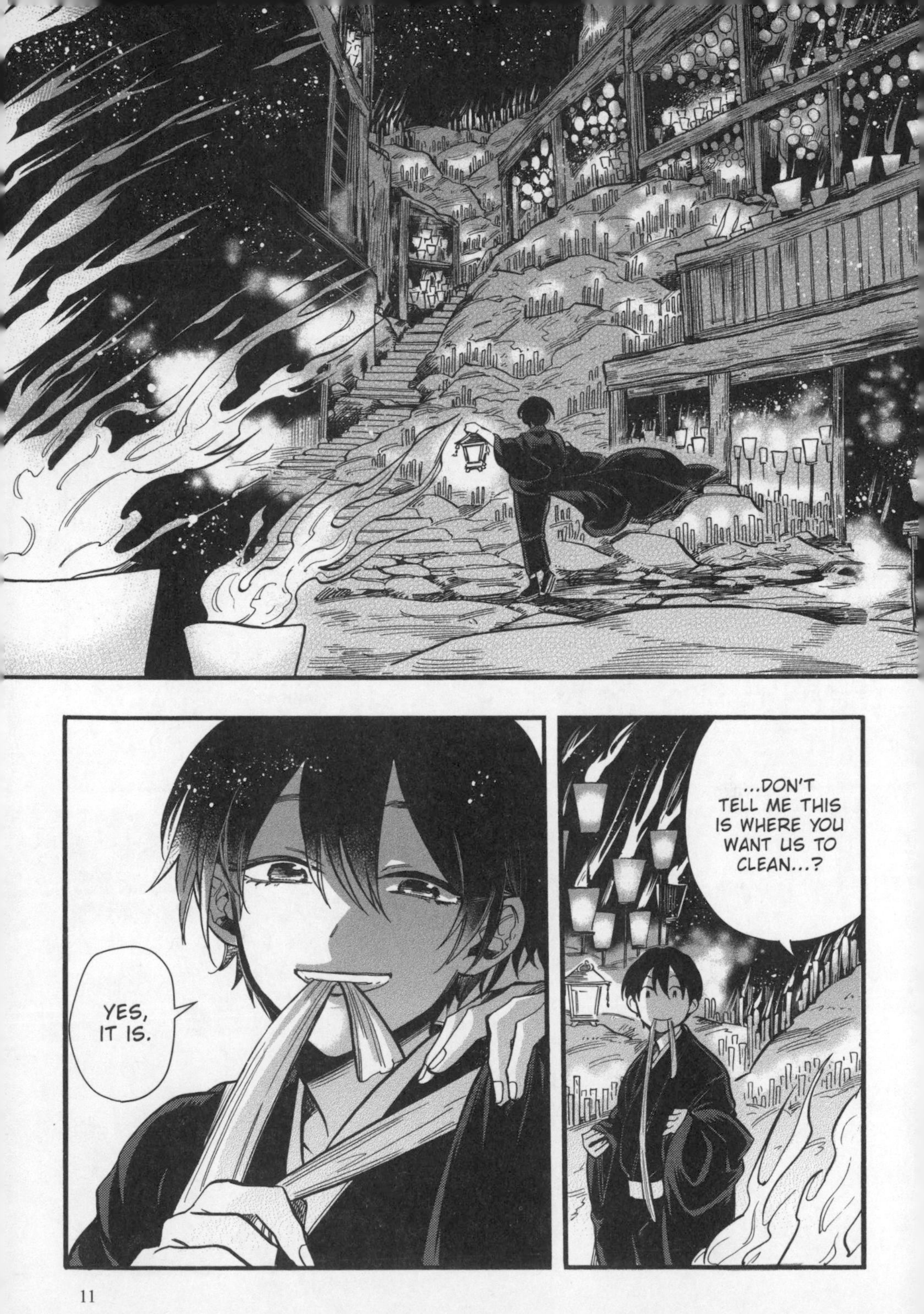
...DON'T TELL ME THIS IS WHERE YOU WANT US TO CLEAN...?
YES, IT IS.

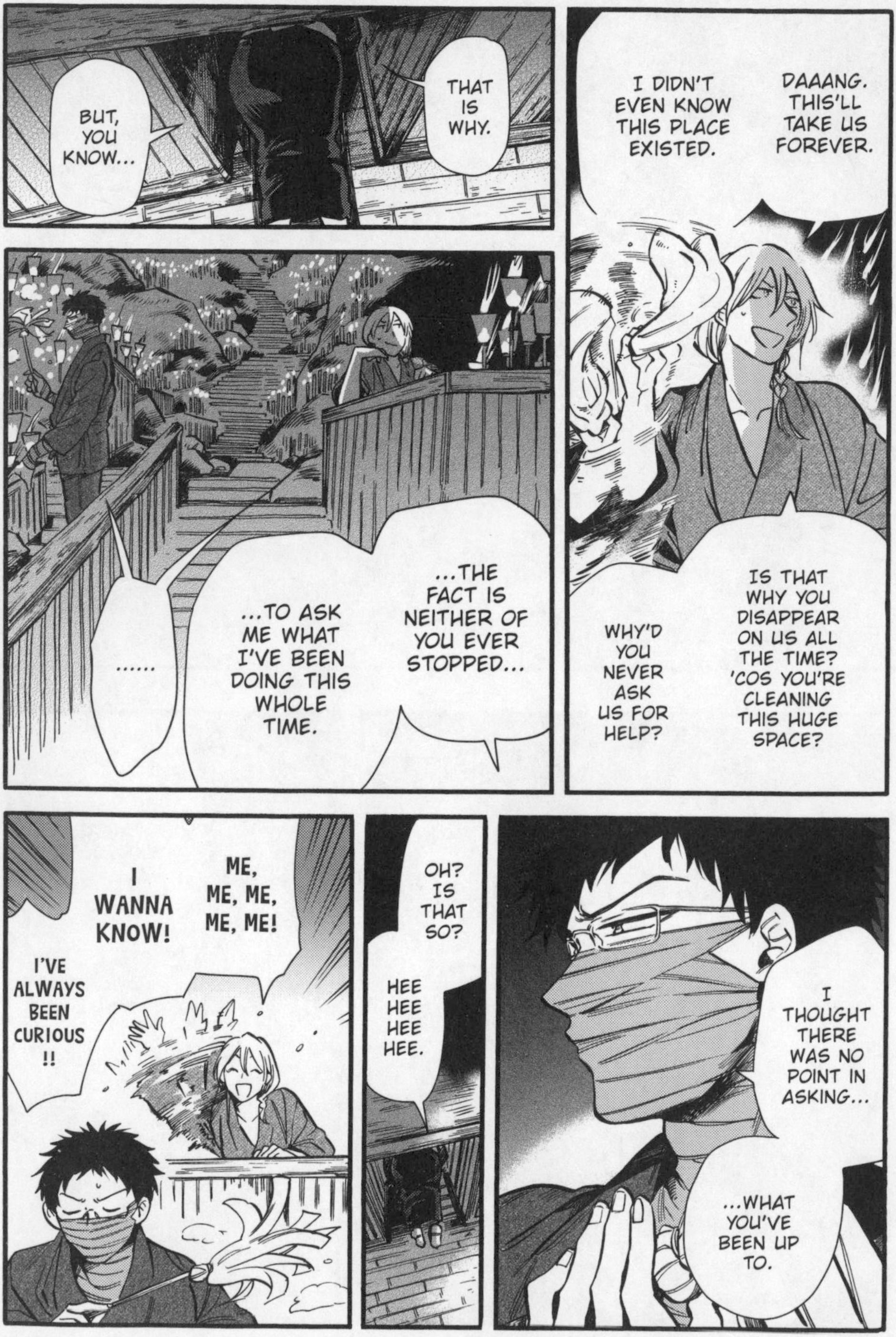
DAAANG. THIS'LL TAKE US FOREVER.
I DIDN'T EVEN KNOW THIS PLACE EXISTED.
IS THAT WHY YOU DISAPPEAR ON US ALL THE TIME? 'COS YOU'RE CLEANING THIS HUGE SPACE?
WHY'D YOU NEVER ASK US FOR HELP?
THAT IS WHY.
BUT, YOU KNOW...
...THE FACT IS NEITHER OF YOU EVER STOPPED...
...TO ASK ME WHAT I'VE BEEN DOING THIS WHOLE TIME.
......
I THOUGHT THERE WAS NO POINT IN ASKING...
...WHAT YOU'VE BEEN UP TO.
OH? IS THAT SO?
HEE HEE HEE HEE.
ME, ME, ME, ME, ME!
I WANNA KNOW!
I'VE ALWAYS BEEN CURIOUS !!

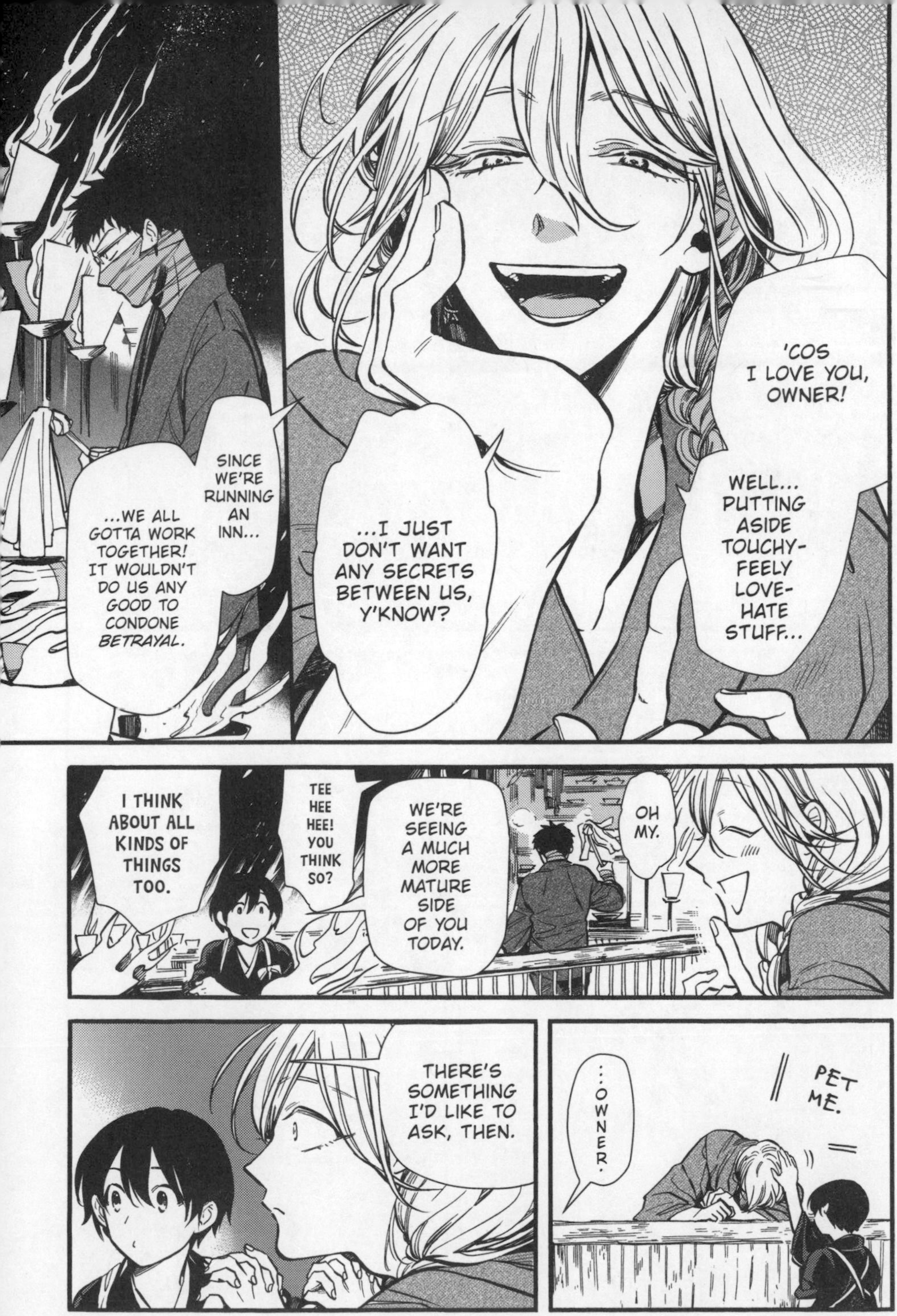
'COS I LOVE YOU, OWNER!
WELL... PUTTING ASIDE TOUCHY-FEELY LOVE-HATE STUFF...
...I JUST DON'T WANT ANY SECRETS BETWEEN US, Y'KNOW?
SINCE WE'RE RUNNING AN INN...
...WE ALL GOTTA WORK TOGETHER! IT WOULDN'T DO US ANY GOOD TO CONDONE *BETRAYAL.*
OH MY.
WE'RE SEEING A MUCH MORE MATURE SIDE OF YOU TODAY.
TEE HEE HEE! YOU THINK SO?
I THINK ABOUT ALL KINDS OF THINGS TOO.
PET ME.
...OWNER.
THERE'S SOMETHING I'D LIKE TO ASK, THEN.

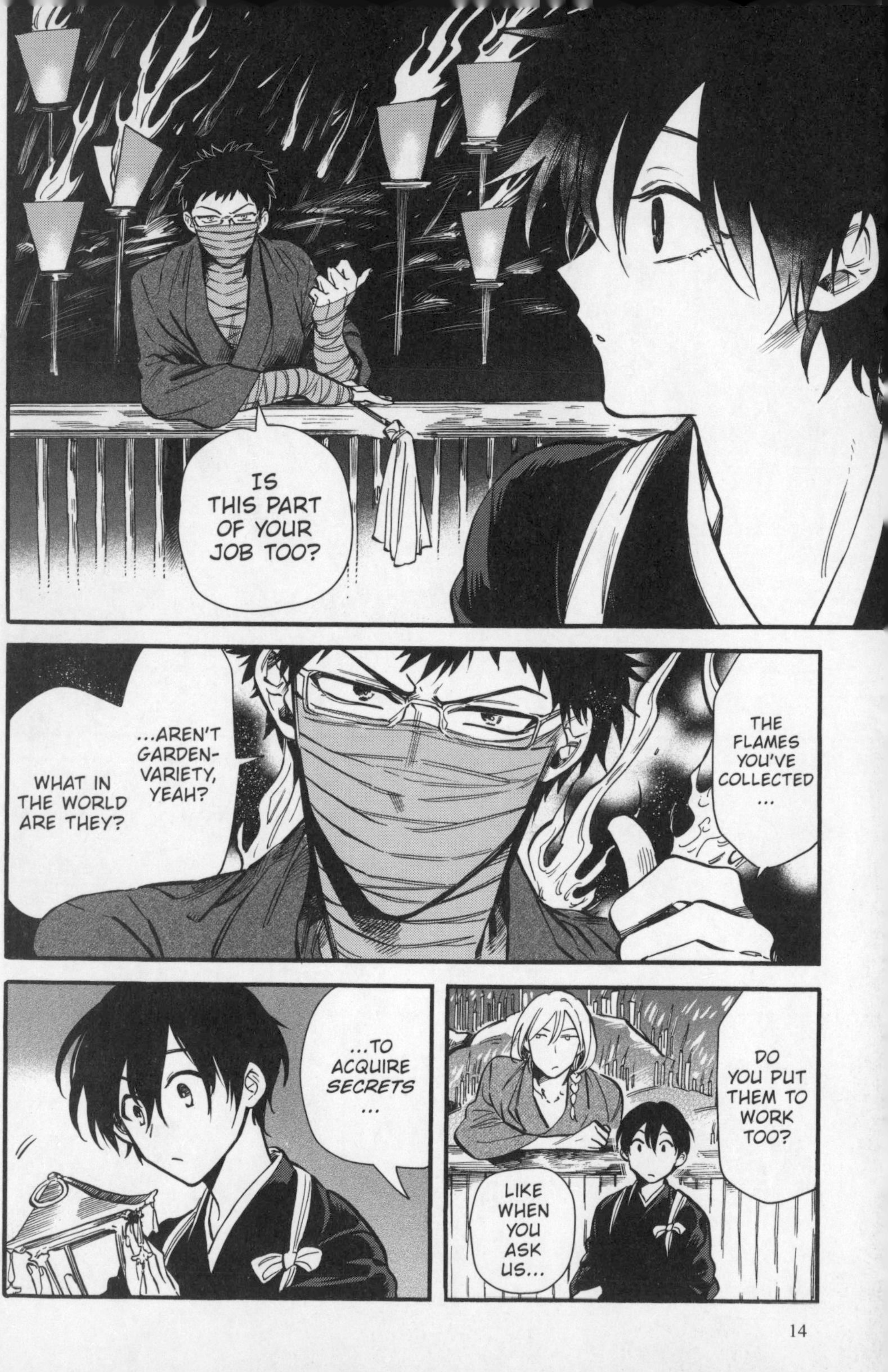
IS THIS PART OF YOUR JOB TOO?
THE FLAMES YOU'VE COLLECTED ...
...AREN'T GARDEN-VARIETY, YEAH?
WHAT IN THE WORLD ARE THEY?
DO YOU PUT THEM TO WORK TOO?
LIKE WHEN YOU ASK US...
...TO ACQUIRE *SECRETS* ...

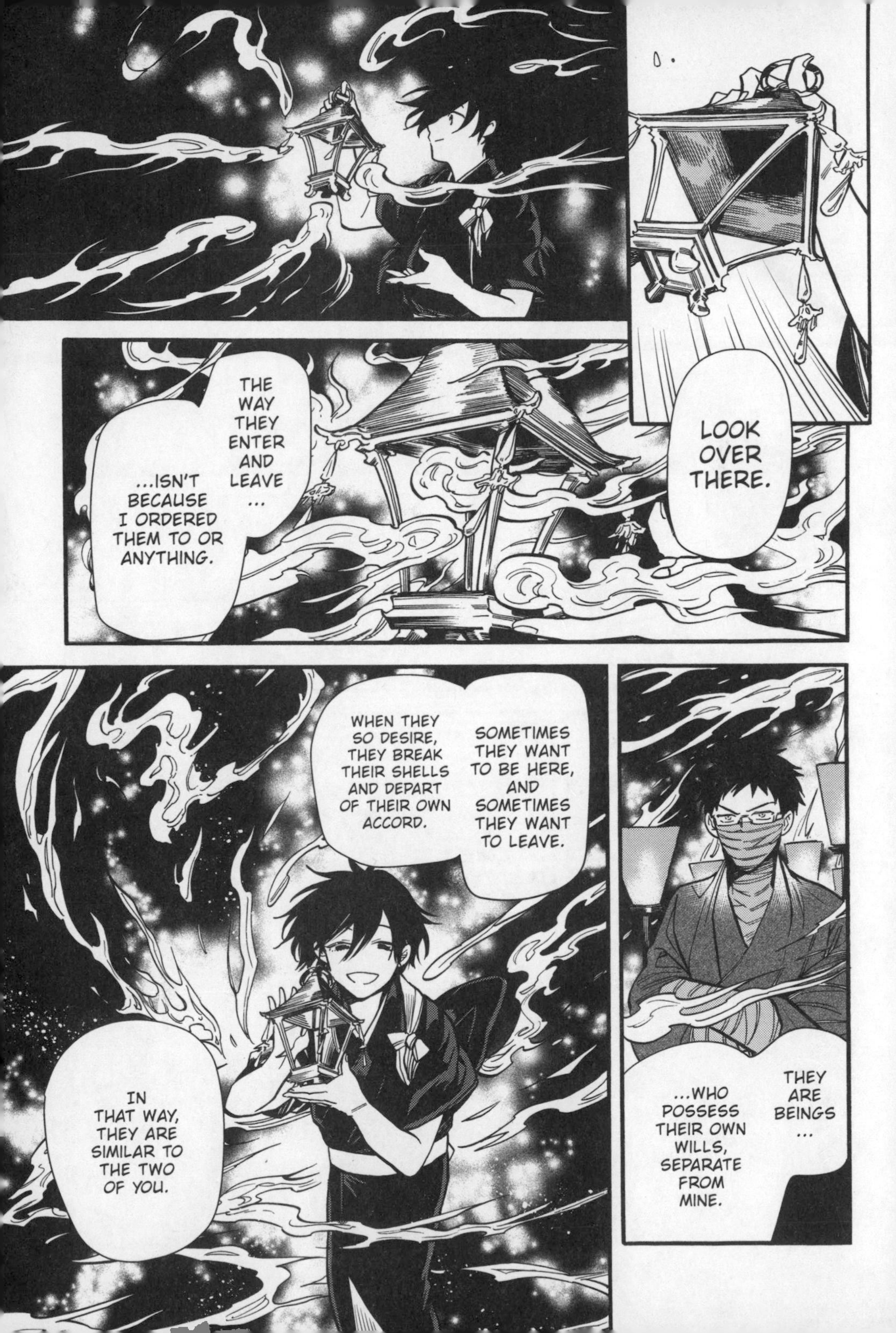
LOOK OVER THERE.
THE WAY THEY ENTER AND LEAVE...
...ISN'T BECAUSE I ORDERED THEM TO OR ANYTHING.
THEY ARE BEINGS...
...WHO POSSESS THEIR OWN WILLS, SEPARATE FROM MINE.
SOMETIMES THEY WANT TO BE HERE, AND SOMETIMES THEY WANT TO LEAVE.
WHEN THEY SO DESIRE, THEY BREAK THEIR SHELLS AND DEPART OF THEIR OWN ACCORD.
IN THAT WAY, THEY ARE SIMILAR TO THE TWO OF YOU.

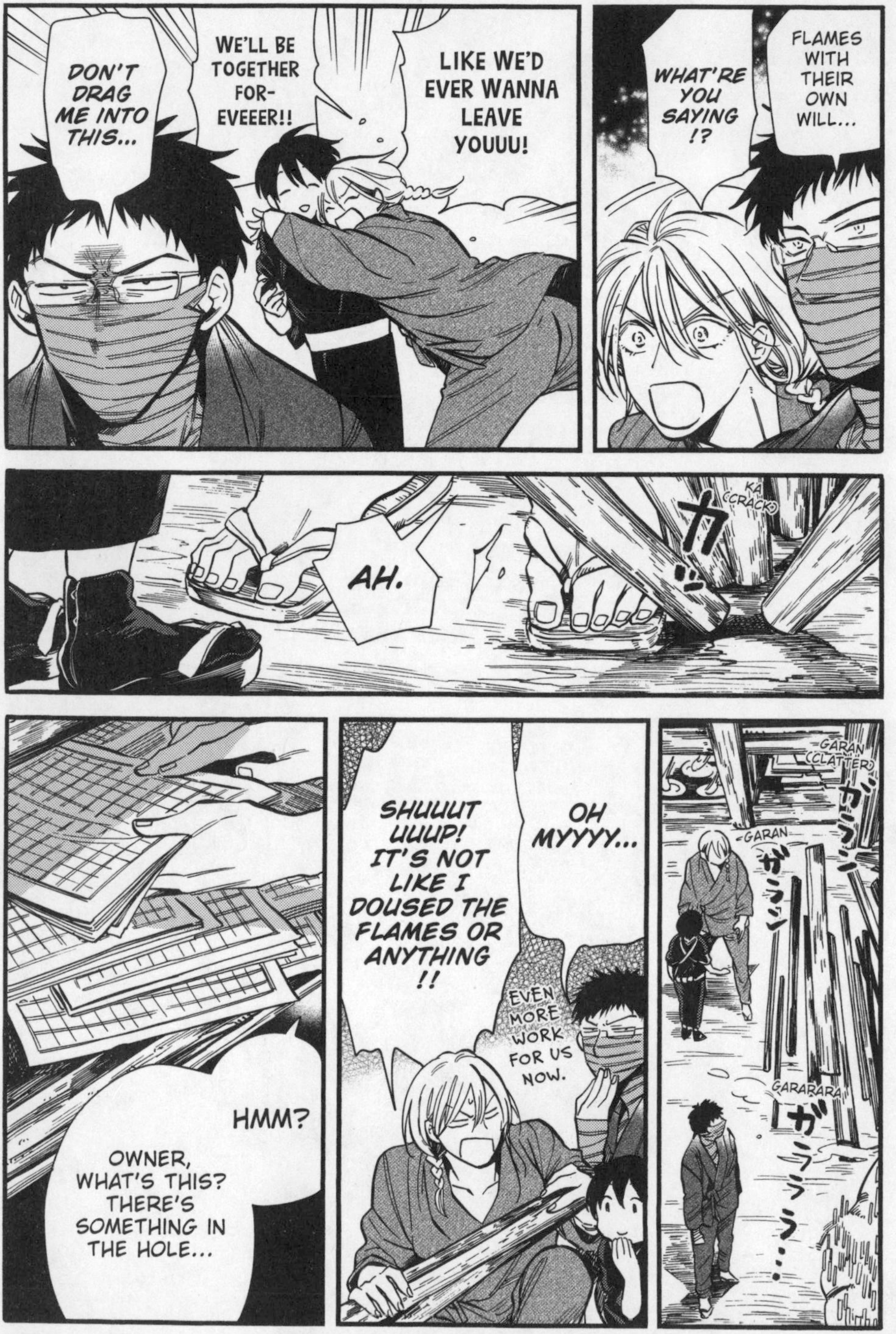
FLAMES WITH THEIR OWN WILL...
WHAT'RE YOU SAYING !?
LIKE WE'D EVER WANNA LEAVE YOUUU!
WE'LL BE TOGETHER FOR-EVEEER!!
DON'T DRAG ME INTO THIS...
KA (CRACK)
AH.
GARAN (CLATTER)
GARAN
GARARARA
OH MYYYY...
SHUUUT UUUP! IT'S NOT LIKE I DOUSED THE FLAMES OR ANYTHING !!
EVEN MORE WORK FOR US NOW.
HMM?
OWNER, WHAT'S THIS? THERE'S SOMETHING IN THE HOLE...

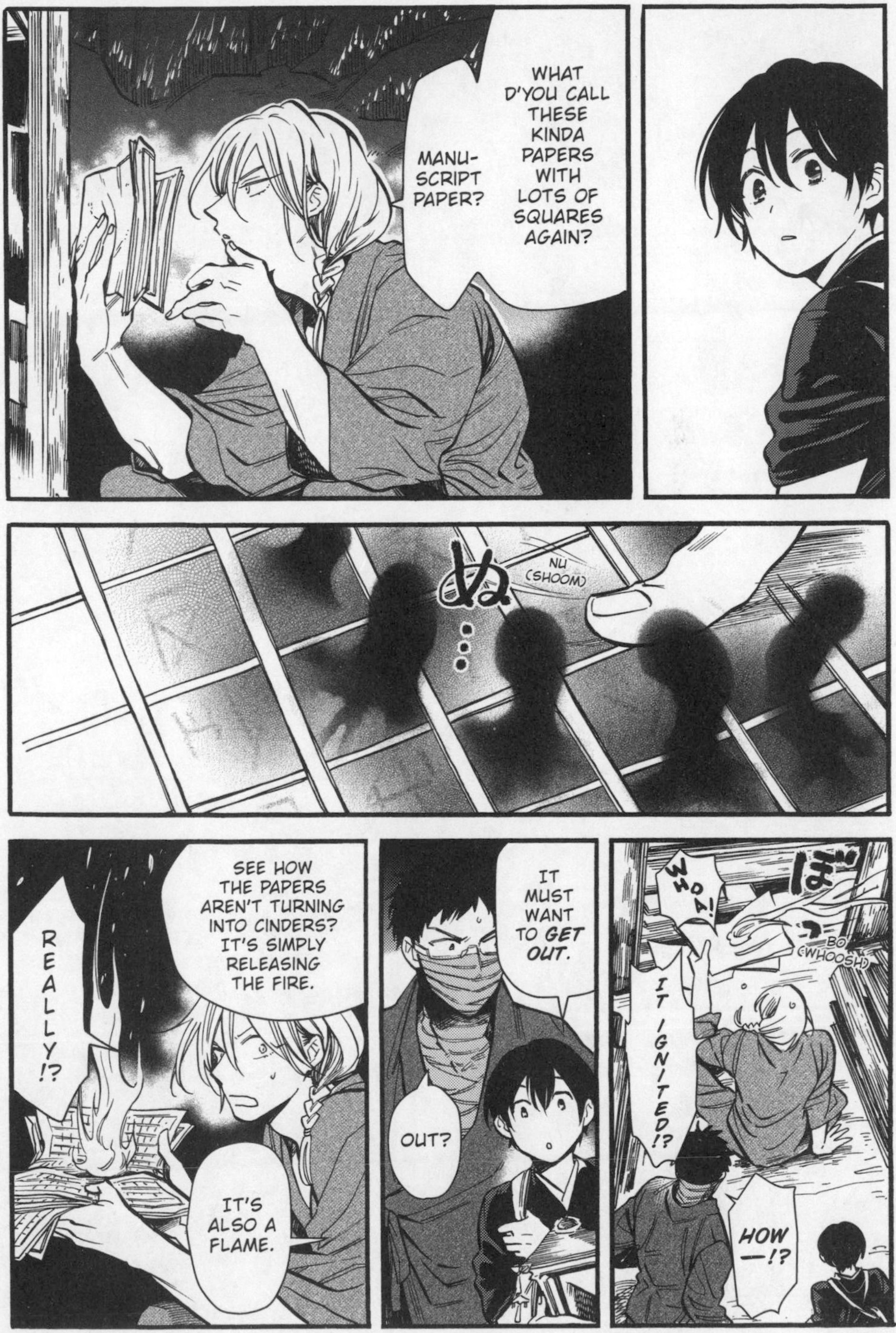
WHAT D'YOU CALL THESE KINDA PAPERS WITH LOTS OF SQUARES AGAIN?
MANU-SCRIPT PAPER?
ぬ
NU (SHOOM)
...
ぼっ
BO (WHOOSH)
WHOA!
IT IGNITED!?
HOW—!?
IT MUST WANT TO *GET OUT*.
OUT?
SEE HOW THE PAPERS AREN'T TURNING INTO CINDERS? IT'S SIMPLY RELEASING THE FIRE.
REALLY!?
IT'S ALSO A FLAME.

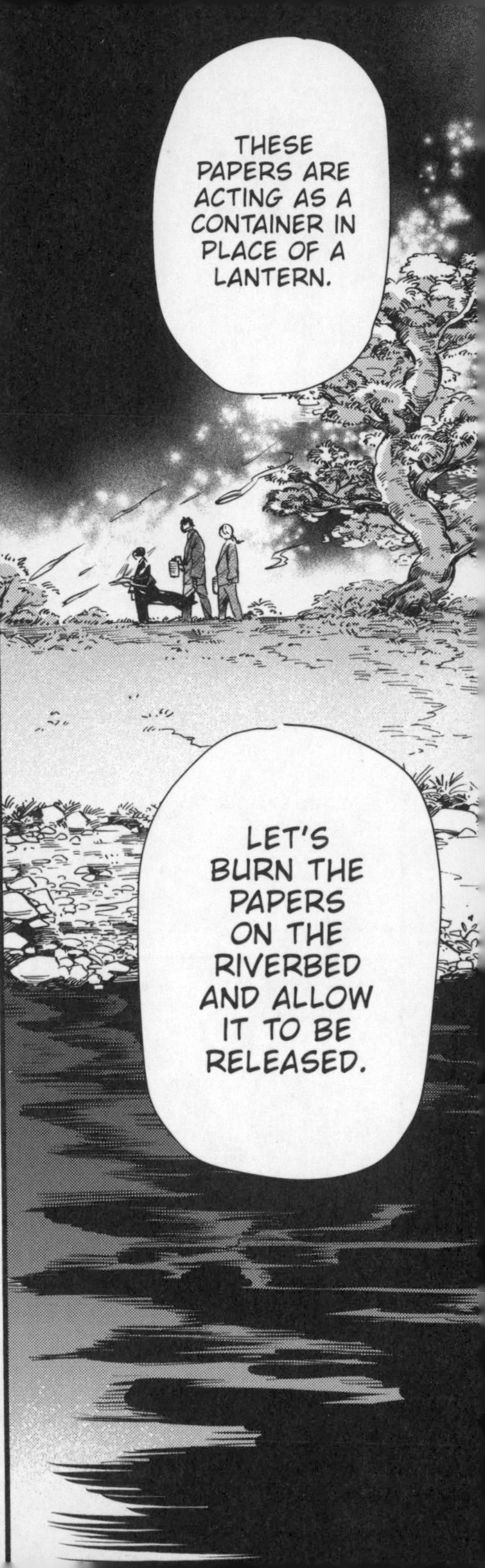
THESE PAPERS ARE ACTING AS A CONTAINER IN PLACE OF A LANTERN.
LET'S BURN THE PAPERS ON THE RIVERBED AND ALLOW IT TO BE RELEASED.

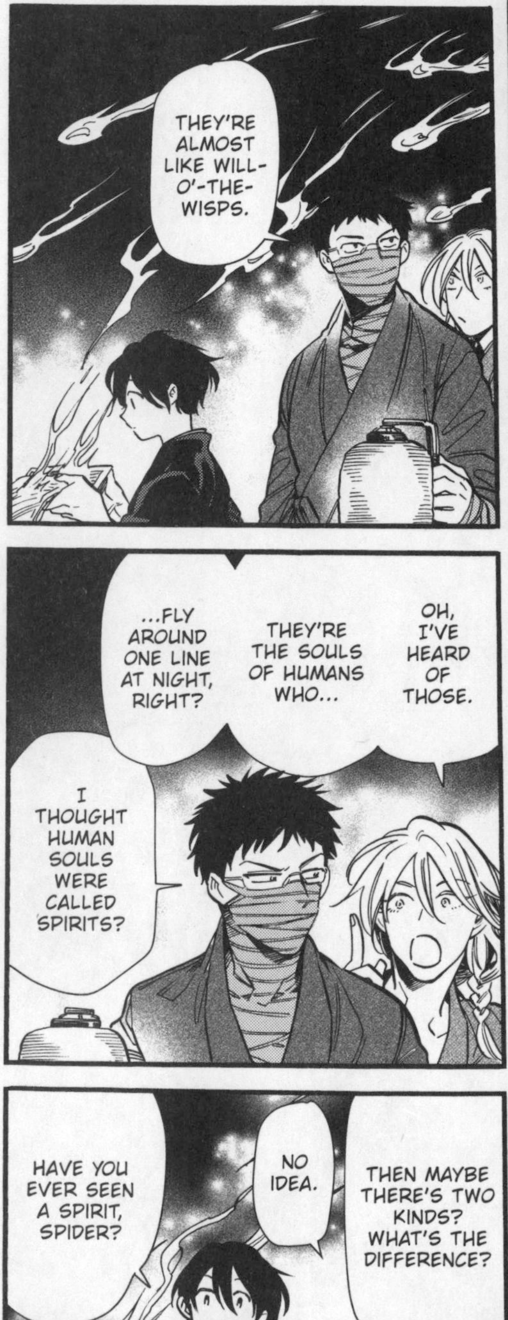
THEY'RE ALMOST LIKE WILL-O'-THE-WISPS.
OH, I'VE HEARD OF THOSE.
THEY'RE THE SOULS OF HUMANS WHO...
...FLY AROUND ONE LINE AT NIGHT, RIGHT?
I THOUGHT HUMAN SOULS WERE CALLED SPIRITS?
THEN MAYBE THERE'S TWO KINDS? WHAT'S THE DIFFERENCE?
NO IDEA.
HAVE YOU EVER SEEN A SPIRIT, SPIDER?

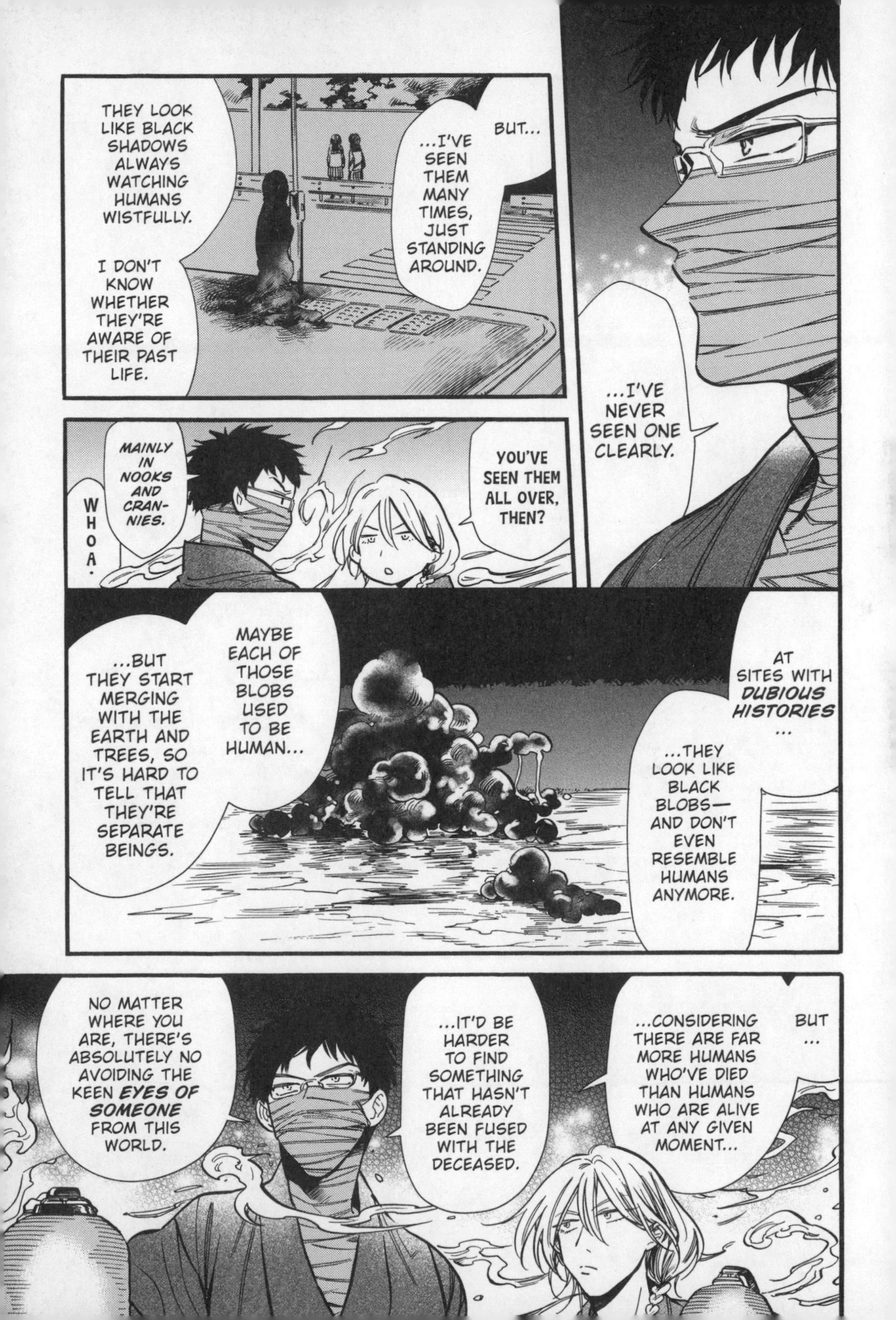
...I'VE NEVER SEEN ONE CLEARLY.
BUT...
...I'VE SEEN THEM MANY TIMES, JUST STANDING AROUND.
THEY LOOK LIKE BLACK SHADOWS ALWAYS WATCHING HUMANS WISTFULLY.
I DON'T KNOW WHETHER THEY'RE AWARE OF THEIR PAST LIFE.
YOU'VE SEEN THEM ALL OVER, THEN?
MAINLY IN NOOKS AND CRAN-NIES.
WHOA.
AT SITES WITH ***DUBIOUS HISTORIES***...
...THEY LOOK LIKE BLACK BLOBS—AND DON'T EVEN RESEMBLE HUMANS ANYMORE.
MAYBE EACH OF THOSE BLOBS USED TO BE HUMAN...
...BUT THEY START MERGING WITH THE EARTH AND TREES, SO IT'S HARD TO TELL THAT THEY'RE SEPARATE BEINGS.
BUT...
...CONSIDERING THERE ARE FAR MORE HUMANS WHO'VE DIED THAN HUMANS WHO ARE ALIVE AT ANY GIVEN MOMENT...
...IT'D BE HARDER TO FIND SOMETHING THAT HASN'T ALREADY BEEN FUSED WITH THE DECEASED.
NO MATTER WHERE YOU ARE, THERE'S ABSOLUTELY NO AVOIDING THE KEEN ***EYES OF SOMEONE*** FROM THIS WORLD.

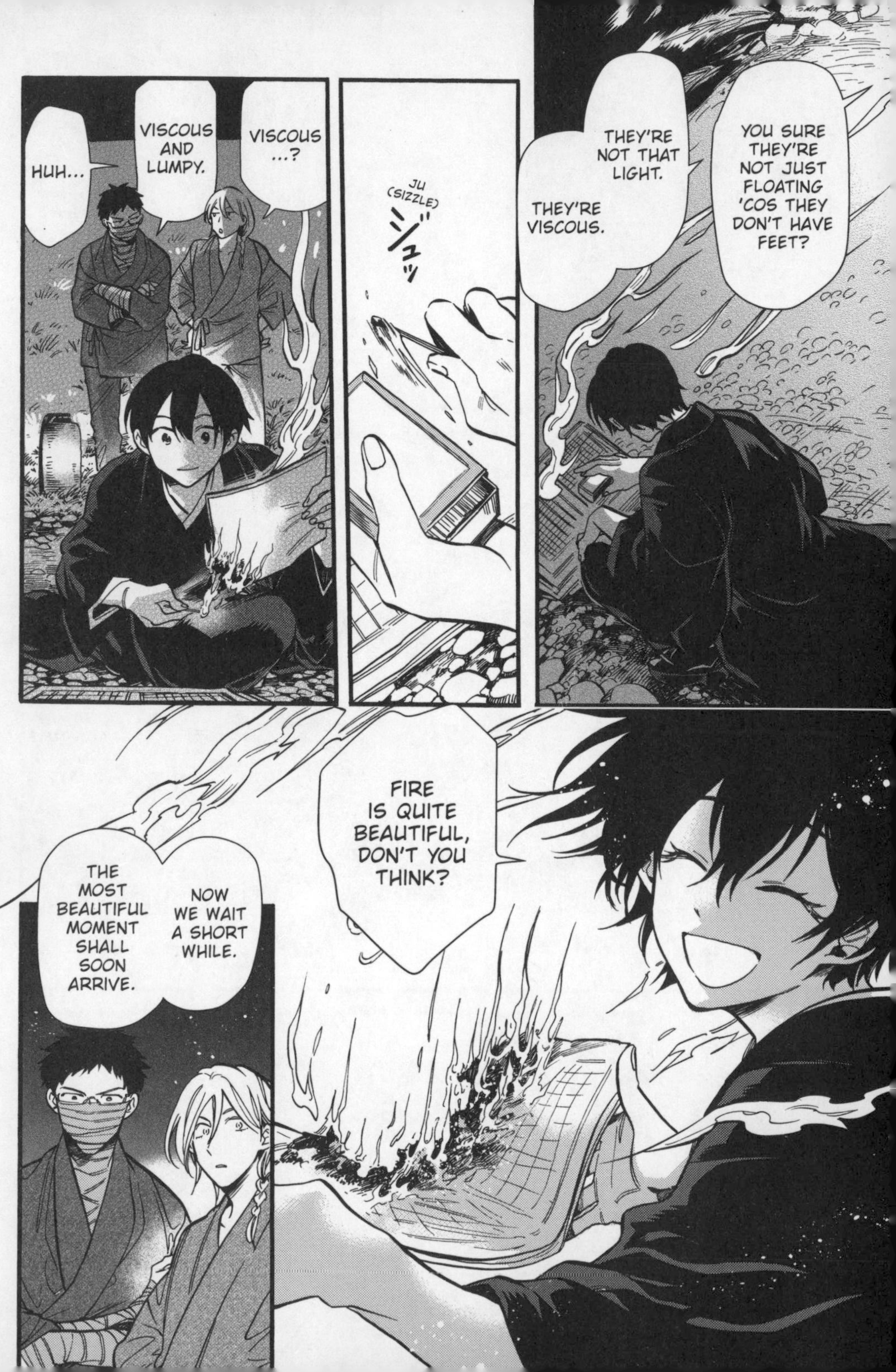
YOU SURE THEY'RE NOT JUST FLOATING 'COS THEY DON'T HAVE FEET?
THEY'RE NOT THAT LIGHT.
THEY'RE VISCOUS.
ジュッ
JU (SIZZLE)
VISCOUS ...?
VISCOUS AND LUMPY.
HUH...
FIRE IS QUITE BEAUTIFUL, DON'T YOU THINK?
NOW WE WAIT A SHORT WHILE.
THE MOST BEAUTIFUL MOMENT SHALL SOON ARRIVE.

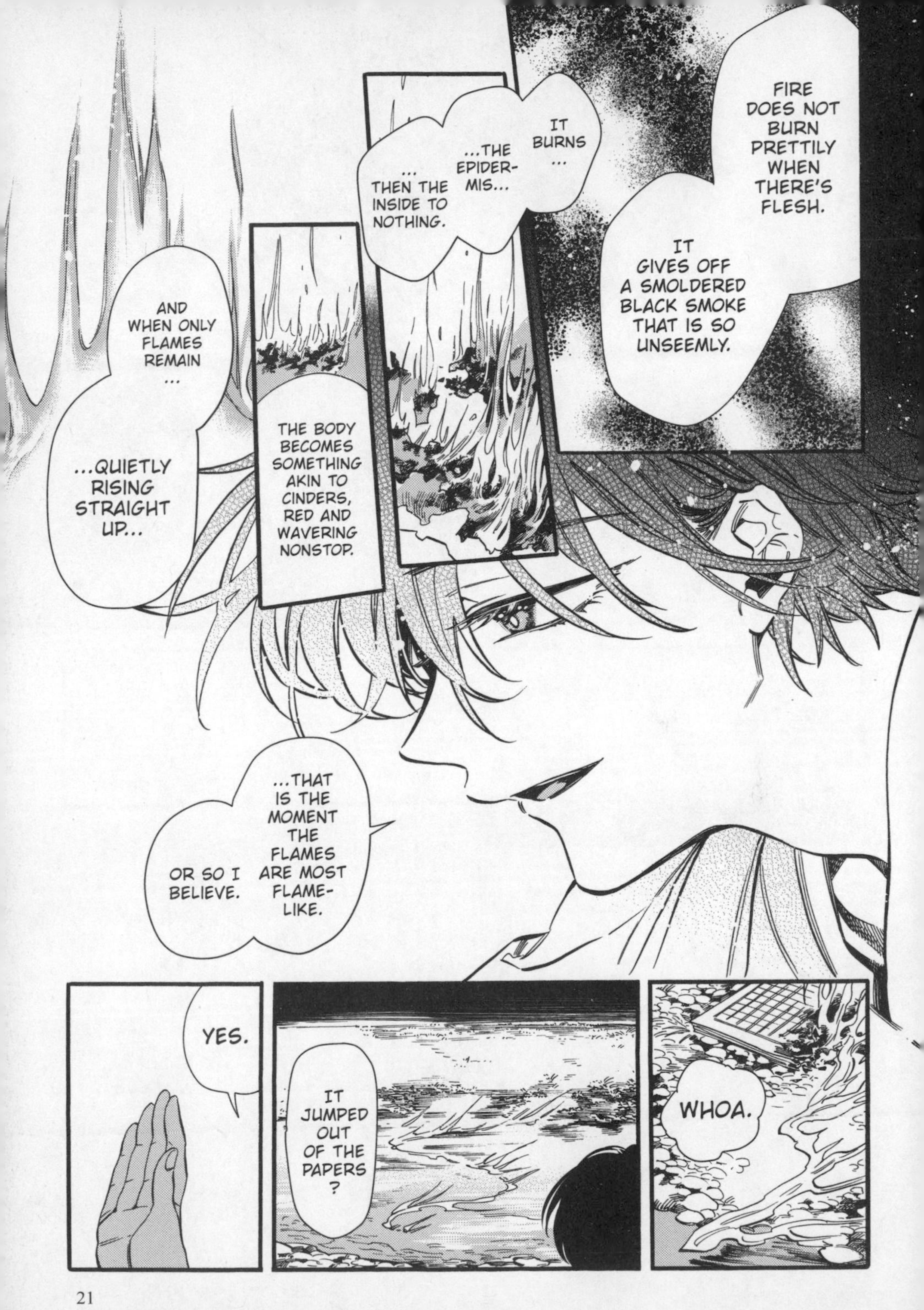
FIRE DOES NOT BURN PRETTILY WHEN THERE'S FLESH.
IT GIVES OFF A SMOLDERED BLACK SMOKE THAT IS SO UNSEEMLY.
IT BURNS ...
...THE EPIDER-MIS...
... THEN THE INSIDE TO NOTHING.
THE BODY BECOMES SOMETHING AKIN TO CINDERS, RED AND WAVERING NONSTOP.
AND WHEN ONLY FLAMES REMAIN ...
...QUIETLY RISING STRAIGHT UP...
...THAT IS THE MOMENT THE FLAMES ARE MOST FLAME-LIKE.
OR SO I BELIEVE.
WHOA.
IT JUMPED OUT OF THE PAPERS ?
YES.

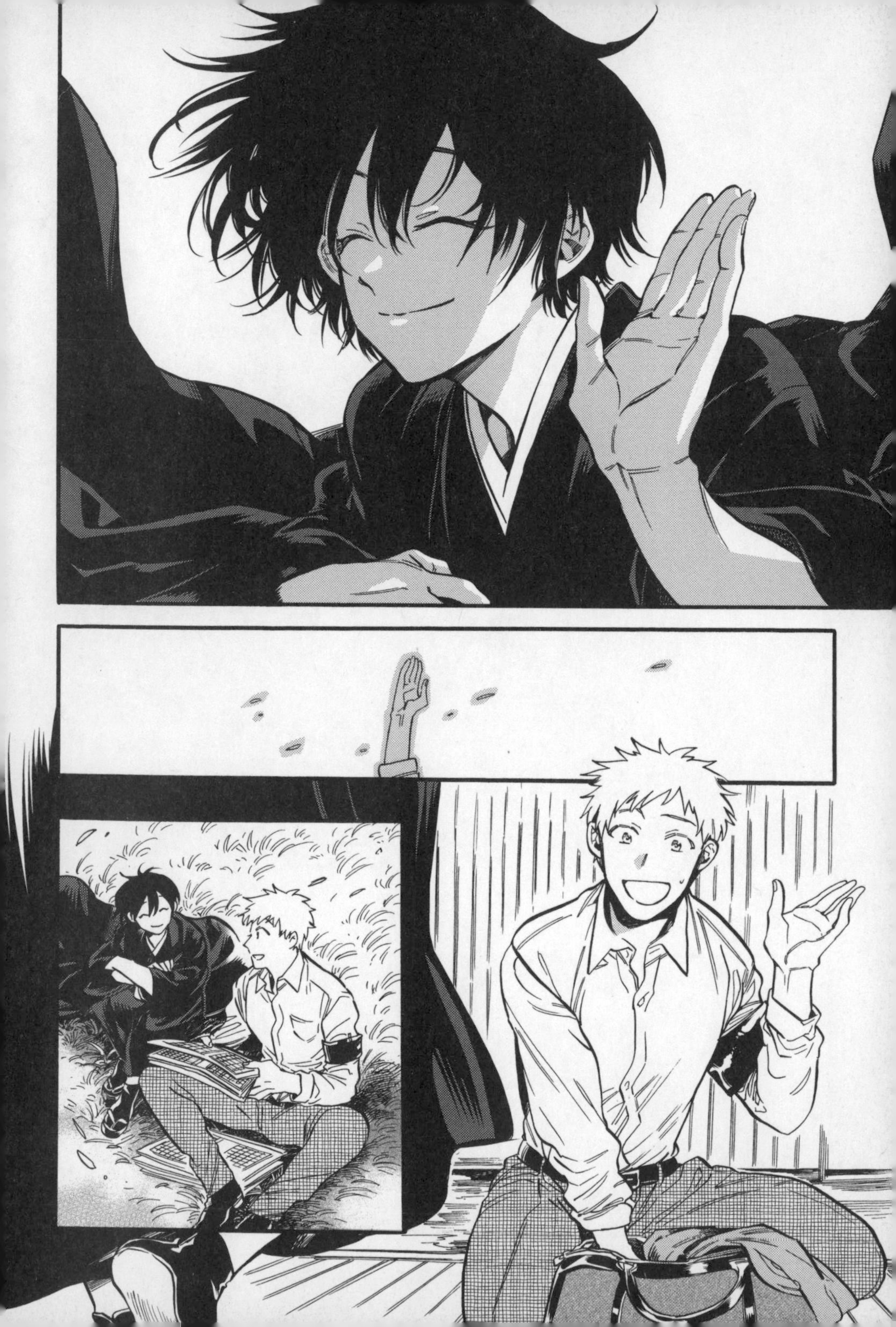

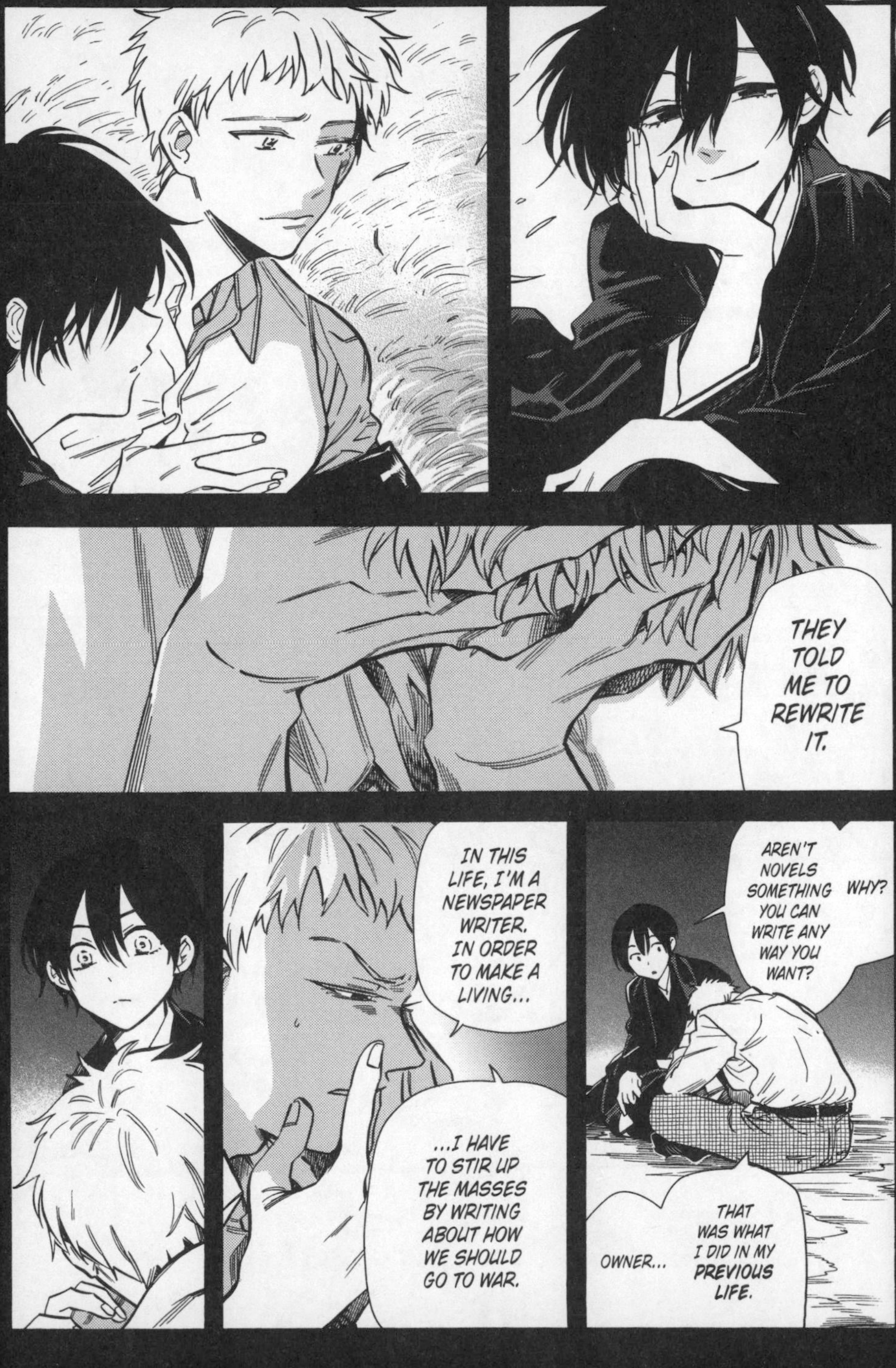
THEY TOLD ME TO REWRITE IT.
WHY?
AREN'T NOVELS SOMETHING YOU CAN WRITE ANY WAY YOU WANT?
THAT WAS WHAT I DID IN MY PREVIOUS LIFE.
OWNER...
IN THIS LIFE, I'M A NEWSPAPER WRITER. IN ORDER TO MAKE A LIVING...
...I HAVE TO STIR UP THE MASSES BY WRITING ABOUT HOW WE SHOULD GO TO WAR.

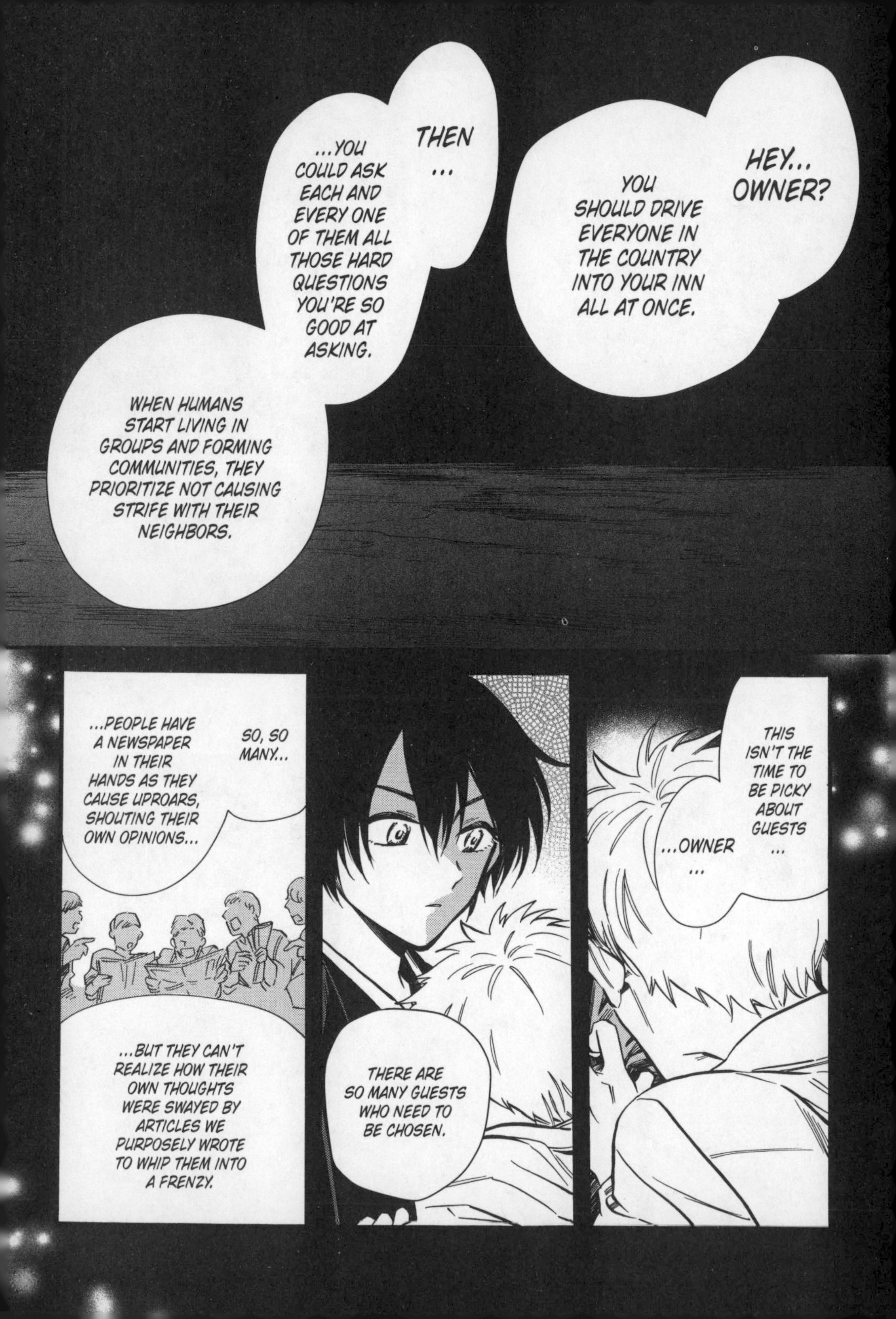
HEY... OWNER?
YOU SHOULD DRIVE EVERYONE IN THE COUNTRY INTO YOUR INN ALL AT ONCE.
THEN...
...YOU COULD ASK EACH AND EVERY ONE OF THEM ALL THOSE HARD QUESTIONS YOU'RE SO GOOD AT ASKING.
WHEN HUMANS START LIVING IN GROUPS AND FORMING COMMUNITIES, THEY PRIORITIZE NOT CAUSING STRIFE WITH THEIR NEIGHBORS.
THIS ISN'T THE TIME TO BE PICKY ABOUT GUESTS...
...OWNER...
THERE ARE SO MANY GUESTS WHO NEED TO BE CHOSEN.
SO, SO MANY...
...PEOPLE HAVE A NEWSPAPER IN THEIR HANDS AS THEY CAUSE UPROARS, SHOUTING THEIR OWN OPINIONS...
...BUT THEY CAN'T REALIZE HOW THEIR OWN THOUGHTS WERE SWAYED BY ARTICLES WE PURPOSELY WROTE TO WHIP THEM INTO A FRENZY.

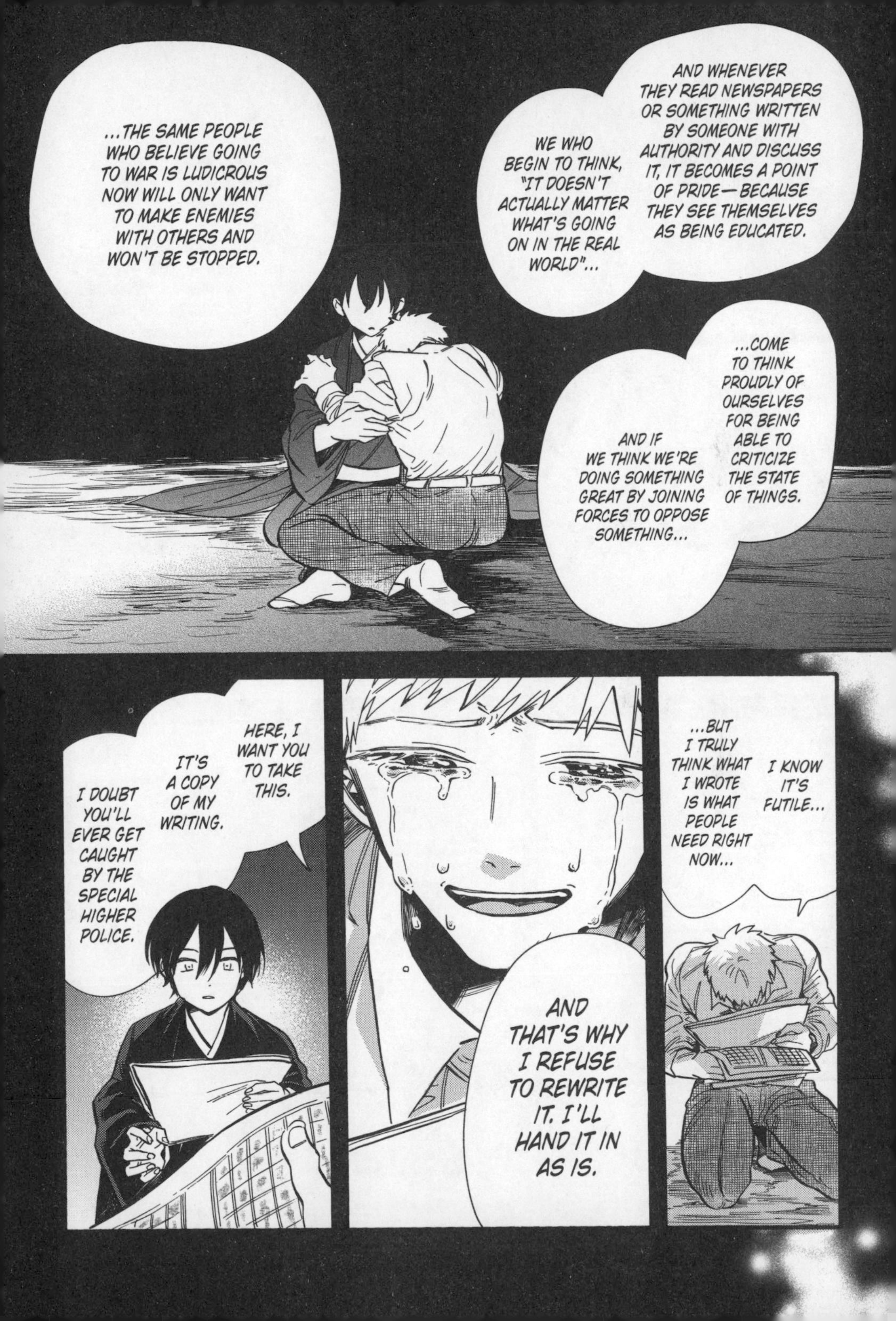
AND WHENEVER THEY READ NEWSPAPERS OR SOMETHING WRITTEN BY SOMEONE WITH AUTHORITY AND DISCUSS IT, IT BECOMES A POINT OF PRIDE—BECAUSE THEY SEE THEMSELVES AS BEING EDUCATED.
WE WHO BEGIN TO THINK, "IT DOESN'T ACTUALLY MATTER WHAT'S GOING ON IN THE REAL WORLD"...
...THE SAME PEOPLE WHO BELIEVE GOING TO WAR IS LUDICROUS NOW WILL ONLY WANT TO MAKE ENEMIES WITH OTHERS AND WON'T BE STOPPED.
...COME TO THINK PROUDLY OF OURSELVES FOR BEING ABLE TO CRITICIZE THE STATE OF THINGS.
AND IF WE THINK WE'RE DOING SOMETHING GREAT BY JOINING FORCES TO OPPOSE SOMETHING...
I KNOW IT'S FUTILE...
...BUT I TRULY THINK WHAT I WROTE IS WHAT PEOPLE NEED RIGHT NOW...
AND THAT'S WHY I REFUSE TO REWRITE IT. I'LL HAND IT IN AS IS.
HERE, I WANT YOU TO TAKE THIS.
IT'S A COPY OF MY WRITING.
I DOUBT YOU'LL EVER GET CAUGHT BY THE SPECIAL HIGHER POLICE.

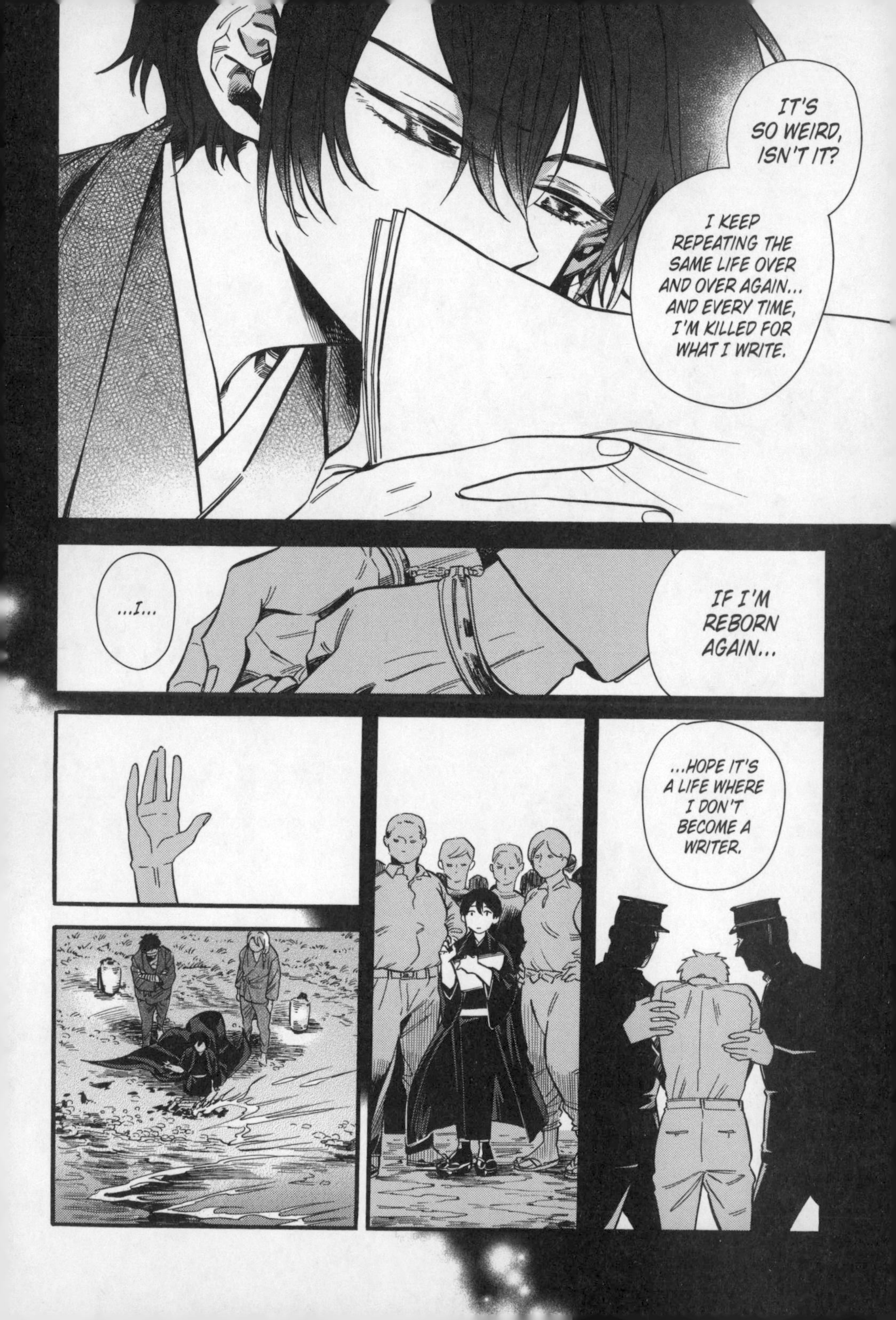
IT'S SO WEIRD, ISN'T IT?
I KEEP REPEATING THE SAME LIFE OVER AND OVER AGAIN... AND EVERY TIME, I'M KILLED FOR WHAT I WRITE.
IF I'M REBORN AGAIN...
...I...
...HOPE IT'S A LIFE WHERE I DON'T BECOME A WRITER.

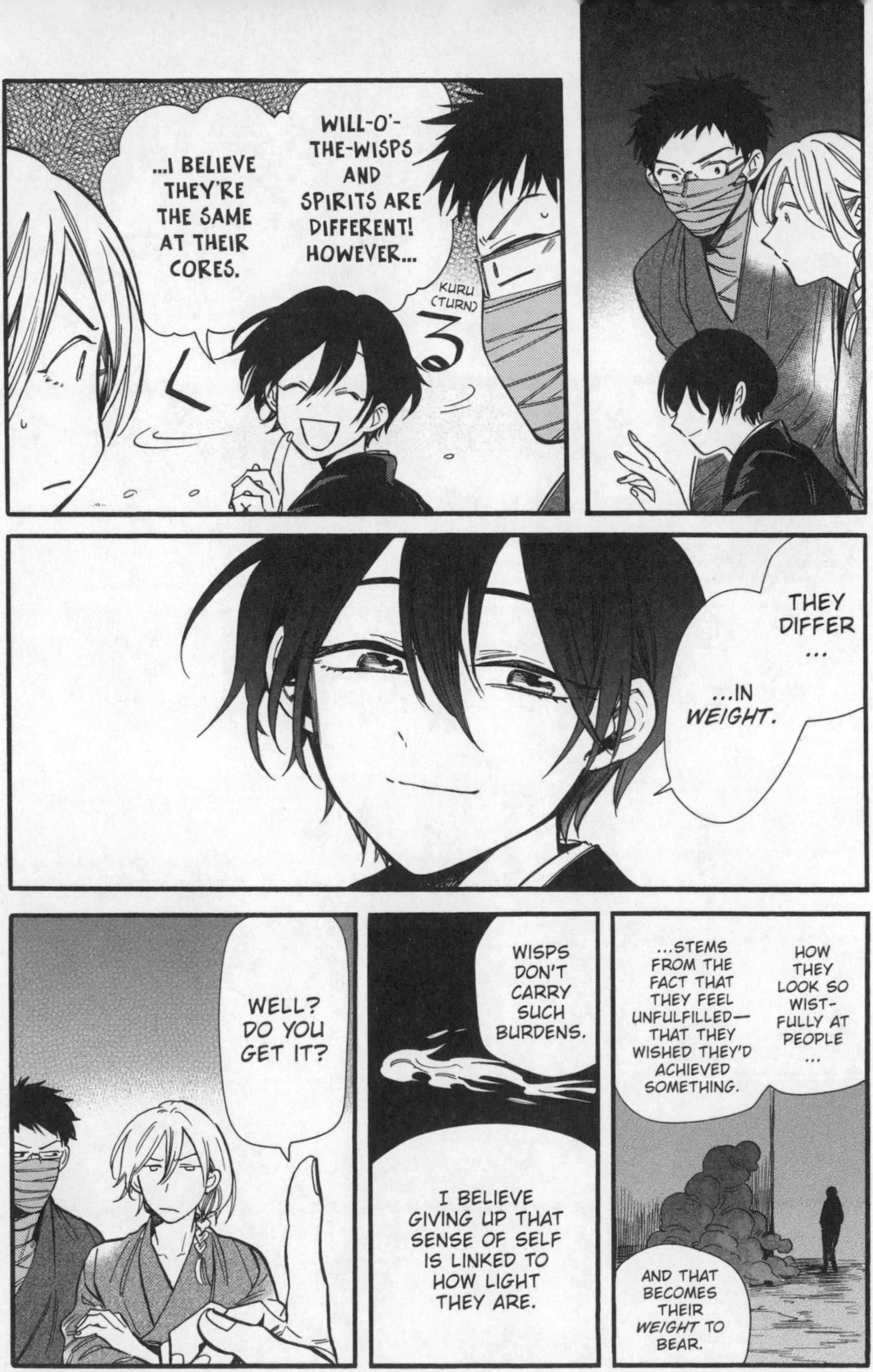
WILL-O'-THE-WISPS AND SPIRITS ARE DIFFERENT! HOWEVER...
...I BELIEVE THEY'RE THE SAME AT THEIR CORES.
KURU (TURN)
THEY DIFFER ...
...IN *WEIGHT*.
HOW THEY LOOK SO WISTFULLY AT PEOPLE ...
...STEMS FROM THE FACT THAT THEY FEEL UNFULFILLED—THAT THEY WISHED THEY'D ACHIEVED SOMETHING.
AND THAT BECOMES THEIR *WEIGHT* TO BEAR.
WISPS DON'T CARRY SUCH BURDENS.
I BELIEVE GIVING UP THAT SENSE OF SELF IS LINKED TO HOW LIGHT THEY ARE.
WELL? DO YOU GET IT?

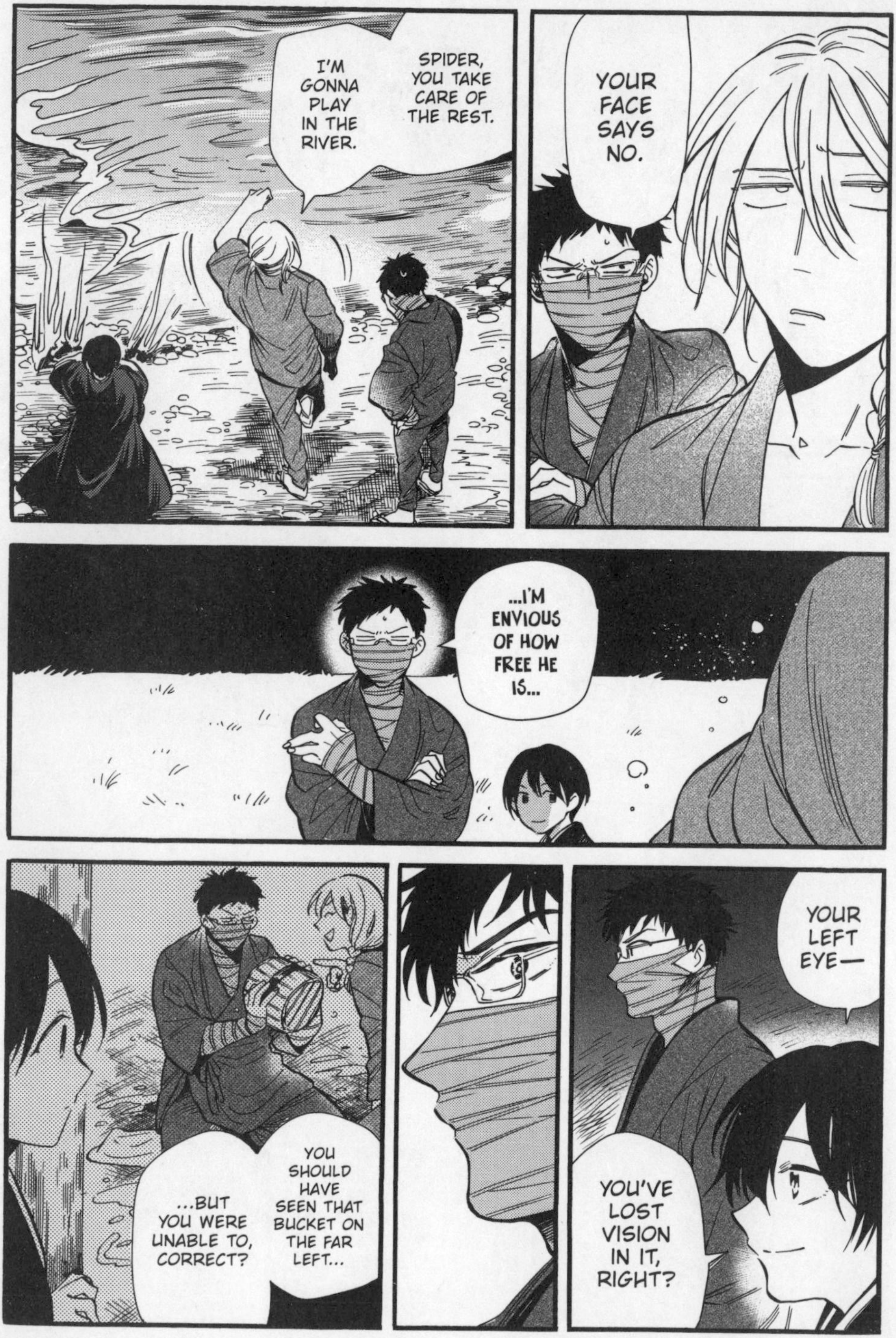
YOUR FACE SAYS NO.
SPIDER, YOU TAKE CARE OF THE REST.
I'M GONNA PLAY IN THE RIVER.
...I'M ENVIOUS OF HOW FREE HE IS...
YOUR LEFT EYE—
YOU'VE LOST VISION IN IT, RIGHT?
YOU SHOULD HAVE SEEN THAT BUCKET ON THE FAR LEFT...
...BUT YOU WERE UNABLE TO, CORRECT?

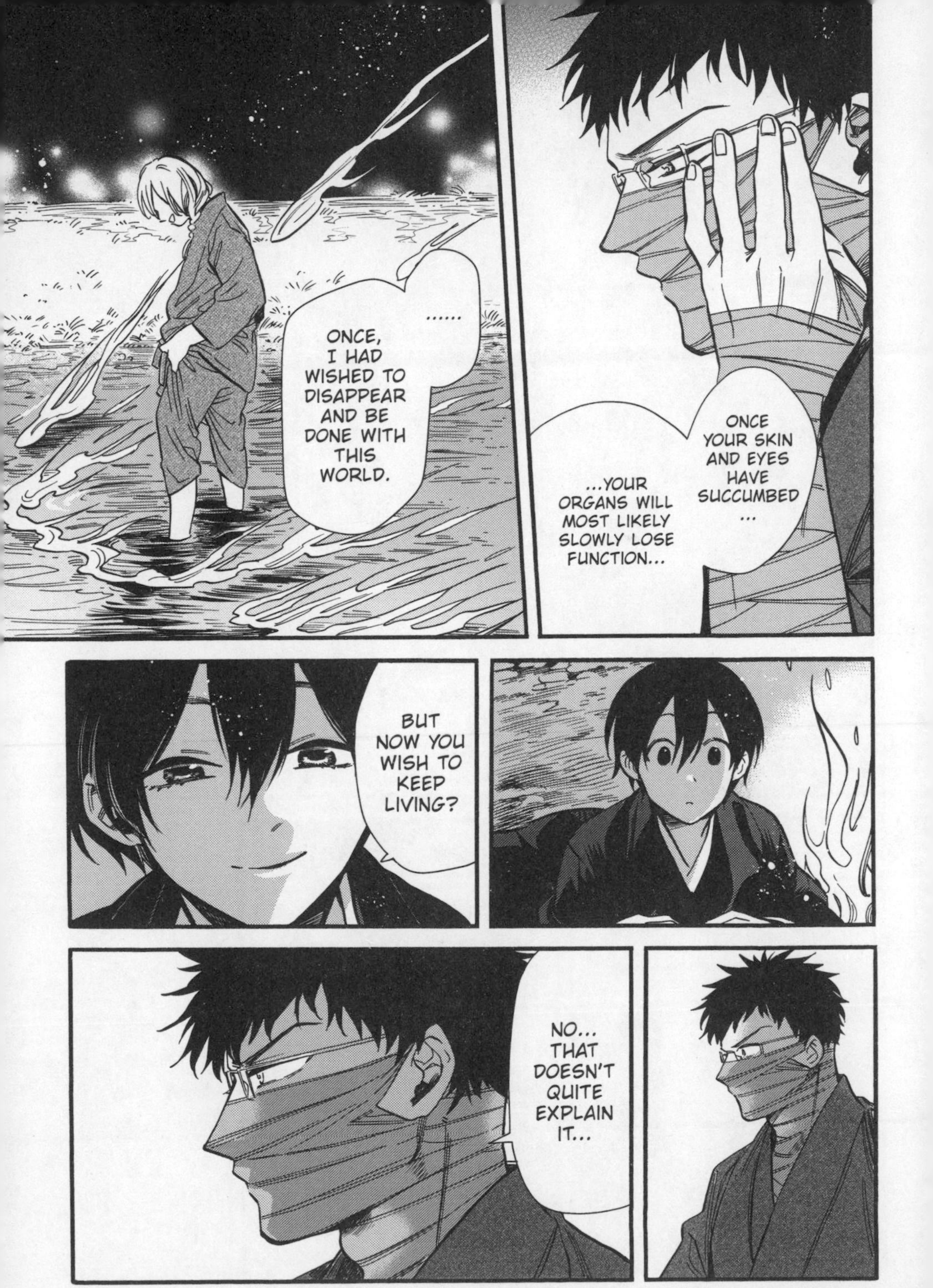
ONCE YOUR SKIN AND EYES HAVE SUCCUMBED ...
...YOUR ORGANS WILL MOST LIKELY SLOWLY LOSE FUNCTION...
......
ONCE, I HAD WISHED TO DISAPPEAR AND BE DONE WITH THIS WORLD.
BUT NOW YOU WISH TO KEEP LIVING?
NO... THAT DOESN'T QUITE EXPLAIN IT...

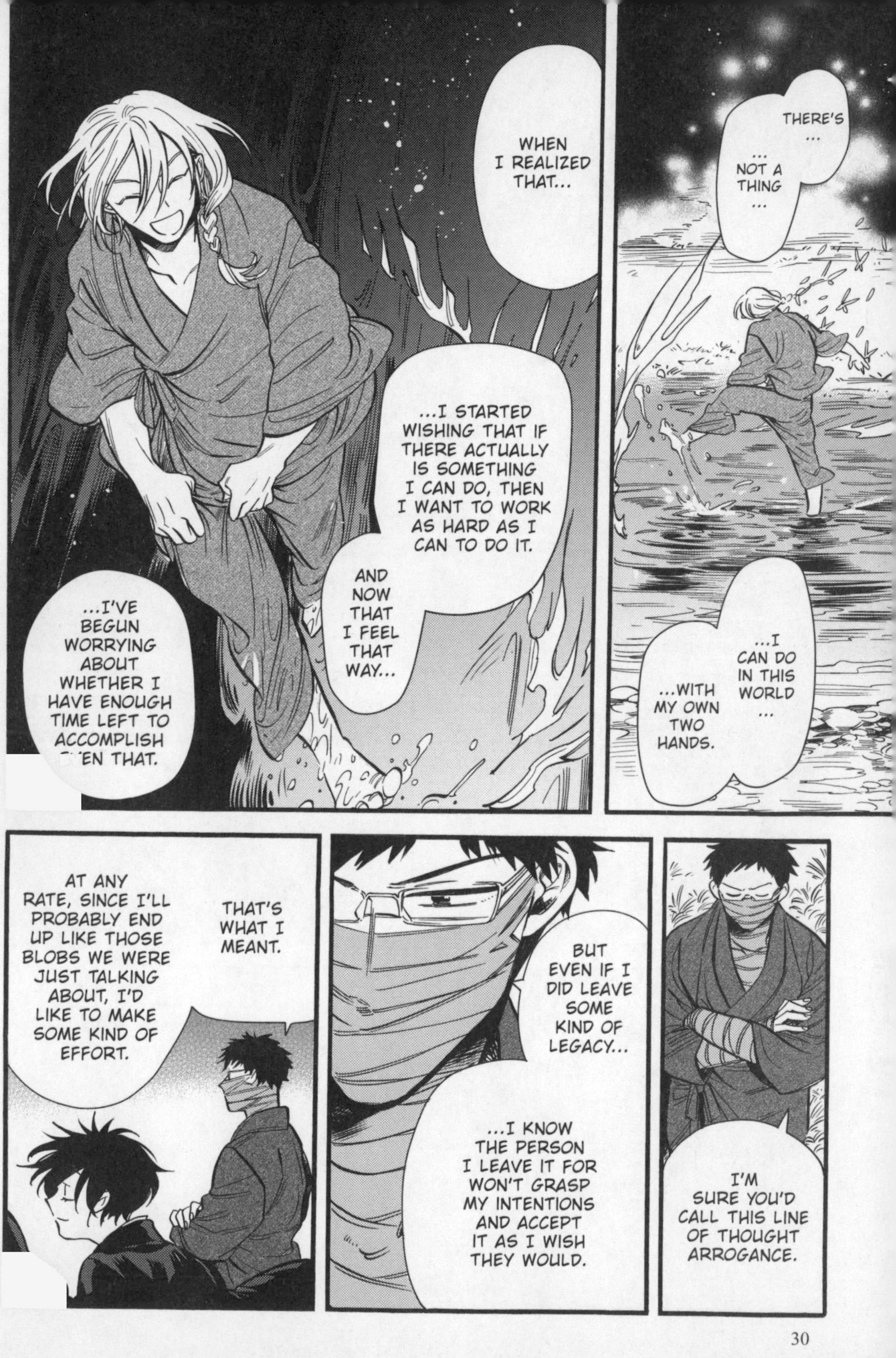
THERE'S ... ... NOT A THING ...
...I CAN DO IN THIS WORLD ...
...WITH MY OWN TWO HANDS.
WHEN I REALIZED THAT...
...I STARTED WISHING THAT IF THERE ACTUALLY IS SOMETHING I CAN DO, THEN I WANT TO WORK AS HARD AS I CAN TO DO IT.
AND NOW THAT I FEEL THAT WAY...
...I'VE BEGUN WORRYING ABOUT WHETHER I HAVE ENOUGH TIME LEFT TO ACCOMPLISH
EN THAT.
I'M SURE YOU'D CALL THIS LINE OF THOUGHT ARROGANCE.
BUT EVEN IF I DID LEAVE SOME KIND OF LEGACY...
...I KNOW THE PERSON I LEAVE IT FOR WON'T GRASP MY INTENTIONS AND ACCEPT IT AS I WISH THEY WOULD.
THAT'S WHAT I MEANT.
AT ANY RATE, SINCE I'LL PROBABLY END UP LIKE THOSE BLOBS WE WERE JUST TALKING ABOUT, I'D LIKE TO MAKE SOME KIND OF EFFORT.

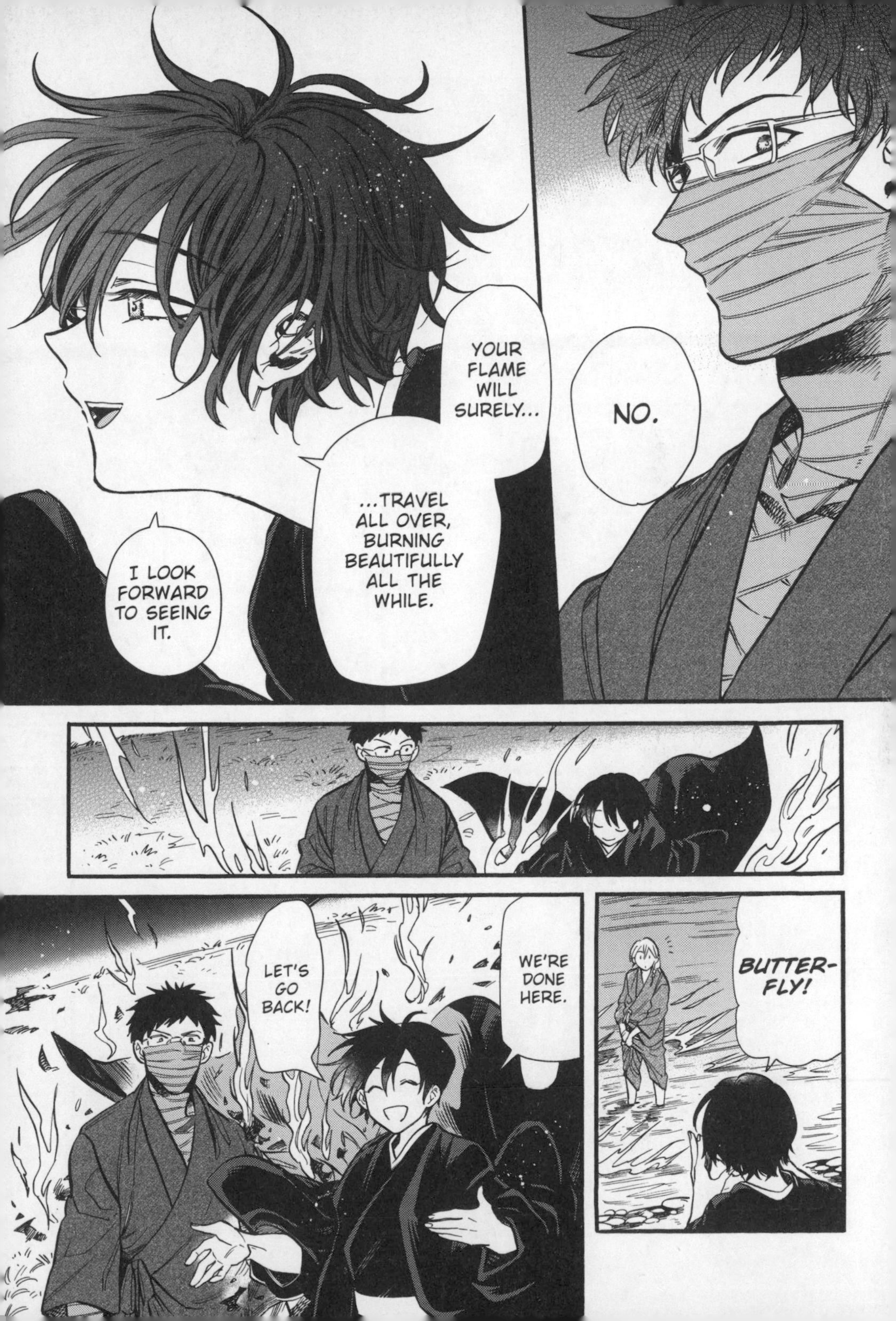
NO.
YOUR FLAME WILL SURELY...
...TRAVEL ALL OVER, BURNING BEAUTIFULLY ALL THE WHILE.
I LOOK FORWARD TO SEEING IT.
BUTTER-FLY!
WE'RE DONE HERE.
LET'S GO BACK!

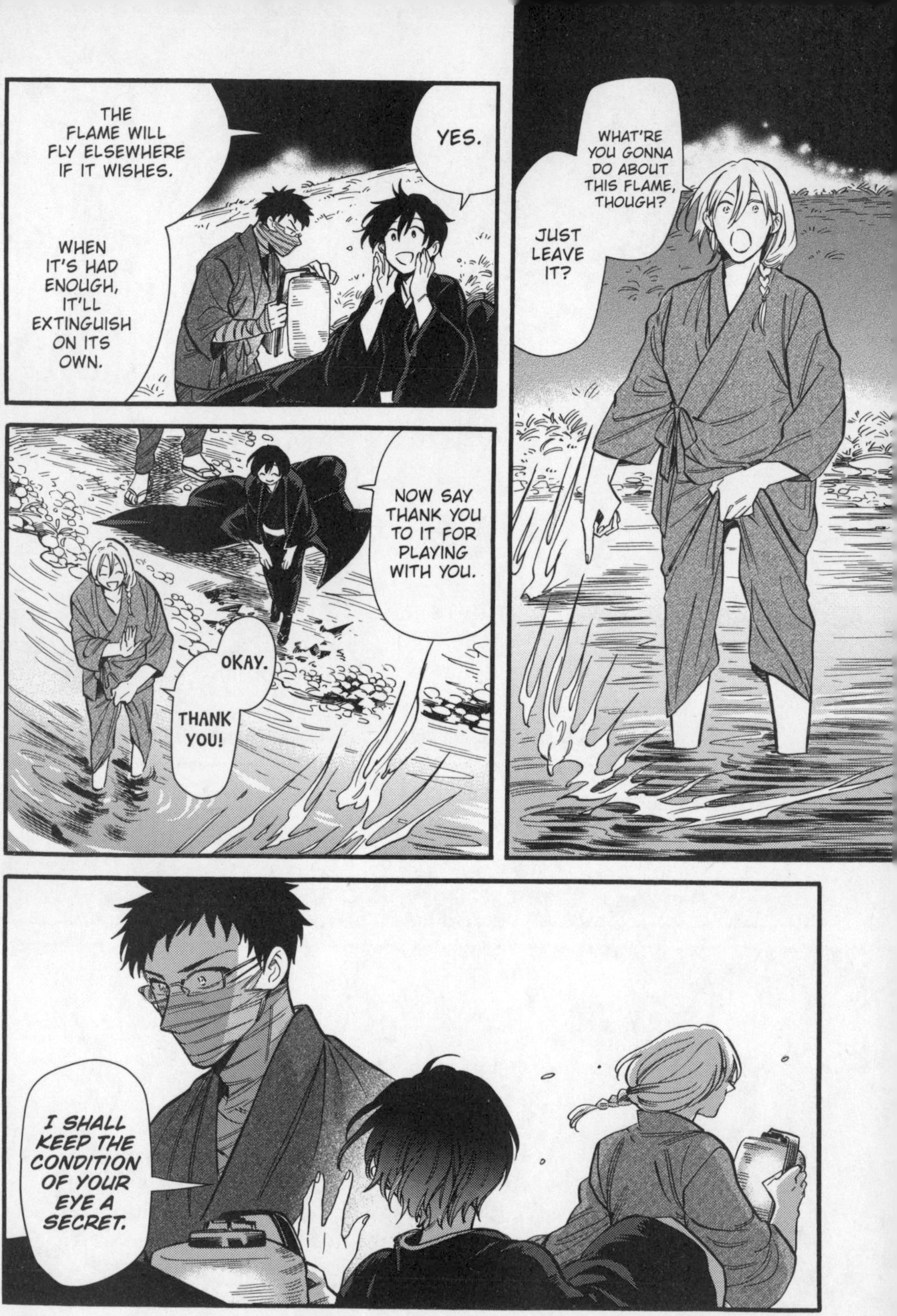

WHAT'RE YOU GONNA DO ABOUT THIS FLAME, THOUGH?
JUST LEAVE IT?
YES.
THE FLAME WILL FLY ELSEWHERE IF IT WISHES.
WHEN IT'S HAD ENOUGH, IT'LL EXTINGUISH ON ITS OWN.
NOW SAY THANK YOU TO IT FOR PLAYING WITH YOU.
OKAY.
THANK YOU!
I SHALL KEEP THE CONDITION OF YOUR EYE A SECRET.

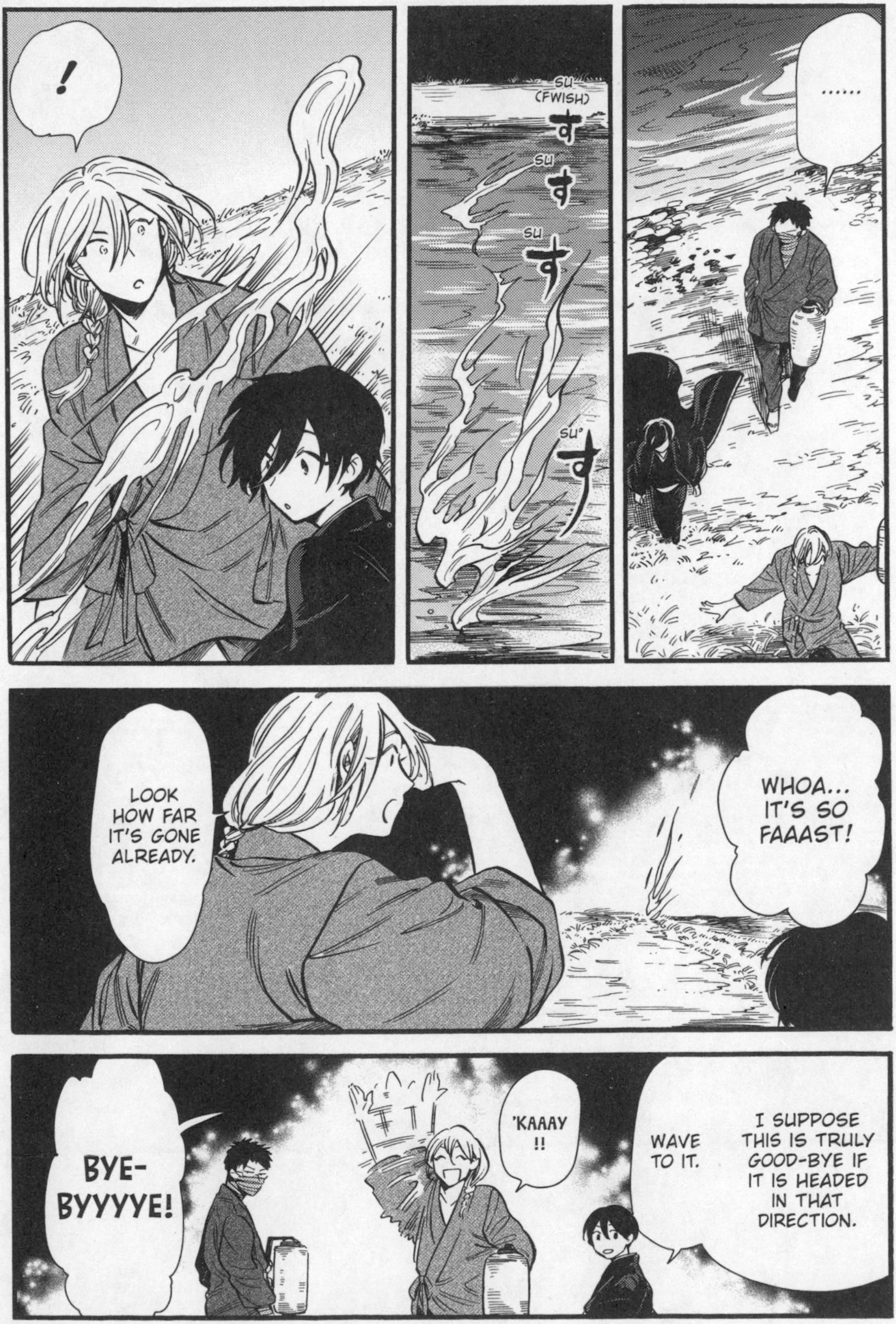
......
SU (FWISH)
す
SU
す
SU
す
SU'
す
!
WHOA... IT'S SO FAAAST!
LOOK HOW FAR IT'S GONE ALREADY.
I SUPPOSE THIS IS TRULY GOOD-BYE IF IT IS HEADED IN THAT DIRECTION.
WAVE TO IT.
'KAAAY !!
BYE-BYYYYE!

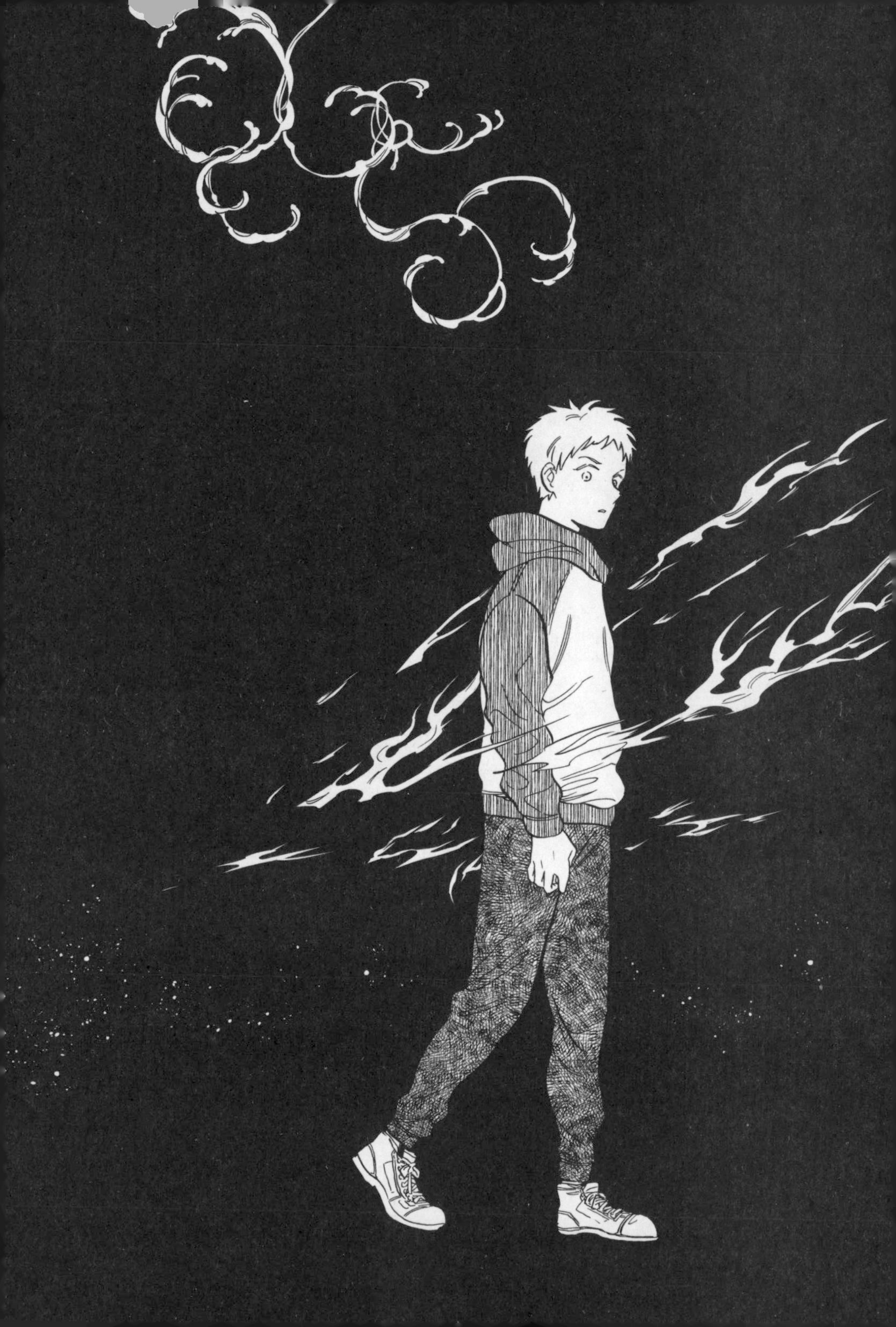

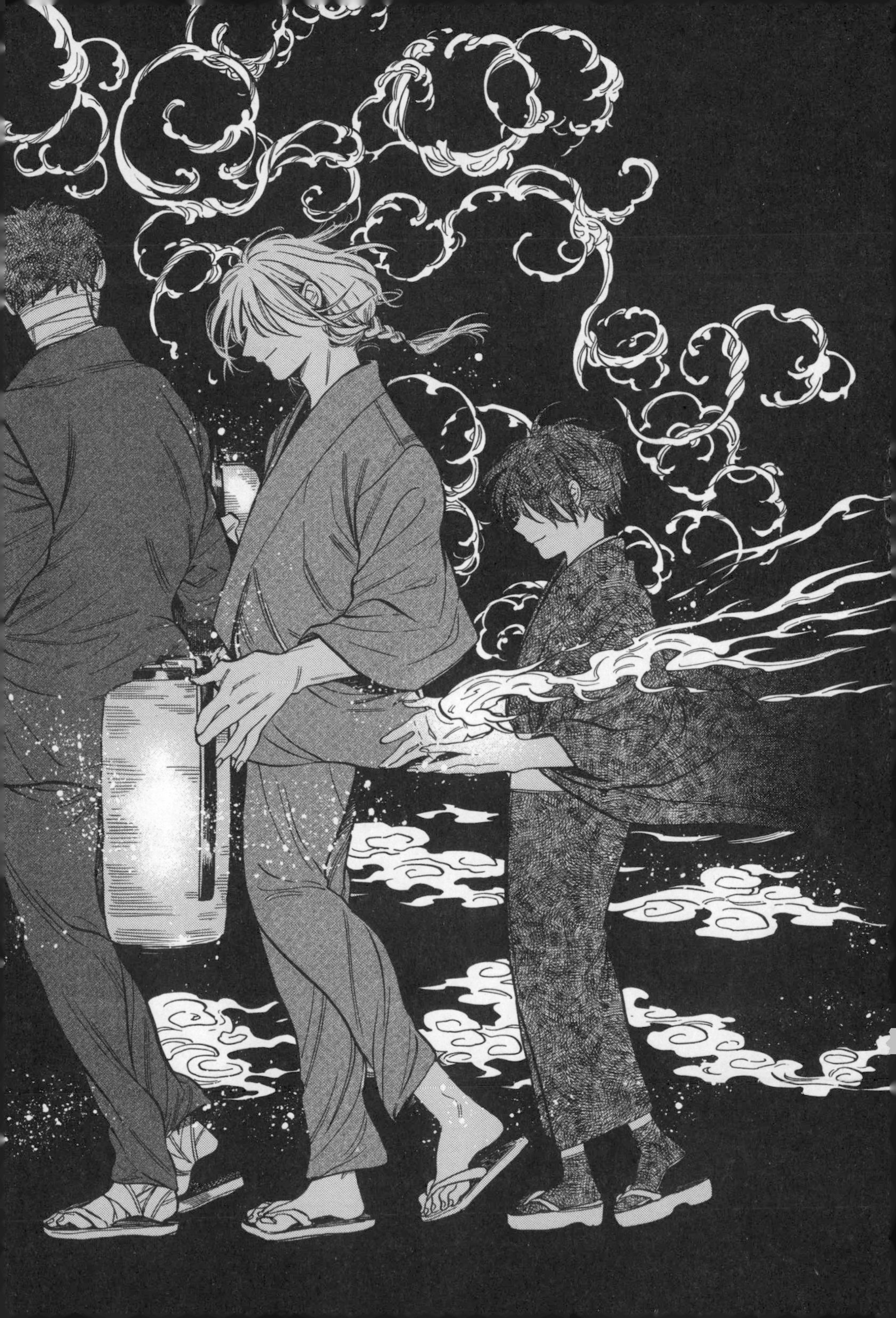

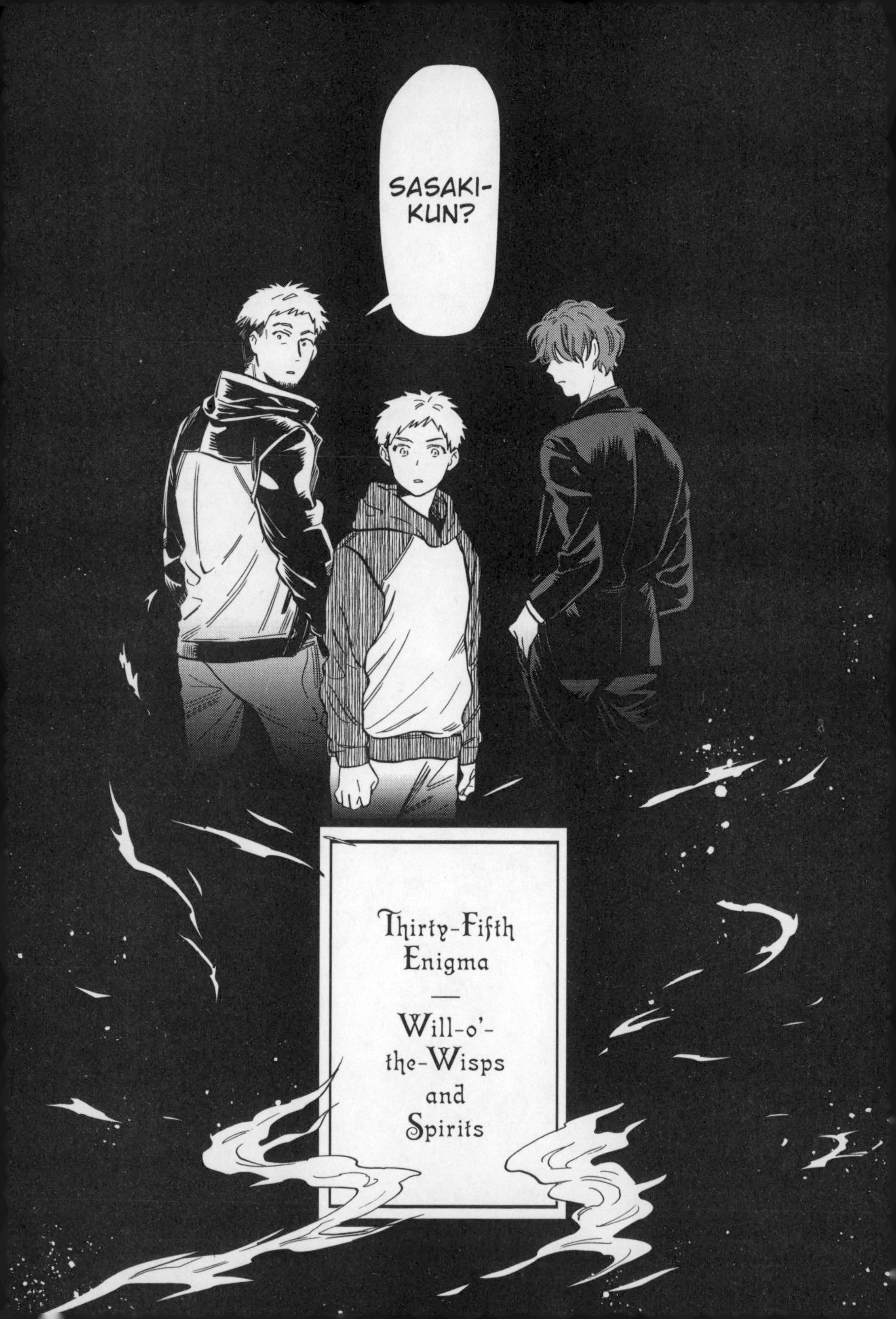
SASAKI-KUN?
Thirty-Fifth Enigma
—
Will-o'-the-Wisps and Spirits

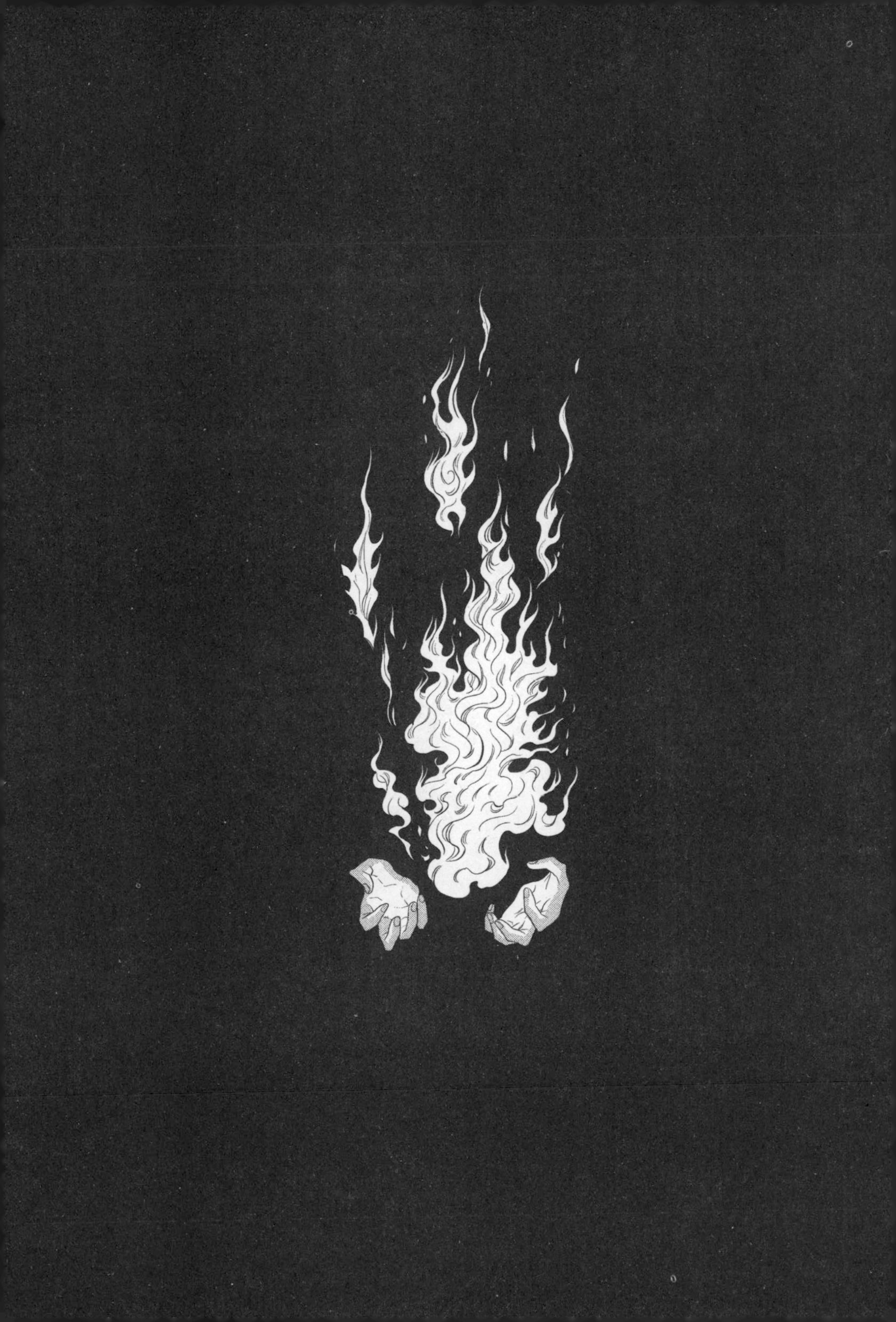

Phantom Tales of the Night

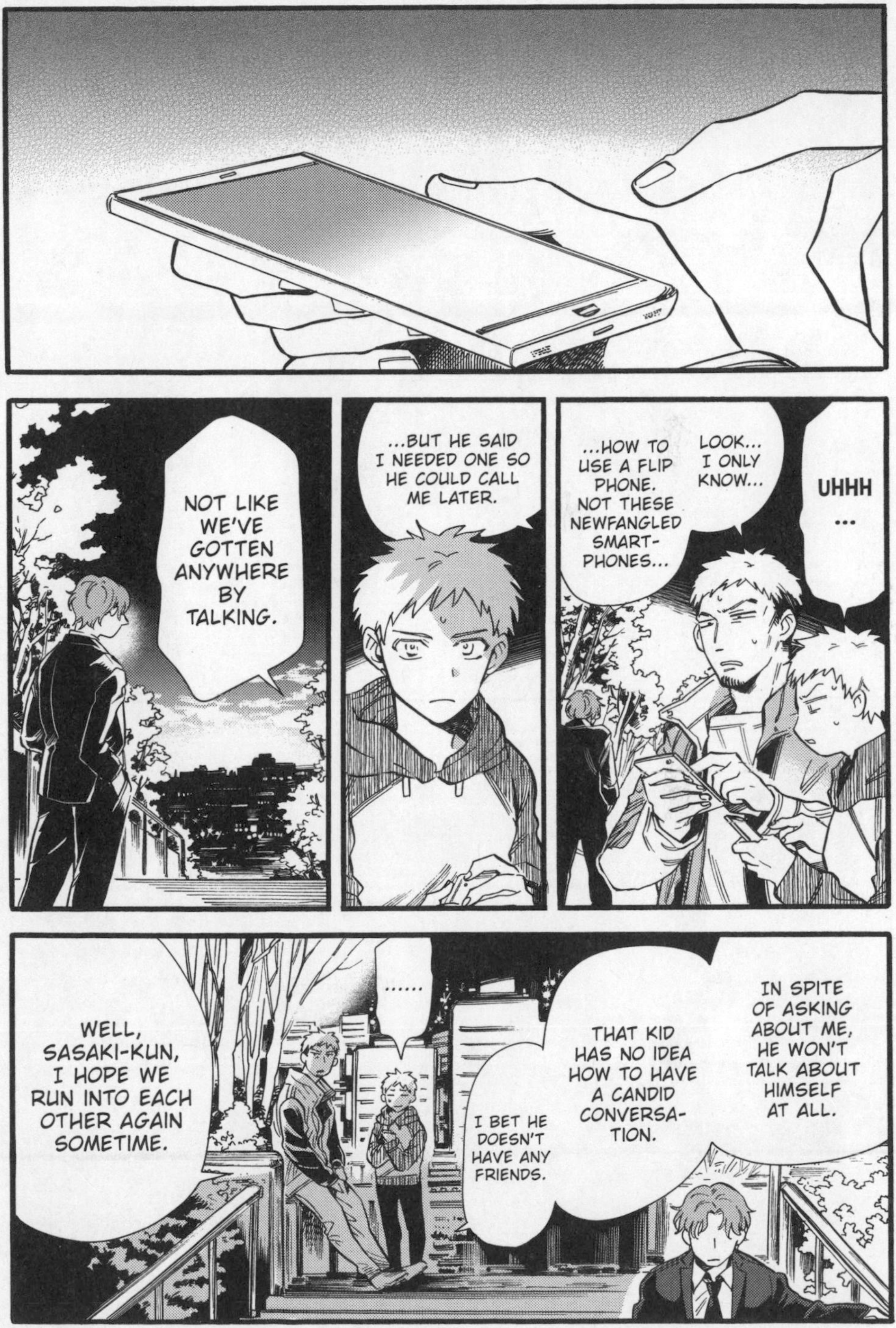
UHHH ...
LOOK... I ONLY KNOW...
...HOW TO USE A FLIP PHONE. NOT THESE NEWFANGLED SMART-PHONES...
...BUT HE SAID I NEEDED ONE SO HE COULD CALL ME LATER.
NOT LIKE WE'VE GOTTEN ANYWHERE BY TALKING.
IN SPITE OF ASKING ABOUT ME, HE WON'T TALK ABOUT HIMSELF AT ALL.
THAT KID HAS NO IDEA HOW TO HAVE A CANDID CONVERSA-TION.
I BET HE DOESN'T HAVE ANY FRIENDS.
......
WELL, SASAKI-KUN, I HOPE WE RUN INTO EACH OTHER AGAIN SOMETIME.

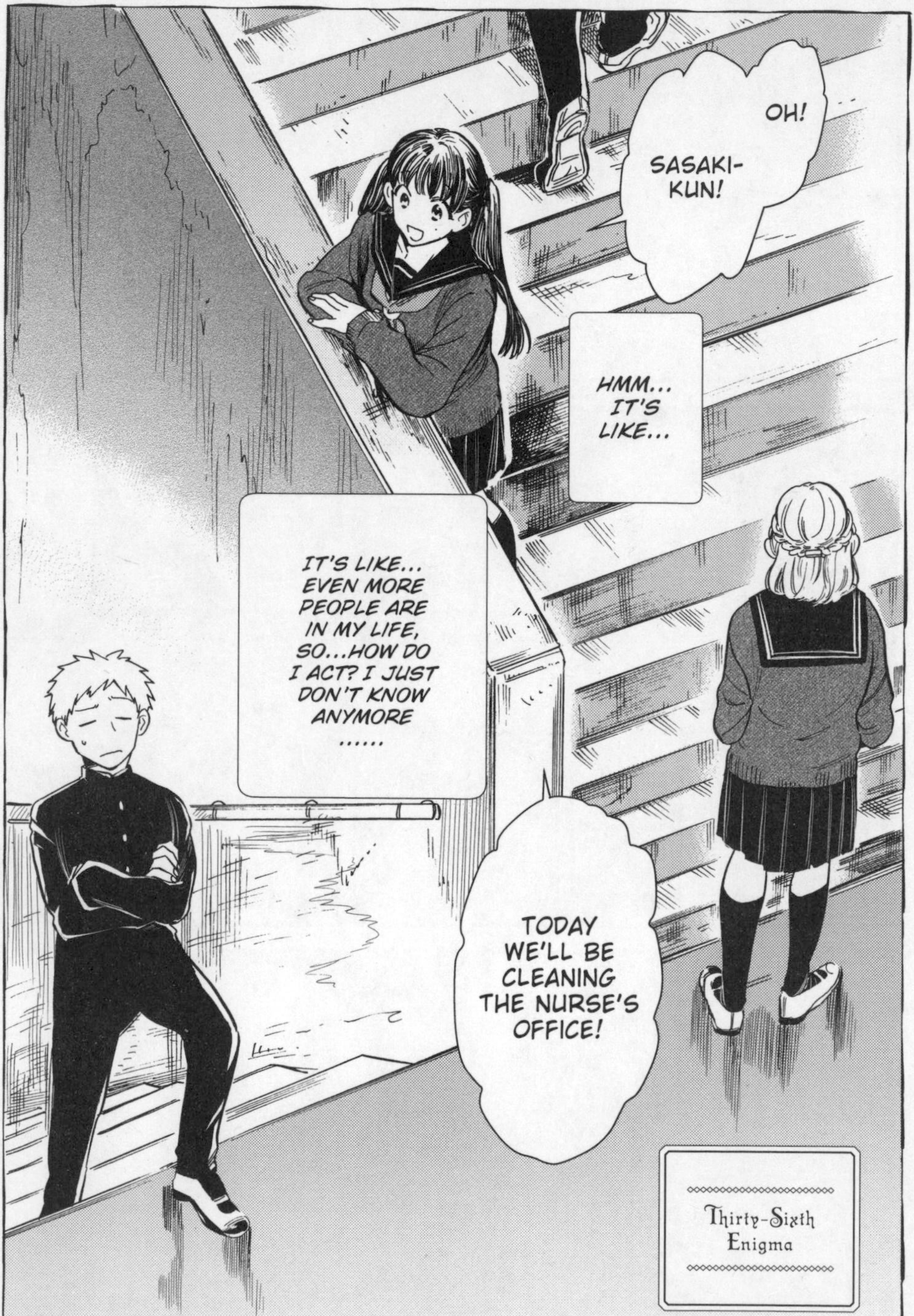
OH! SASAKI-KUN!
HMM... IT'S LIKE...
IT'S LIKE... EVEN MORE PEOPLE ARE IN MY LIFE, SO...HOW DO I ACT? I JUST DON'T KNOW ANYMORE ......
TODAY WE'LL BE CLEANING THE NURSE'S OFFICE!
Thirty-Sixth Enigma

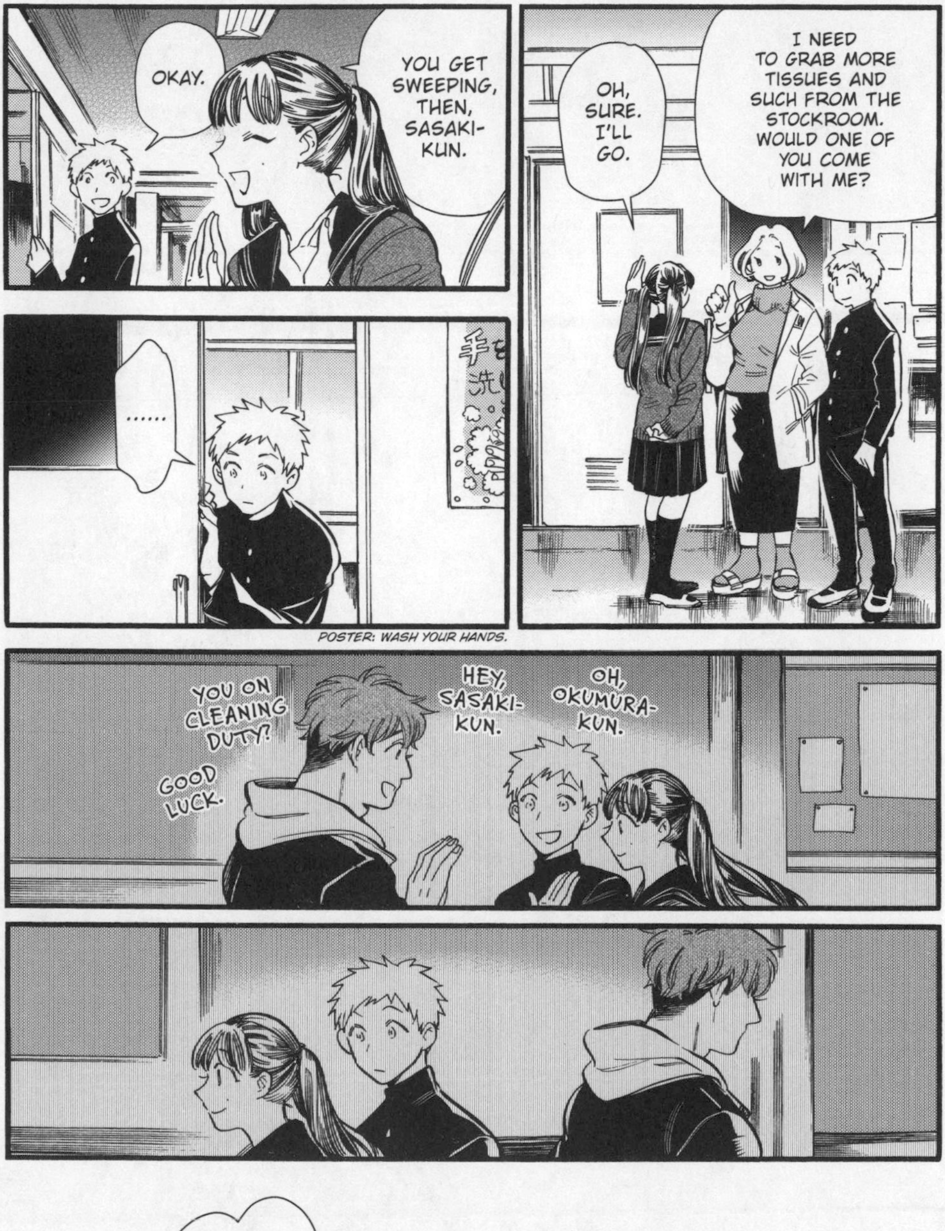
I NEED TO GRAB MORE TISSUES AND SUCH FROM THE STOCKROOM. WOULD ONE OF YOU COME WITH ME?
OH, SURE. I'LL GO.
YOU GET SWEEPING, THEN, SASAKI-KUN.
OKAY.
......
POSTER: WASH YOUR HANDS.
OH, OKUMURA-KUN.
HEY, SASAKI-KUN.
YOU ON CLEANING DUTY?
GOOD LUCK.
......
HUH?

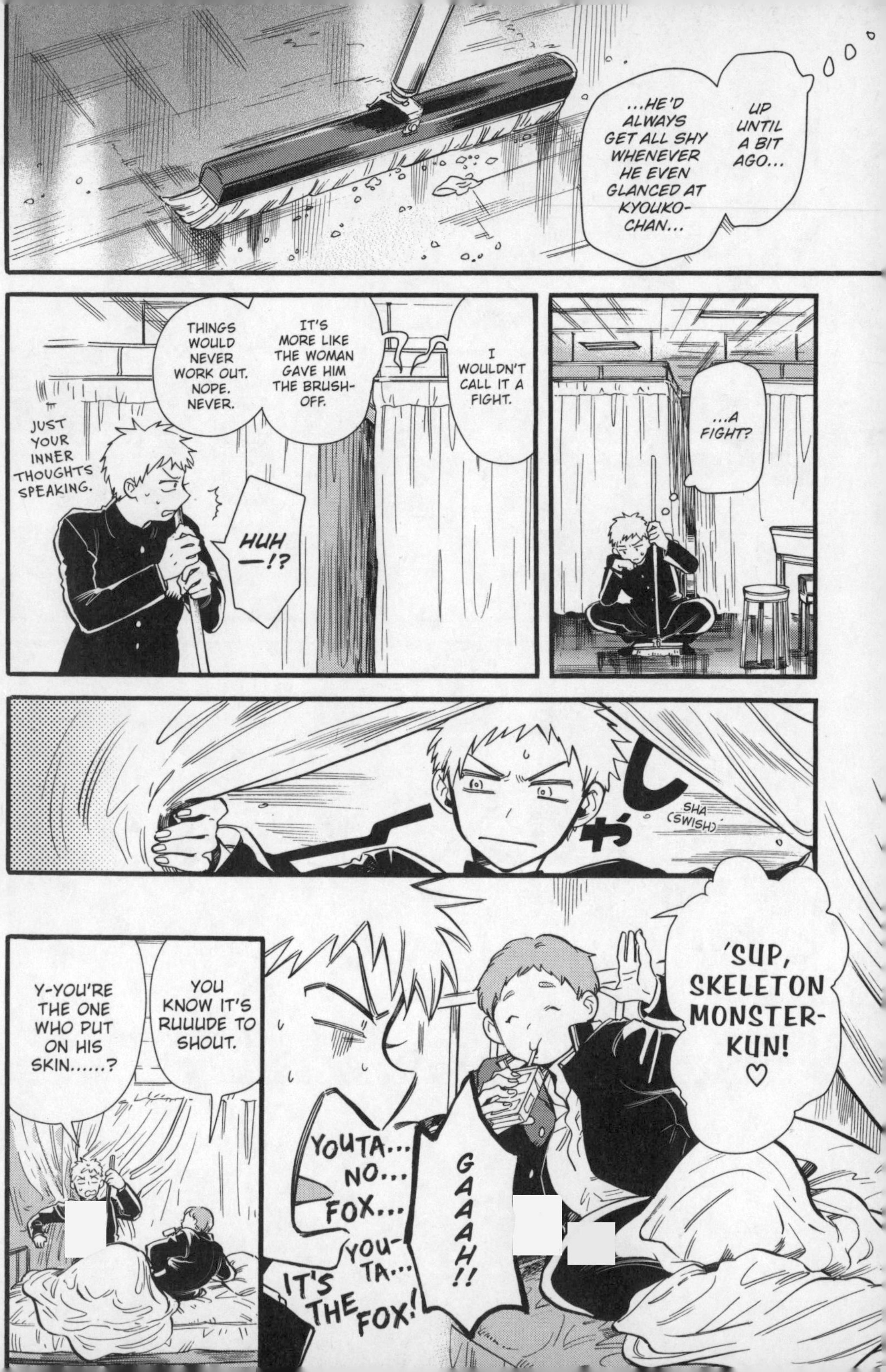
UP UNTIL A BIT AGO...
...HE'D ALWAYS GET ALL SHY WHENEVER HE EVEN GLANCED AT KYOUKO-CHAN...
...A FIGHT?
I WOULDN'T CALL IT A FIGHT.
IT'S MORE LIKE THE WOMAN GAVE HIM THE BRUSH-OFF.
THINGS WOULD NEVER WORK OUT. NOPE. NEVER.
HUH—!?
JUST YOUR INNER THOUGHTS SPEAKING.
SHA (SWISH)
'SUP, SKELETON MONSTER-KUN! ♡
GAAAAH!!
YOUTA... NO... FOX... YOU-TA... IT'S THE FOX!
YOU KNOW IT'S RUUUDE TO SHOUT.
Y-YOU'RE THE ONE WHO PUT ON HIS SKIN......?

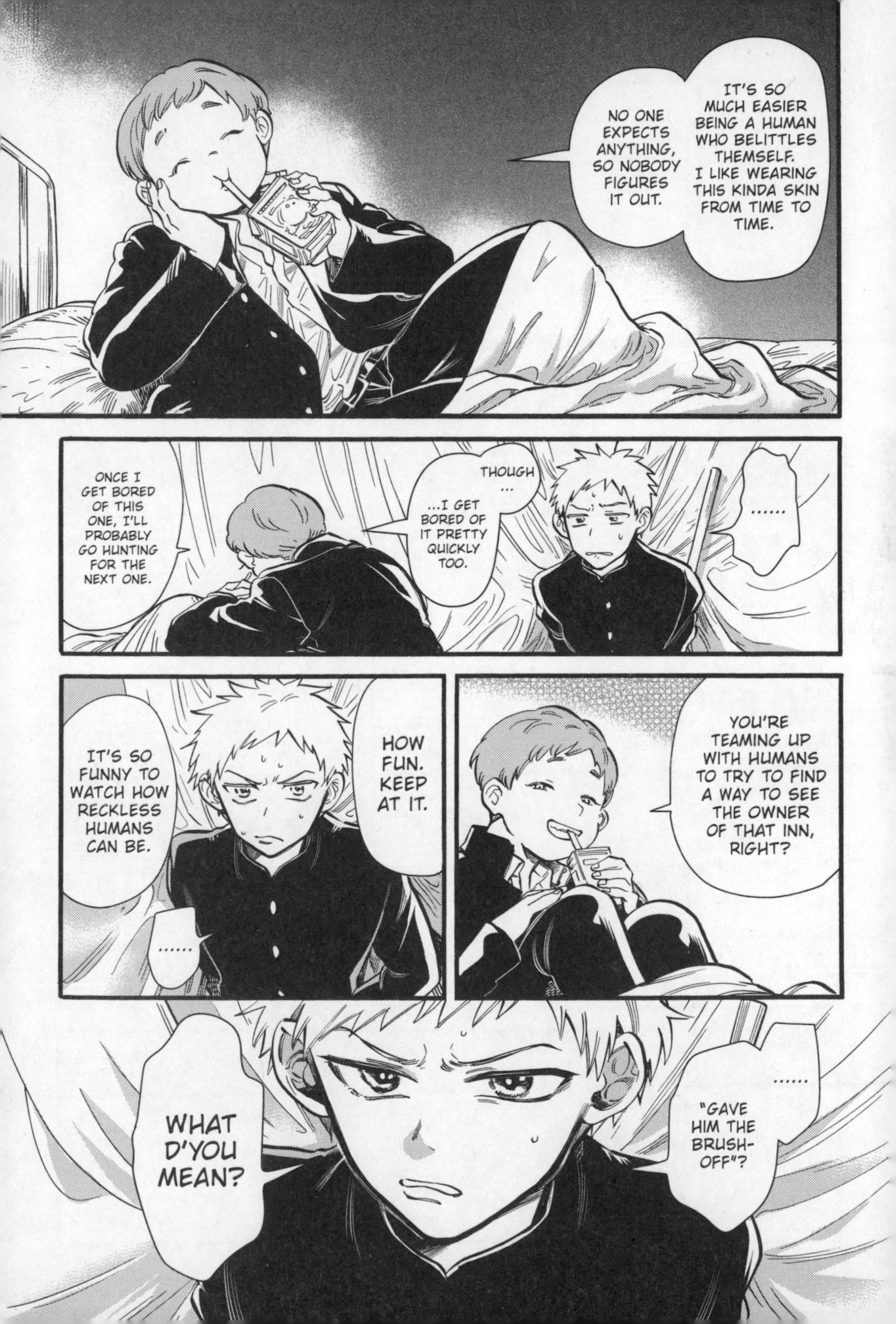
IT'S SO MUCH EASIER BEING A HUMAN WHO BELITTLES THEMSELF. I LIKE WEARING THIS KINDA SKIN FROM TIME TO TIME.
NO ONE EXPECTS ANYTHING, SO NOBODY FIGURES IT OUT.
......
THOUGH ...
...I GET BORED OF IT PRETTY QUICKLY TOO.
ONCE I GET BORED OF THIS ONE, I'LL PROBABLY GO HUNTING FOR THE NEXT ONE.
YOU'RE TEAMING UP WITH HUMANS TO TRY TO FIND A WAY TO SEE THE OWNER OF THAT INN, RIGHT?
HOW FUN. KEEP AT IT.
IT'S SO FUNNY TO WATCH HOW RECKLESS HUMANS CAN BE.
......
......
"GAVE HIM THE BRUSH-OFF"?
WHAT D'YOU MEAN?

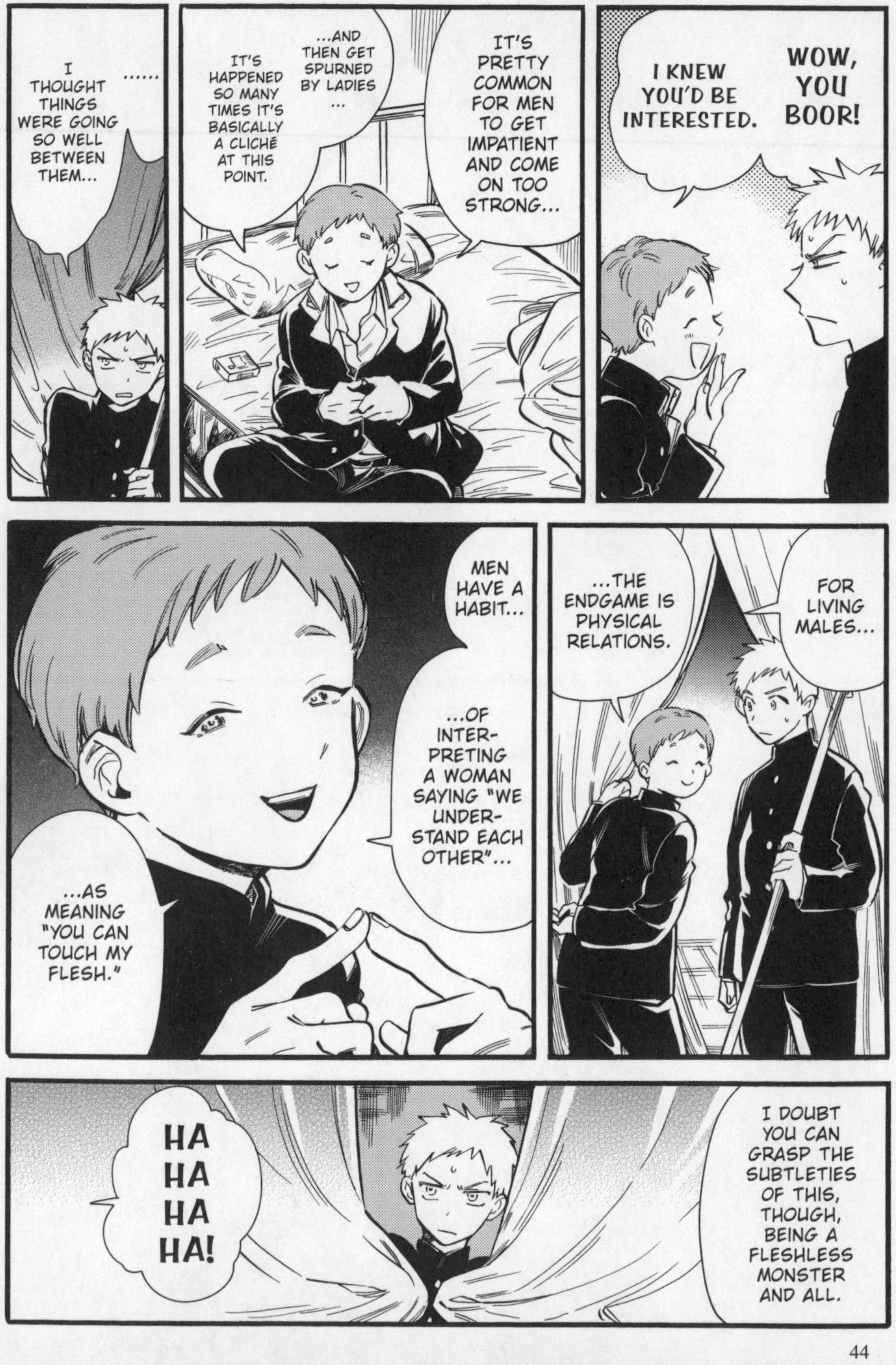
WOW, YOU BOOR!
I KNEW YOU'D BE INTERESTED.
IT'S PRETTY COMMON FOR MEN TO GET IMPATIENT AND COME ON TOO STRONG...
...AND THEN GET SPURNED BY LADIES...
IT'S HAPPENED SO MANY TIMES IT'S BASICALLY A CLICHÉ AT THIS POINT.
......
I THOUGHT THINGS WERE GOING SO WELL BETWEEN THEM...
FOR LIVING MALES...
...THE ENDGAME IS PHYSICAL RELATIONS.
MEN HAVE A HABIT...
...OF INTERPRETING A WOMAN SAYING "WE UNDERSTAND EACH OTHER"...
...AS MEANING "YOU CAN TOUCH MY FLESH."
I DOUBT YOU CAN GRASP THE SUBTLETIES OF THIS, THOUGH, BEING A FLESHLESS MONSTER AND ALL.
HA HA HA HA!

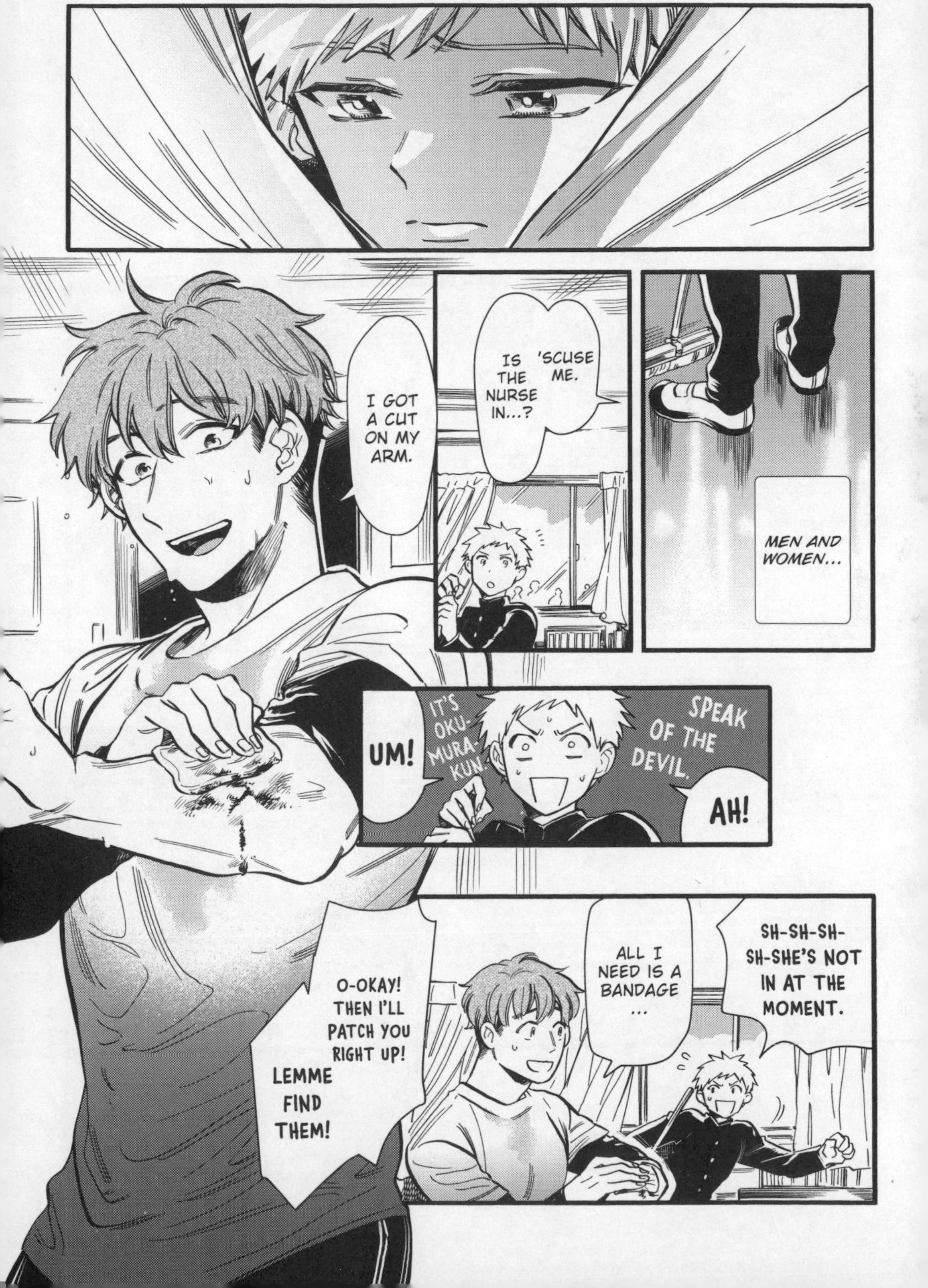

MEN AND WOMEN…
'SCUSE ME.
IS THE NURSE IN…?
I GOT A CUT ON MY ARM.
SPEAK OF THE DEVIL.
AH!
IT'S OKU-MURA-KUN.
UM!
SH-SH-SH-SH-SHE'S NOT IN AT THE MOMENT.
ALL I NEED IS A BANDAGE …
O-OKAY! THEN I'LL PATCH YOU RIGHT UP!
LEMME FIND THEM!

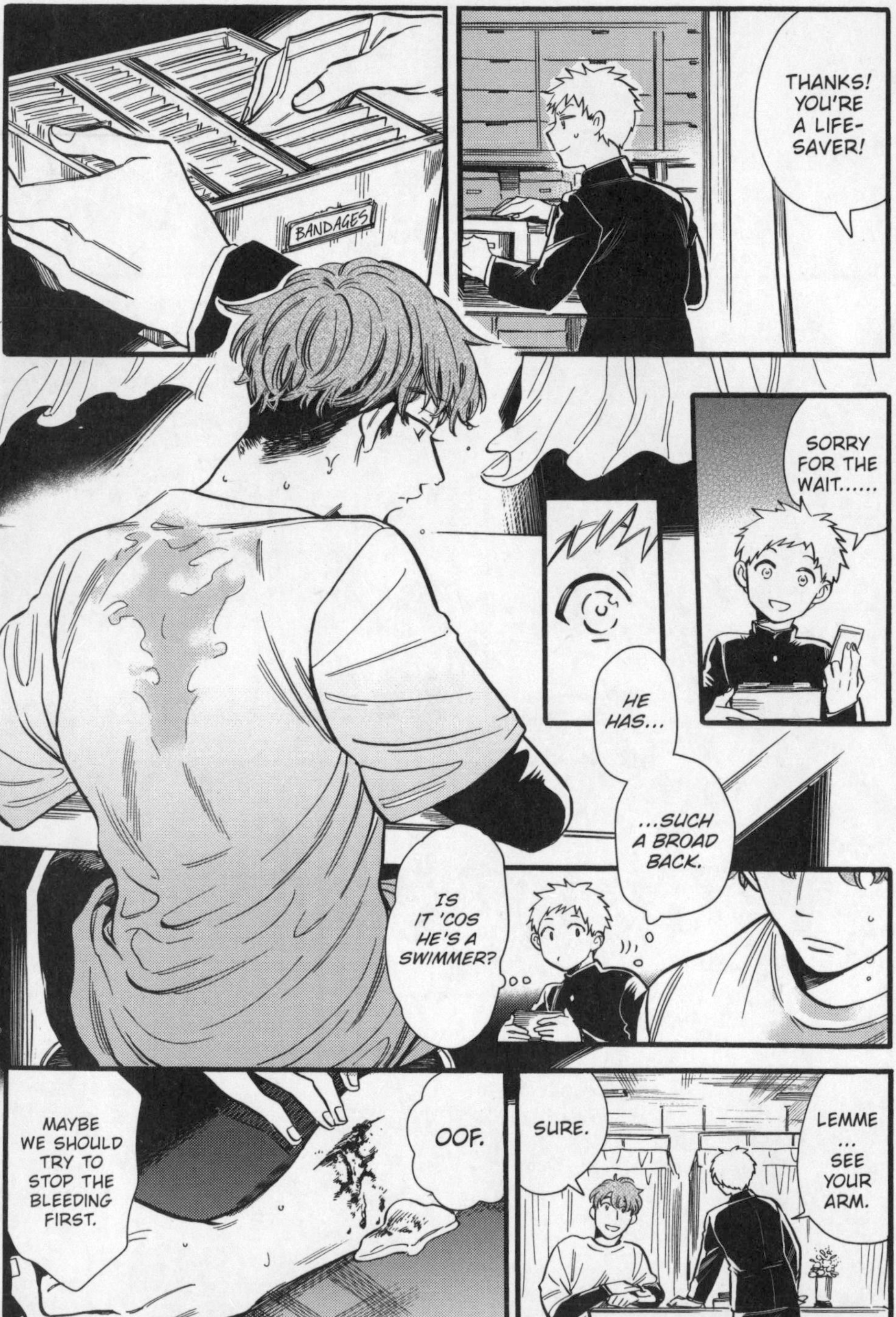
THANKS! YOU'RE A LIFE-SAVER!
BANDAGES
SORRY FOR THE WAIT......
HE HAS...
...SUCH A BROAD BACK.
IS IT 'COS HE'S A SWIMMER?
LEMME ... SEE YOUR ARM.
SURE.
OOF.
MAYBE WE SHOULD TRY TO STOP THE BLEEDING FIRST.

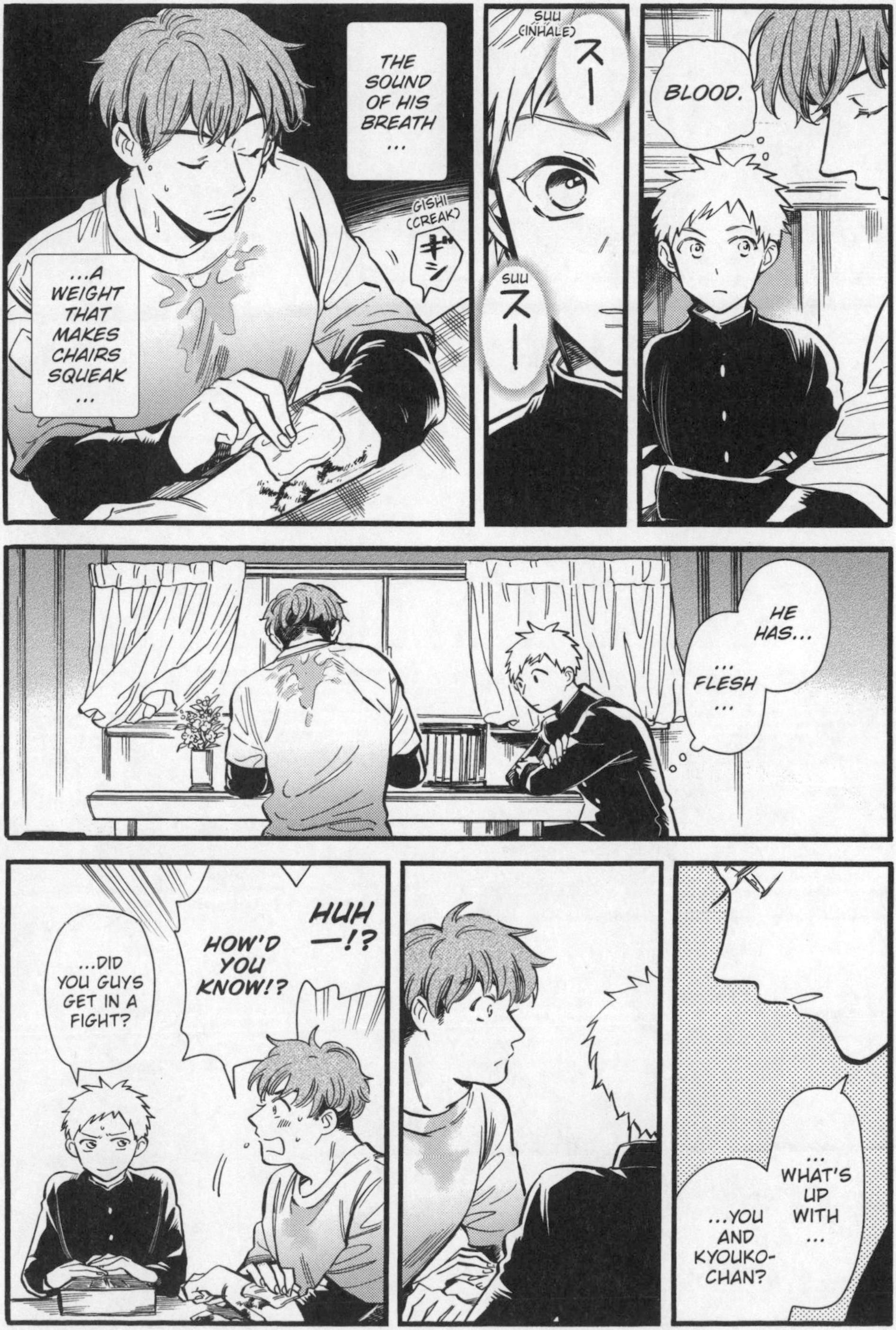
BLOOD.
SUU (INHALE)
スー
SUU
スー
THE SOUND OF HIS BREATH ...
GISHI (CREAK)
ギシ
...A WEIGHT THAT MAKES CHAIRS SQUEAK ...
HE HAS... ...FLESH ...
... WHAT'S UP WITH ...
...YOU AND KYOUKO-CHAN?
HUH —!?
HOW'D YOU KNOW!?
...DID YOU GUYS GET IN A FIGHT?

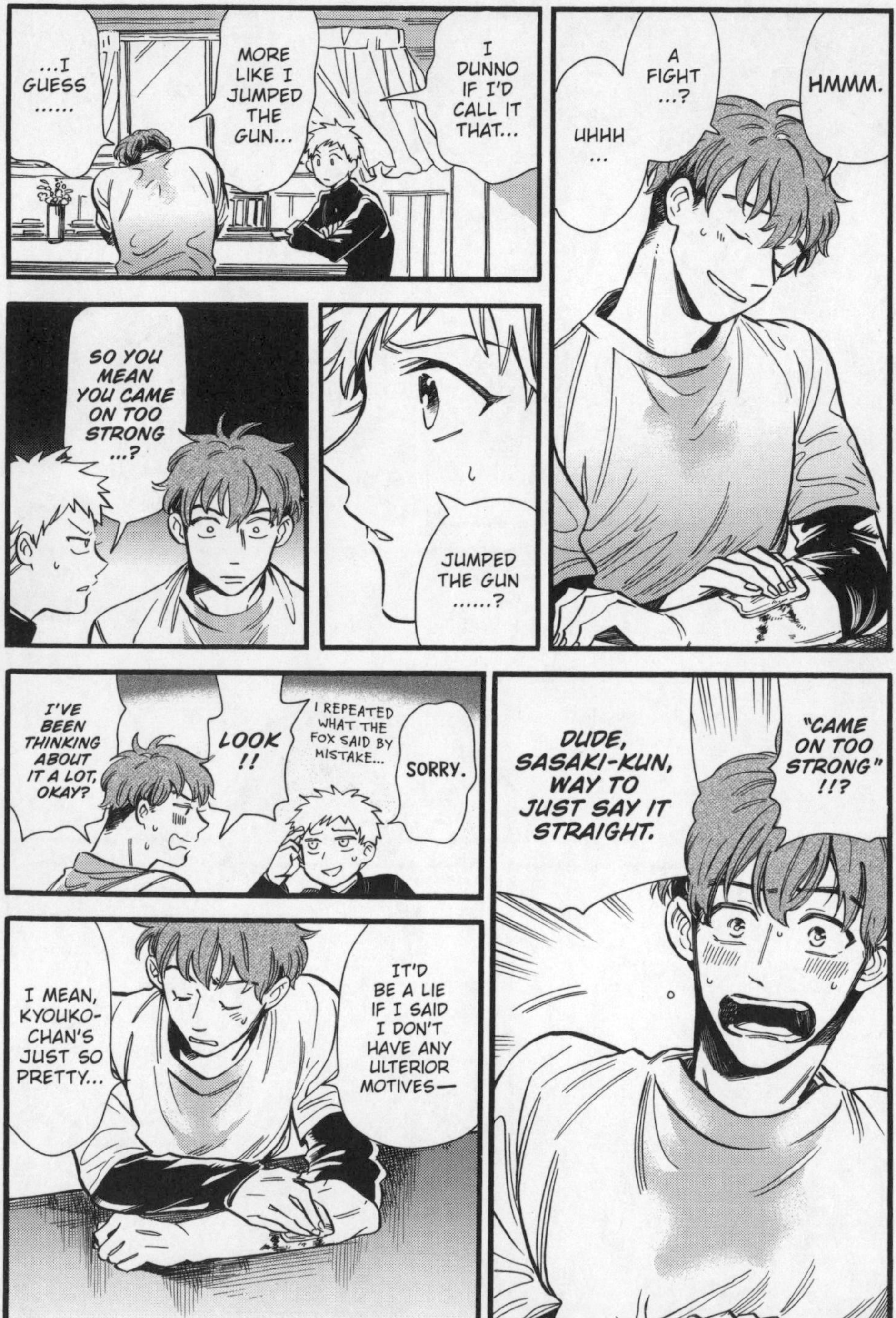
HMMM.
A FIGHT ...?
UHHH ...
I DUNNO IF I'D CALL IT THAT...
MORE LIKE I JUMPED THE GUN...
...I GUESS ......
JUMPED THE GUN ......?
SO YOU MEAN YOU CAME ON TOO STRONG ...?
"CAME ON TOO STRONG" !!?
DUDE, SASAKI-KUN, WAY TO JUST SAY IT STRAIGHT.
SORRY.
I REPEATED WHAT THE FOX SAID BY MISTAKE...
LOOK !!
I'VE BEEN THINKING ABOUT IT A LOT, OKAY?
IT'D BE A LIE IF I SAID I DON'T HAVE ANY ULTERIOR MOTIVES—
I MEAN, KYOUKO-CHAN'S JUST SO PRETTY...

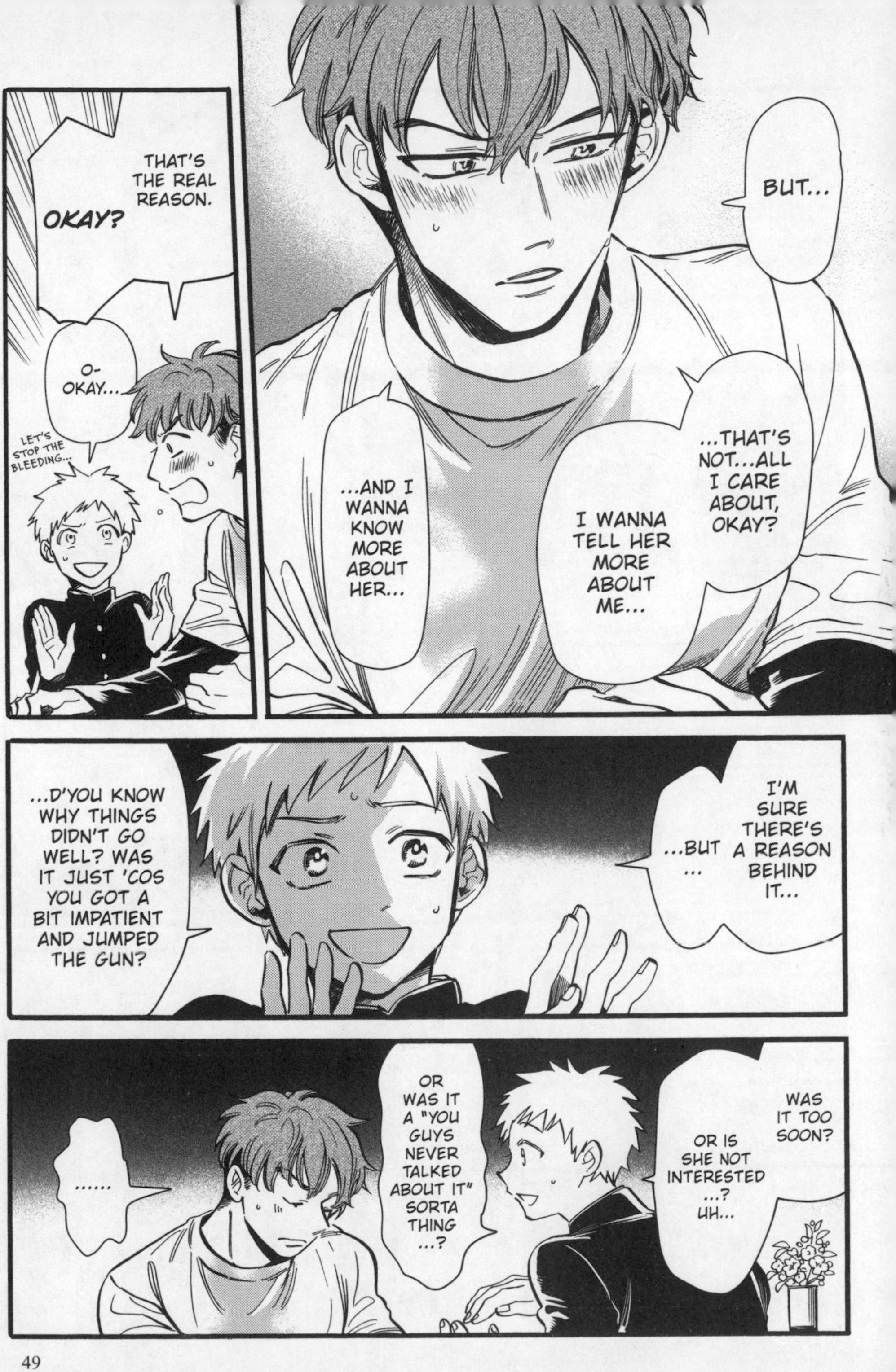
BUT...
...THAT'S NOT...ALL I CARE ABOUT, OKAY?
I WANNA TELL HER MORE ABOUT ME...
...AND I WANNA KNOW MORE ABOUT HER...
THAT'S THE REAL REASON. OKAY?
O-OKAY...
LET'S STOP THE BLEEDING...
I'M SURE THERE'S A REASON BEHIND IT...
...BUT ...
...D'YOU KNOW WHY THINGS DIDN'T GO WELL? WAS IT JUST 'COS YOU GOT A BIT IMPATIENT AND JUMPED THE GUN?
WAS IT TOO SOON?
OR IS SHE NOT INTERESTED ...? UH...
OR WAS IT A "YOU GUYS NEVER TALKED ABOUT IT" SORTA THING ...?
......

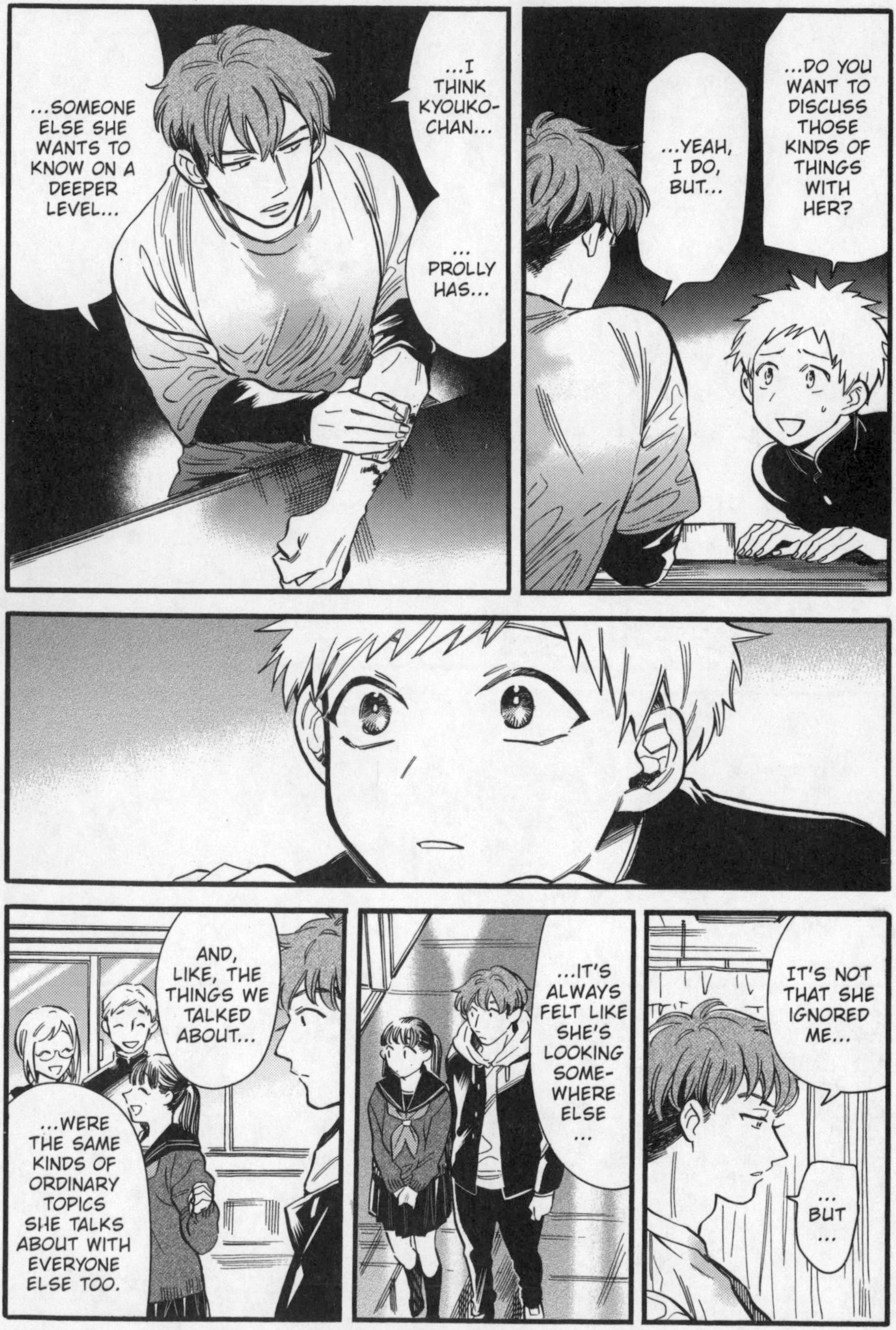
...DO YOU WANT TO DISCUSS THOSE KINDS OF THINGS WITH HER?
...YEAH, I DO, BUT...
...I THINK KYOUKO-CHAN...
... PROLLY HAS...
...SOMEONE ELSE SHE WANTS TO KNOW ON A DEEPER LEVEL...
IT'S NOT THAT SHE IGNORED ME...
... BUT ...
...IT'S ALWAYS FELT LIKE SHE'S LOOKING SOME-WHERE ELSE ...
AND, LIKE, THE THINGS WE TALKED ABOUT...
...WERE THE SAME KINDS OF ORDINARY TOPICS SHE TALKS ABOUT WITH EVERYONE ELSE TOO.

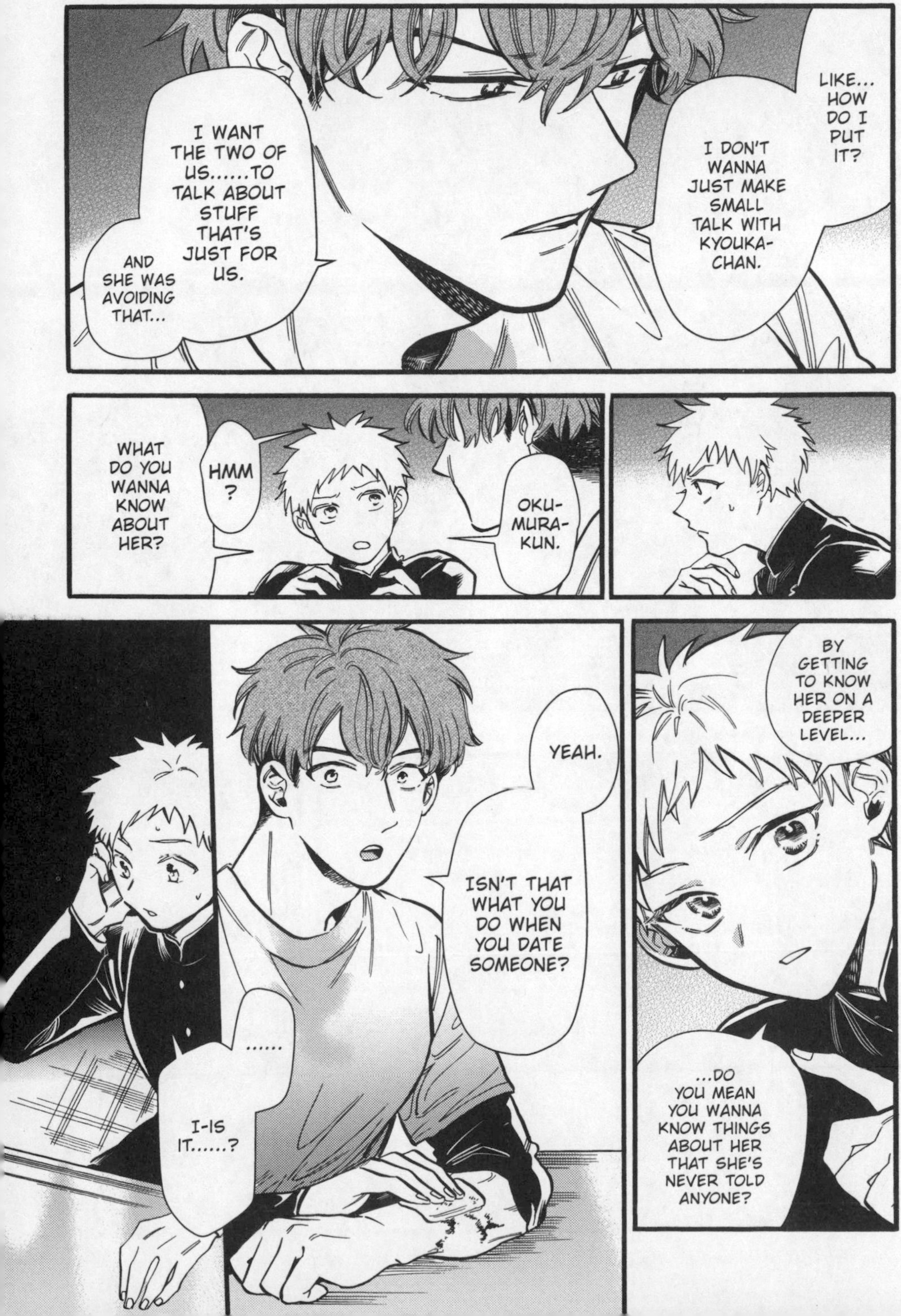
LIKE... HOW DO I PUT IT?
I DON'T WANNA JUST MAKE SMALL TALK WITH KYOUKA-CHAN.
I WANT THE TWO OF US......TO TALK ABOUT STUFF THAT'S JUST FOR US.
AND SHE WAS AVOIDING THAT...
OKU-MURA-KUN.
HMM ?
WHAT DO YOU WANNA KNOW ABOUT HER?
BY GETTING TO KNOW HER ON A DEEPER LEVEL...
...DO YOU MEAN YOU WANNA KNOW THINGS ABOUT HER THAT SHE'S NEVER TOLD ANYONE?
YEAH.
ISN'T THAT WHAT YOU DO WHEN YOU DATE SOMEONE?
......
I-IS IT......?

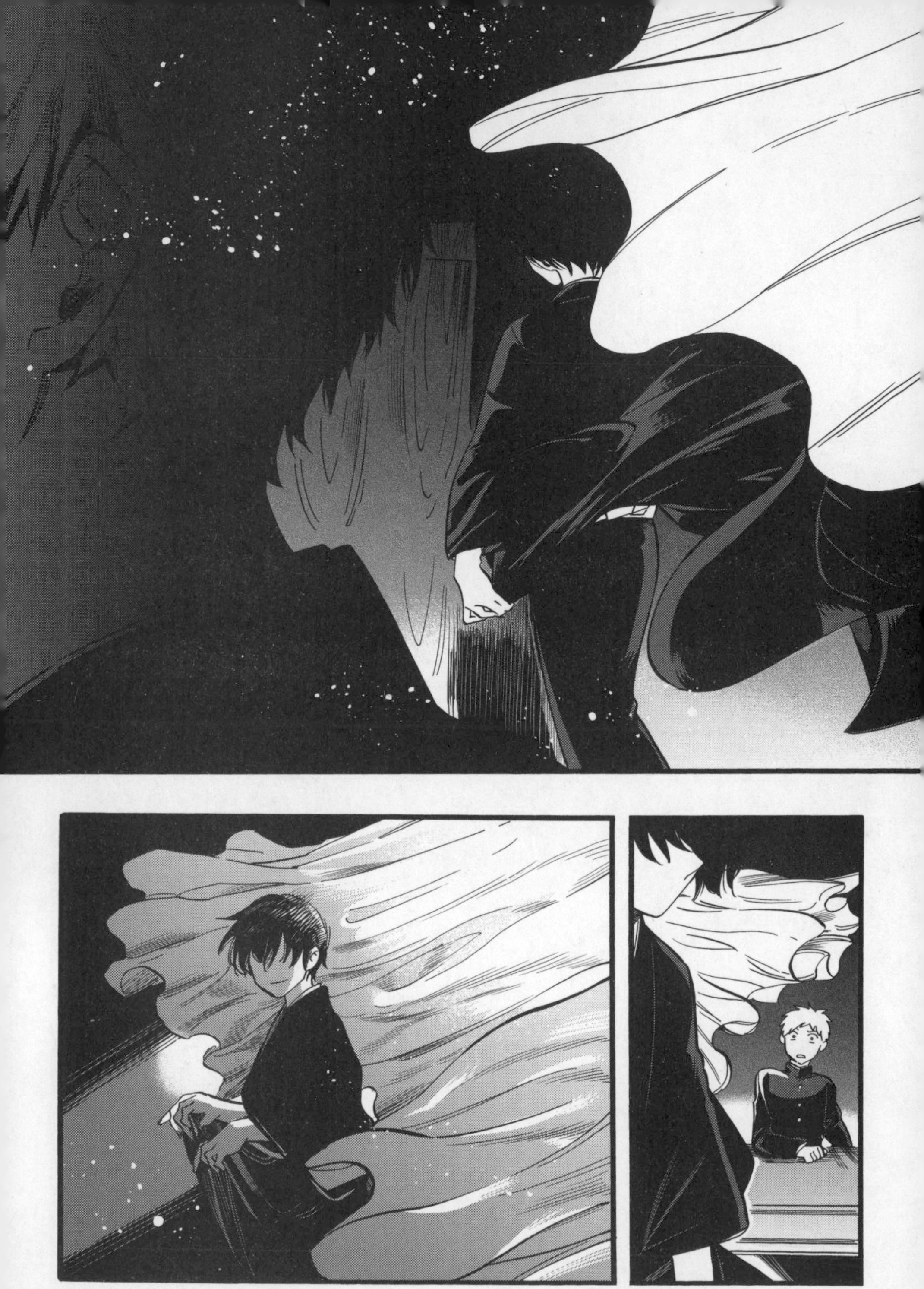

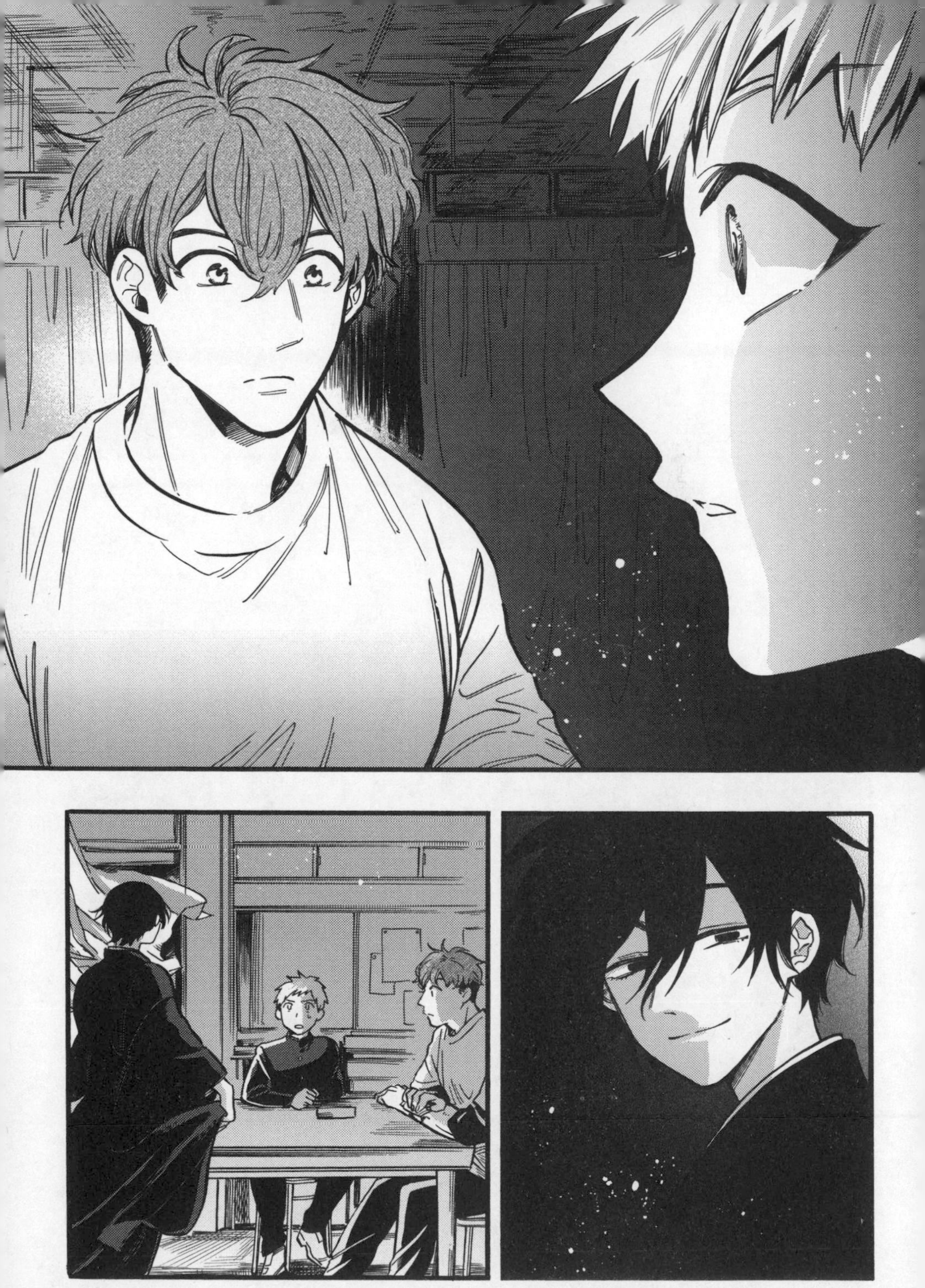

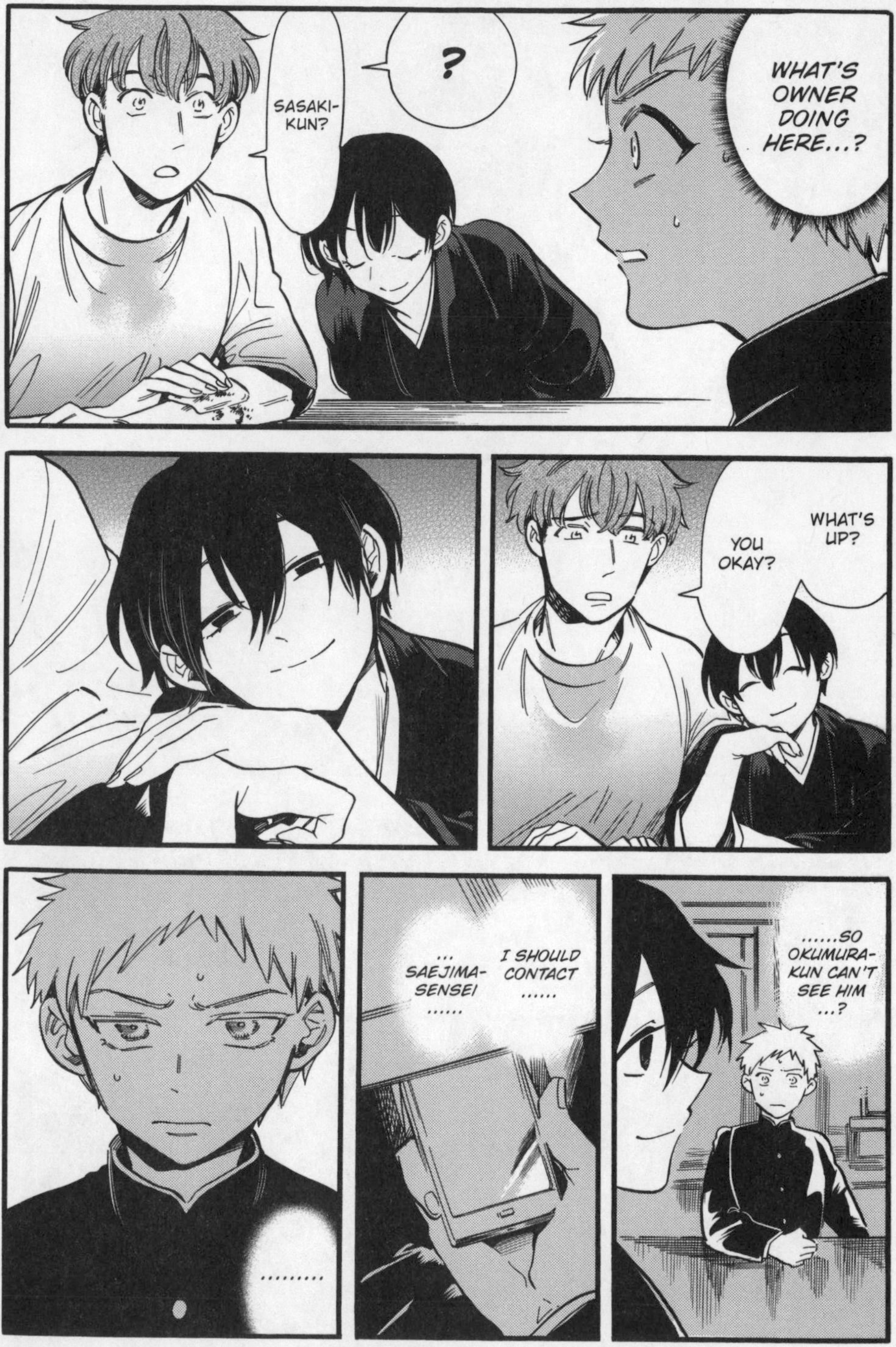
WHAT'S OWNER DOING HERE...?
?
SASAKI-KUN?
WHAT'S UP?
YOU OKAY?
......SO OKUMURA-KUN CAN'T SEE HIM ...?
I SHOULD CONTACT ......
... SAEJIMA-SENSEI ......
....

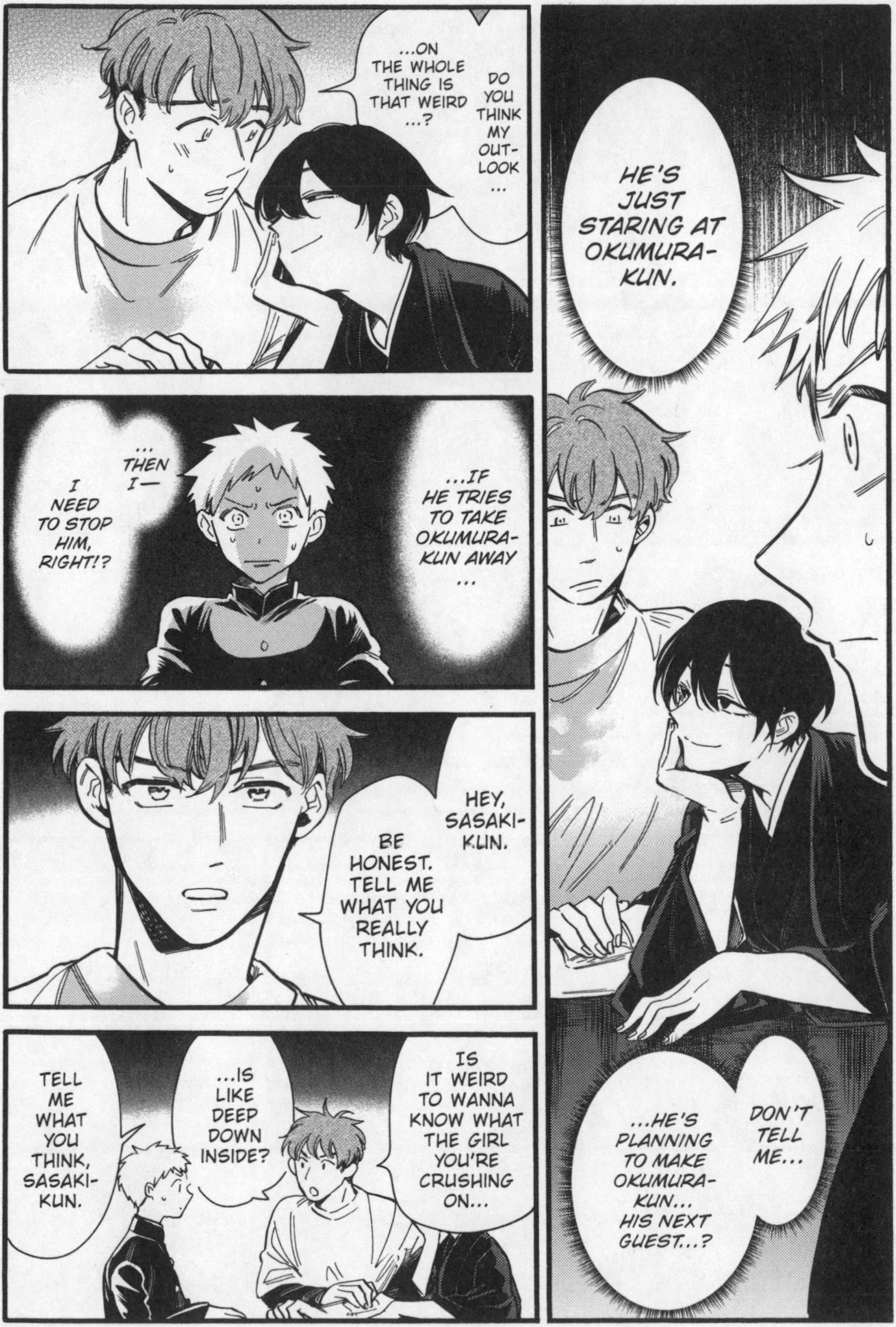
HE'S JUST STARING AT OKUMURA-KUN.
DON'T TELL ME...
...HE'S PLANNING TO MAKE OKUMURA-KUN... HIS NEXT GUEST...?
DO YOU THINK MY OUT-LOOK...
...ON THE WHOLE THING IS THAT WEIRD ...?
...IF HE TRIES TO TAKE OKUMURA-KUN AWAY...
...THEN I—
I NEED TO STOP HIM, RIGHT!?
HEY, SASAKI-KUN.
BE HONEST. TELL ME WHAT YOU REALLY THINK.
IS IT WEIRD TO WANNA KNOW WHAT THE GIRL YOU'RE CRUSHING ON...
...IS LIKE DEEP DOWN INSIDE?
TELL ME WHAT YOU THINK, SASAKI-KUN.

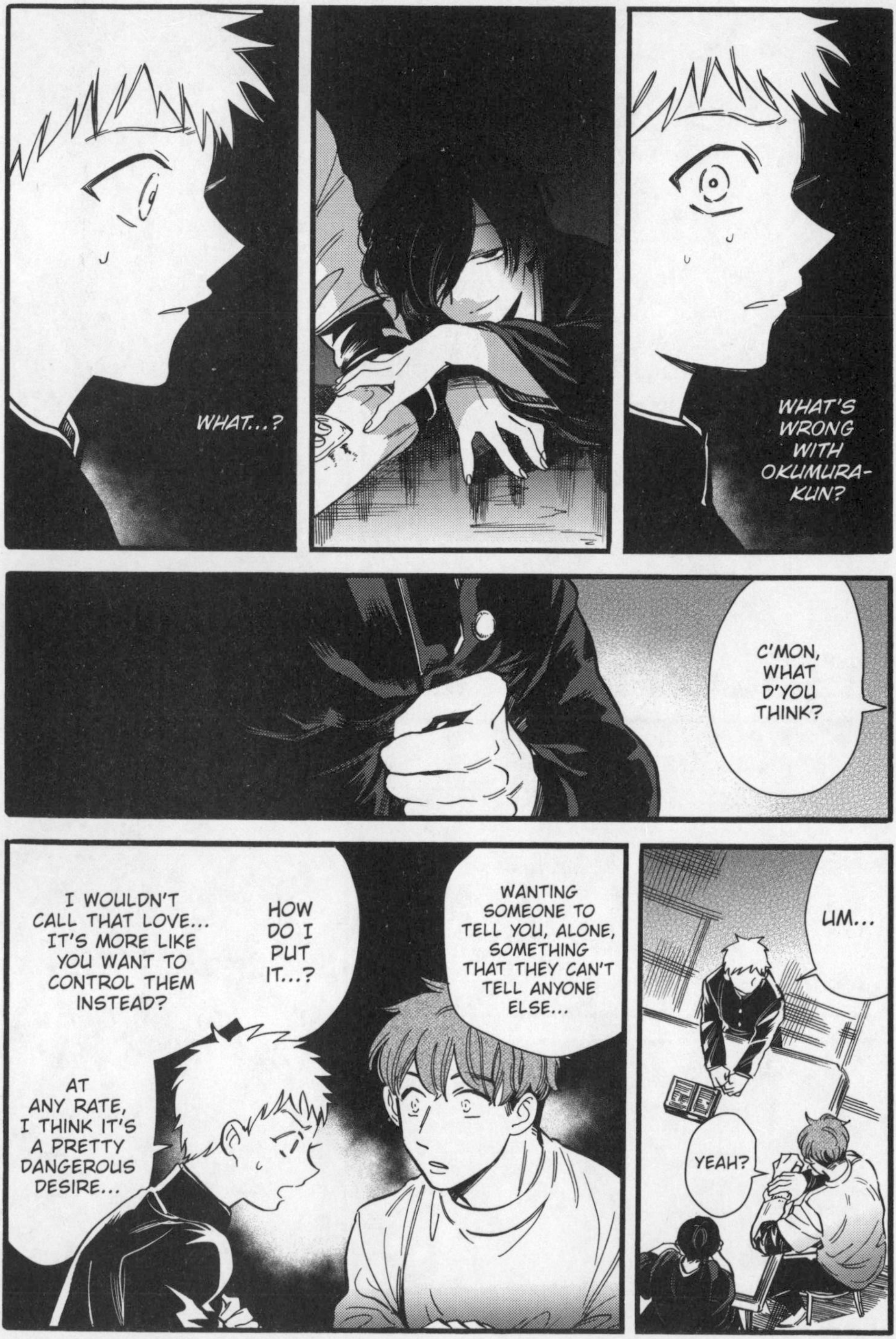
WHAT'S WRONG WITH OKUMURA-KUN?
WHAT...?
C'MON, WHAT D'YOU THINK?
UM...
YEAH?
WANTING SOMEONE TO TELL YOU, ALONE, SOMETHING THAT THEY CAN'T TELL ANYONE ELSE...
HOW DO I PUT IT...?
I WOULDN'T CALL THAT LOVE... IT'S MORE LIKE YOU WANT TO CONTROL THEM INSTEAD?
AT ANY RATE, I THINK IT'S A PRETTY DANGEROUS DESIRE...

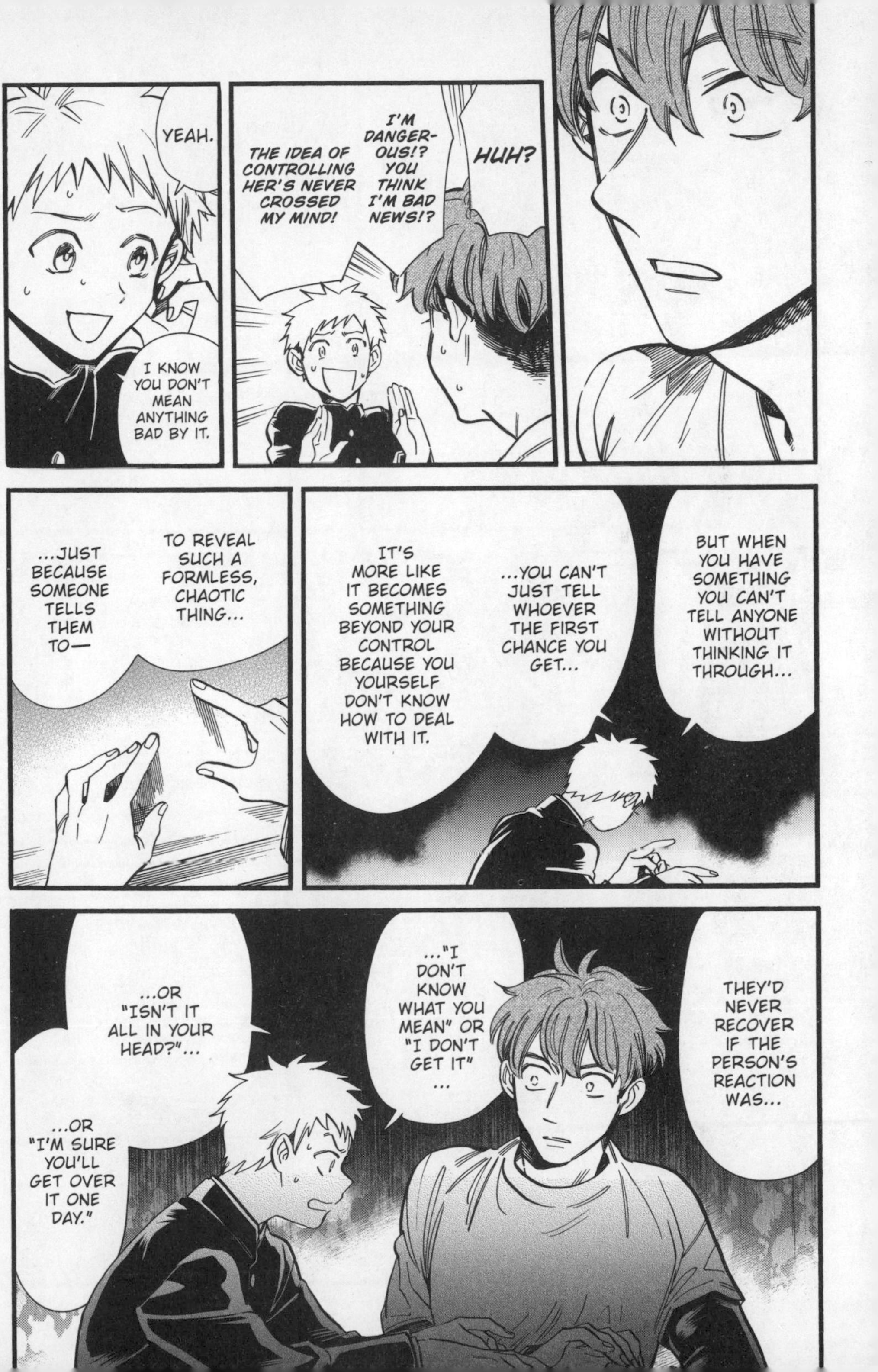
HUH?
I'M DANGEROUS!? YOU THINK I'M BAD NEWS!?
THE IDEA OF CONTROLLING HER'S NEVER CROSSED MY MIND!
YEAH.
I KNOW YOU DON'T MEAN ANYTHING BAD BY IT.
BUT WHEN YOU HAVE SOMETHING YOU CAN'T TELL ANYONE WITHOUT THINKING IT THROUGH...
...YOU CAN'T JUST TELL WHOEVER THE FIRST CHANCE YOU GET...
IT'S MORE LIKE IT BECOMES SOMETHING BEYOND YOUR CONTROL BECAUSE YOU YOURSELF DON'T KNOW HOW TO DEAL WITH IT.
TO REVEAL SUCH A FORMLESS, CHAOTIC THING...
...JUST BECAUSE SOMEONE TELLS THEM TO—
THEY'D NEVER RECOVER IF THE PERSON'S REACTION WAS...
..."I DON'T KNOW WHAT YOU MEAN" OR "I DON'T GET IT"...
...OR "ISN'T IT ALL IN YOUR HEAD?"...
...OR "I'M SURE YOU'LL GET OVER IT ONE DAY."

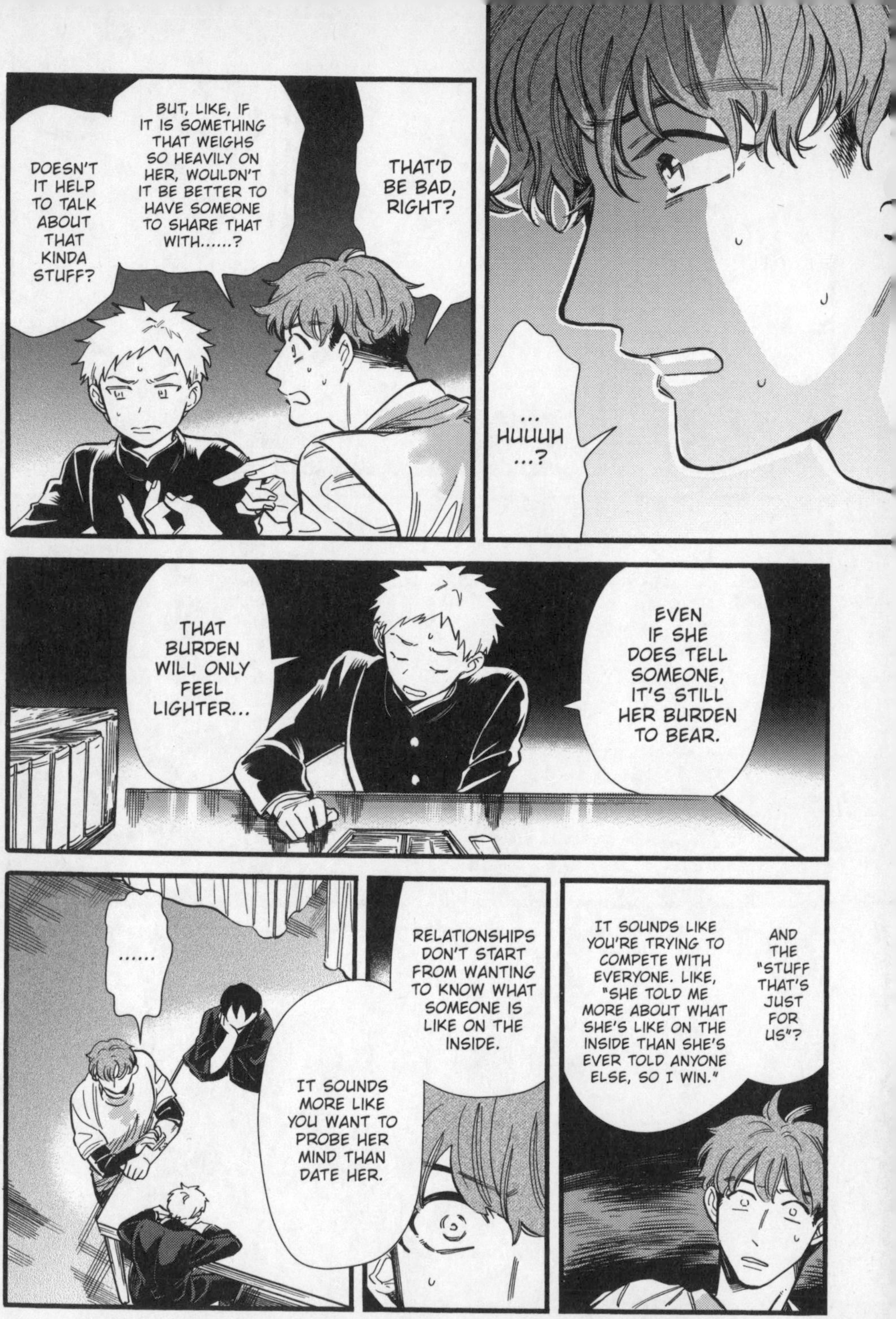
... HUUUH ...?
THAT'D BE BAD, RIGHT?
BUT, LIKE, IF IT IS SOMETHING THAT WEIGHS SO HEAVILY ON HER, WOULDN'T IT BE BETTER TO HAVE SOMEONE TO SHARE THAT WITH......?
DOESN'T IT HELP TO TALK ABOUT THAT KINDA STUFF?
EVEN IF SHE DOES TELL SOMEONE, IT'S STILL HER BURDEN TO BEAR.
THAT BURDEN WILL ONLY FEEL LIGHTER...
AND THE "STUFF THAT'S JUST FOR US"?
IT SOUNDS LIKE YOU'RE TRYING TO COMPETE WITH EVERYONE. LIKE, "SHE TOLD ME MORE ABOUT WHAT SHE'S LIKE ON THE INSIDE THAN SHE'S EVER TOLD ANYONE ELSE, SO I WIN."
RELATIONSHIPS DON'T START FROM WANTING TO KNOW WHAT SOMEONE IS LIKE ON THE INSIDE.
IT SOUNDS MORE LIKE YOU WANT TO PROBE HER MIND THAN DATE HER.
......

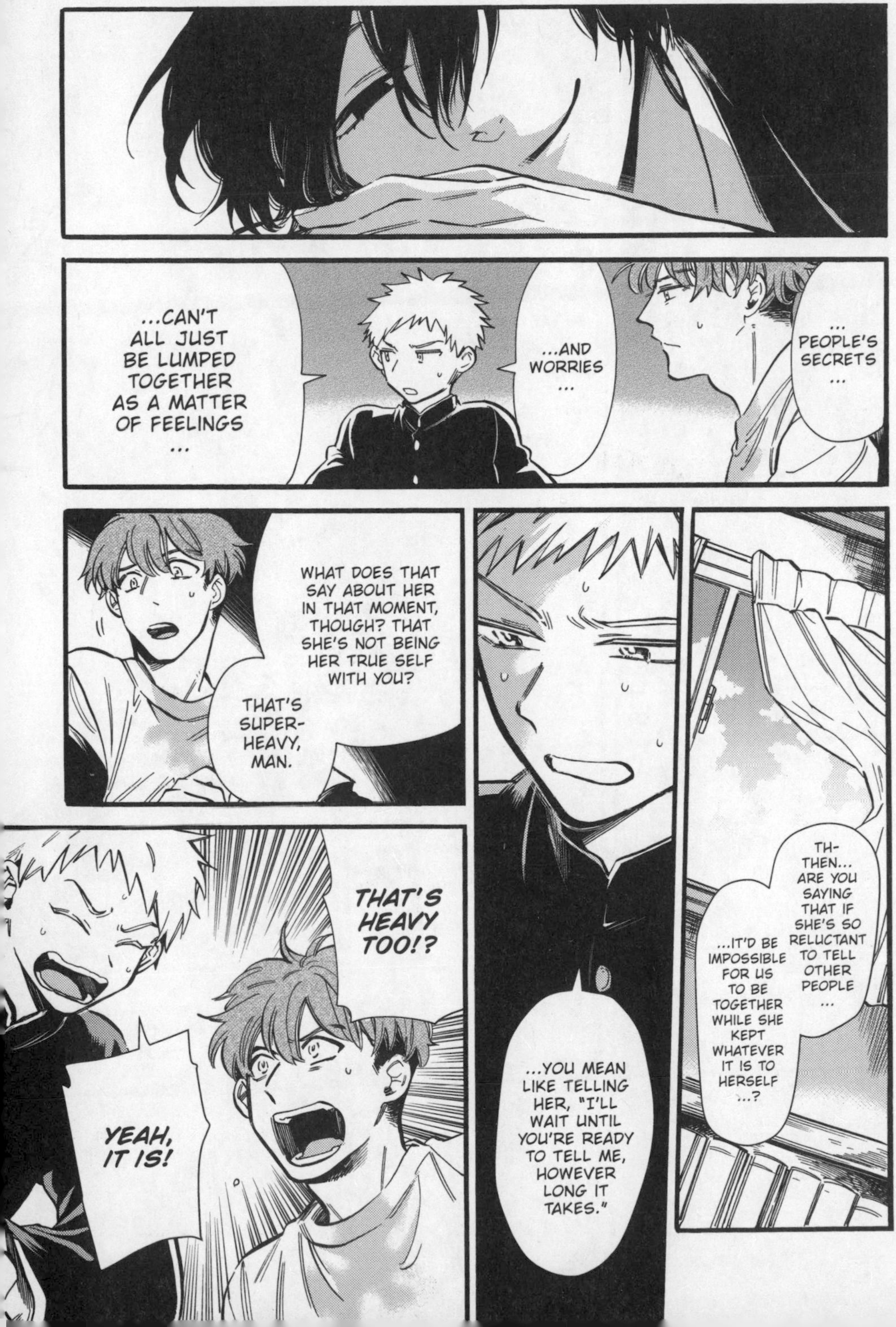
...PEOPLE'S SECRETS...
...AND WORRIES...
...CAN'T ALL JUST BE LUMPED TOGETHER AS A MATTER OF FEELINGS...
TH-THEN... ARE YOU SAYING THAT IF SHE'S SO RELUCTANT TO TELL OTHER PEOPLE...
...IT'D BE IMPOSSIBLE FOR US TO BE TOGETHER WHILE SHE KEPT WHATEVER IT IS TO HERSELF...?
...YOU MEAN LIKE TELLING HER, "I'LL WAIT UNTIL YOU'RE READY TO TELL ME, HOWEVER LONG IT TAKES."
WHAT DOES THAT SAY ABOUT HER IN THAT MOMENT, THOUGH? THAT SHE'S NOT BEING HER TRUE SELF WITH YOU?
THAT'S SUPER-HEAVY, MAN.
THAT'S HEAVY TOO!?
YEAH, IT IS!

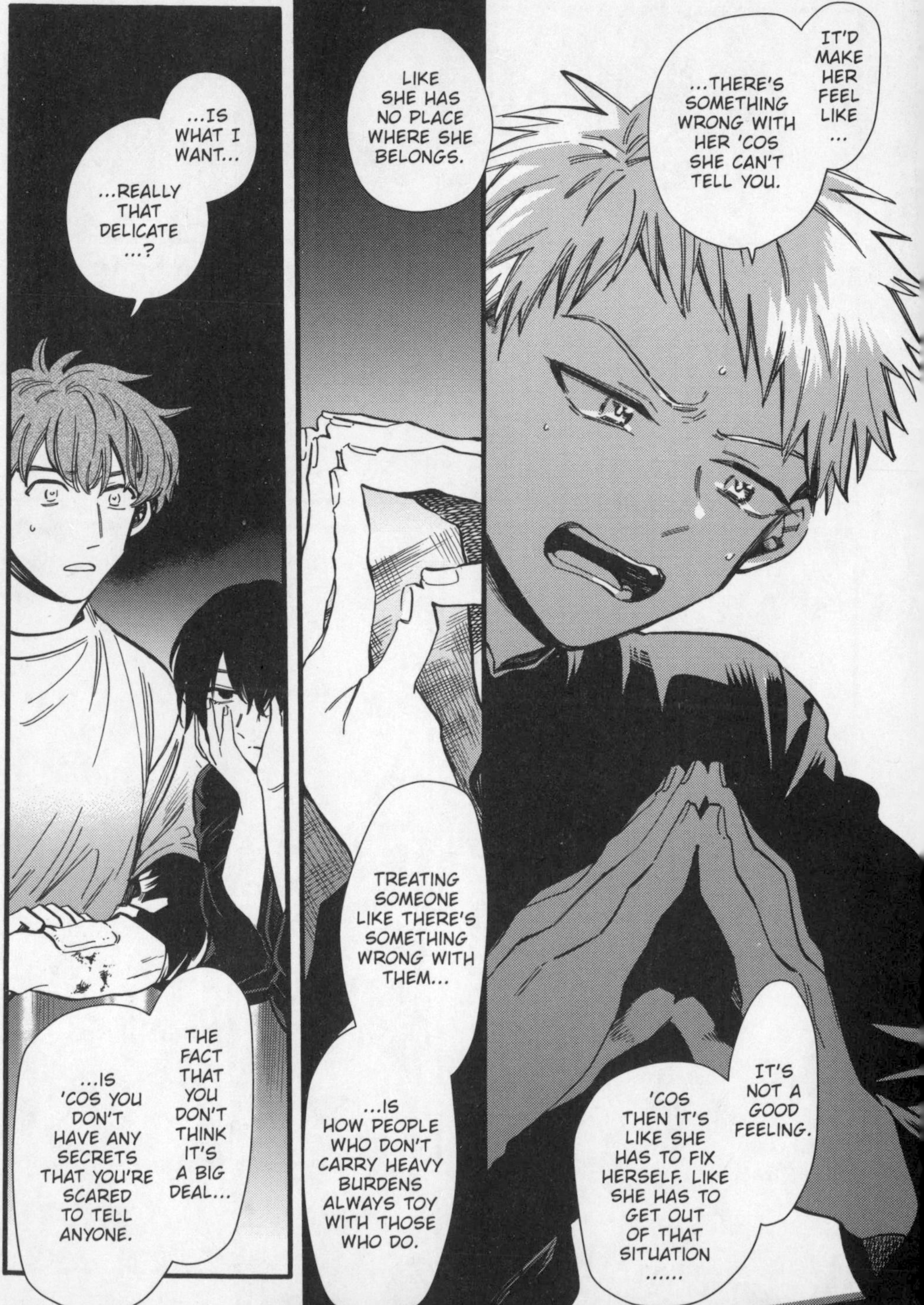
IT'D MAKE HER FEEL LIKE ...
...THERE'S SOMETHING WRONG WITH HER 'COS SHE CAN'T TELL YOU.
LIKE SHE HAS NO PLACE WHERE SHE BELONGS.
IT'S NOT A GOOD FEELING.
'COS THEN IT'S LIKE SHE HAS TO FIX HERSELF. LIKE SHE HAS TO GET OUT OF THAT SITUATION ......
TREATING SOMEONE LIKE THERE'S SOMETHING WRONG WITH THEM...
...IS HOW PEOPLE WHO DON'T CARRY HEAVY BURDENS ALWAYS TOY WITH THOSE WHO DO.
...IS WHAT I WANT...
...REALLY THAT DELICATE ...?
THE FACT THAT YOU DON'T THINK IT'S A BIG DEAL...
...IS 'COS YOU DON'T HAVE ANY SECRETS THAT YOU'RE SCARED TO TELL ANYONE.

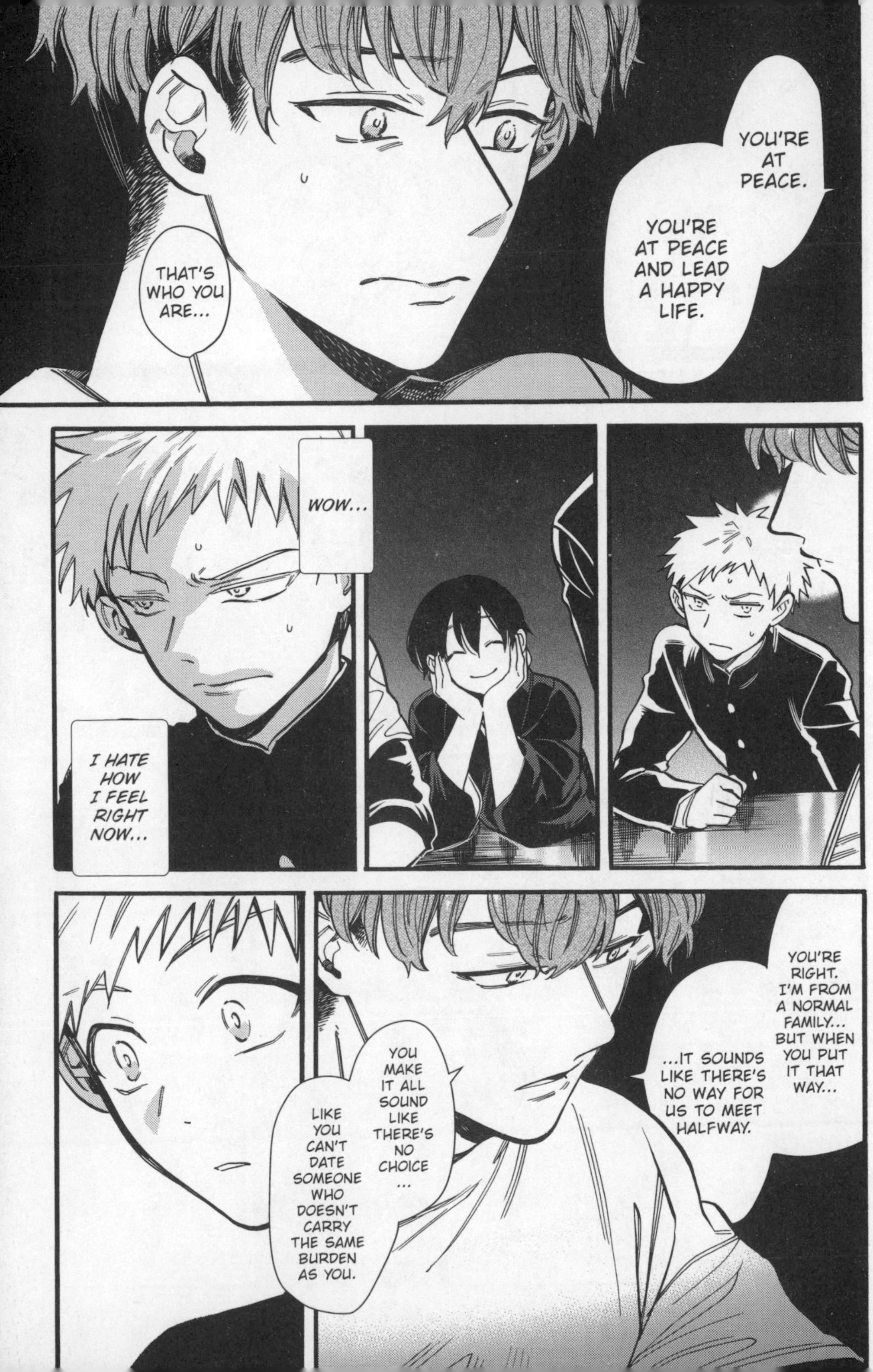
YOU'RE AT PEACE.
YOU'RE AT PEACE AND LEAD A HAPPY LIFE.
THAT'S WHO YOU ARE...
WOW...
I HATE HOW I FEEL RIGHT NOW...
YOU'RE RIGHT. I'M FROM A NORMAL FAMILY... BUT WHEN YOU PUT IT THAT WAY...
...IT SOUNDS LIKE THERE'S NO WAY FOR US TO MEET HALFWAY.
YOU MAKE IT ALL SOUND LIKE THERE'S NO CHOICE ...
LIKE YOU CAN'T DATE SOMEONE WHO DOESN'T CARRY THE SAME BURDEN AS YOU.

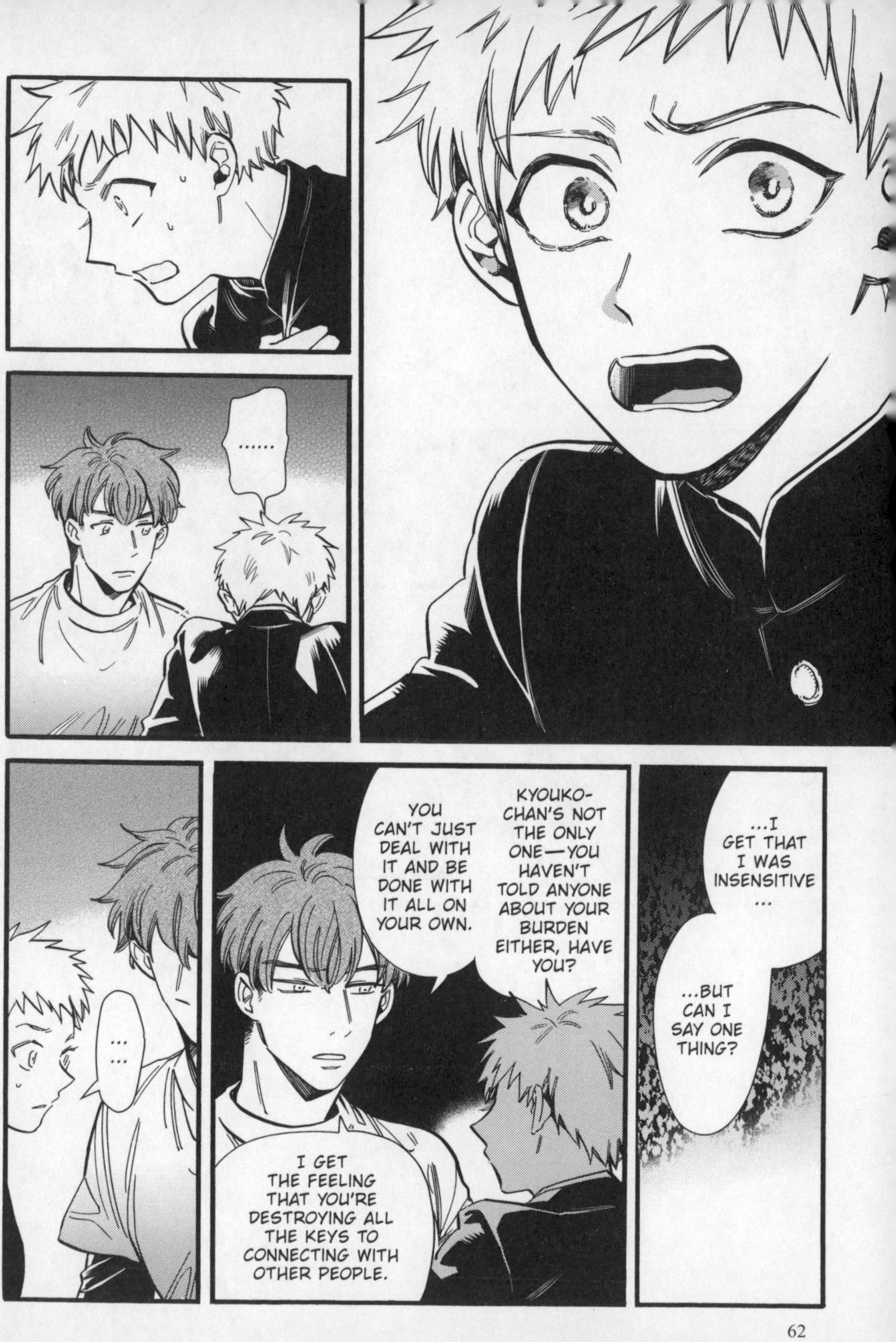
......
...I GET THAT I WAS INSENSITIVE ...
...BUT CAN I SAY ONE THING?
KYOUKO-CHAN'S NOT THE ONLY ONE—YOU HAVEN'T TOLD ANYONE ABOUT YOUR BURDEN EITHER, HAVE YOU?
YOU CAN'T JUST DEAL WITH IT AND BE DONE WITH IT ALL ON YOUR OWN.
I GET THE FEELING THAT YOU'RE DESTROYING ALL THE KEYS TO CONNECTING WITH OTHER PEOPLE.
... ...

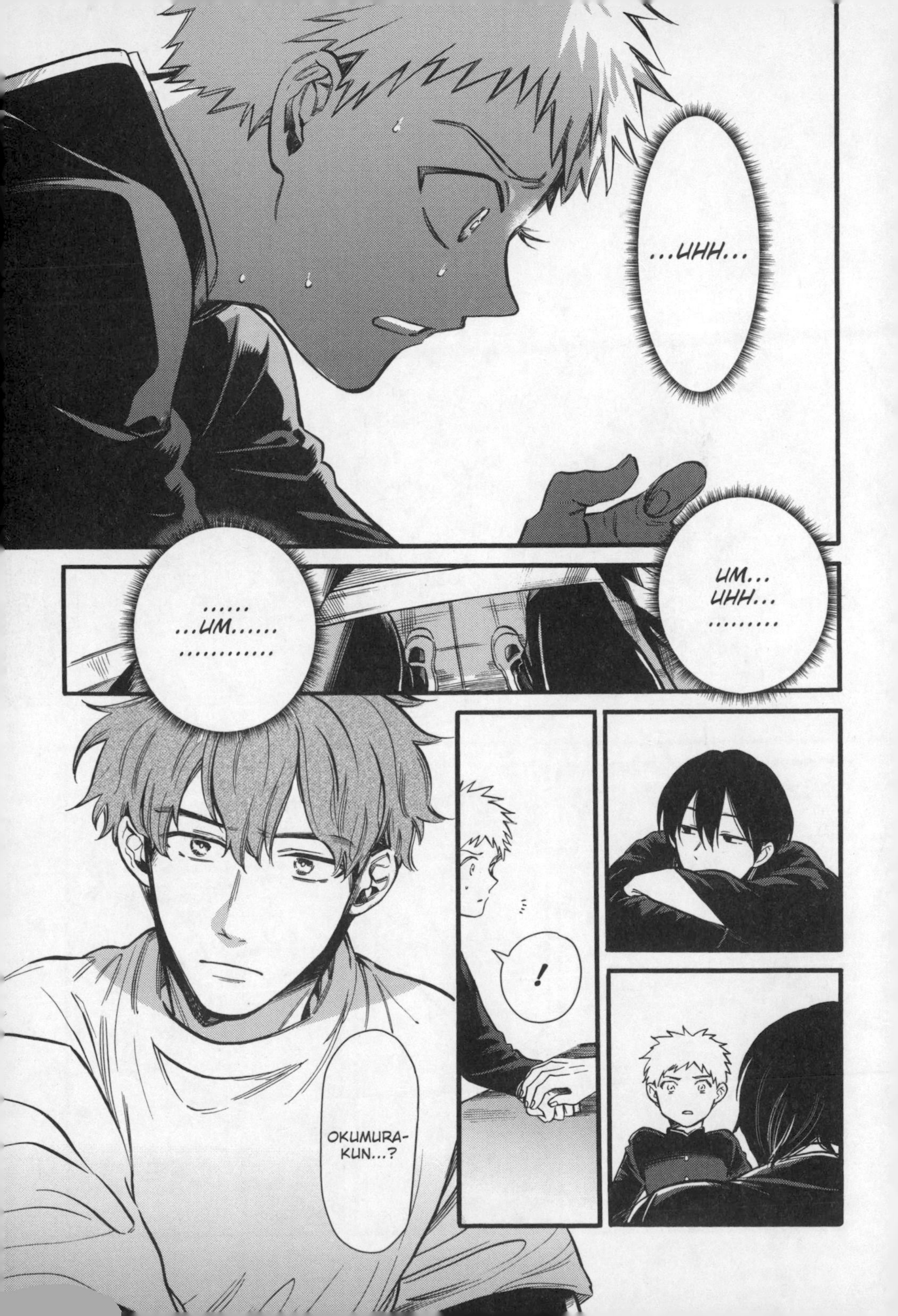
...UHH...
UM... UHH... ....
....UM...... ....
!
OKUMURA-KUN...?

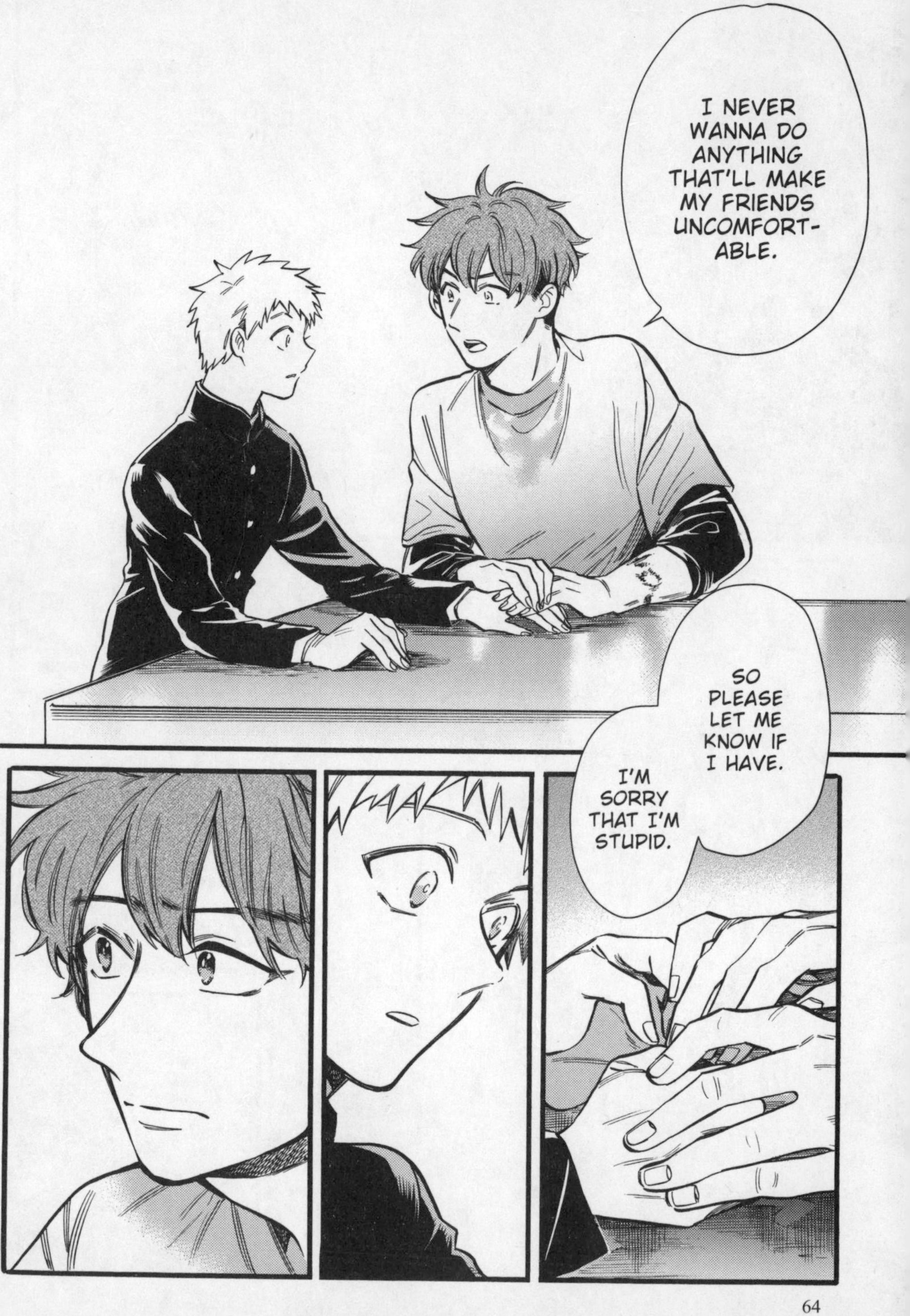
I NEVER WANNA DO ANYTHING THAT'LL MAKE MY FRIENDS UNCOMFORT-ABLE.
SO PLEASE LET ME KNOW IF I HAVE.
I'M SORRY THAT I'M STUPID.

HA-HA-HA!

SORRY. IT'S SO HARD TO GIVE ADVICE!

UM...

I WAS JUST IMAGINING WHAT IT WAS LIKE FOR KYOUKO-CHAN.

THANKS.

OKAY...

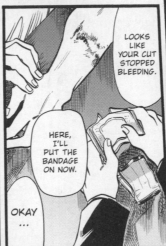

LOOKS LIKE YOUR CUT STOPPED BLEEDING.

HERE, I'LL PUT THE BANDAGE ON NOW.

WHAT SHE MIGHT ACTUALLY BE THINKING... I GUESS.

HEY, SASAKI-KUN......?

NOW WHERE'S HE GOING...?

OWNER...?

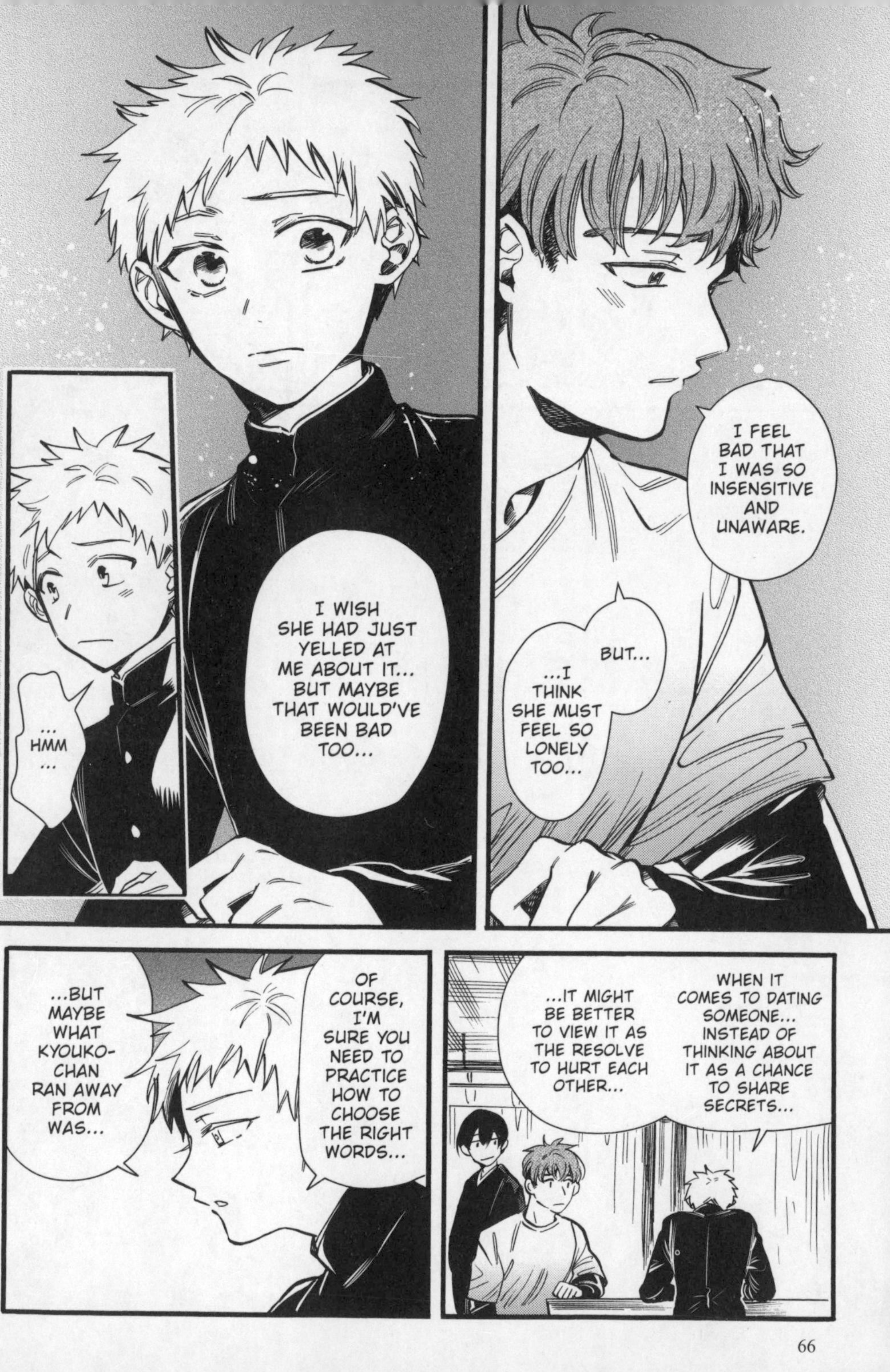
I FEEL BAD THAT I WAS SO INSENSITIVE AND UNAWARE.
BUT...
...I THINK SHE MUST FEEL SO LONELY TOO...
I WISH SHE HAD JUST YELLED AT ME ABOUT IT... BUT MAYBE THAT WOULD'VE BEEN BAD TOO...
...HMM...
WHEN IT COMES TO DATING SOMEONE... INSTEAD OF THINKING ABOUT IT AS A CHANCE TO SHARE SECRETS...
...IT MIGHT BE BETTER TO VIEW IT AS THE RESOLVE TO HURT EACH OTHER...
OF COURSE, I'M SURE YOU NEED TO PRACTICE HOW TO CHOOSE THE RIGHT WORDS...
...BUT MAYBE WHAT KYOUKO-CHAN RAN AWAY FROM WAS...

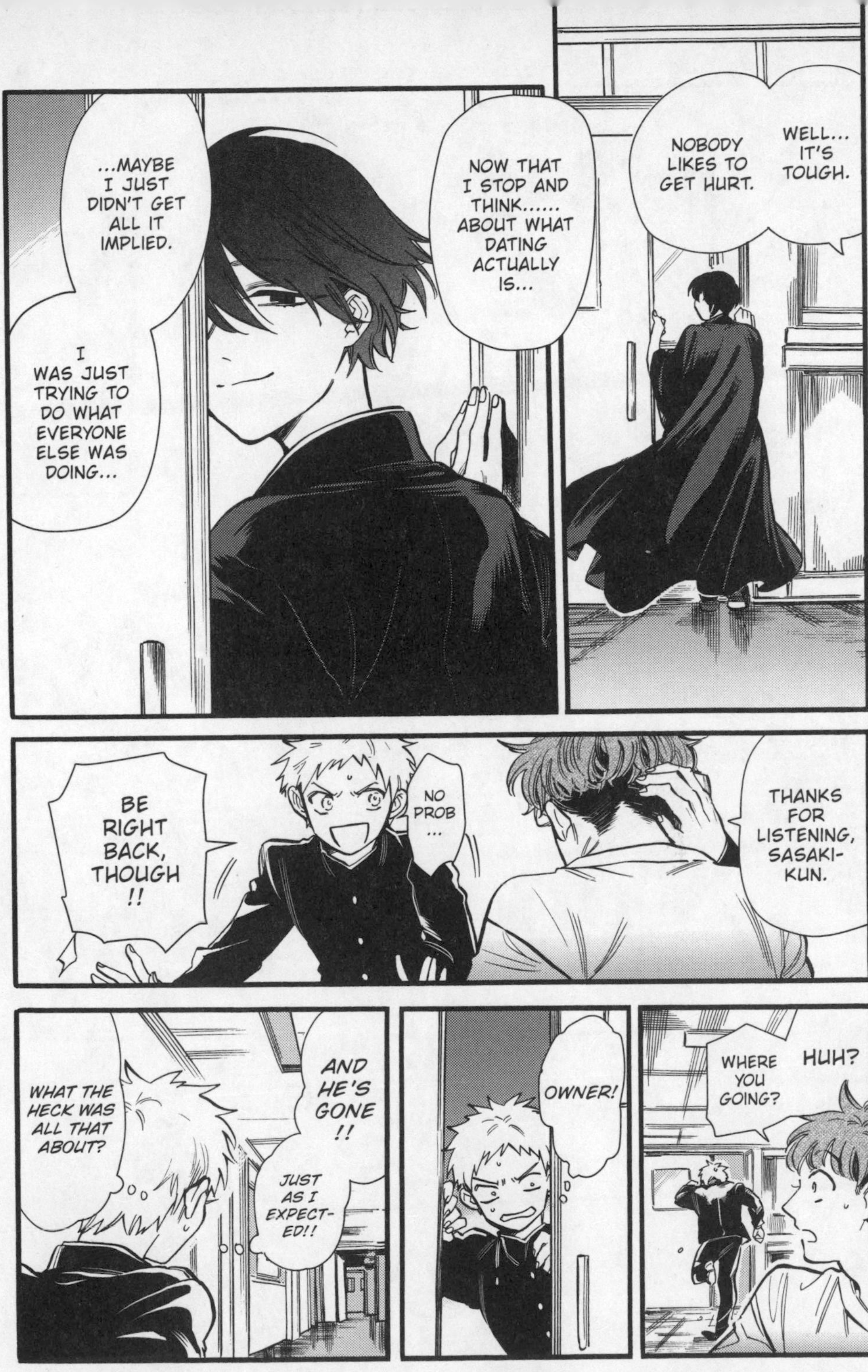
WELL... IT'S TOUGH.
NOBODY LIKES TO GET HURT.
NOW THAT I STOP AND THINK...... ABOUT WHAT DATING ACTUALLY IS...
...MAYBE I JUST DIDN'T GET ALL IT IMPLIED.
I WAS JUST TRYING TO DO WHAT EVERYONE ELSE WAS DOING...
THANKS FOR LISTENING, SASAKI-KUN.
NO PROB...
BE RIGHT BACK, THOUGH!!
HUH?
WHERE YOU GOING?
OWNER!
AND HE'S GONE!!
JUST AS I EXPECTED!!
WHAT THE HECK WAS ALL THAT ABOUT?

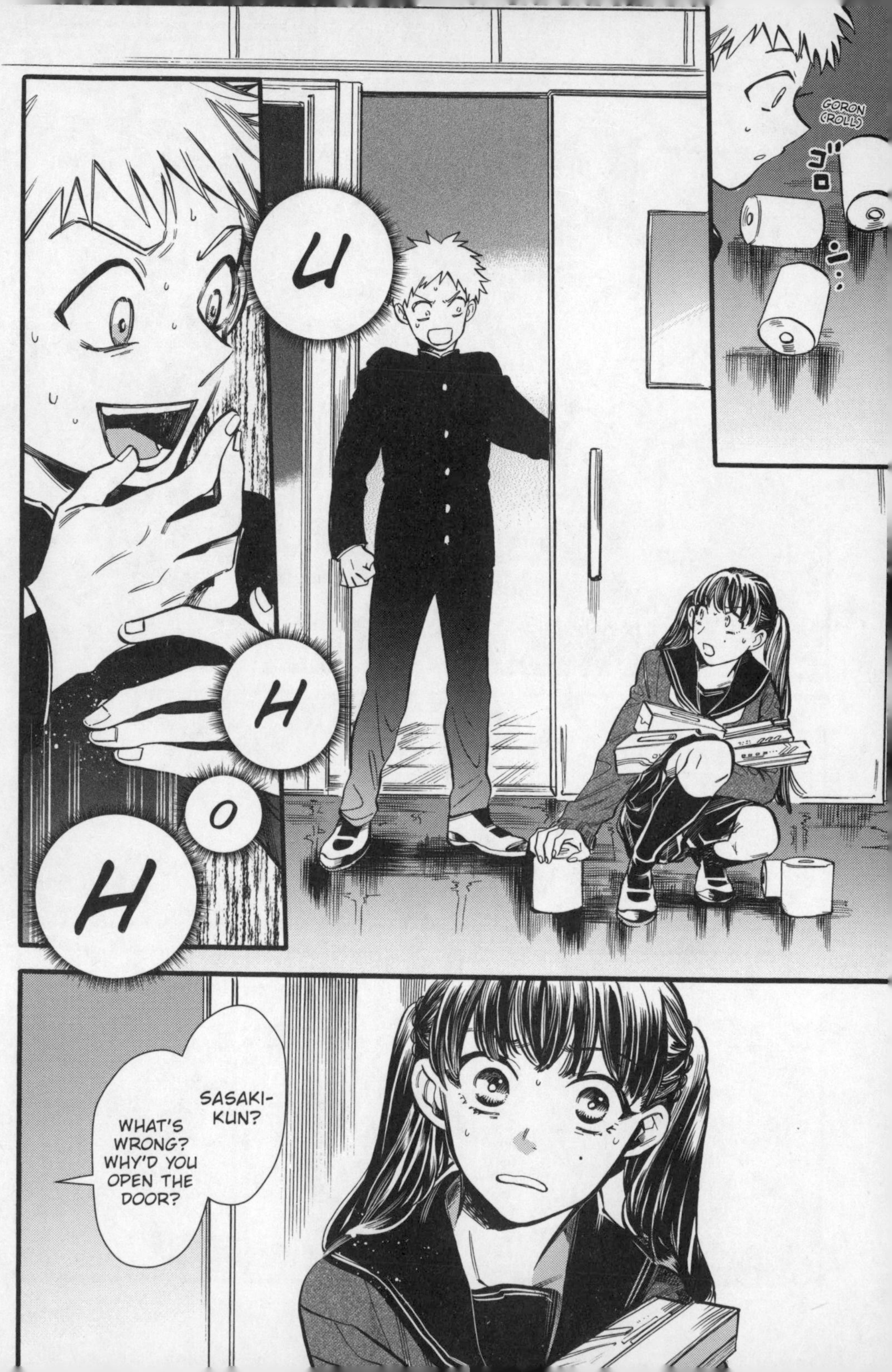
GORON (ROLLS)
ゴロ
U
H
O
H
SASAKI-KUN?
WHAT'S WRONG? WHY'D YOU OPEN THE DOOR?

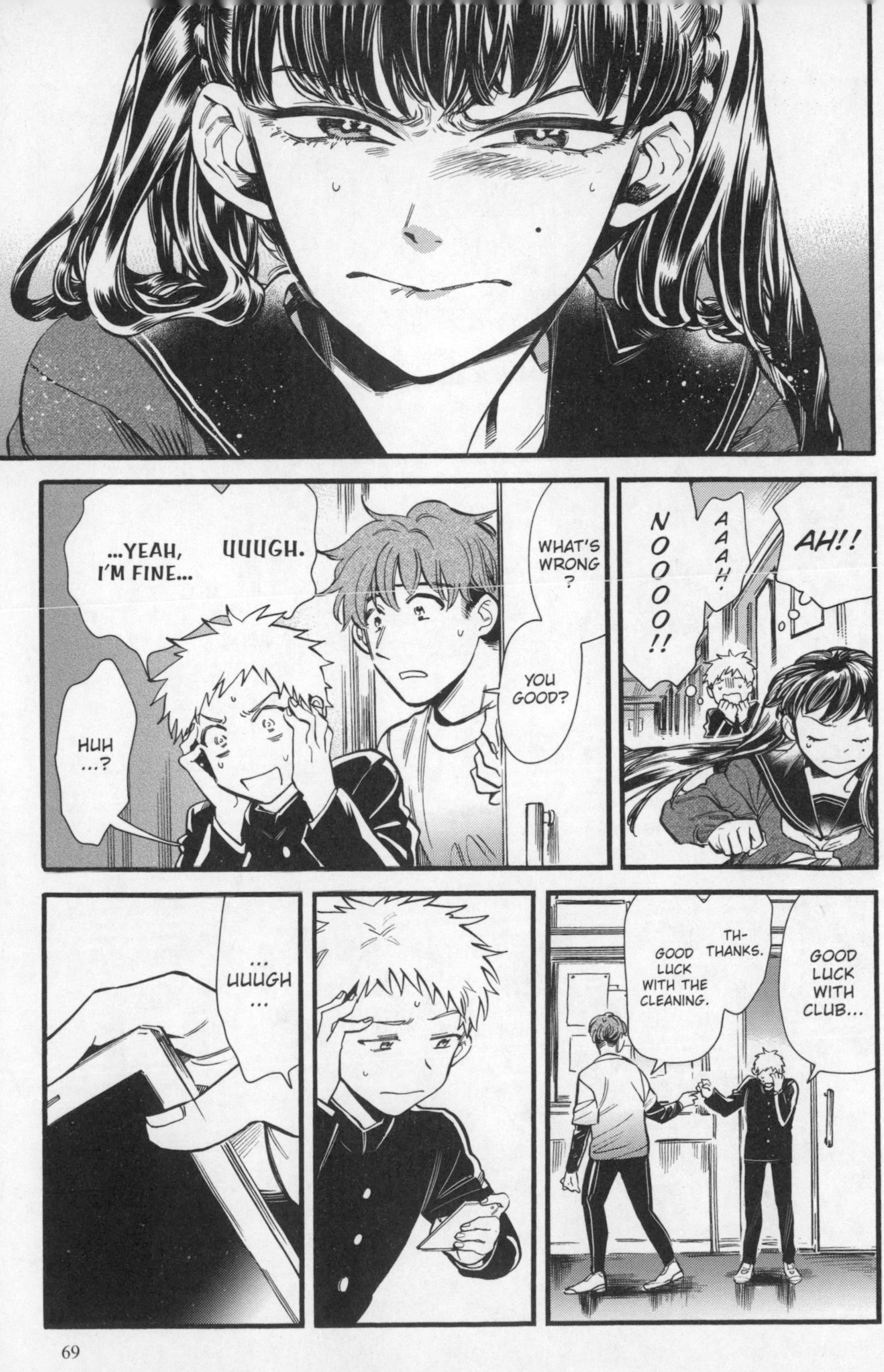
AH!!
AAAAH!
NOOOOO!!
WHAT'S WRONG?
YOU GOOD?
UUUGH.
...YEAH, I'M FINE...
HUH ...?
GOOD LUCK WITH CLUB...
TH- THANKS.
GOOD LUCK WITH THE CLEANING.
... UUUGH ...

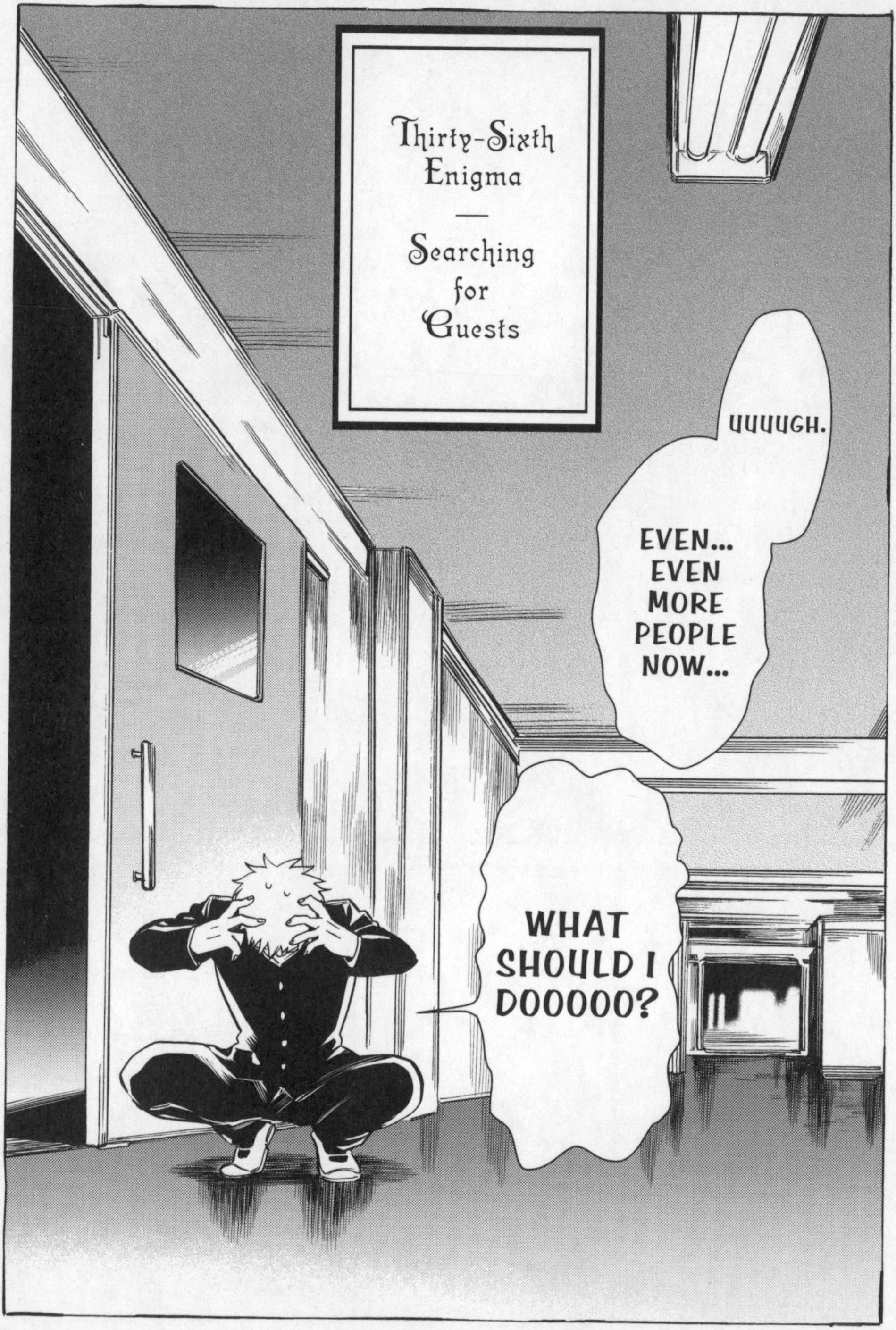
Thirty-Sixth Enigma
—
Searching for Guests
UUUUGH.
EVEN... EVEN MORE PEOPLE NOW...
WHAT SHOULD I DOOOOO?

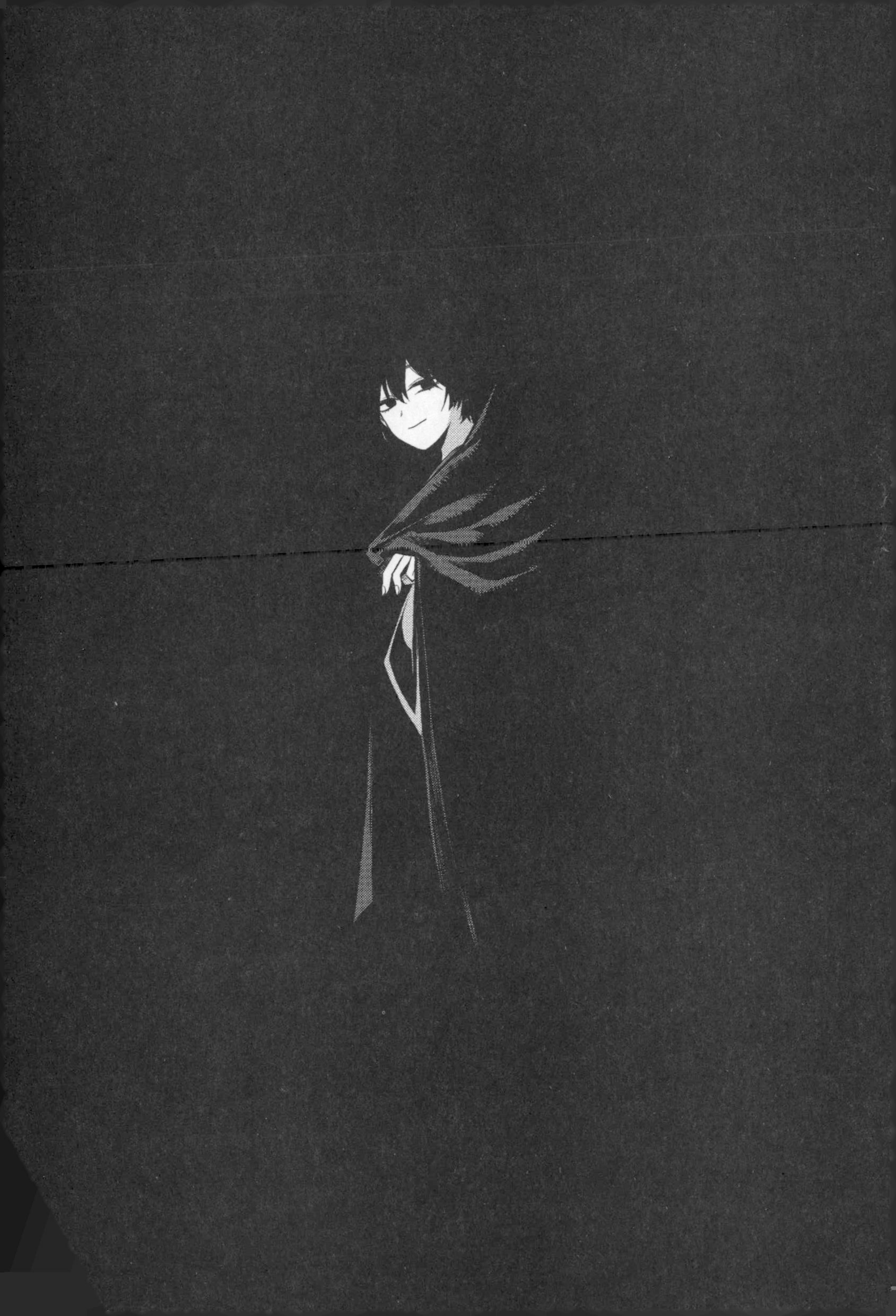

Phantom Tales of the Night

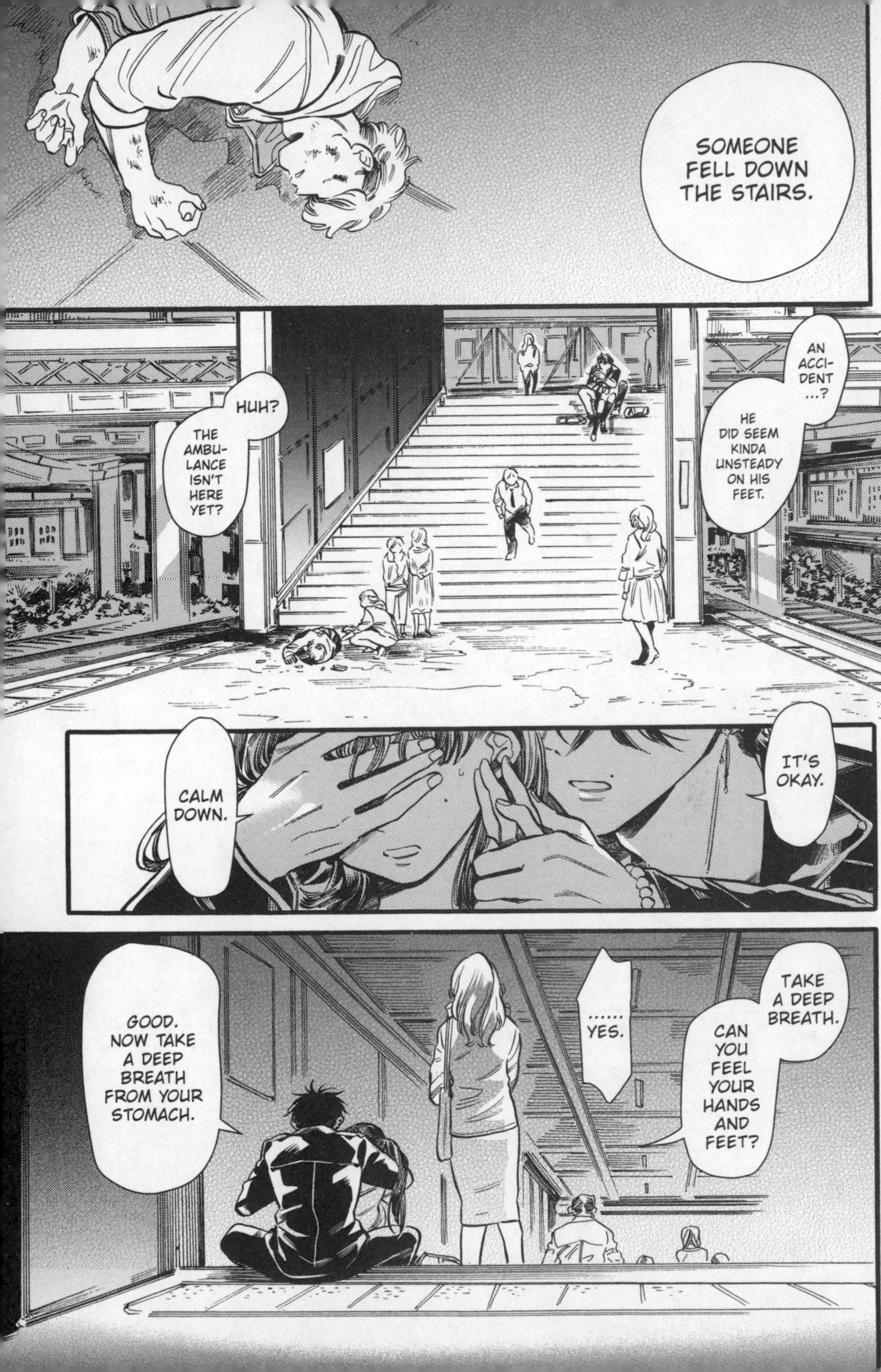
SOMEONE FELL DOWN THE STAIRS.
AN ACCIDENT ...?
HE DID SEEM KINDA UNSTEADY ON HIS FEET.
HUH?
THE AMBULANCE ISN'T HERE YET?
IT'S OKAY.
CALM DOWN.
TAKE A DEEP BREATH.
CAN YOU FEEL YOUR HANDS AND FEET?
......YES.
GOOD. NOW TAKE A DEEP BREATH FROM YOUR STOMACH.

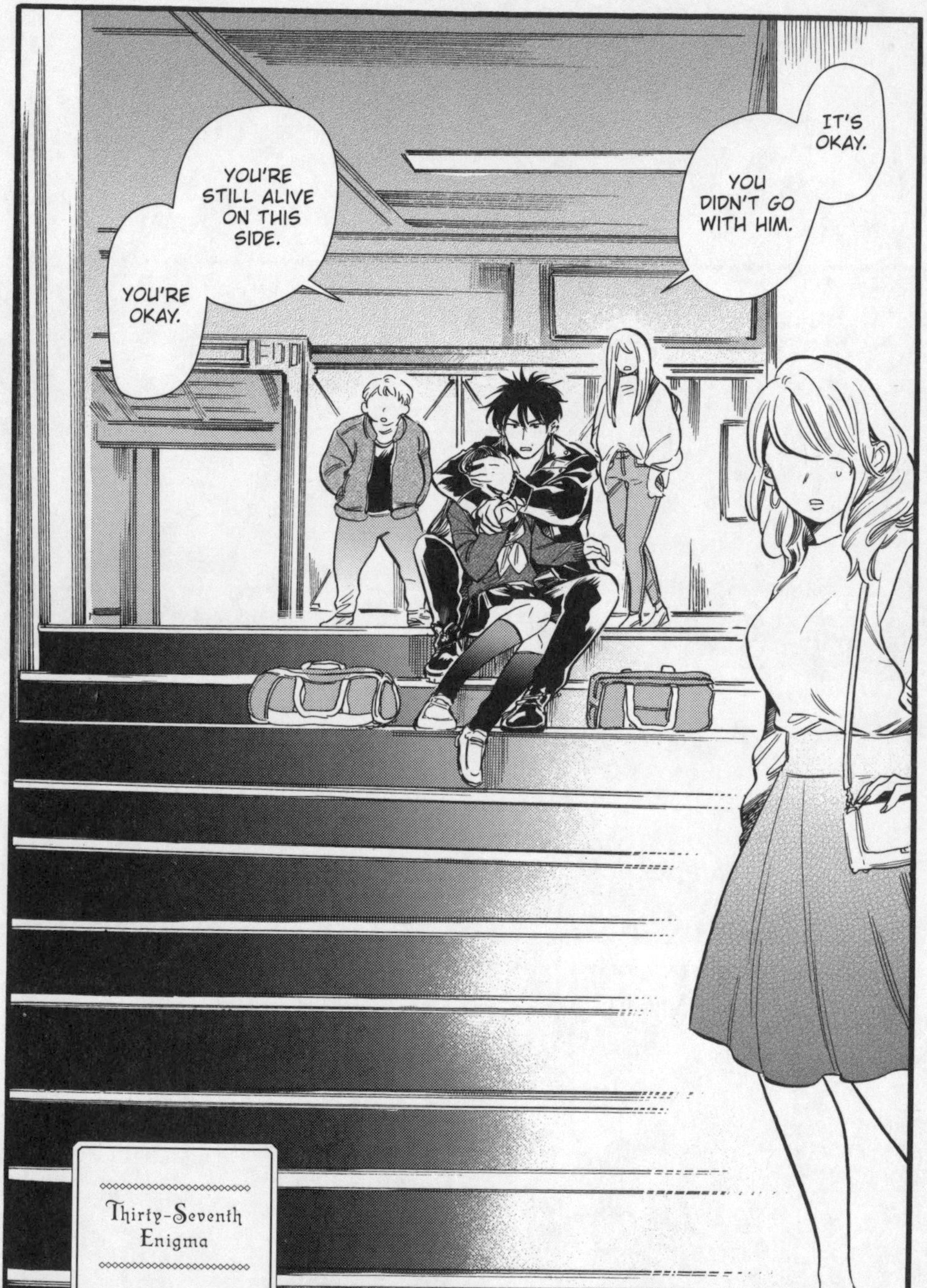
IT'S OKAY.
YOU DIDN'T GO WITH HIM.
YOU'RE STILL ALIVE ON THIS SIDE.
YOU'RE OKAY.
Thirty-Seventh Enigma

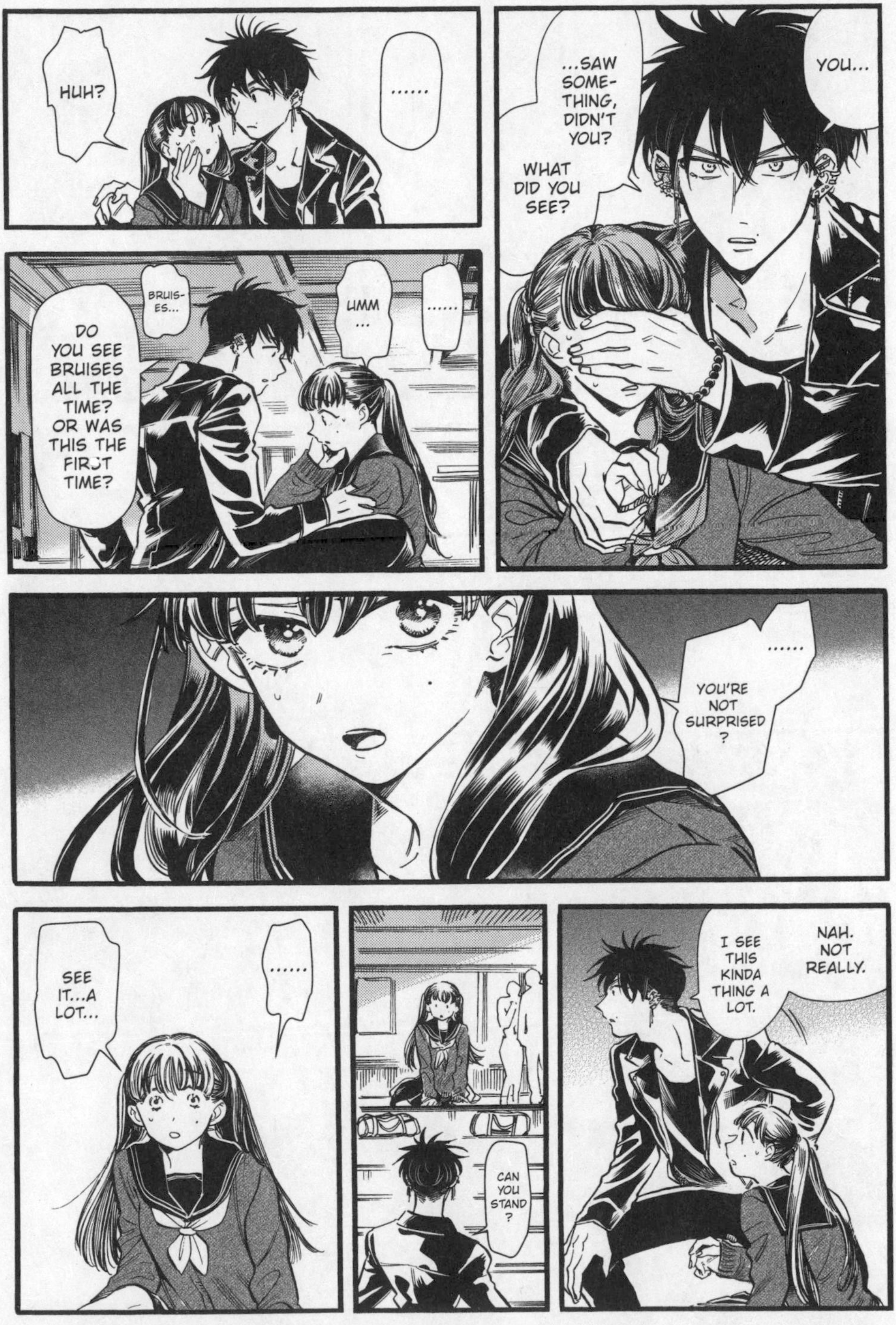
YOU...
...SAW SOMETHING, DIDN'T YOU?
WHAT DID YOU SEE?
......
HUH?
......
UMM ...
BRUISES...
DO YOU SEE BRUISES ALL THE TIME? OR WAS THIS THE FIRST TIME?
......
YOU'RE NOT SURPRISED?
NAH. NOT REALLY.
I SEE THIS KINDA THING A LOT.
CAN YOU STAND?
......
SEE IT...A LOT...

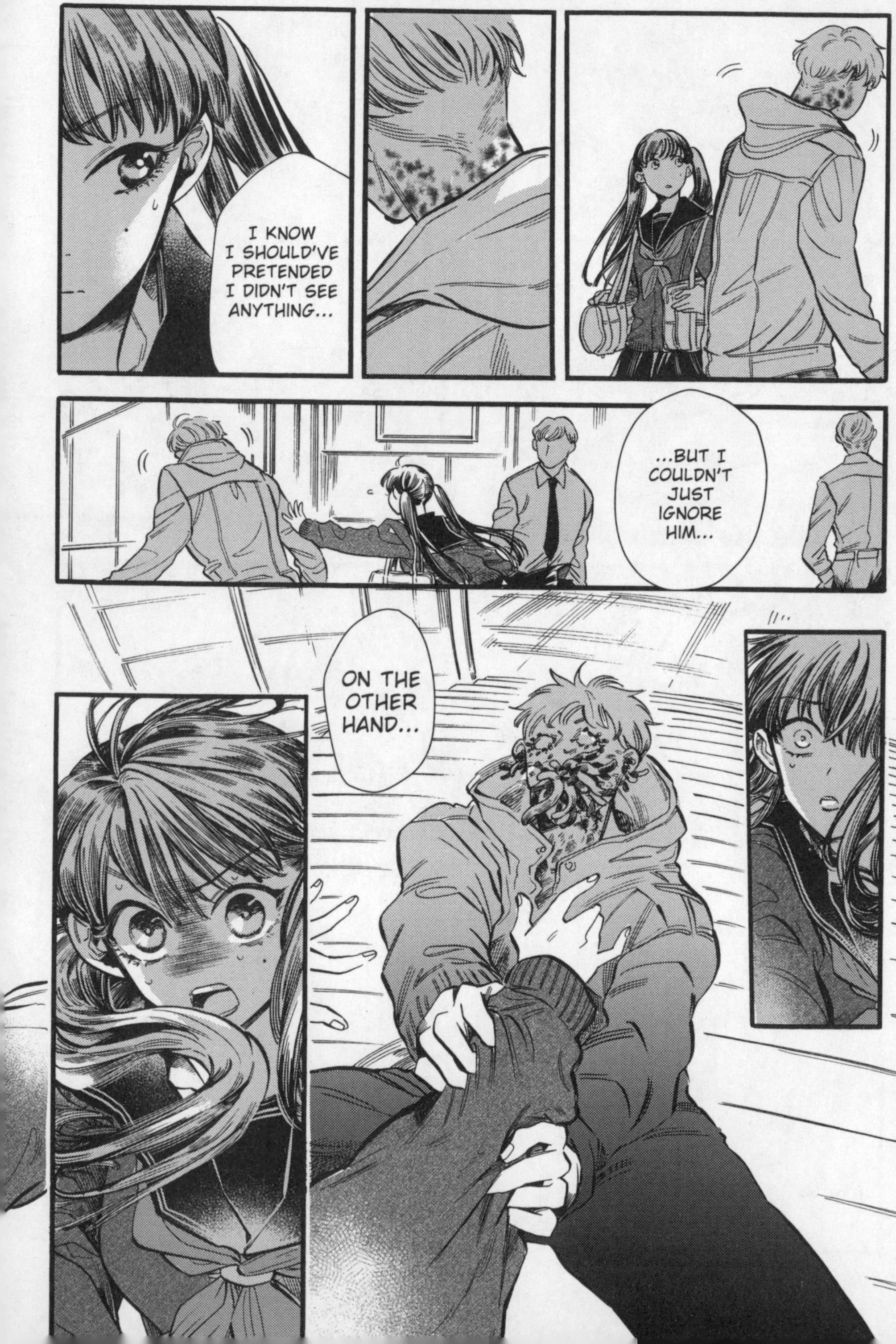
I KNOW I SHOULD'VE PRETENDED I DIDN'T SEE ANYTHING...
...BUT I COULDN'T JUST IGNORE HIM...
ON THE OTHER HAND...

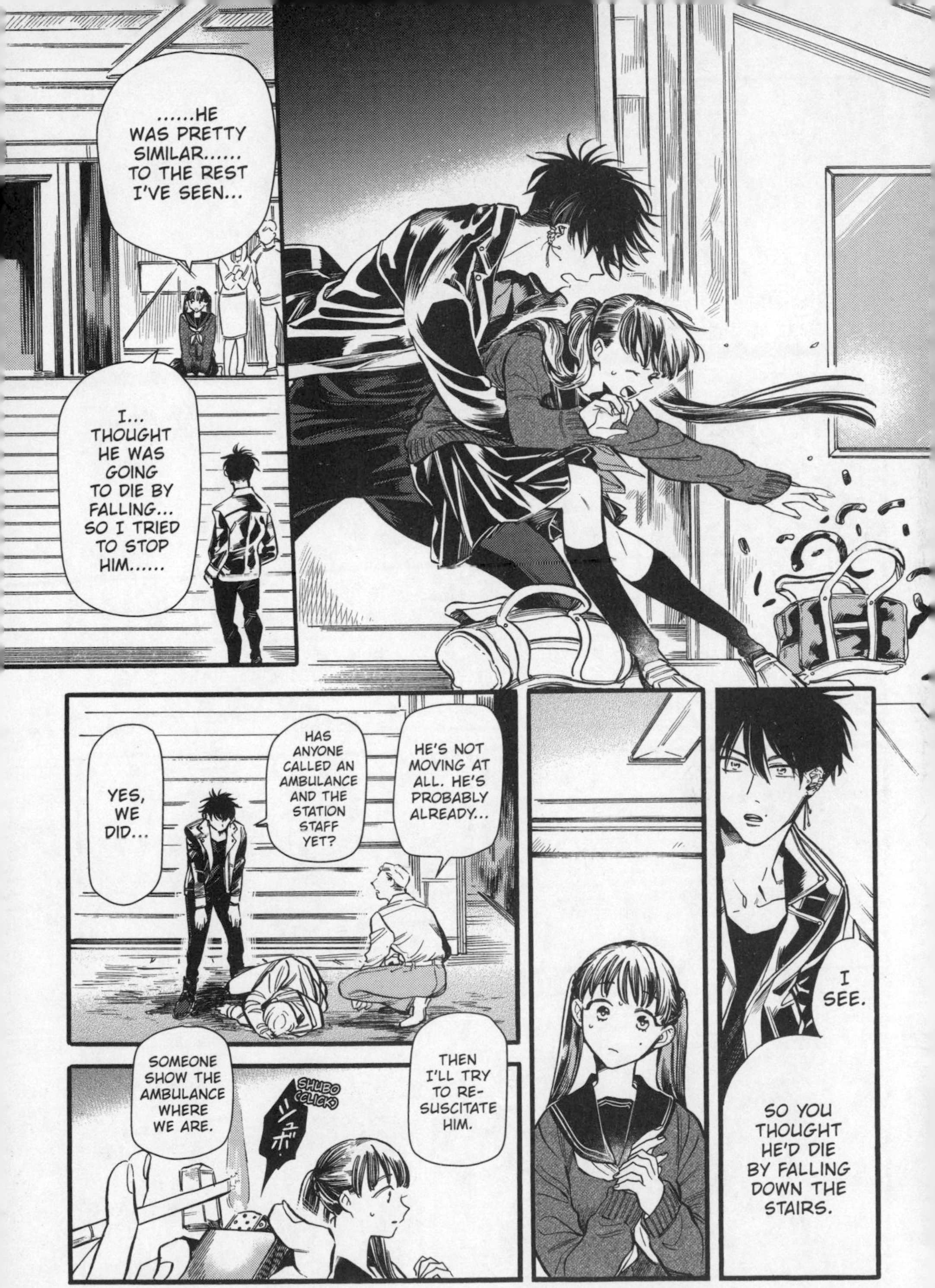
......HE WAS PRETTY SIMILAR...... TO THE REST I'VE SEEN...
I... THOUGHT HE WAS GOING TO DIE BY FALLING... SO I TRIED TO STOP HIM......
I SEE.
SO YOU THOUGHT HE'D DIE BY FALLING DOWN THE STAIRS.
HE'S NOT MOVING AT ALL. HE'S PROBABLY ALREADY...
HAS ANYONE CALLED AN AMBULANCE AND THE STATION STAFF YET?
YES, WE DID...
THEN I'LL TRY TO RE-SUSCITATE HIM.
SHUBO (CLICK)
シュボ
SOMEONE SHOW THE AMBULANCE WHERE WE ARE.

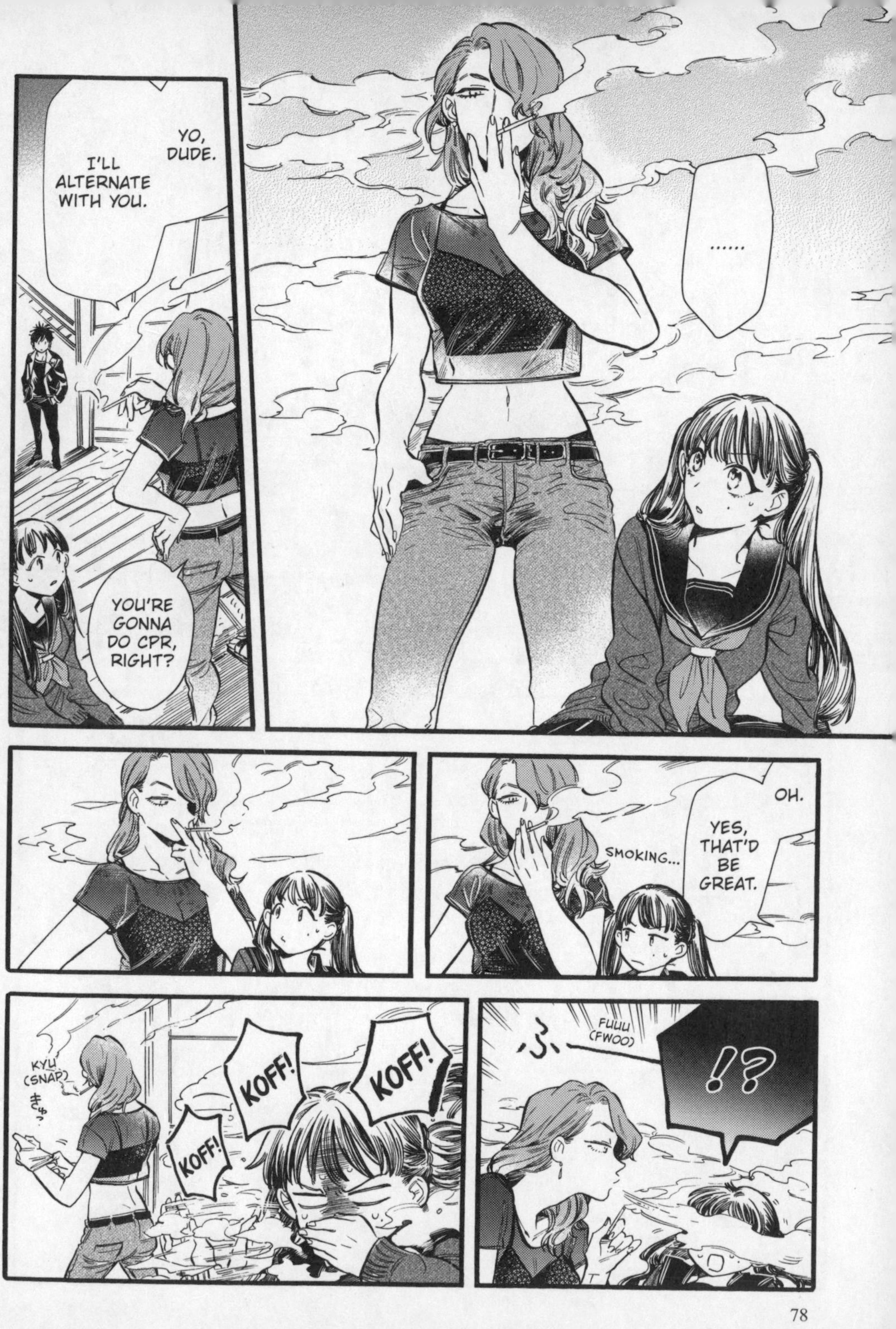
......
YO, DUDE.
I'LL ALTERNATE WITH YOU.
YOU'RE GONNA DO CPR, RIGHT?
OH.
YES, THAT'D BE GREAT.
SMOKING...
FUUU (FWOO)
ふ
!?
KOFF!
KOFF!
KOFF!
KYU (SNAP)
きゅ

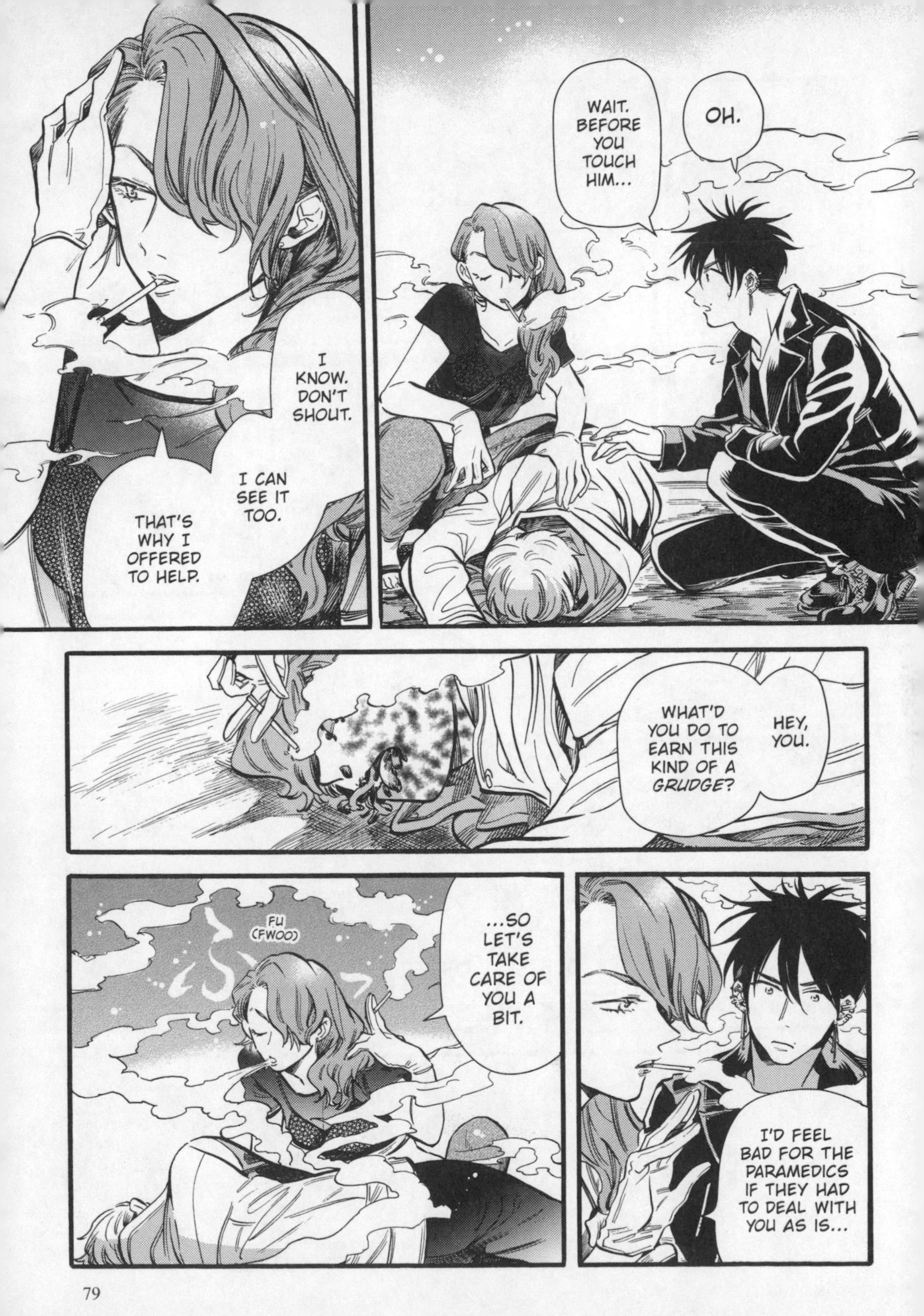
OH.
WAIT. BEFORE YOU TOUCH HIM...
I KNOW. DON'T SHOUT.
I CAN SEE IT TOO.
THAT'S WHY I OFFERED TO HELP.
HEY, YOU.
WHAT'D YOU DO TO EARN THIS KIND OF A GRUDGE?
I'D FEEL BAD FOR THE PARAMEDICS IF THEY HAD TO DEAL WITH YOU AS IS...
...SO LET'S TAKE CARE OF YOU A BIT.
FU (FWOO)

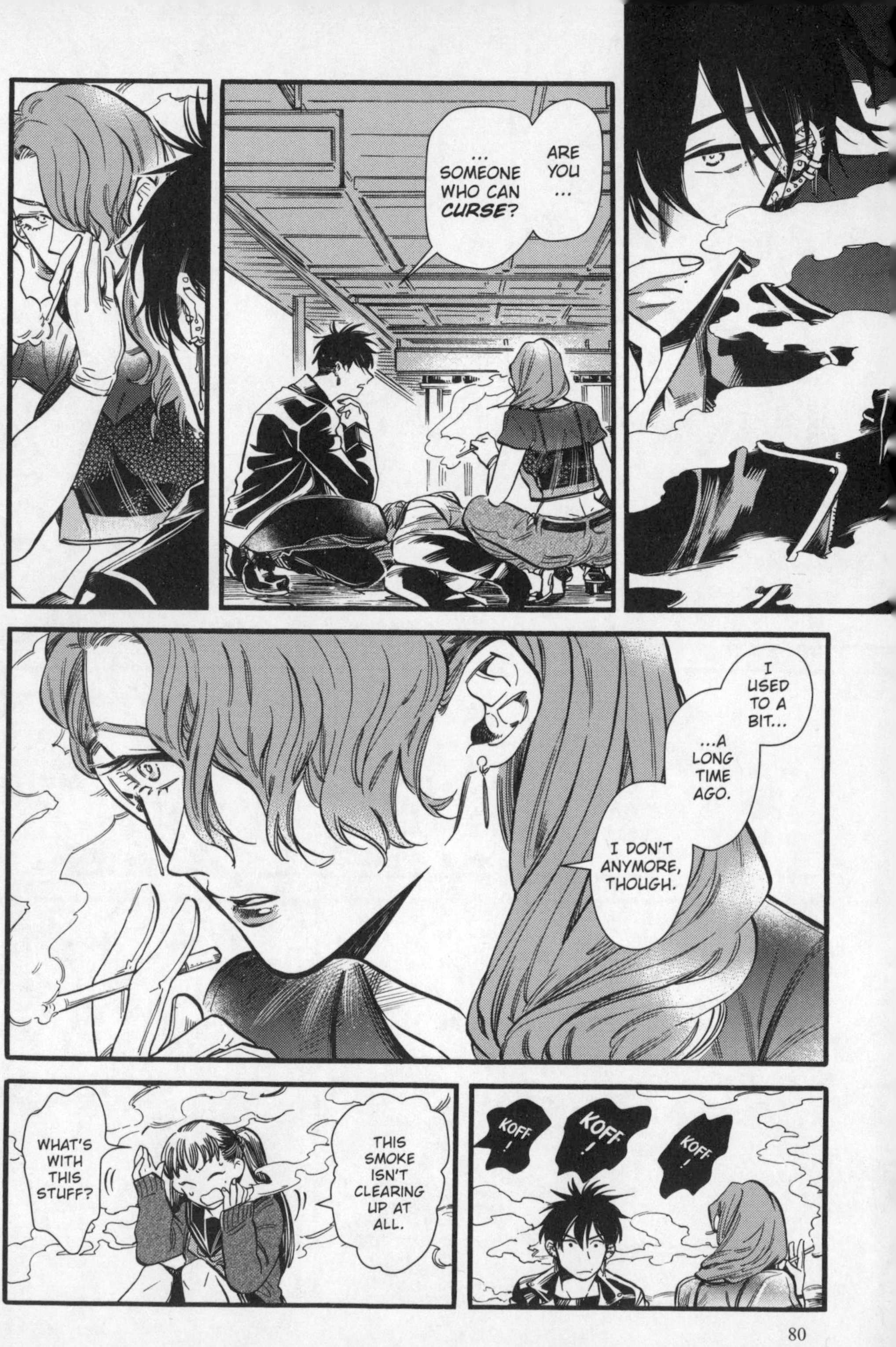
ARE YOU ...
... SOMEONE WHO CAN *CURSE*?
I USED TO A BIT...
...A LONG TIME AGO.
I DON'T ANYMORE, THOUGH.
KOFF!
KOFF!
KOFF!
THIS SMOKE ISN'T CLEARING UP AT ALL.
WHAT'S WITH THIS STUFF?

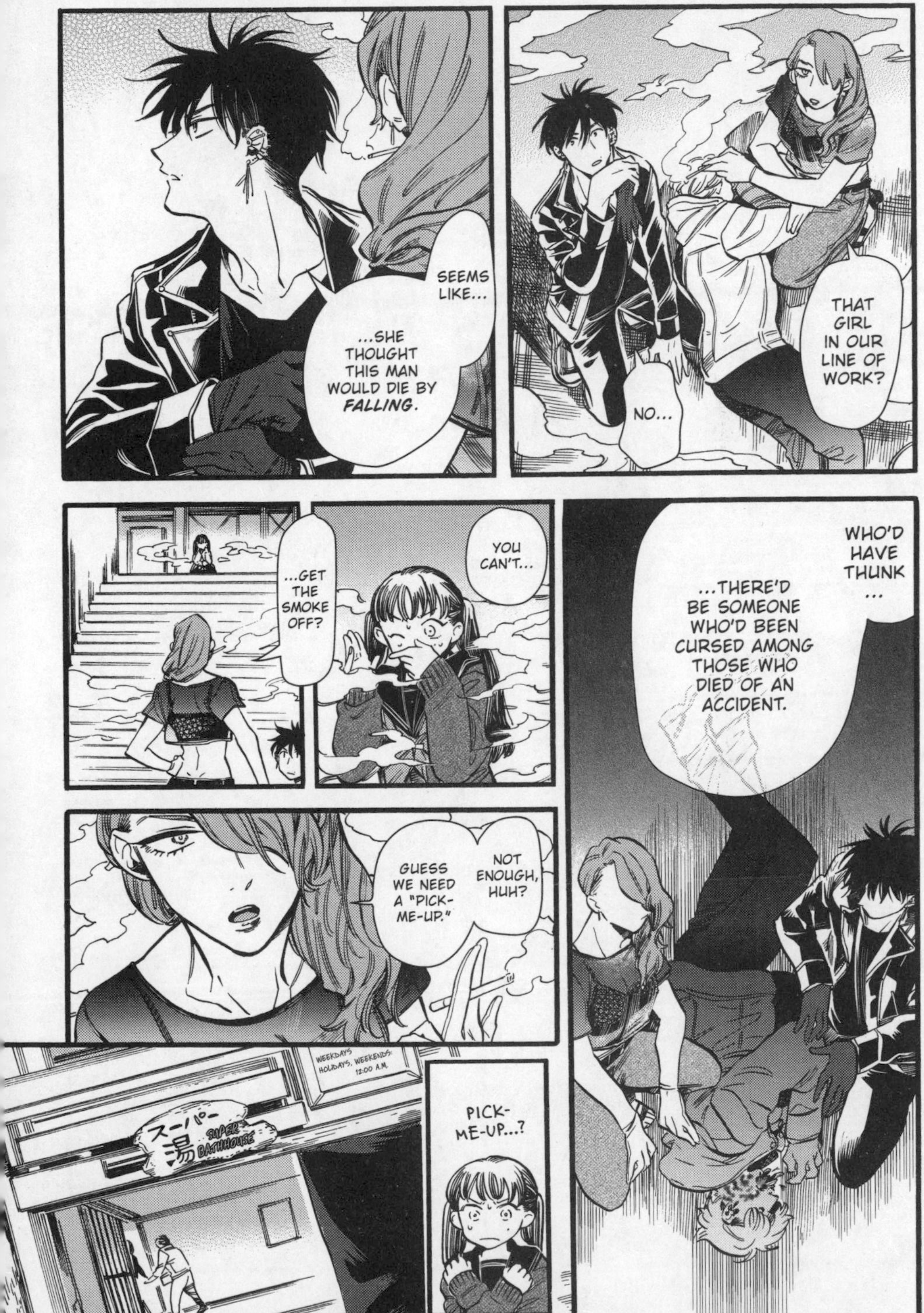
THAT GIRL IN OUR LINE OF WORK?
NO...
SEEMS LIKE...
...SHE THOUGHT THIS MAN WOULD DIE BY *FALLING*.
WHO'D HAVE THUNK...
...THERE'D BE SOMEONE WHO'D BEEN CURSED AMONG THOSE WHO DIED OF AN ACCIDENT.
YOU CAN'T...
...GET THE SMOKE OFF?
NOT ENOUGH, HUH?
GUESS WE NEED A "PICK-ME-UP."
PICK-ME-UP...?
WEEKDAYS HOLIDAYS, WEEKENDS: 12:00 A.M.
スーパー湯 SUPER BATHHOUSE

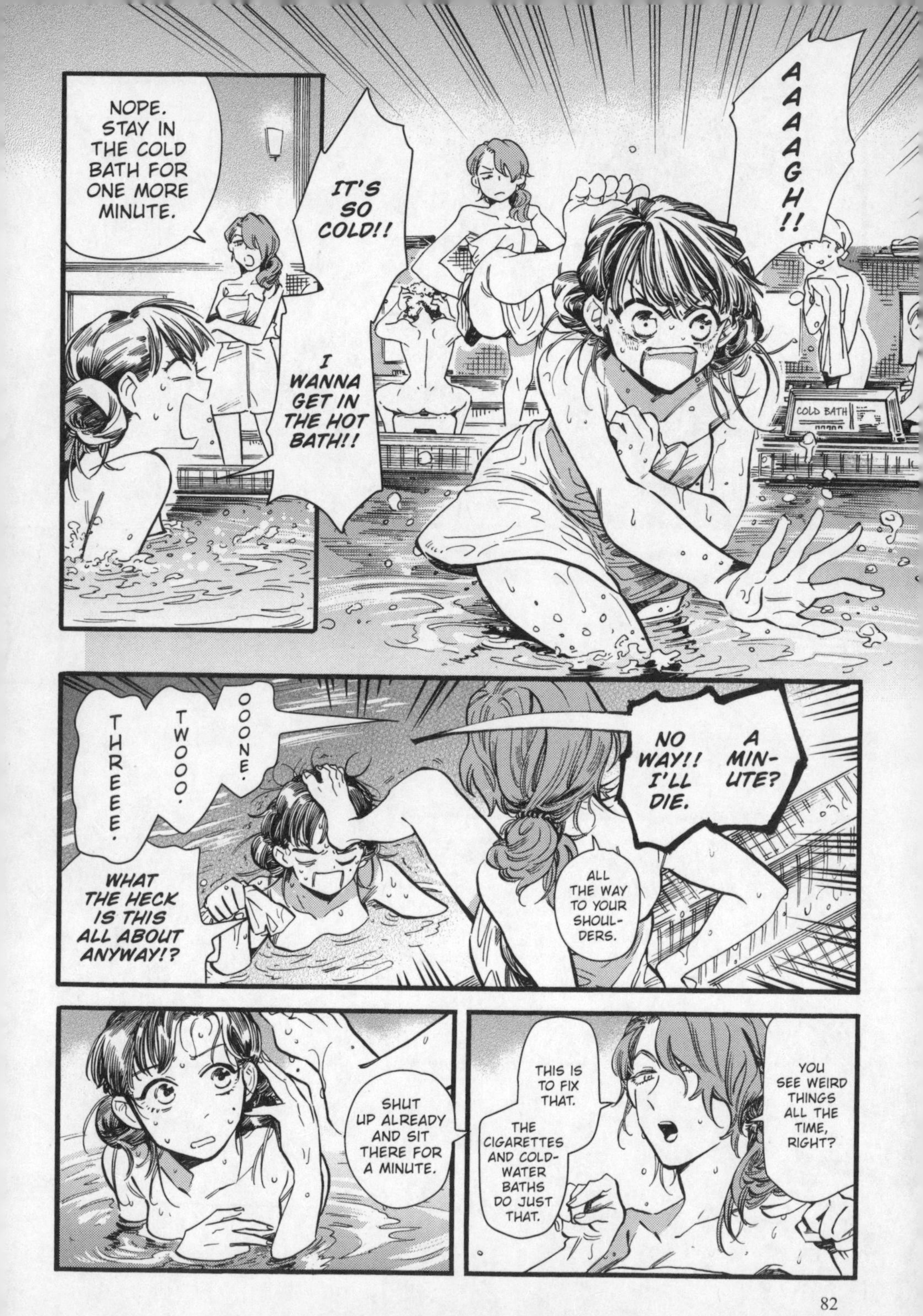
AAAAGH!!
COLD BATH
IT'S SO COLD!!
I WANNA GET IN THE HOT BATH!!
NOPE. STAY IN THE COLD BATH FOR ONE MORE MINUTE.
A MINUTE?
NO WAY!! I'LL DIE.
ALL THE WAY TO YOUR SHOULDERS.
OOONE.
TWOOO.
THREEE.
WHAT THE HECK IS THIS ALL ABOUT ANYWAY!?
YOU SEE WEIRD THINGS ALL THE TIME, RIGHT?
THIS IS TO FIX THAT.
THE CIGARETTES AND COLD-WATER BATHS DO JUST THAT.
SHUT UP ALREADY AND SIT THERE FOR A MINUTE.

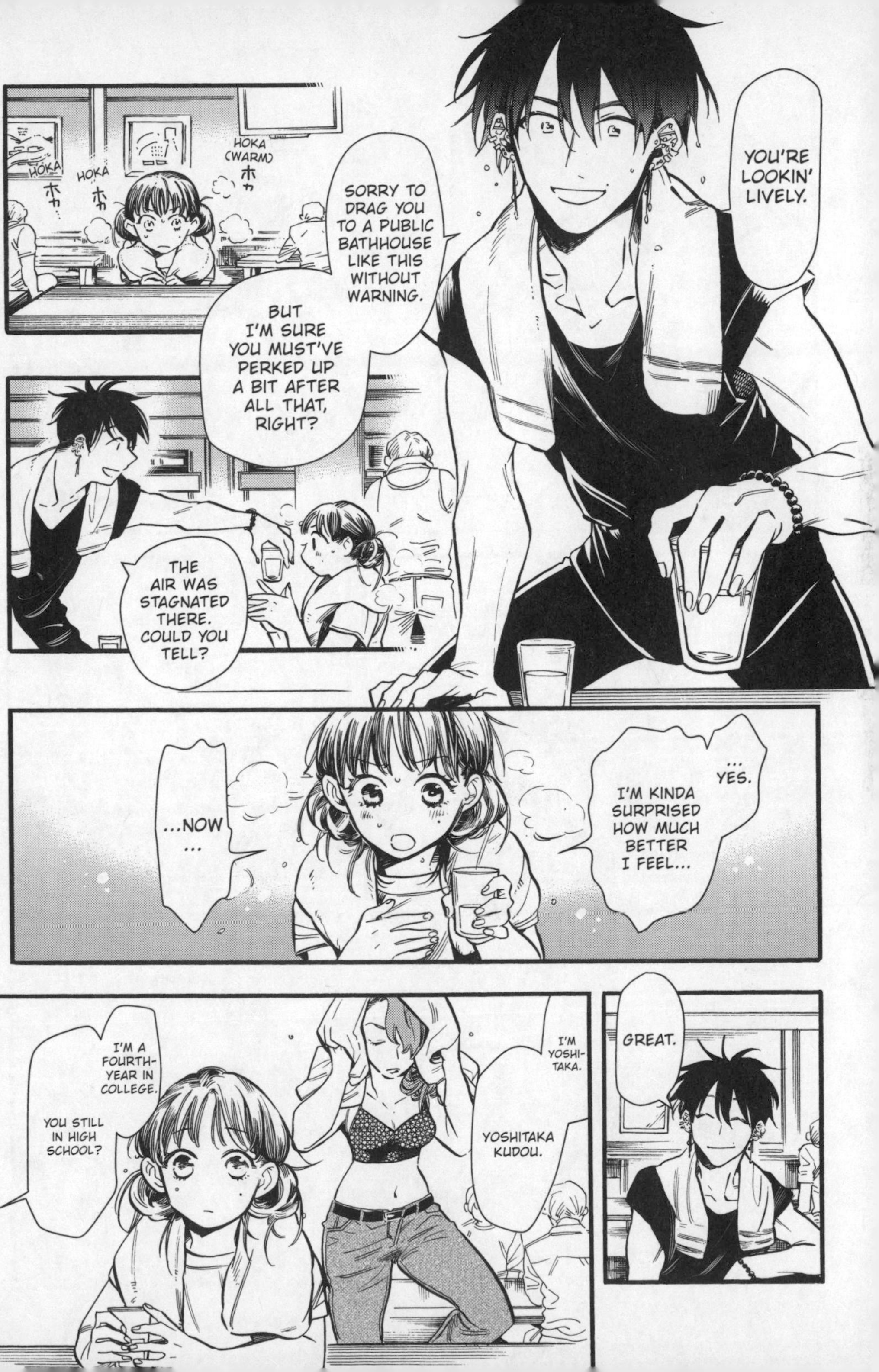
YOU'RE LOOKIN' LIVELY.
HOKA (WARM)
ホカ
HOKA
ホカ
HOKA
ホカ
SORRY TO DRAG YOU TO A PUBLIC BATHHOUSE LIKE THIS WITHOUT WARNING.
BUT I'M SURE YOU MUST'VE PERKED UP A BIT AFTER ALL THAT, RIGHT?
THE AIR WAS STAGNATED THERE. COULD YOU TELL?
... YES.
I'M KINDA SURPRISED HOW MUCH BETTER I FEEL...
...NOW ...
GREAT.
I'M YOSHI-TAKA.
YOSHITAKA KUDOU.
I'M A FOURTH-YEAR IN COLLEGE.
YOU STILL IN HIGH SCHOOL?

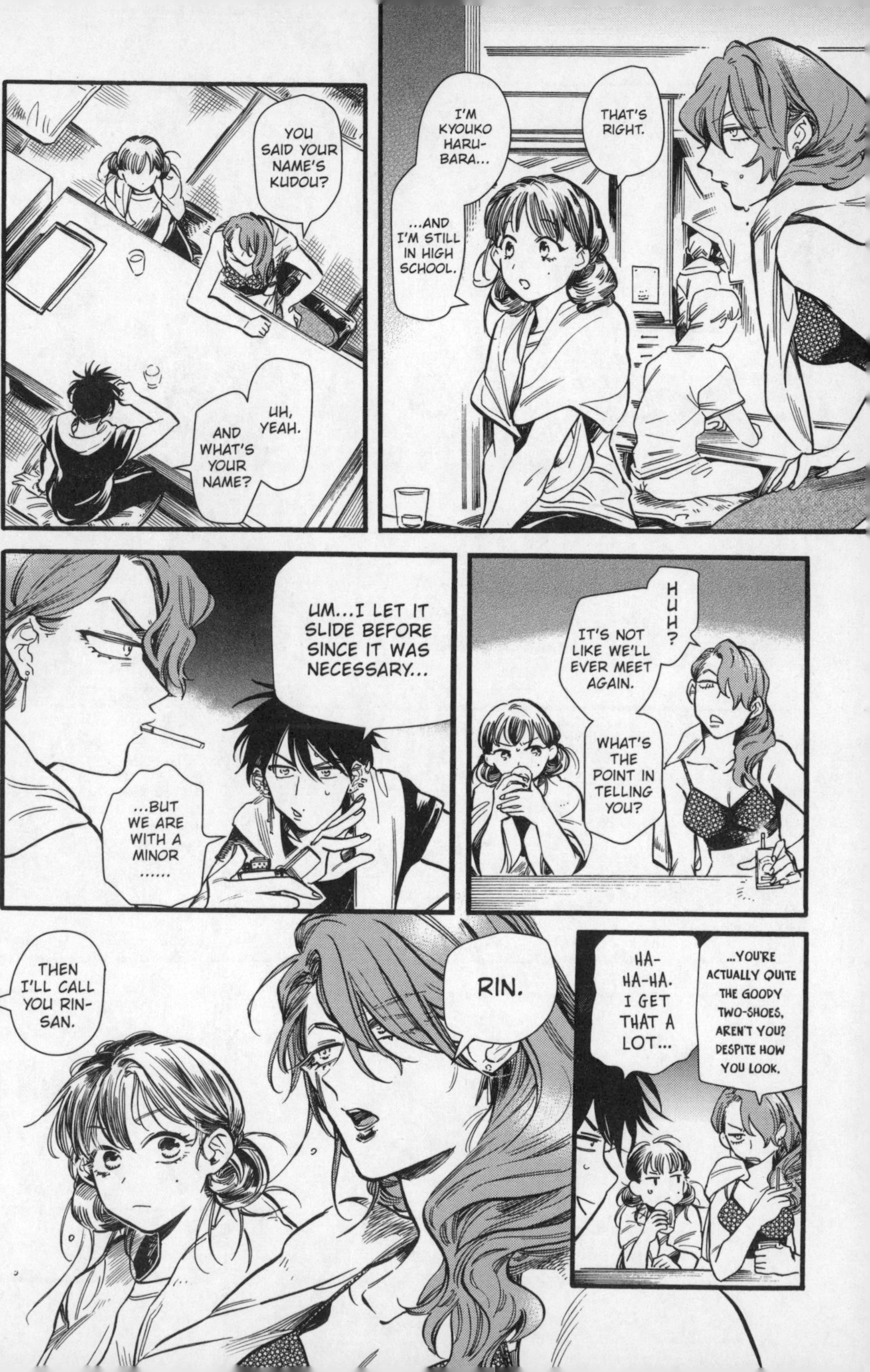
THAT'S RIGHT.
I'M KYOUKO HARU-BARA...
...AND I'M STILL IN HIGH SCHOOL.
YOU SAID YOUR NAME'S KUDOU?
UH, YEAH.
AND WHAT'S YOUR NAME?
HUH?
IT'S NOT LIKE WE'LL EVER MEET AGAIN.
WHAT'S THE POINT IN TELLING YOU?
UM...I LET IT SLIDE BEFORE SINCE IT WAS NECESSARY...
...BUT WE ARE WITH A MINOR ......
...YOU'RE ACTUALLY QUITE THE GOODY TWO-SHOES, AREN'T YOU? DESPITE HOW YOU LOOK.
HA-HA-HA. I GET THAT A LOT...
RIN.
THEN I'LL CALL YOU RIN-SAN.

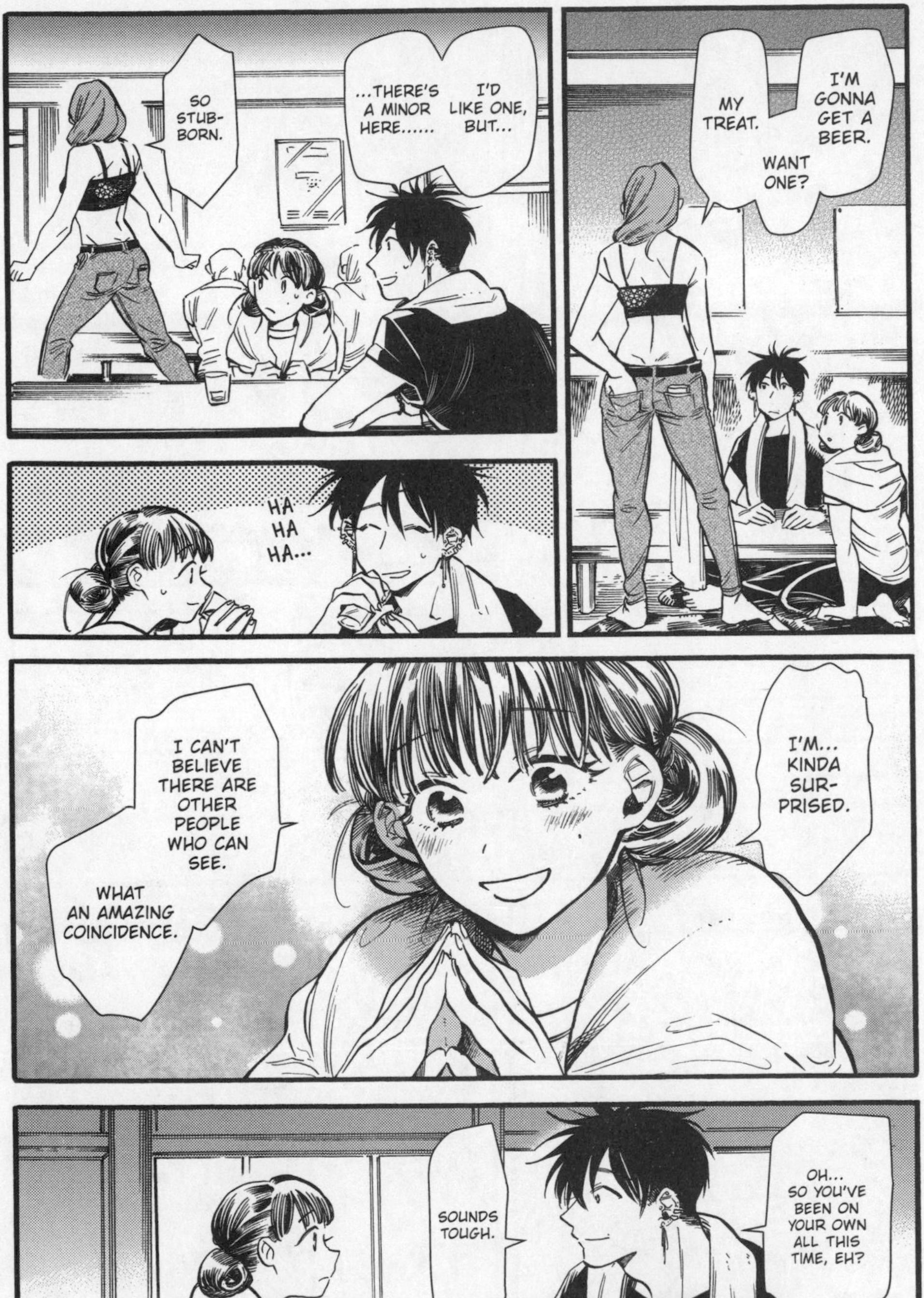
I'M GONNA GET A BEER.
MY TREAT.
WANT ONE?
I'D LIKE ONE, BUT...
...THERE'S A MINOR HERE......
SO STUB-BORN.
HA HA HA...
I'M... KINDA SUR-PRISED.
I CAN'T BELIEVE THERE ARE OTHER PEOPLE WHO CAN SEE.
WHAT AN AMAZING COINCIDENCE.
OH... SO YOU'VE BEEN ON YOUR OWN ALL THIS TIME, EH?
SOUNDS TOUGH.

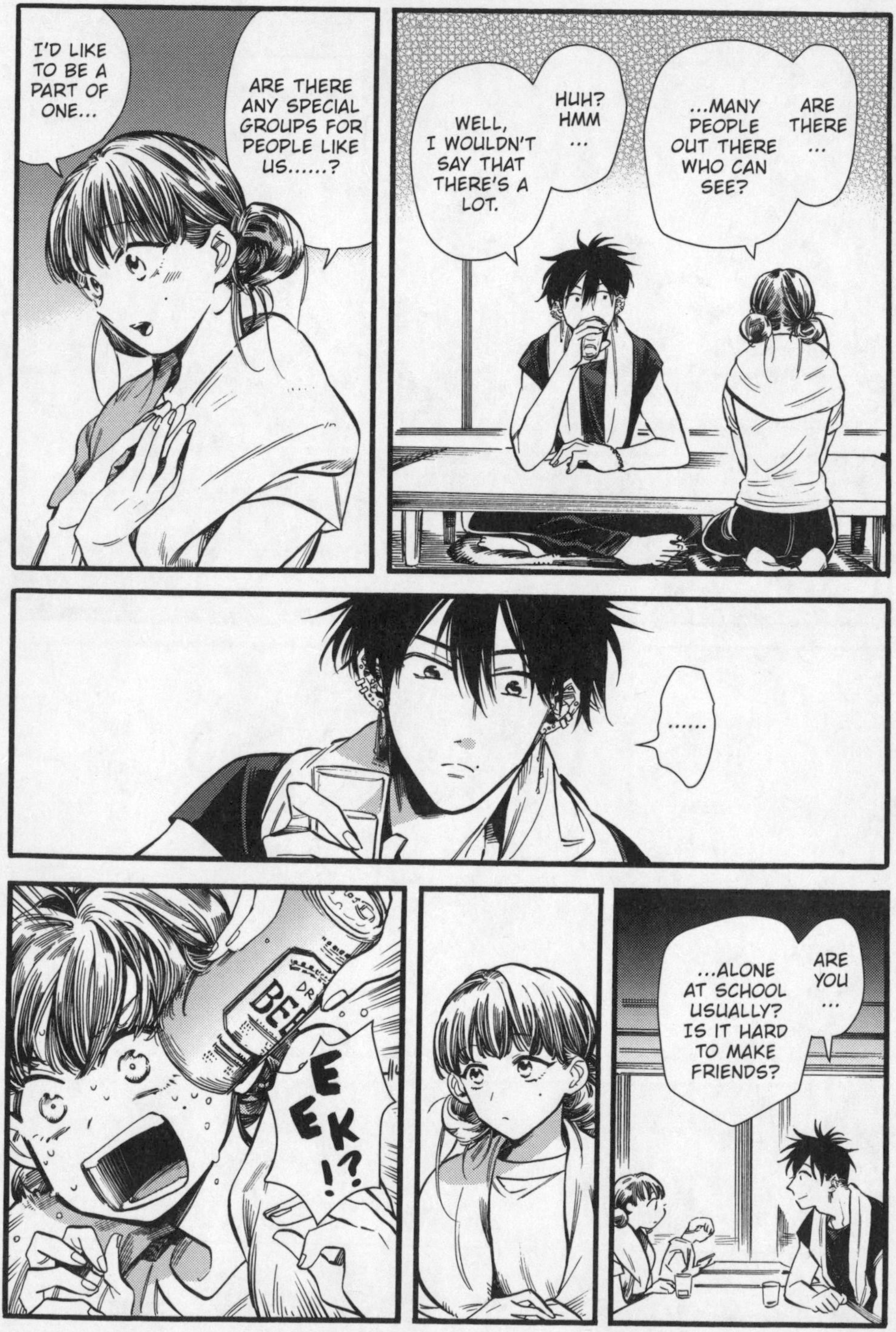
ARE THERE ...
...MANY PEOPLE OUT THERE WHO CAN SEE?
HUH? HMM ...
WELL, I WOULDN'T SAY THAT THERE'S A LOT.
ARE THERE ANY SPECIAL GROUPS FOR PEOPLE LIKE US......?
I'D LIKE TO BE A PART OF ONE...
......
ARE YOU ...
...ALONE AT SCHOOL USUALLY? IS IT HARD TO MAKE FRIENDS?
EEK!?

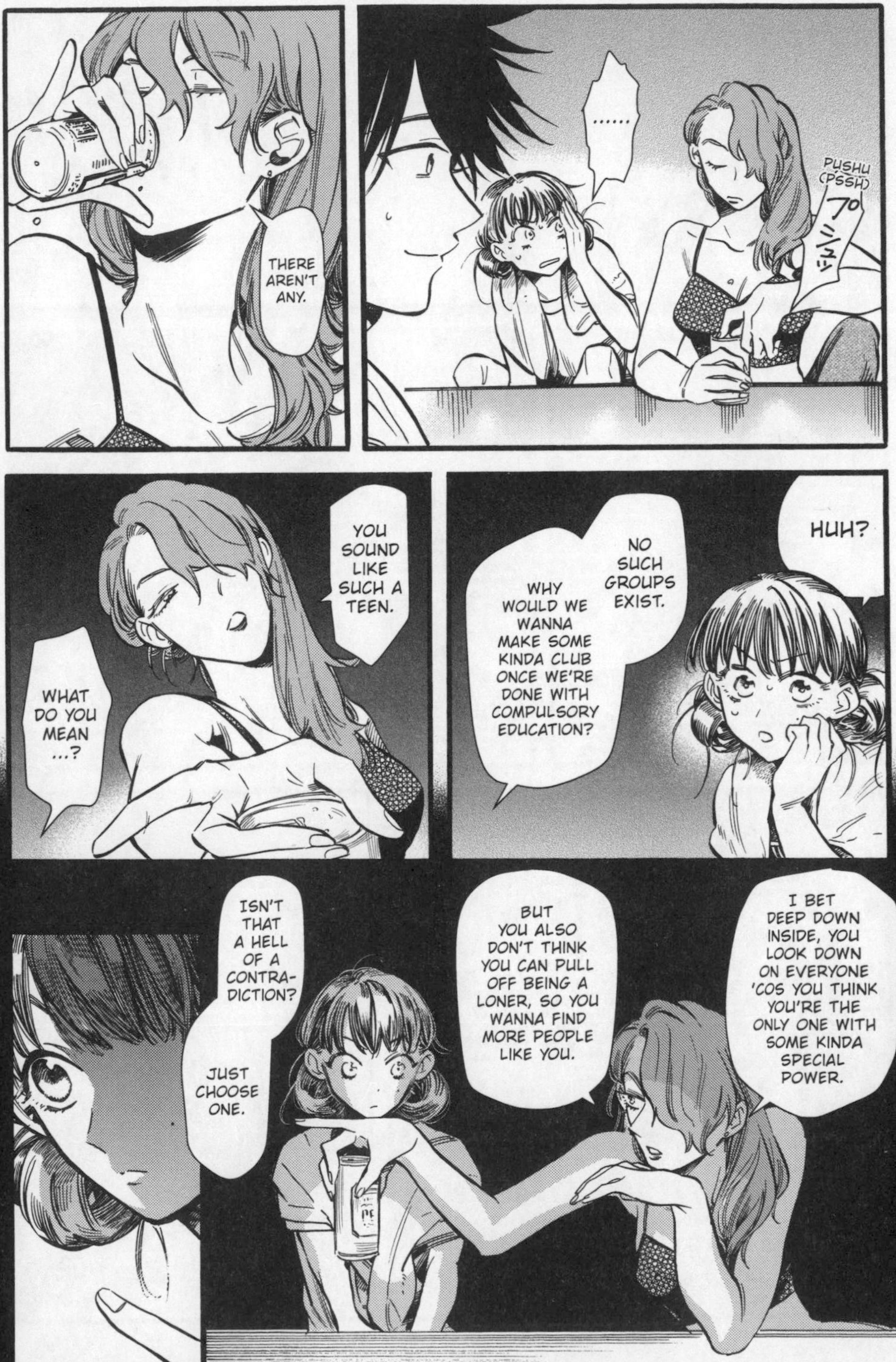

......
PUSHU (PSSH)
THERE AREN'T ANY.
HUH?
NO SUCH GROUPS EXIST.
WHY WOULD WE WANNA MAKE SOME KINDA CLUB ONCE WE'RE DONE WITH COMPULSORY EDUCATION?
YOU SOUND LIKE SUCH A TEEN.
WHAT DO YOU MEAN ...?
I BET DEEP DOWN INSIDE, YOU LOOK DOWN ON EVERYONE 'COS YOU THINK YOU'RE THE ONLY ONE WITH SOME KINDA SPECIAL POWER.
BUT YOU ALSO DON'T THINK YOU CAN PULL OFF BEING A LONER, SO YOU WANNA FIND MORE PEOPLE LIKE YOU.
ISN'T THAT A HELL OF A CONTRA-DICTION?
JUST CHOOSE ONE.

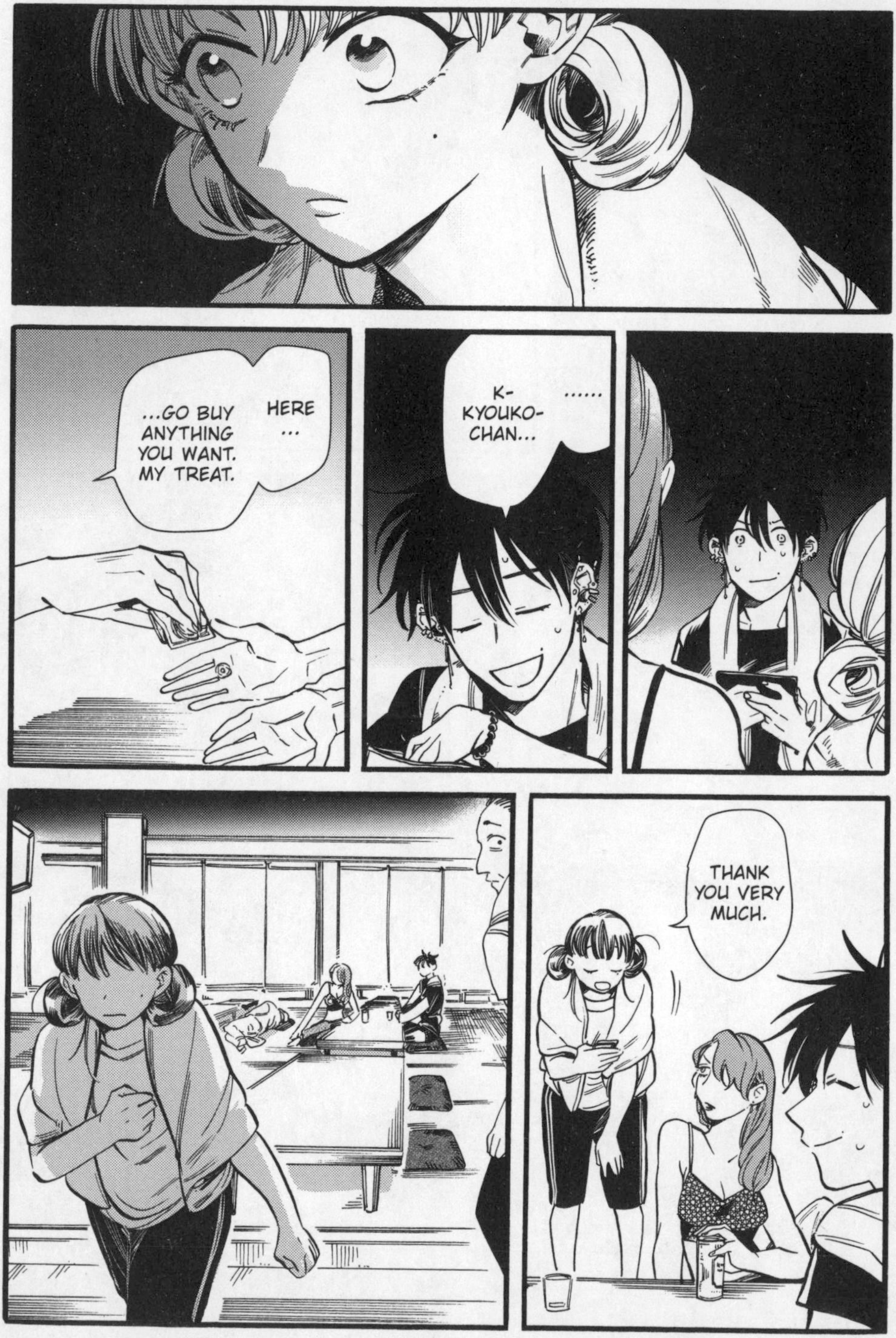
......
K-KYOUKO-CHAN...
HERE ...
...GO BUY ANYTHING YOU WANT. MY TREAT.
THANK YOU VERY MUCH.

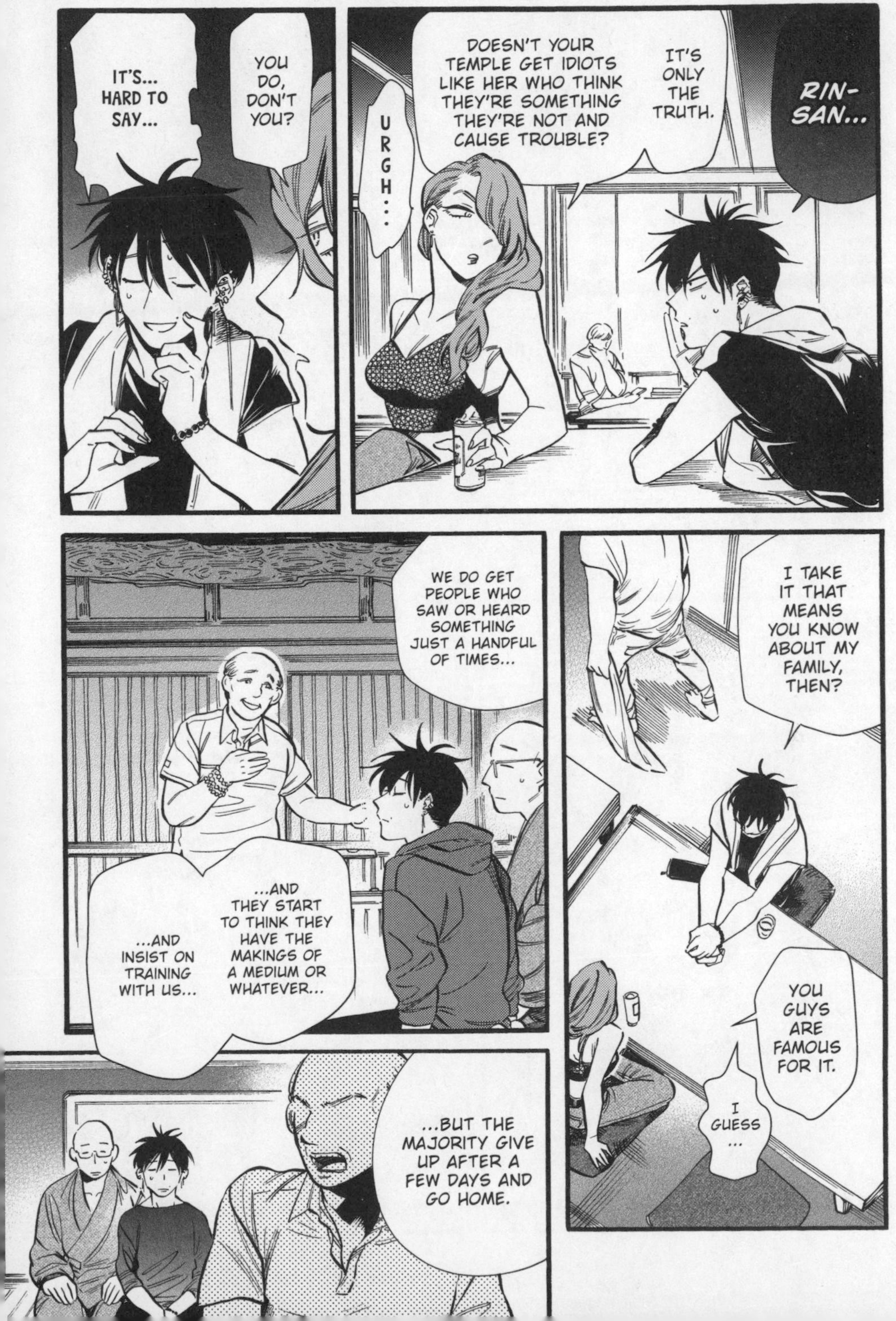
RIN-SAN...
IT'S ONLY THE TRUTH.
DOESN'T YOUR TEMPLE GET IDIOTS LIKE HER WHO THINK THEY'RE SOMETHING THEY'RE NOT AND CAUSE TROUBLE?
URGH...
YOU DO, DON'T YOU?
IT'S... HARD TO SAY...
I TAKE IT THAT MEANS YOU KNOW ABOUT MY FAMILY, THEN?
YOU GUYS ARE FAMOUS FOR IT.
I GUESS...
WE DO GET PEOPLE WHO SAW OR HEARD SOMETHING JUST A HANDFUL OF TIMES...
...AND THEY START TO THINK THEY HAVE THE MAKINGS OF A MEDIUM OR WHATEVER...
...AND INSIST ON TRAINING WITH US...
...BUT THE MAJORITY GIVE UP AFTER A FEW DAYS AND GO HOME.

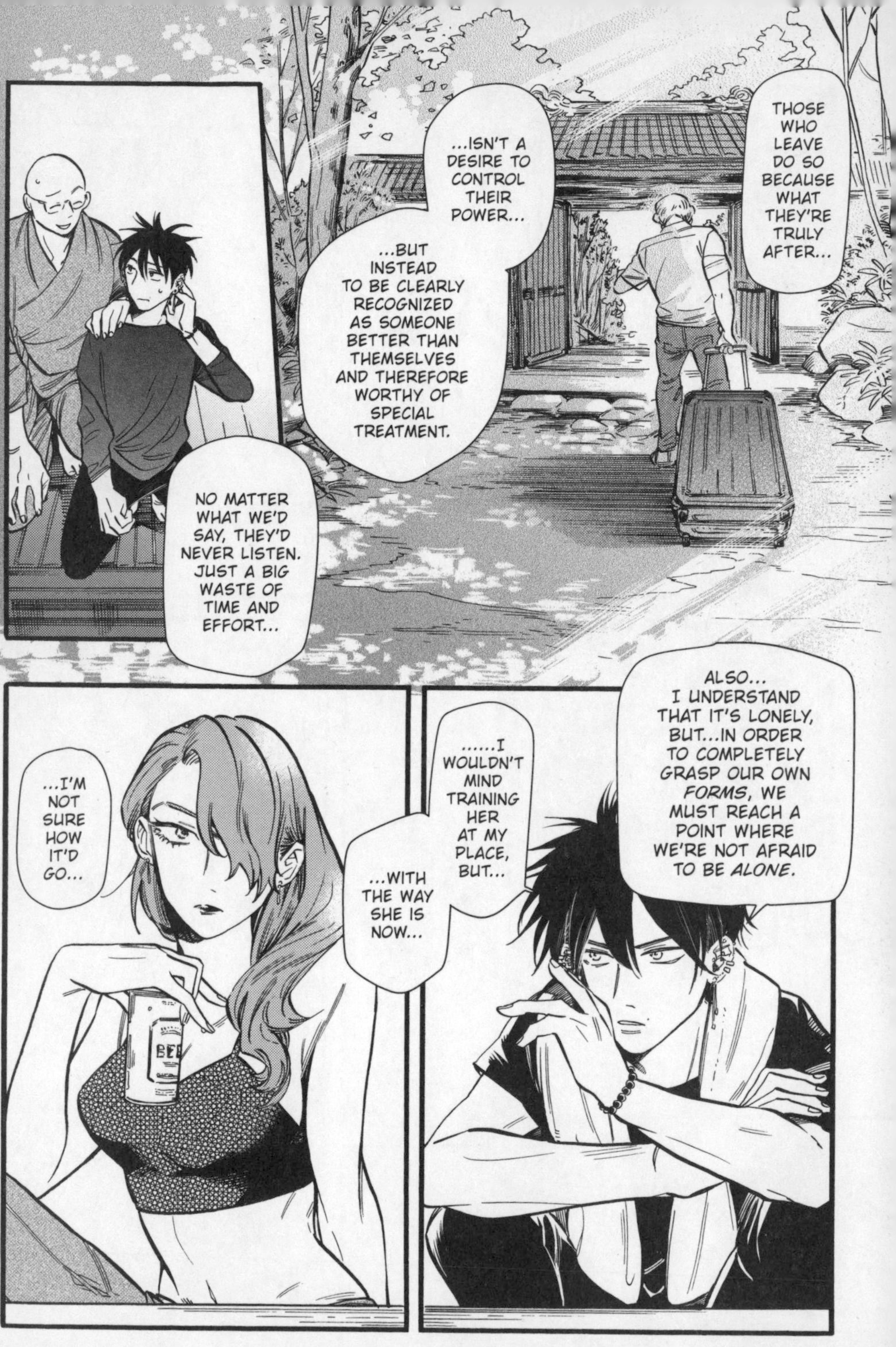
THOSE WHO LEAVE DO SO BECAUSE WHAT THEY'RE TRULY AFTER...
...ISN'T A DESIRE TO CONTROL THEIR POWER...
...BUT INSTEAD TO BE CLEARLY RECOGNIZED AS SOMEONE BETTER THAN THEMSELVES AND THEREFORE WORTHY OF SPECIAL TREATMENT.
NO MATTER WHAT WE'D SAY, THEY'D NEVER LISTEN. JUST A BIG WASTE OF TIME AND EFFORT...
ALSO... I UNDERSTAND THAT IT'S LONELY, BUT...IN ORDER TO COMPLETELY GRASP OUR OWN *FORMS*, WE MUST REACH A POINT WHERE WE'RE NOT AFRAID TO BE *ALONE*.
......I WOULDN'T MIND TRAINING HER AT MY PLACE, BUT...
...WITH THE WAY SHE IS NOW...
...I'M NOT SURE HOW IT'D GO...

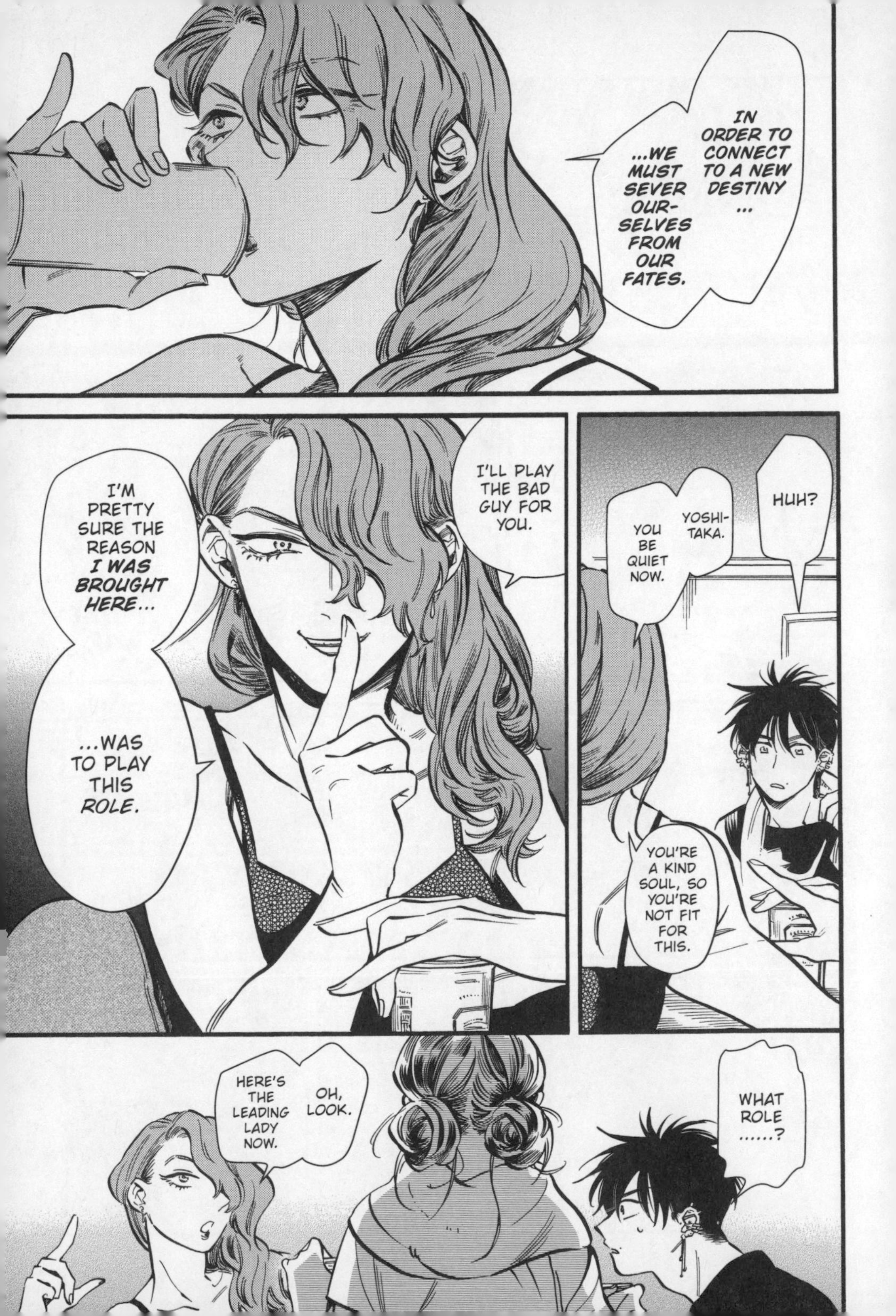
IN ORDER TO CONNECT TO A NEW DESTINY ...
...WE MUST SEVER OURSELVES FROM OUR FATES.
HUH?
YOSHITAKA.
YOU BE QUIET NOW.
YOU'RE A KIND SOUL, SO YOU'RE NOT FIT FOR THIS.
I'LL PLAY THE BAD GUY FOR YOU.
I'M PRETTY SURE THE REASON *I WAS BROUGHT HERE*...
...WAS TO PLAY THIS *ROLE*.
WHAT ROLE ......?
OH, LOOK.
HERE'S THE LEADING LADY NOW.

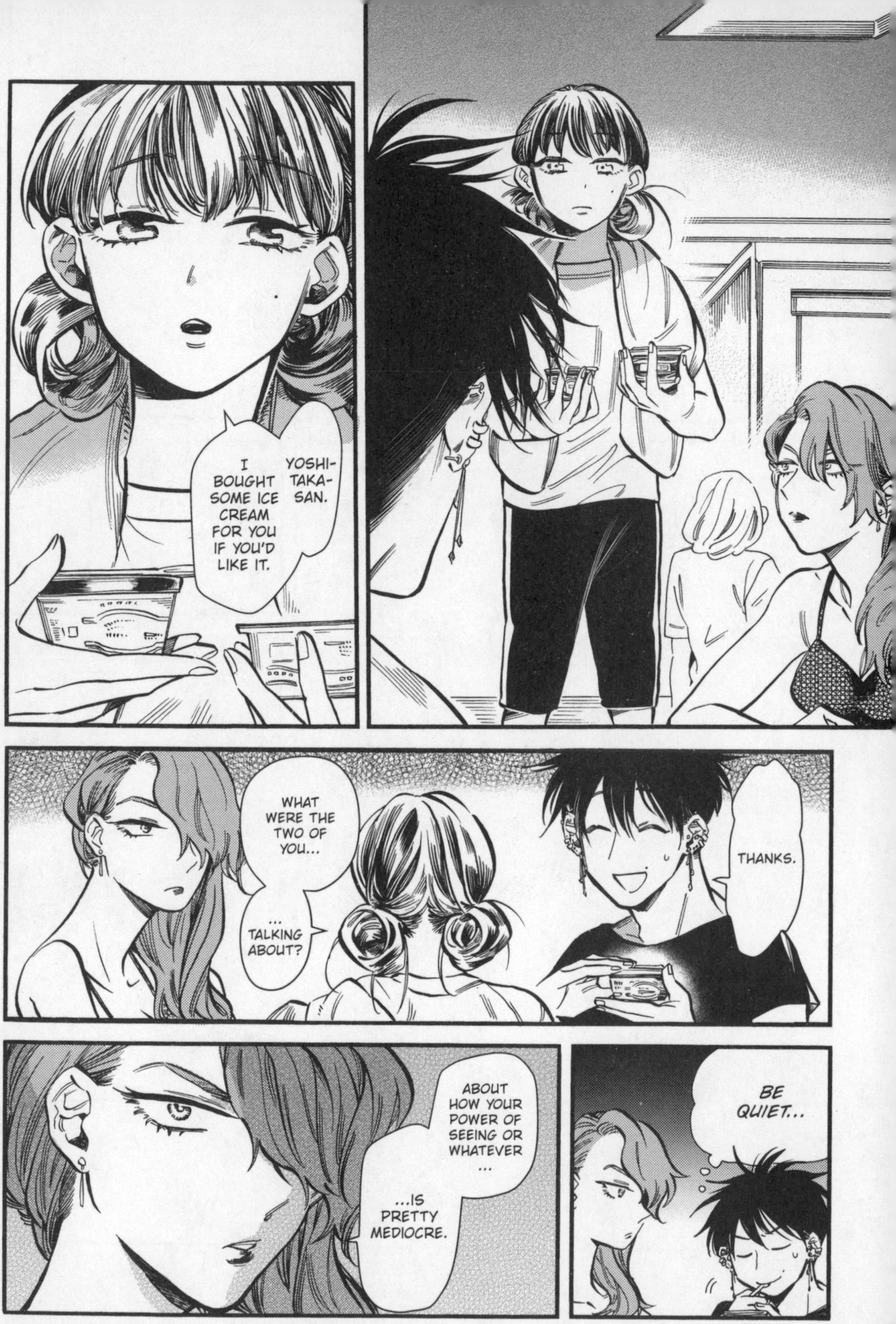
YOSHI-TAKA-SAN.
I BOUGHT SOME ICE CREAM FOR YOU IF YOU'D LIKE IT.
THANKS.
WHAT WERE THE TWO OF YOU...
...TALKING ABOUT?
BE QUIET...
ABOUT HOW YOUR POWER OF SEEING OR WHATEVER...
...IS PRETTY MEDIOCRE.

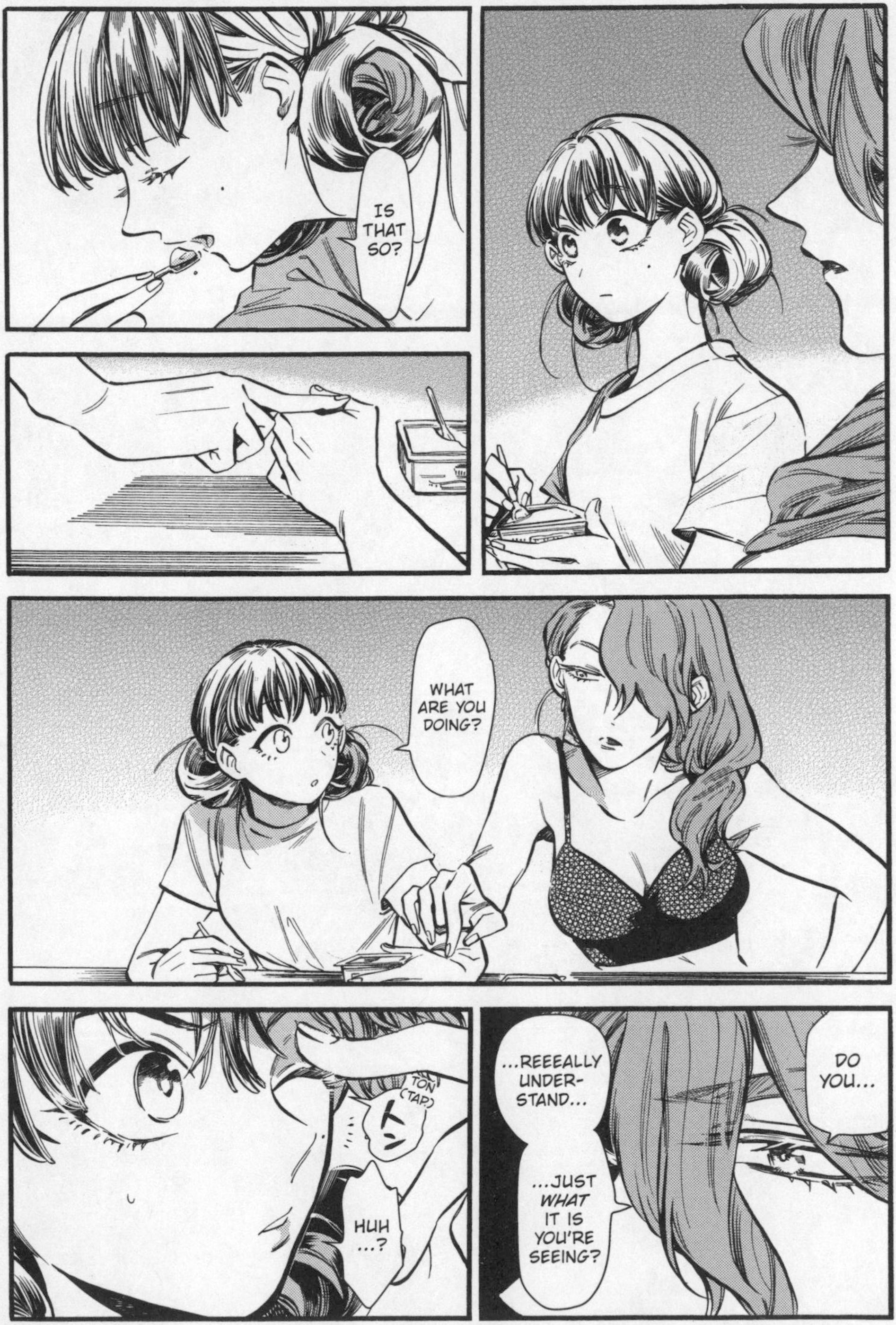
IS THAT SO?
WHAT ARE YOU DOING?
DO YOU...
...REEEALLY UNDER-STAND...
...JUST *WHAT* IT IS YOU'RE SEEING?
TON (TAP)
HUH ...?

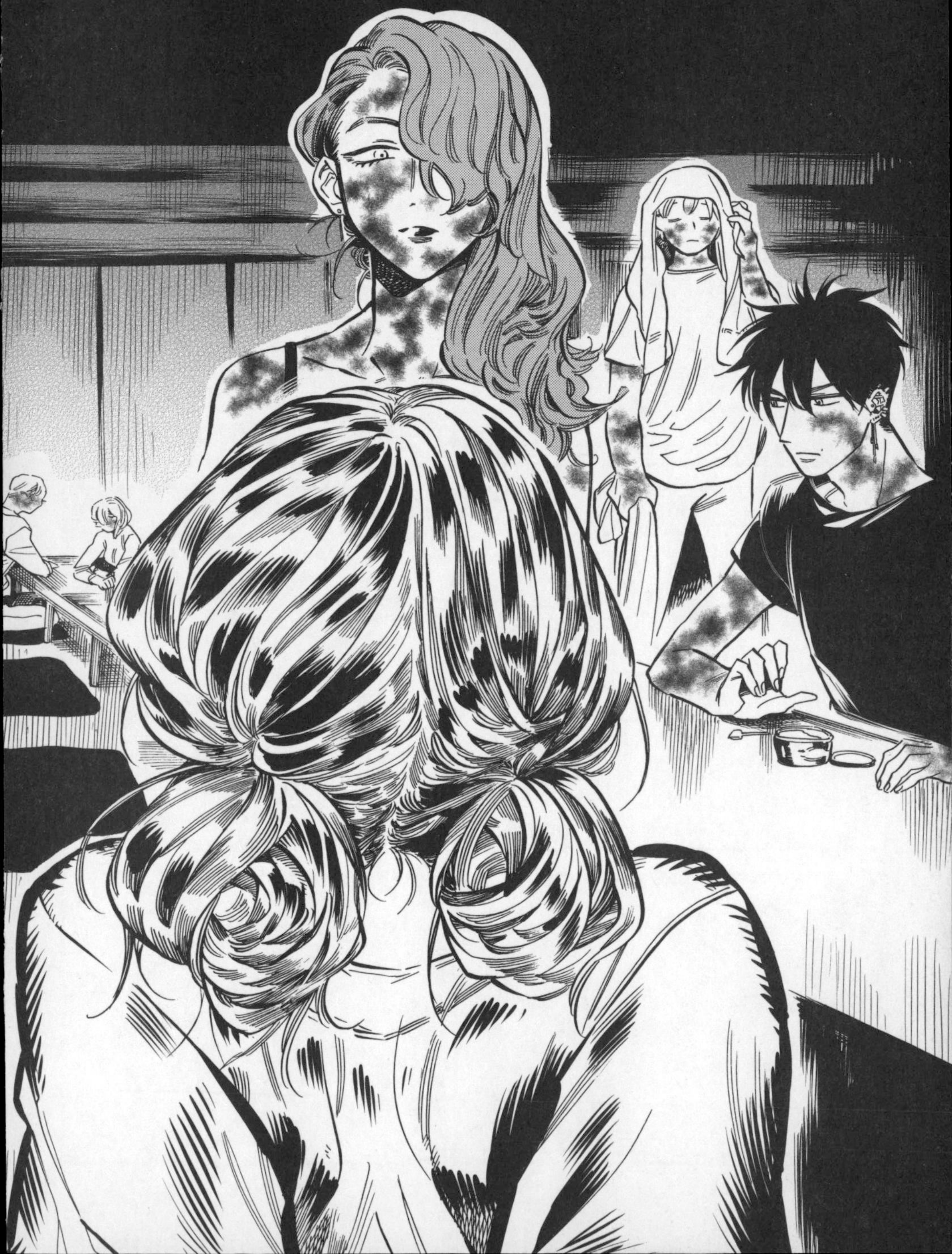

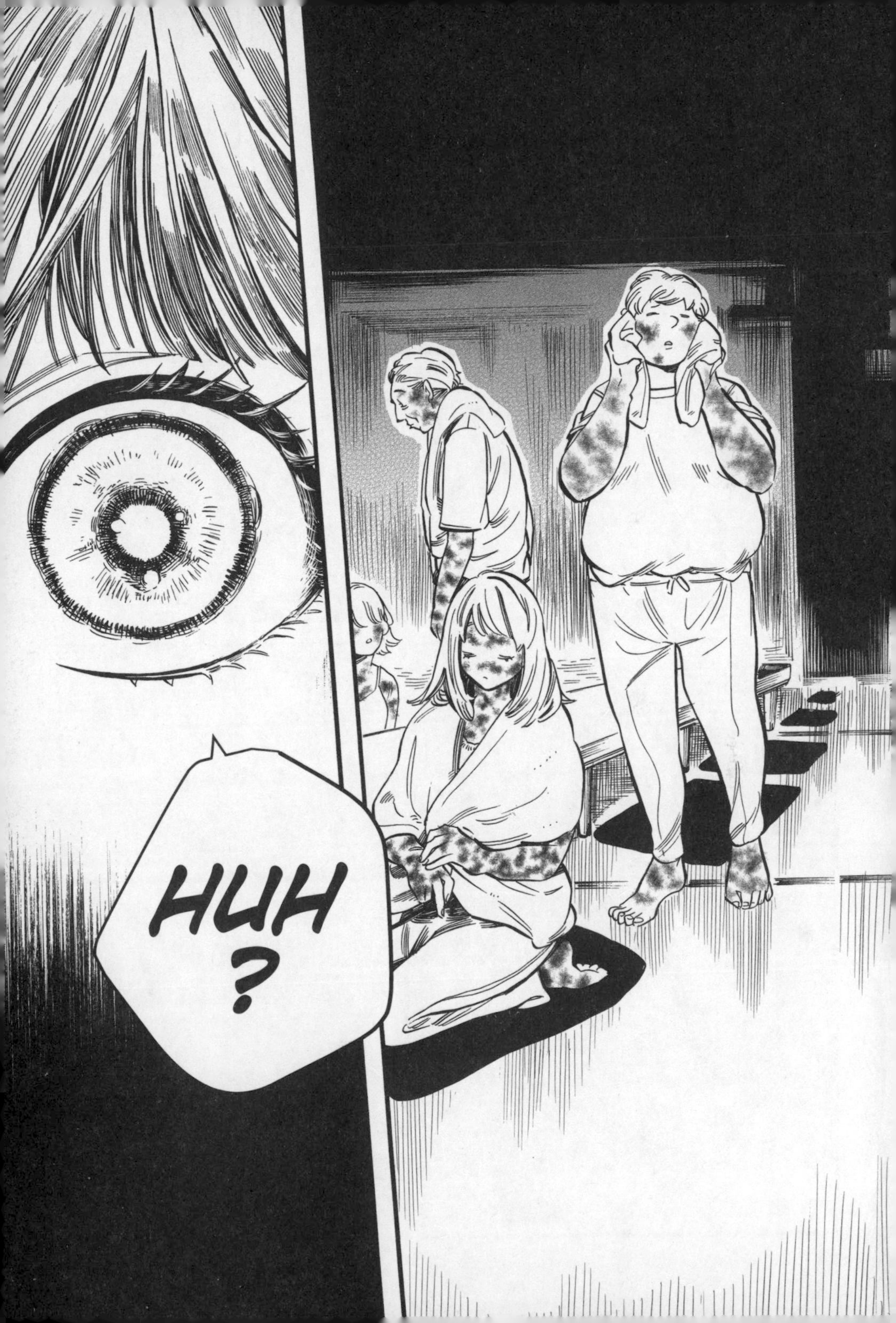
HUH?

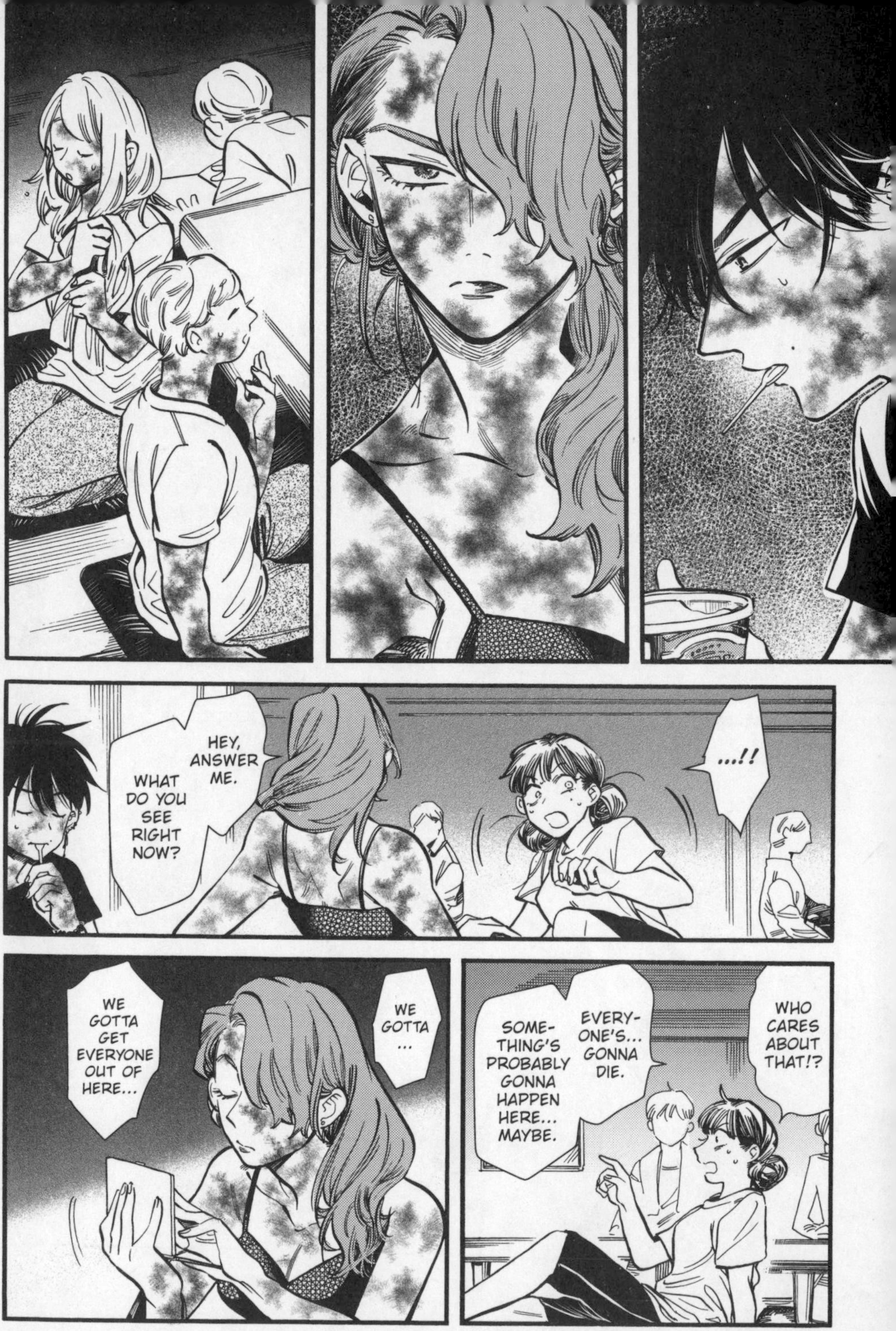
...!!
HEY, ANSWER ME.
WHAT DO YOU SEE RIGHT NOW?
WHO CARES ABOUT THAT!?
EVERY-ONE'S... GONNA DIE.
SOME-THING'S PROBABLY GONNA HAPPEN HERE... MAYBE.
WE GOTTA ...
WE GOTTA GET EVERYONE OUT OF HERE...

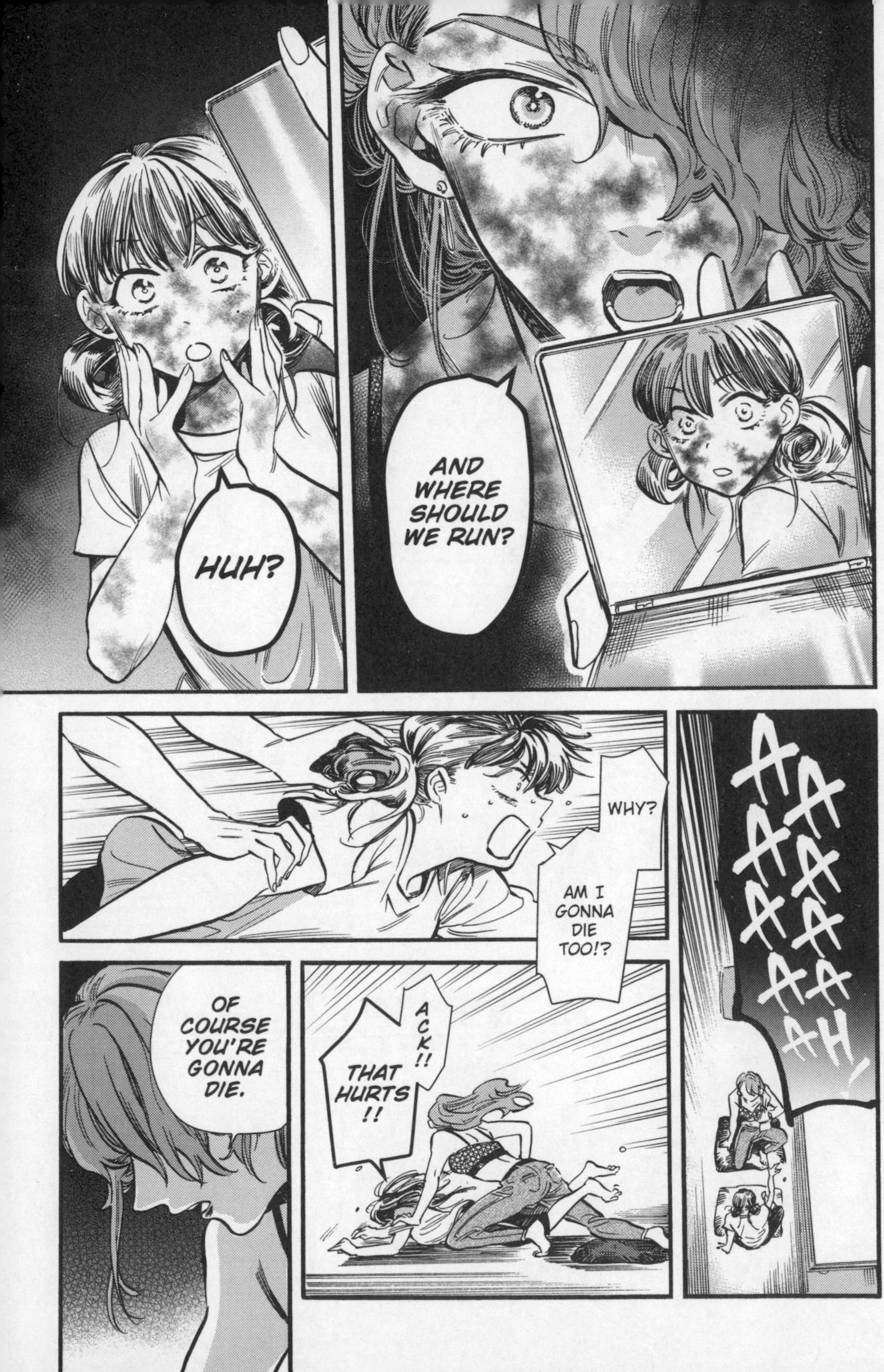
AND WHERE SHOULD WE RUN?
HUH?
AAAAAAAAAAAH!
WHY?
AM I GONNA DIE TOO!?
ACK!!
THAT HURTS!!
OF COURSE YOU'RE GONNA DIE.

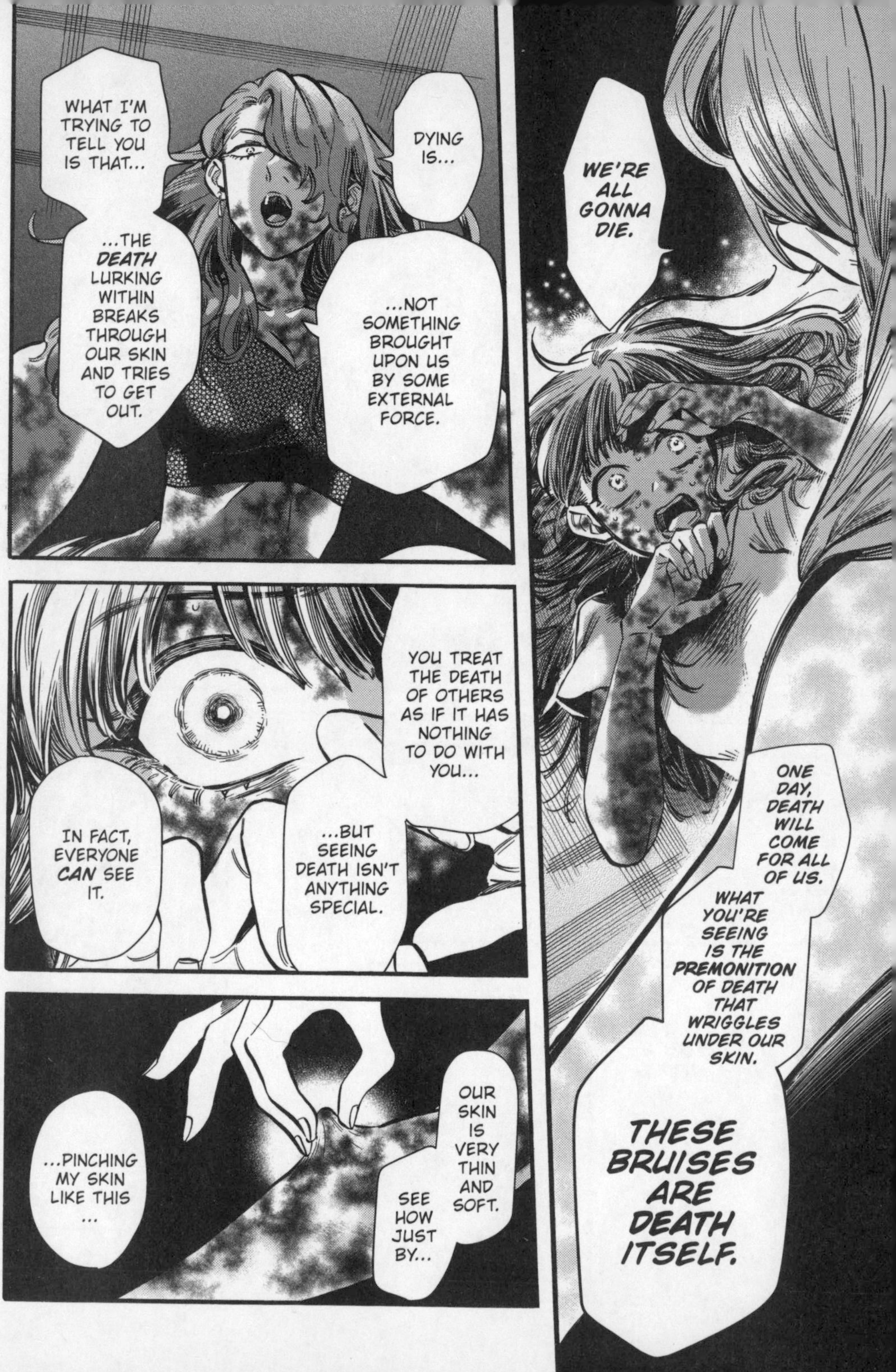
WE'RE ALL GONNA DIE.
ONE DAY, DEATH WILL COME FOR ALL OF US.
WHAT YOU'RE SEEING IS THE PREMONITION OF DEATH THAT WRIGGLES UNDER OUR SKIN.
THESE BRUISES ARE DEATH ITSELF.
WHAT I'M TRYING TO TELL YOU IS THAT...
DYING IS...
...NOT SOMETHING BROUGHT UPON US BY SOME EXTERNAL FORCE.
...THE DEATH LURKING WITHIN BREAKS THROUGH OUR SKIN AND TRIES TO GET OUT.
YOU TREAT THE DEATH OF OTHERS AS IF IT HAS NOTHING TO DO WITH YOU...
...BUT SEEING DEATH ISN'T ANYTHING SPECIAL.
IN FACT, EVERYONE CAN SEE IT.
OUR SKIN IS VERY THIN AND SOFT.
SEE HOW JUST BY...
...PINCHING MY SKIN LIKE THIS ...

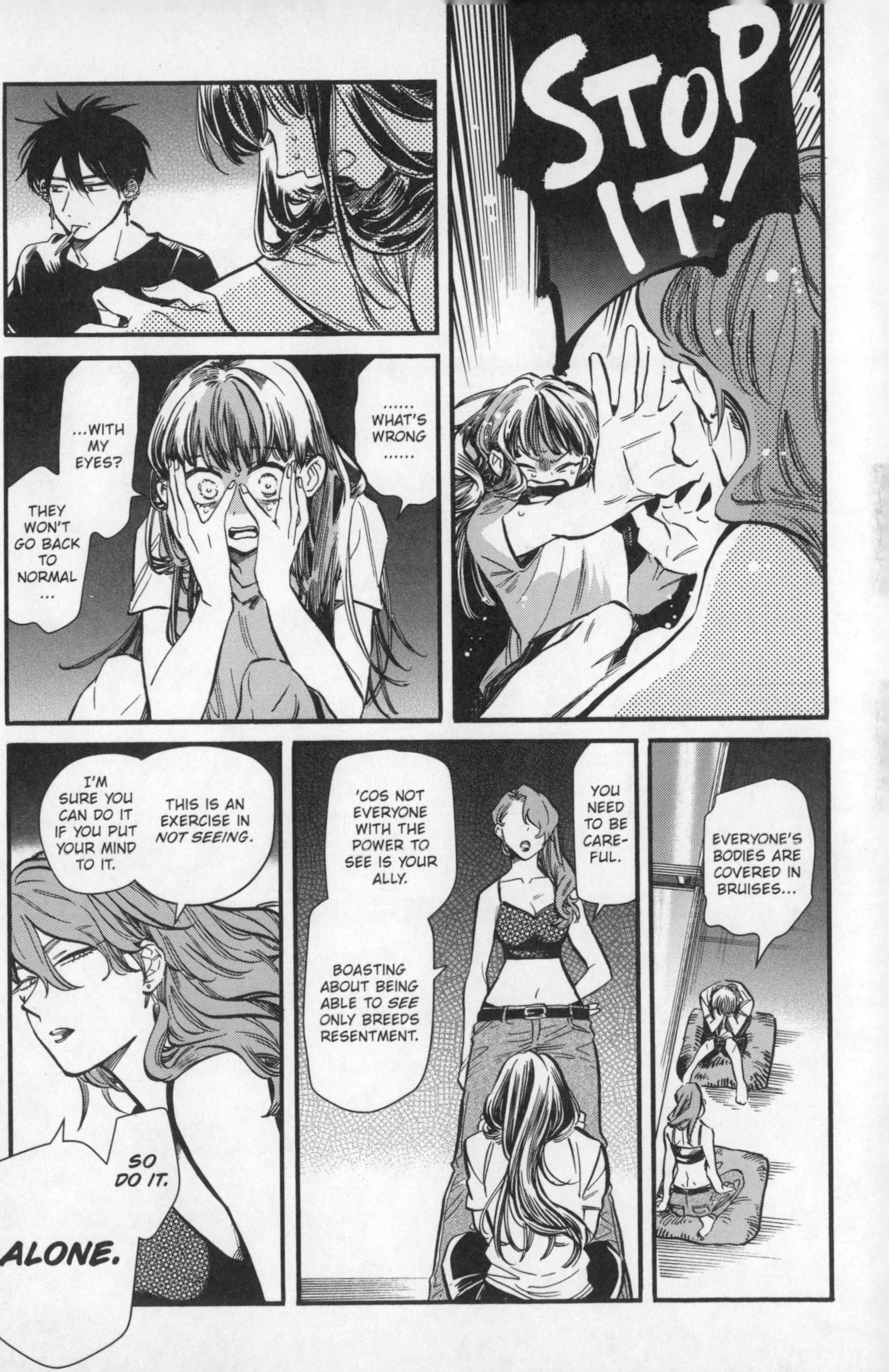
STOP IT!
......WHAT'S WRONG......
...WITH MY EYES?
THEY WON'T GO BACK TO NORMAL...
EVERYONE'S BODIES ARE COVERED IN BRUISES...
YOU NEED TO BE CARE-FUL.
'COS NOT EVERYONE WITH THE POWER TO SEE IS YOUR ALLY.
BOASTING ABOUT BEING ABLE TO *SEE* ONLY BREEDS RESENTMENT.
THIS IS AN EXERCISE IN *NOT SEEING*.
I'M SURE YOU CAN DO IT IF YOU PUT YOUR MIND TO IT.
SO DO IT.
ALONE.

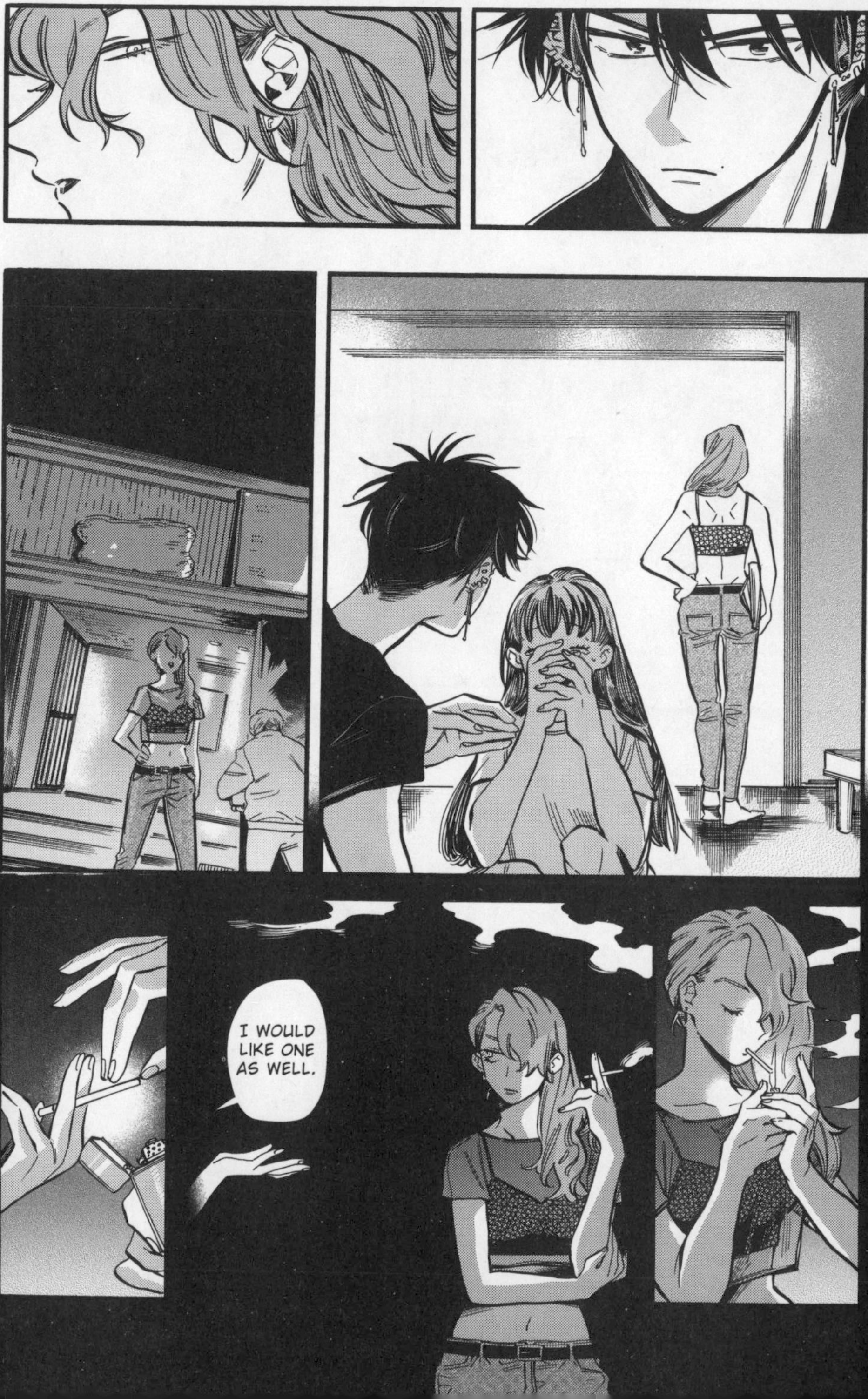
I WOULD LIKE ONE AS WELL.

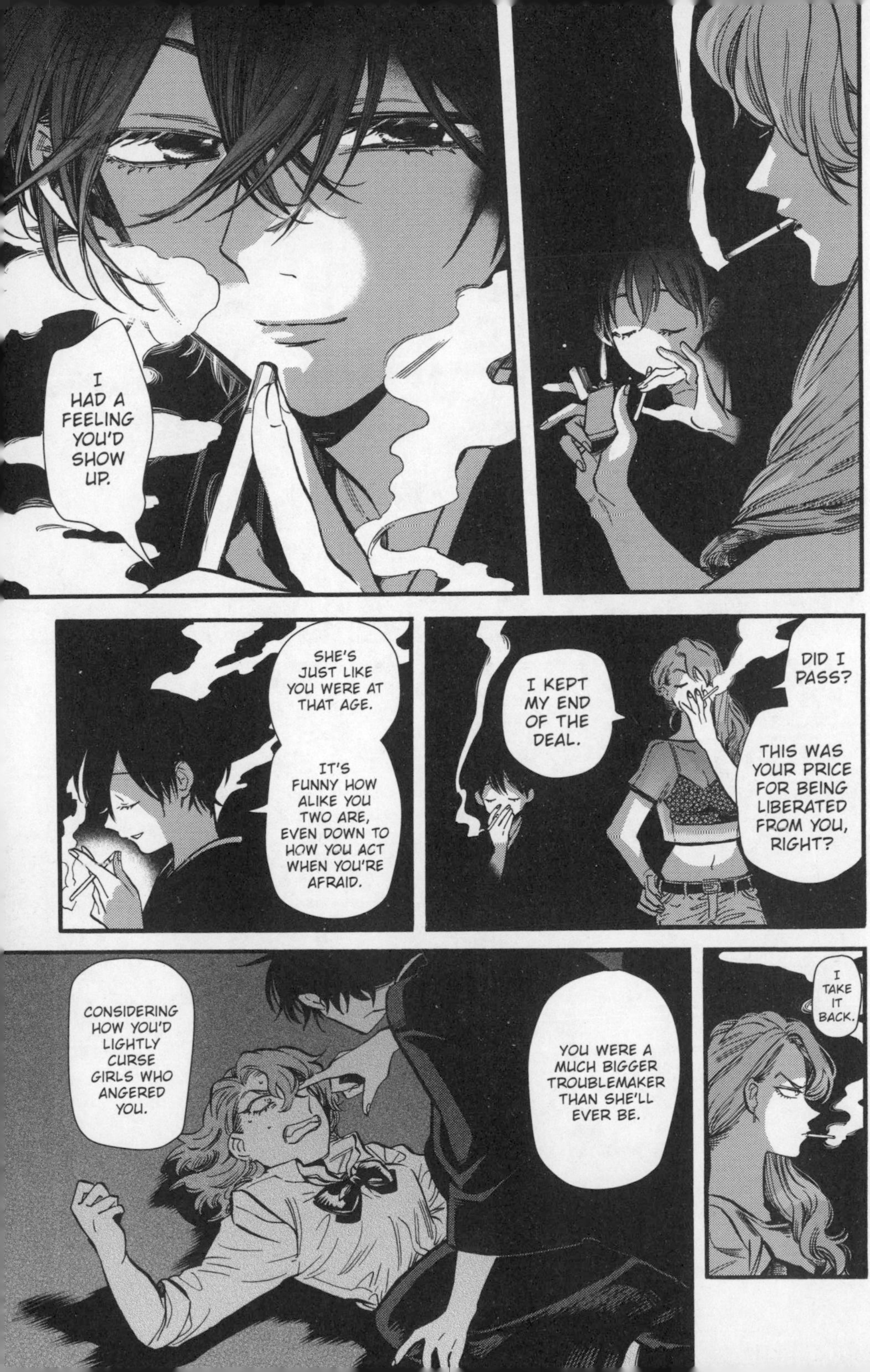
I HAD A FEELING YOU'D SHOW UP.
DID I PASS?
THIS WAS YOUR PRICE FOR BEING LIBERATED FROM YOU, RIGHT?
I KEPT MY END OF THE DEAL.
SHE'S JUST LIKE YOU WERE AT THAT AGE.
IT'S FUNNY HOW ALIKE YOU TWO ARE, EVEN DOWN TO HOW YOU ACT WHEN YOU'RE AFRAID.
I TAKE IT BACK.
YOU WERE A MUCH BIGGER TROUBLEMAKER THAN SHE'LL EVER BE.
CONSIDERING HOW YOU'D LIGHTLY CURSE GIRLS WHO ANGERED YOU.

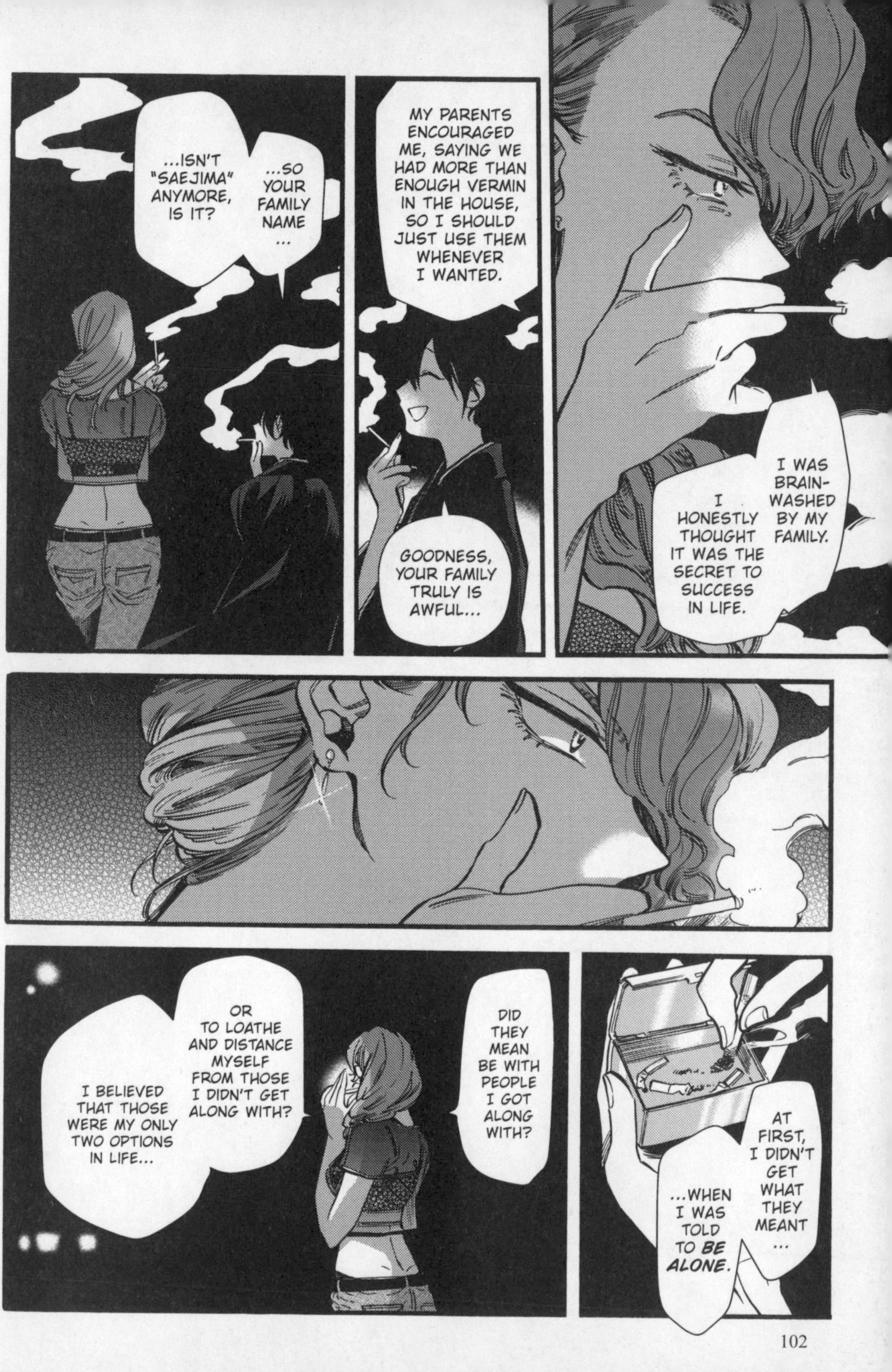
I WAS BRAIN-WASHED BY MY FAMILY.
I HONESTLY THOUGHT IT WAS THE SECRET TO SUCCESS IN LIFE.
MY PARENTS ENCOURAGED ME, SAYING WE HAD MORE THAN ENOUGH VERMIN IN THE HOUSE, SO I SHOULD JUST USE THEM WHENEVER I WANTED.
GOODNESS, YOUR FAMILY TRULY IS AWFUL...
...SO YOUR FAMILY NAME...
...ISN'T "SAEJIMA" ANYMORE, IS IT?
AT FIRST, I DIDN'T GET WHAT THEY MEANT...
...WHEN I WAS TOLD TO ***BE ALONE***.
DID THEY MEAN BE WITH PEOPLE I GOT ALONG WITH?
OR TO LOATHE AND DISTANCE MYSELF FROM THOSE I DIDN'T GET ALONG WITH?
I BELIEVED THAT THOSE WERE MY ONLY TWO OPTIONS IN LIFE...

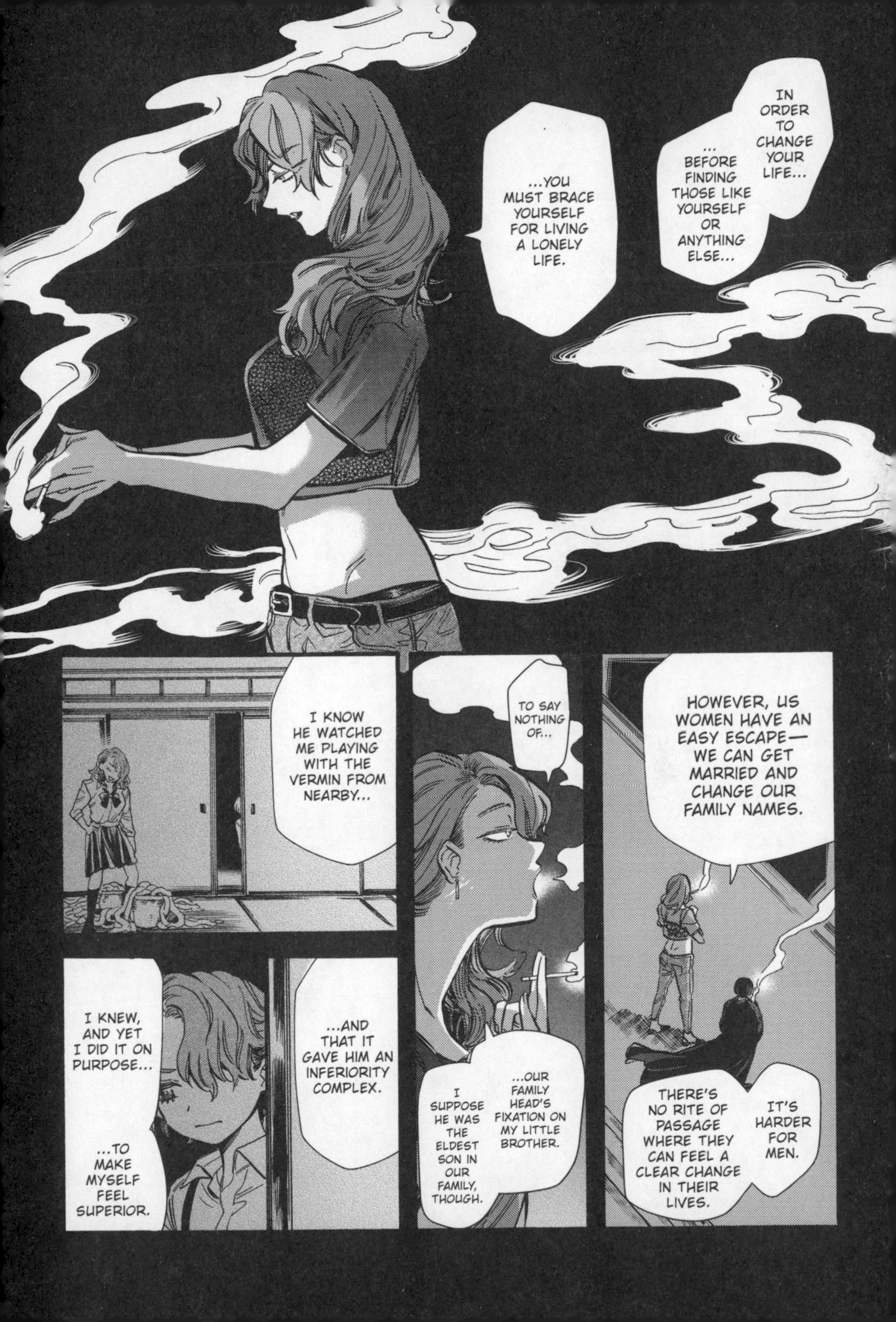
IN ORDER TO CHANGE YOUR LIFE...
...BEFORE FINDING THOSE LIKE YOURSELF OR ANYTHING ELSE...
...YOU MUST BRACE YOURSELF FOR LIVING A LONELY LIFE.
HOWEVER, US WOMEN HAVE AN EASY ESCAPE— WE CAN GET MARRIED AND CHANGE OUR FAMILY NAMES.
IT'S HARDER FOR MEN.
THERE'S NO RITE OF PASSAGE WHERE THEY CAN FEEL A CLEAR CHANGE IN THEIR LIVES.
TO SAY NOTHING OF...
...OUR FAMILY HEAD'S FIXATION ON MY LITTLE BROTHER.
I SUPPOSE HE WAS THE ELDEST SON IN OUR FAMILY, THOUGH.
I KNOW HE WATCHED ME PLAYING WITH THE VERMIN FROM NEARBY...
...AND THAT IT GAVE HIM AN INFERIORITY COMPLEX.
I KNEW, AND YET I DID IT ON PURPOSE...
...TO MAKE MYSELF FEEL SUPERIOR.

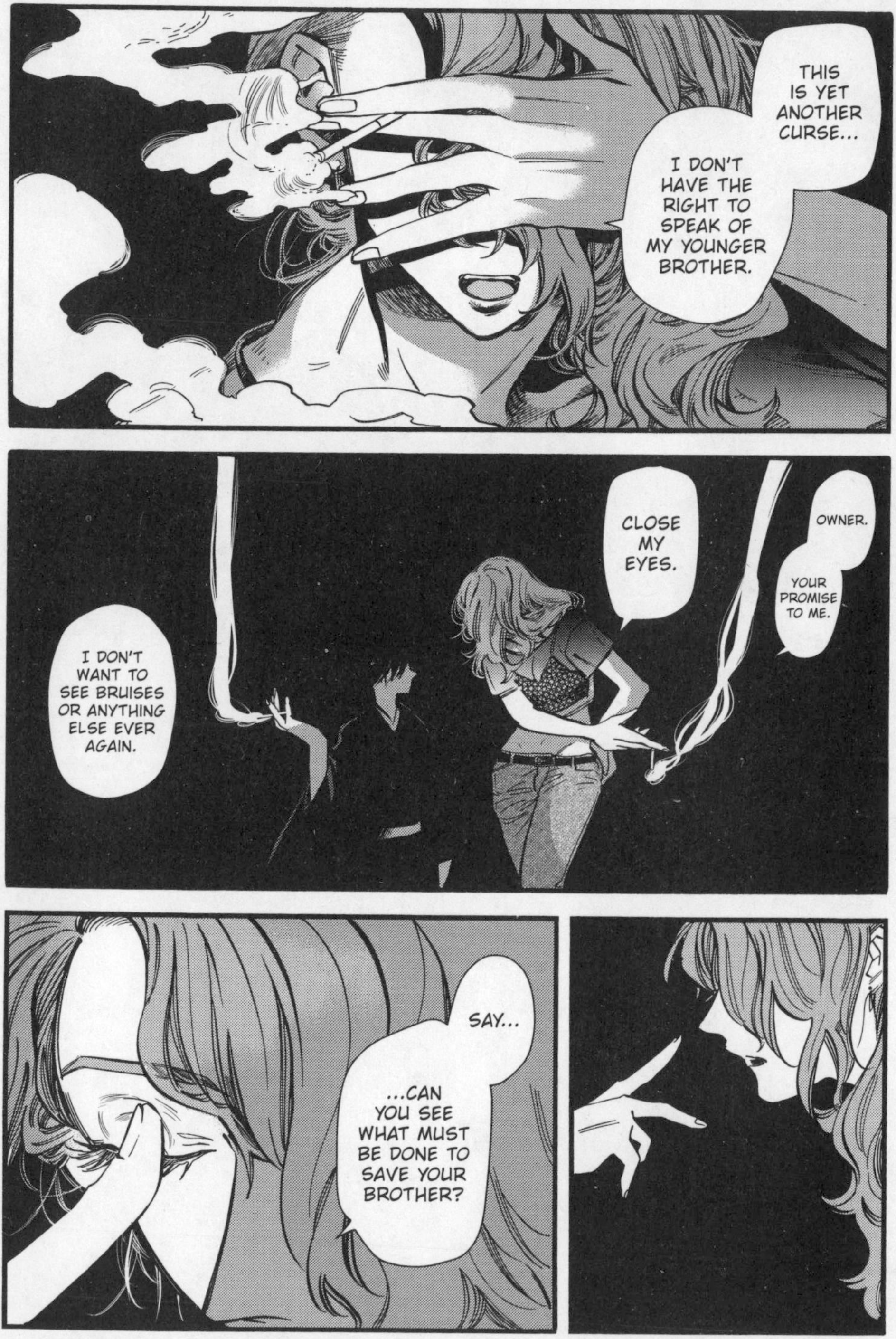
THIS IS YET ANOTHER CURSE...
I DON'T HAVE THE RIGHT TO SPEAK OF MY YOUNGER BROTHER.
OWNER.
YOUR PROMISE TO ME.
CLOSE MY EYES.
I DON'T WANT TO SEE BRUISES OR ANYTHING ELSE EVER AGAIN.
SAY...
...CAN YOU SEE WHAT MUST BE DONE TO SAVE YOUR BROTHER?

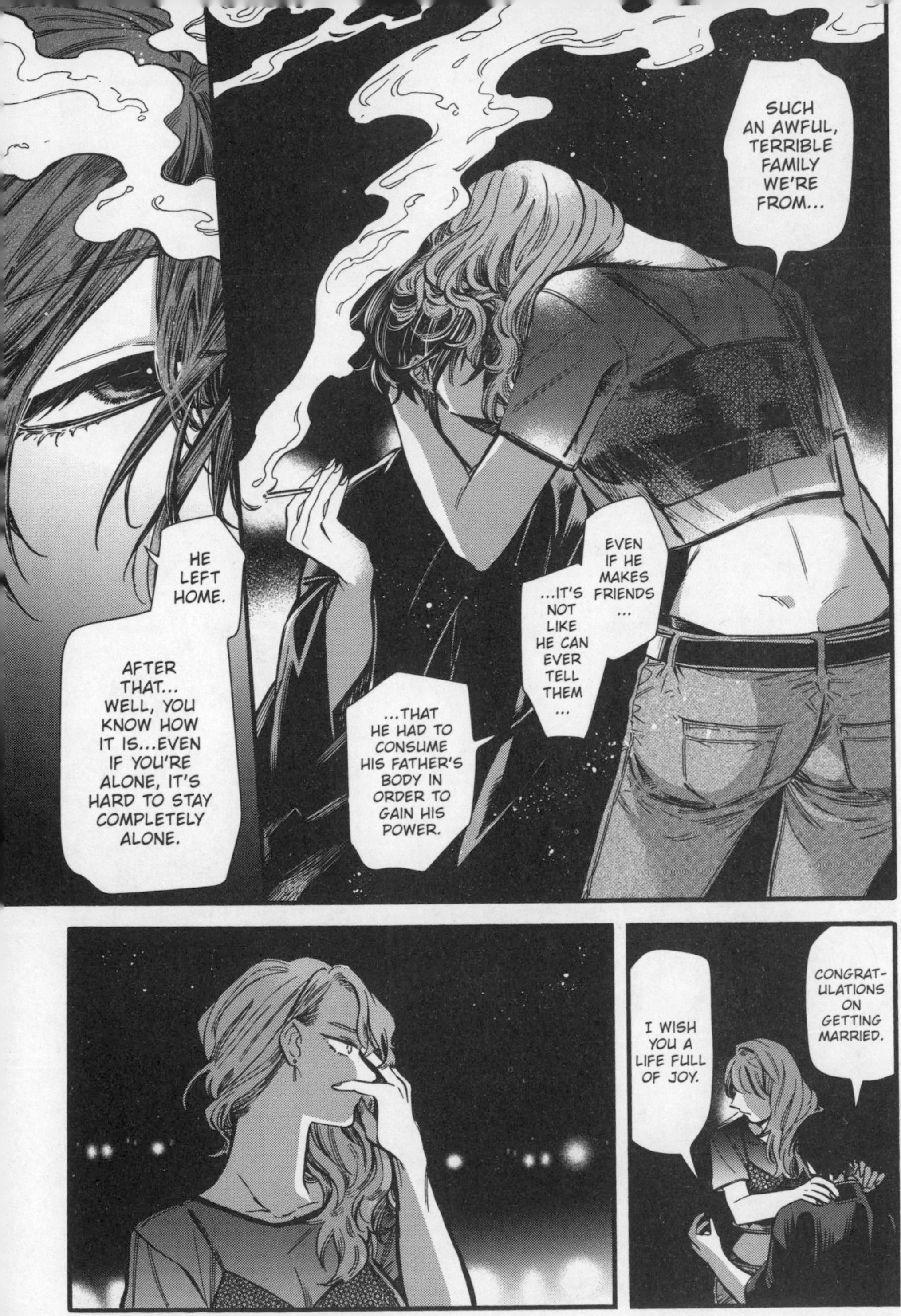
SUCH AN AWFUL, TERRIBLE FAMILY WE'RE FROM...
EVEN IF HE MAKES FRIENDS...
...IT'S NOT LIKE HE CAN EVER TELL THEM...
...THAT HE HAD TO CONSUME HIS FATHER'S BODY IN ORDER TO GAIN HIS POWER.
HE LEFT HOME.
AFTER THAT... WELL, YOU KNOW HOW IT IS...EVEN IF YOU'RE ALONE, IT'S HARD TO STAY COMPLETELY ALONE.
CONGRAT-ULATIONS ON GETTING MARRIED.
I WISH YOU A LIFE FULL OF JOY.

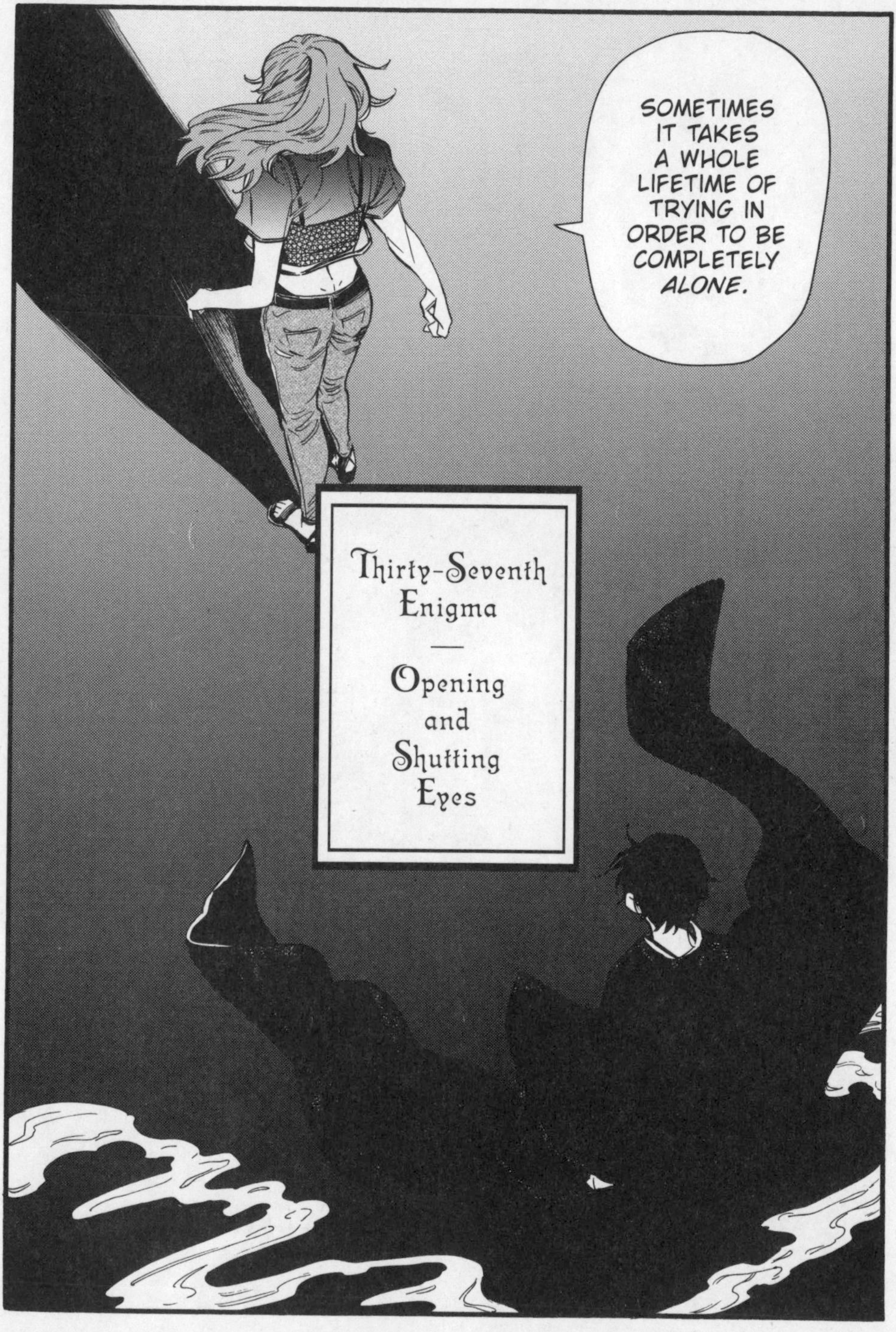
SOMETIMES IT TAKES A WHOLE LIFETIME OF TRYING IN ORDER TO BE COMPLETELY ALONE.
Thirty-Seventh Enigma
—
Opening and Shutting Eyes

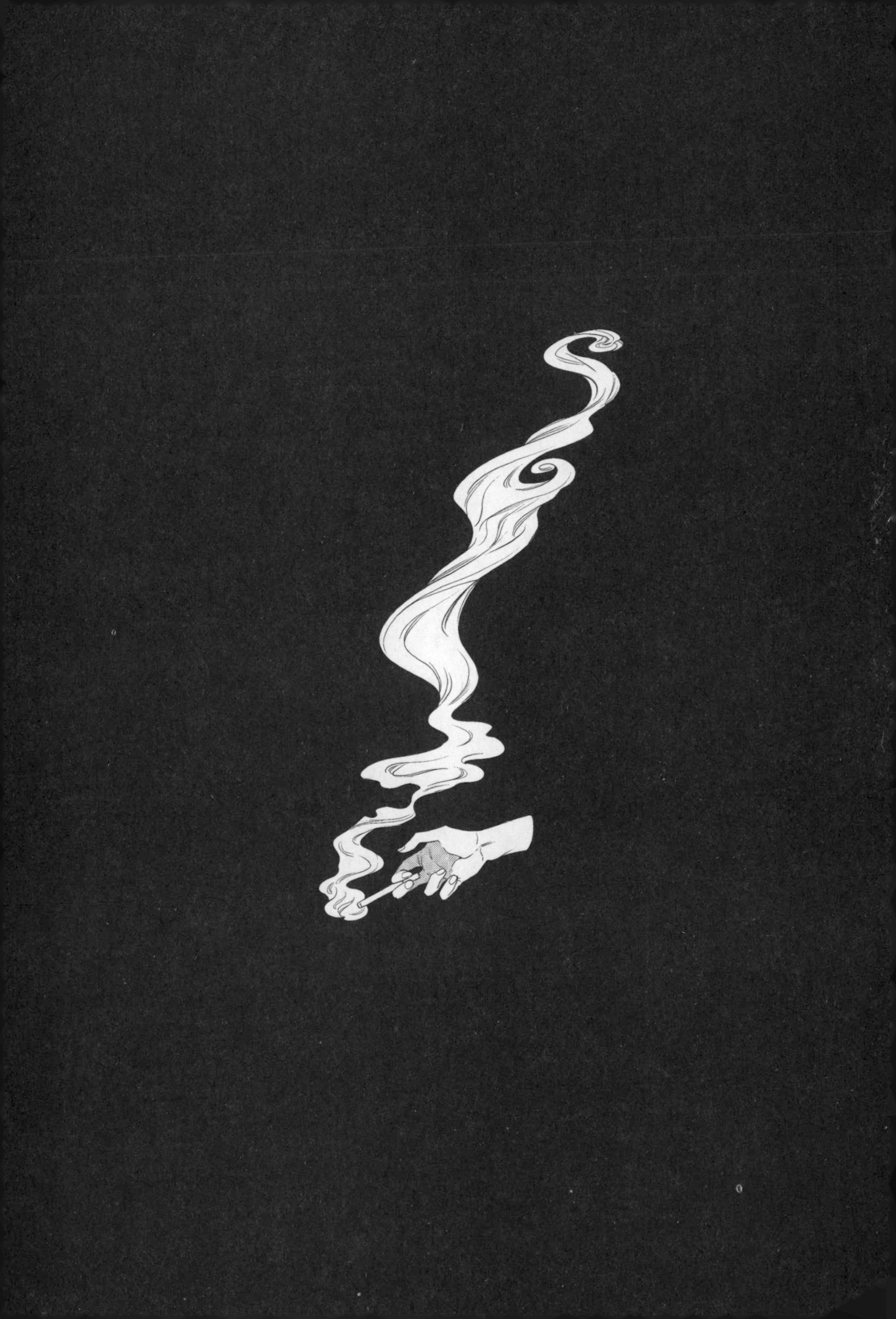

Phantom Tales of the Night

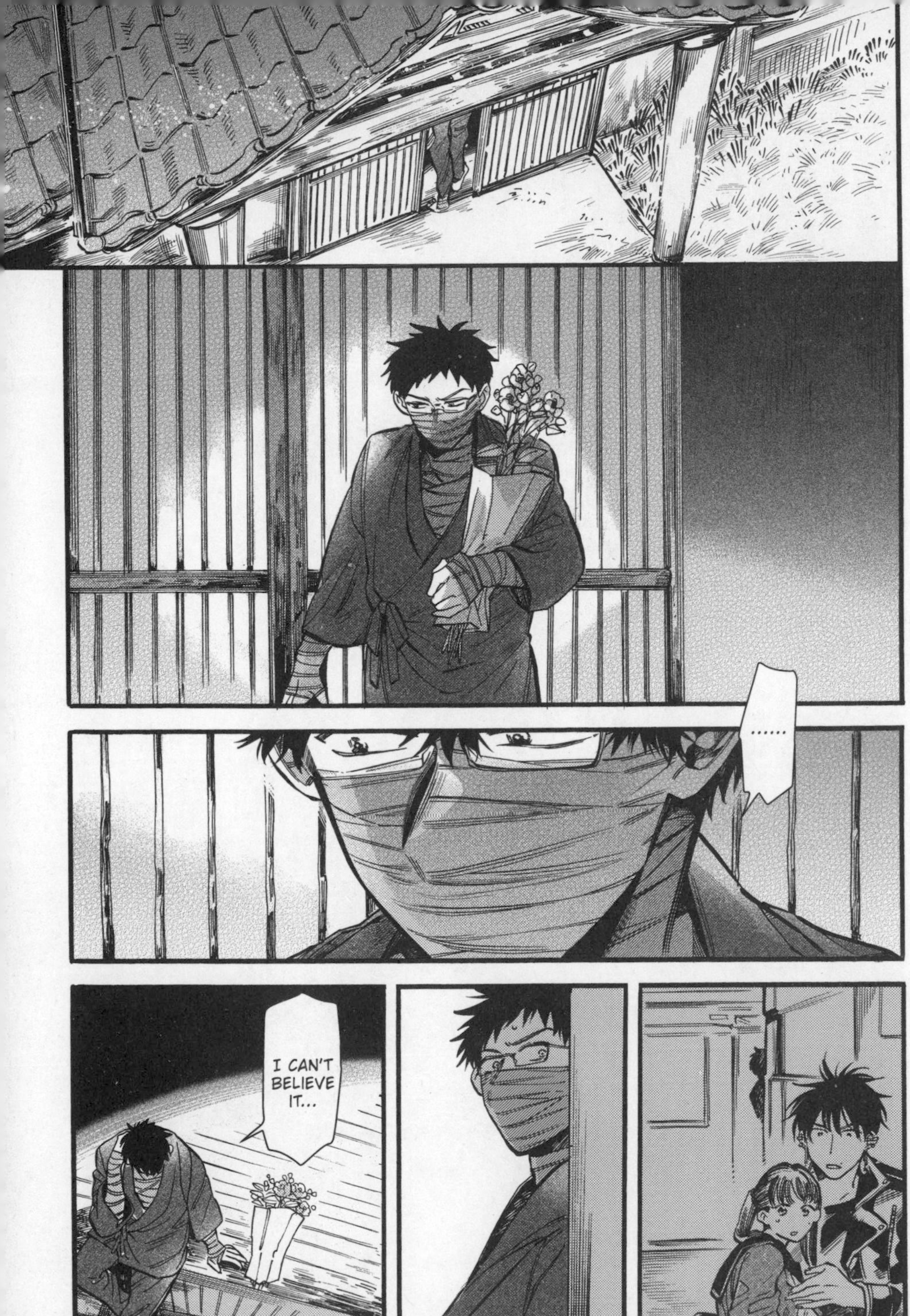
......
I CAN'T BELIEVE IT...

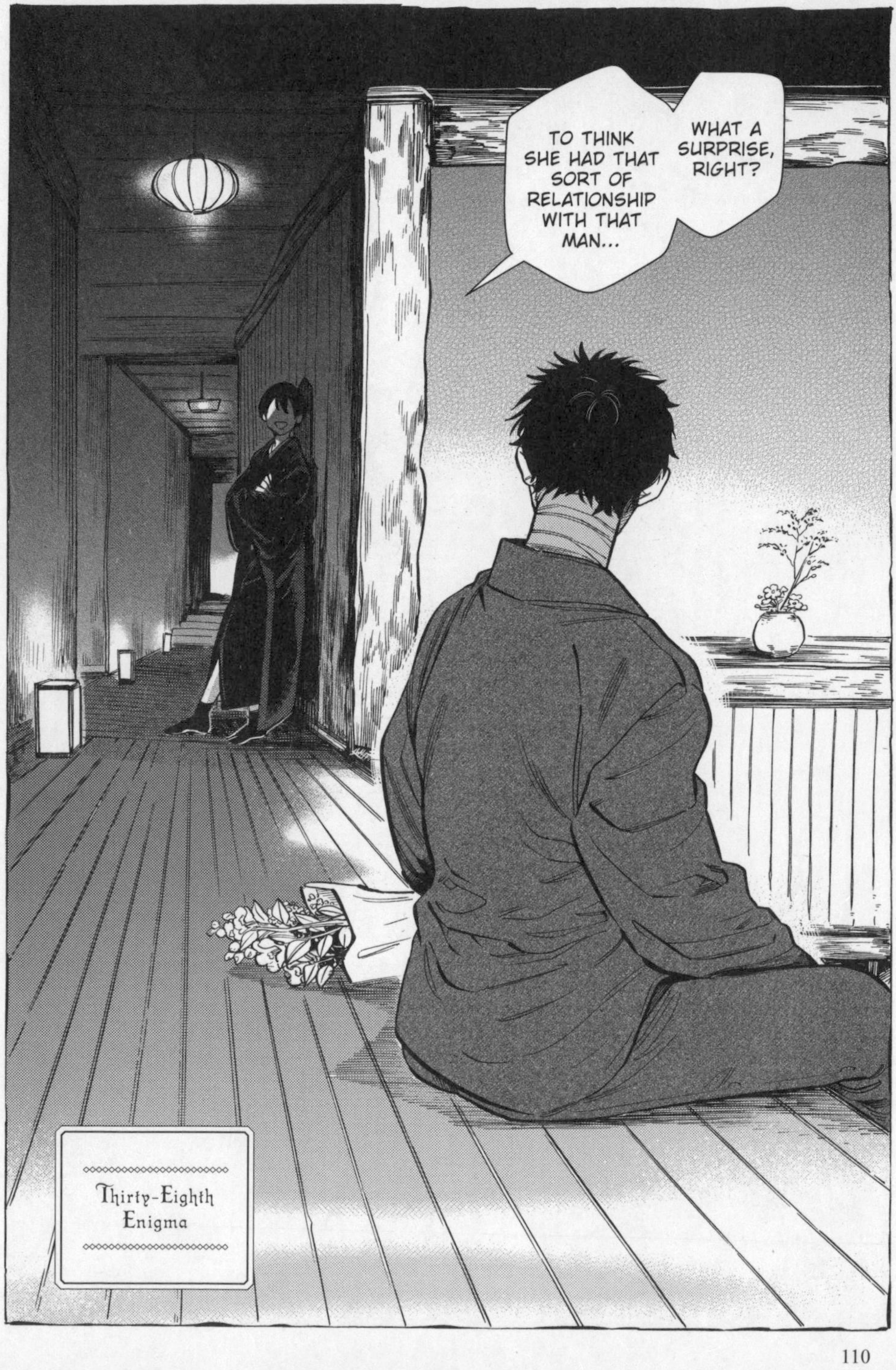
WHAT A SURPRISE, RIGHT?
TO THINK SHE HAD THAT SORT OF RELATIONSHIP WITH THAT MAN...
Thirty-Eighth Enigma

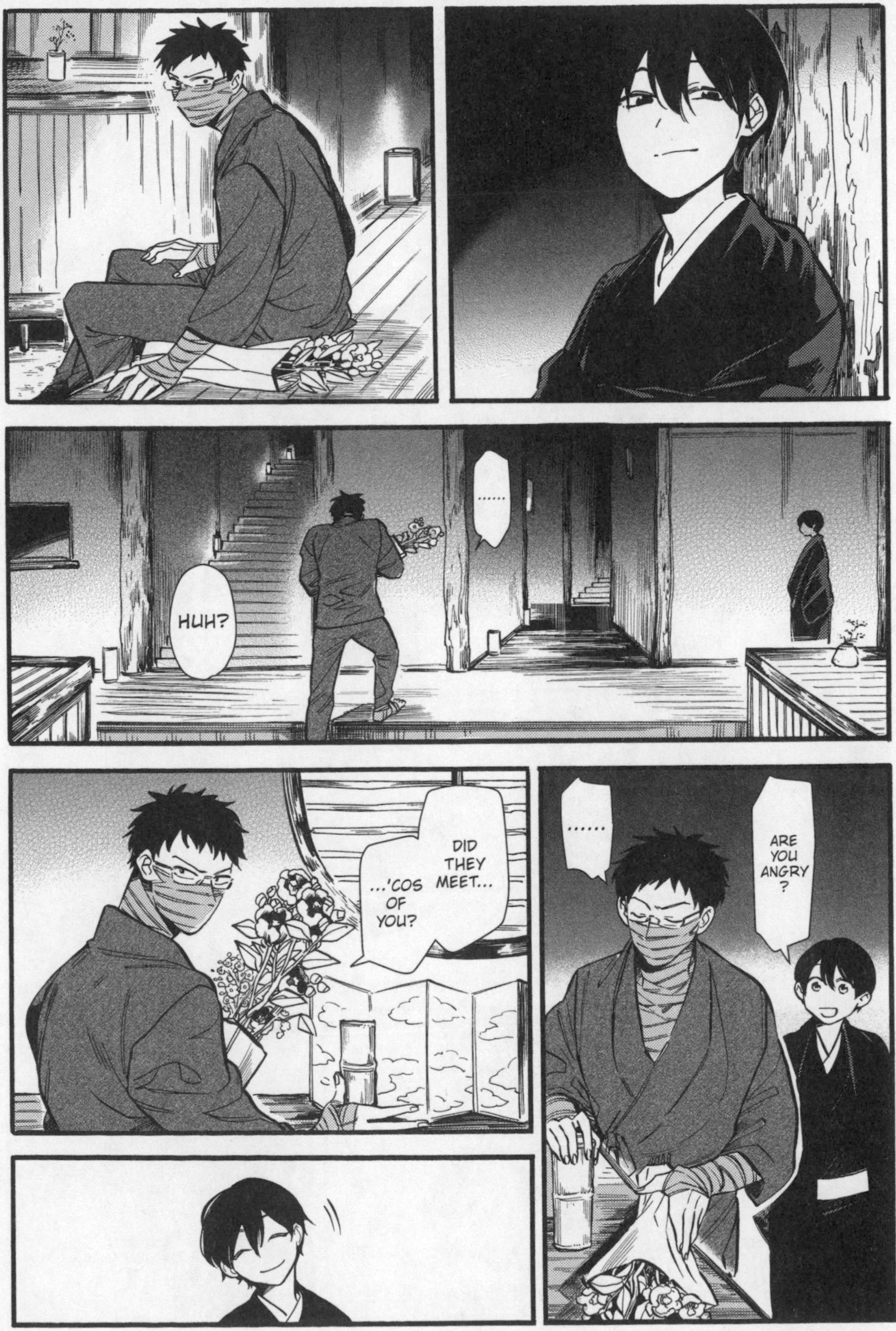
......
HUH?
ARE YOU ANGRY ?
......
DID THEY MEET...
...'COS OF YOU?

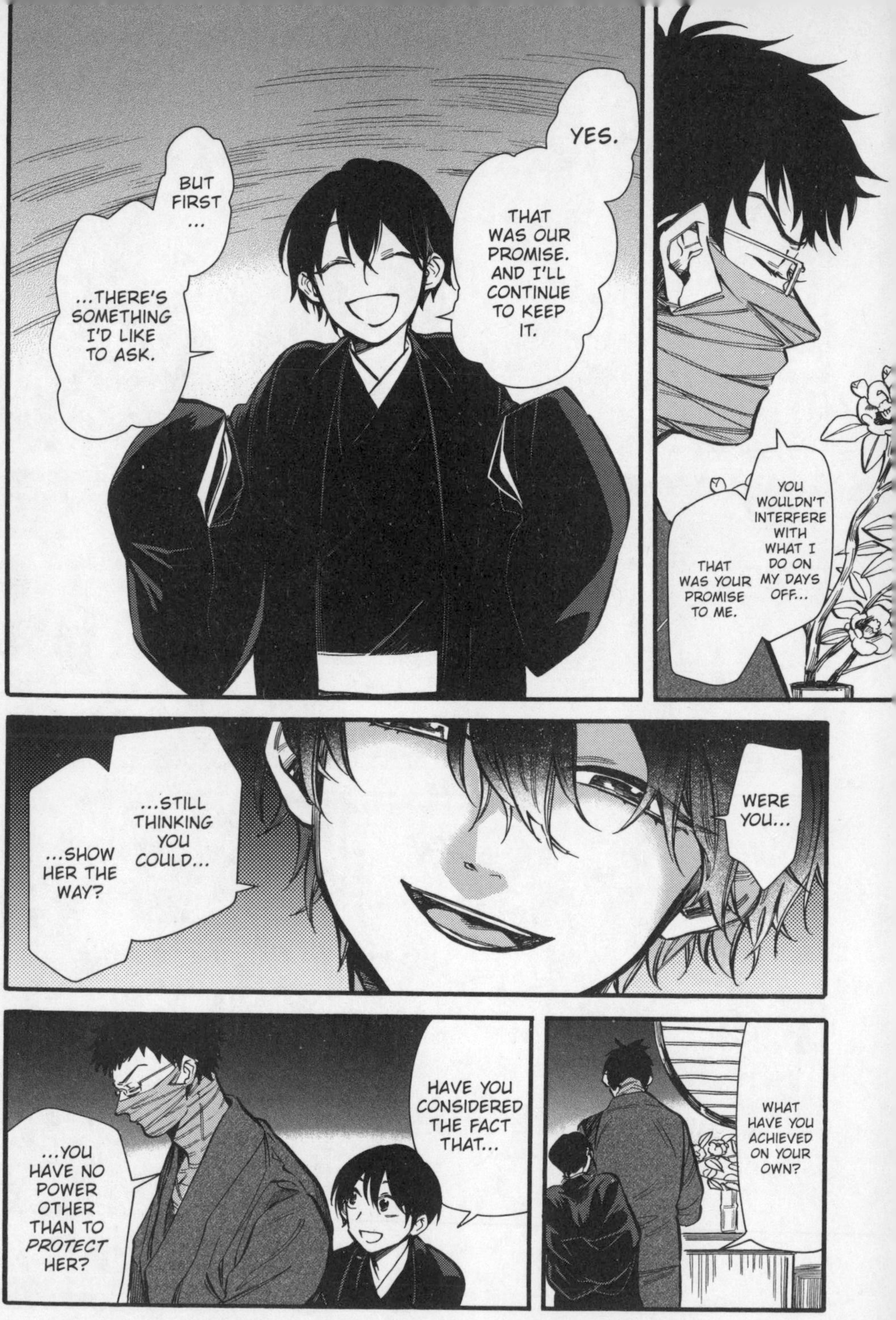
YOU WOULDN'T INTERFERE WITH WHAT I DO ON MY DAYS OFF...
THAT WAS YOUR PROMISE TO ME.
YES.
THAT WAS OUR PROMISE. AND I'LL CONTINUE TO KEEP IT.
BUT FIRST ...
...THERE'S SOMETHING I'D LIKE TO ASK.
WERE YOU...
...STILL THINKING YOU COULD...
...SHOW HER THE WAY?
WHAT HAVE YOU ACHIEVED ON YOUR OWN?
HAVE YOU CONSIDERED THE FACT THAT...
...YOU HAVE NO POWER OTHER THAN TO *PROTECT* HER?

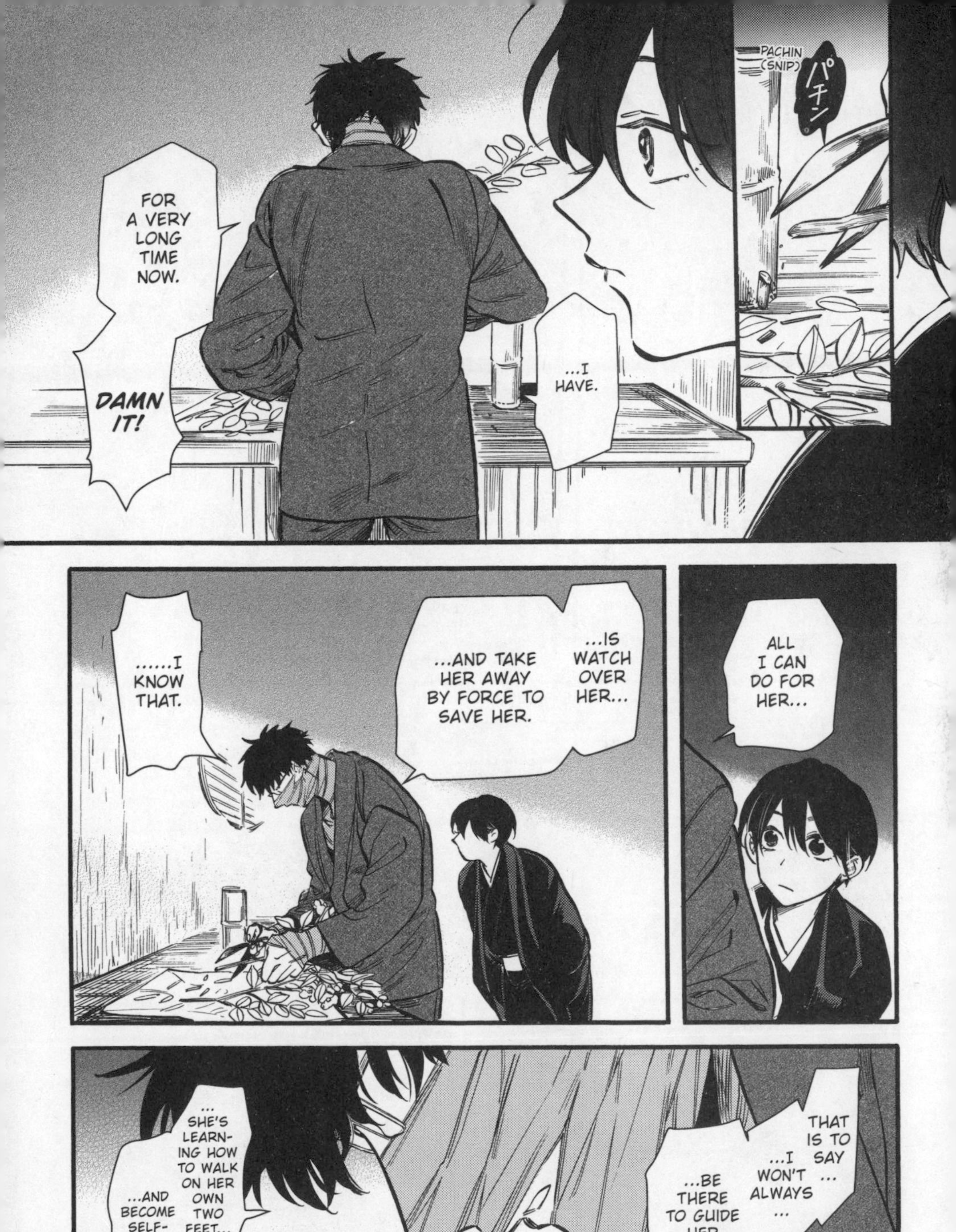
PACHIN (SNIP)
パチン
...I HAVE.
FOR A VERY LONG TIME NOW.
DAMN IT!
ALL I CAN DO FOR HER...
...IS WATCH OVER HER...
...AND TAKE HER AWAY BY FORCE TO SAVE HER.
......I KNOW THAT.
THAT IS TO SAY...
...I WON'T ALWAYS...
...BE THERE TO GUIDE HER WHILE...
...SHE'S LEARNING HOW TO WALK ON HER OWN TWO FEET...
...AND BECOME SELF-RELIANT, OR—

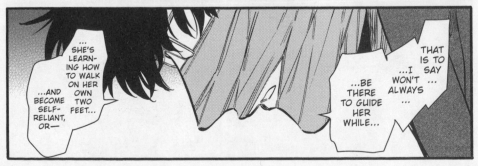

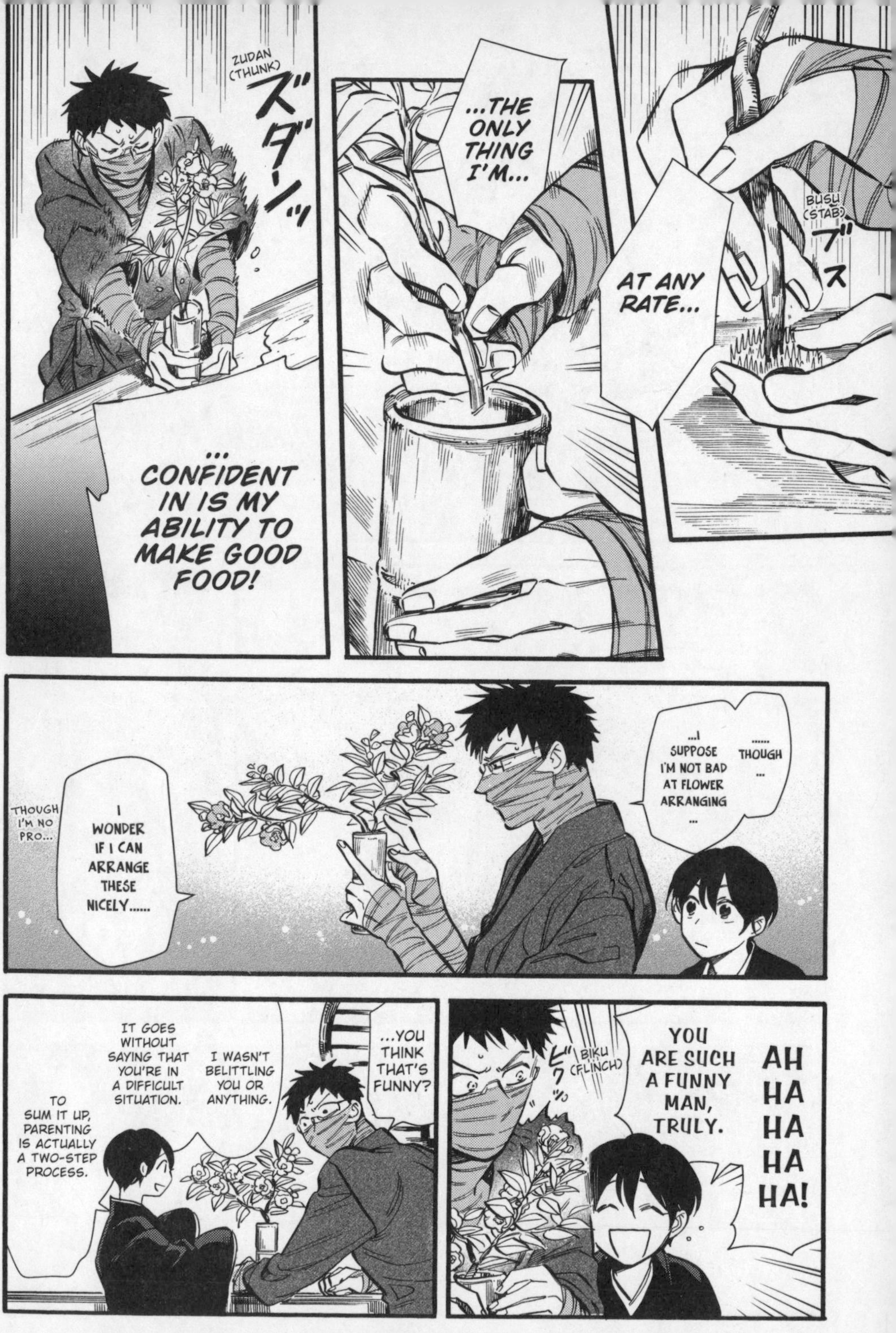
BUSU (STAB)
ブス
AT ANY RATE...
...THE ONLY THING I'M...
ZUDAN (THUNK)
ズダンッ
... CONFIDENT IN IS MY ABILITY TO MAKE GOOD FOOD!
...... THOUGH ...
...I SUPPOSE I'M NOT BAD AT FLOWER ARRANGING ...
I WONDER IF I CAN ARRANGE THESE NICELY......
THOUGH I'M NO PRO...
AH HA HA HA HA!
YOU ARE SUCH A FUNNY MAN, TRULY.
BIKU (FLINCH)
ビクッ
...YOU THINK THAT'S FUNNY?
I WASN'T BELITTLING YOU OR ANYTHING.
IT GOES WITHOUT SAYING THAT YOU'RE IN A DIFFICULT SITUATION.
TO SUM IT UP, PARENTING IS ACTUALLY A TWO-STEP PROCESS.

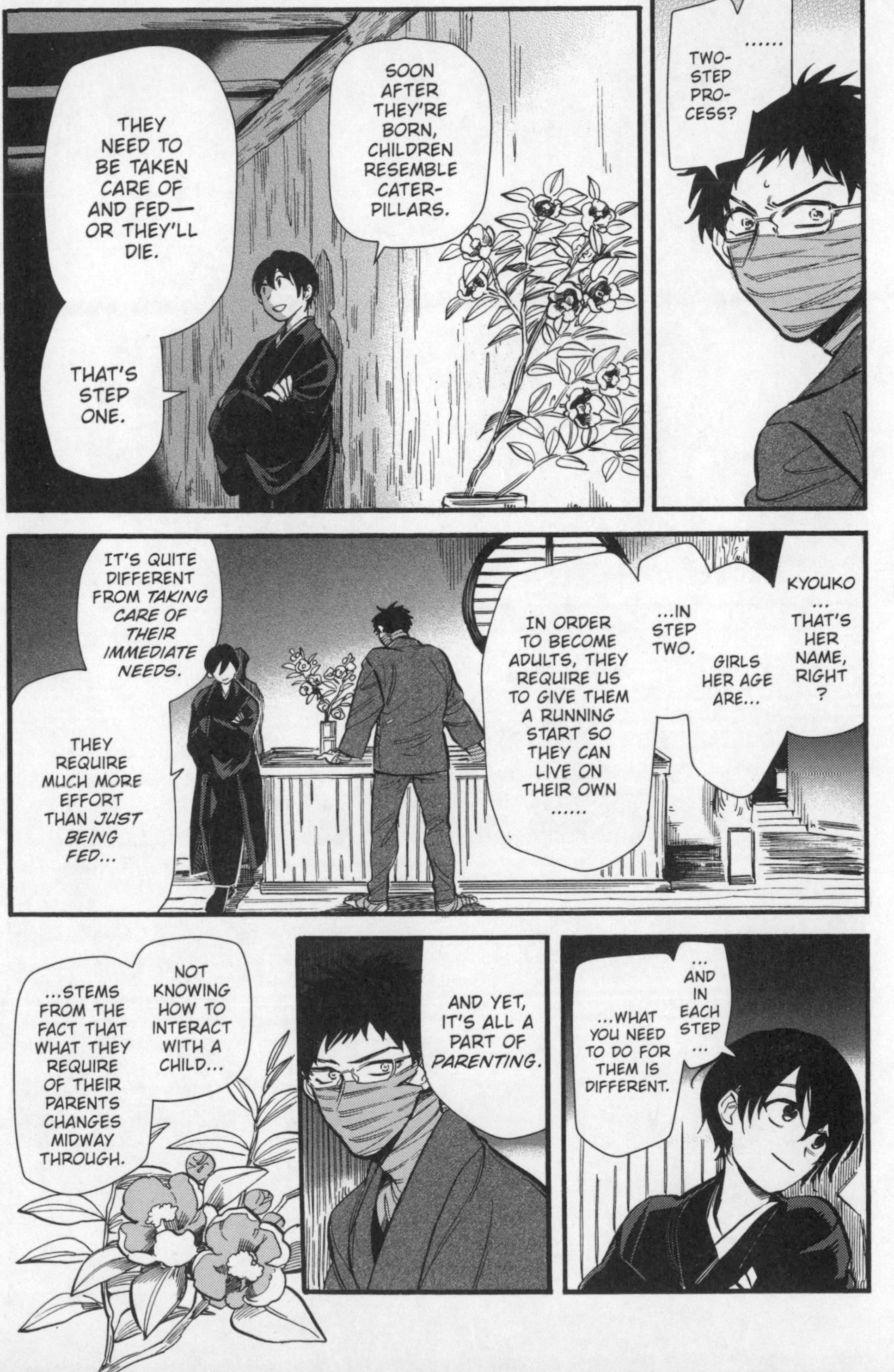
......
TWO-STEP PROCESS?
SOON AFTER THEY'RE BORN, CHILDREN RESEMBLE CATER-PILLARS.
THEY NEED TO BE TAKEN CARE OF AND FED—OR THEY'LL DIE.
THAT'S STEP ONE.
KYOUKO... THAT'S HER NAME, RIGHT?
GIRLS HER AGE ARE...
...IN STEP TWO.
IN ORDER TO BECOME ADULTS, THEY REQUIRE US TO GIVE THEM A RUNNING START SO THEY CAN LIVE ON THEIR OWN......
IT'S QUITE DIFFERENT FROM *TAKING CARE OF THEIR IMMEDIATE NEEDS*.
THEY REQUIRE MUCH MORE EFFORT THAN *JUST BEING FED*...
...AND IN EACH STEP...
...WHAT YOU NEED TO DO FOR THEM IS DIFFERENT.
AND YET, IT'S ALL A PART OF *PARENTING*.
NOT KNOWING HOW TO INTERACT WITH A CHILD...
...STEMS FROM THE FACT THAT WHAT THEY REQUIRE OF THEIR PARENTS CHANGES MIDWAY THROUGH.

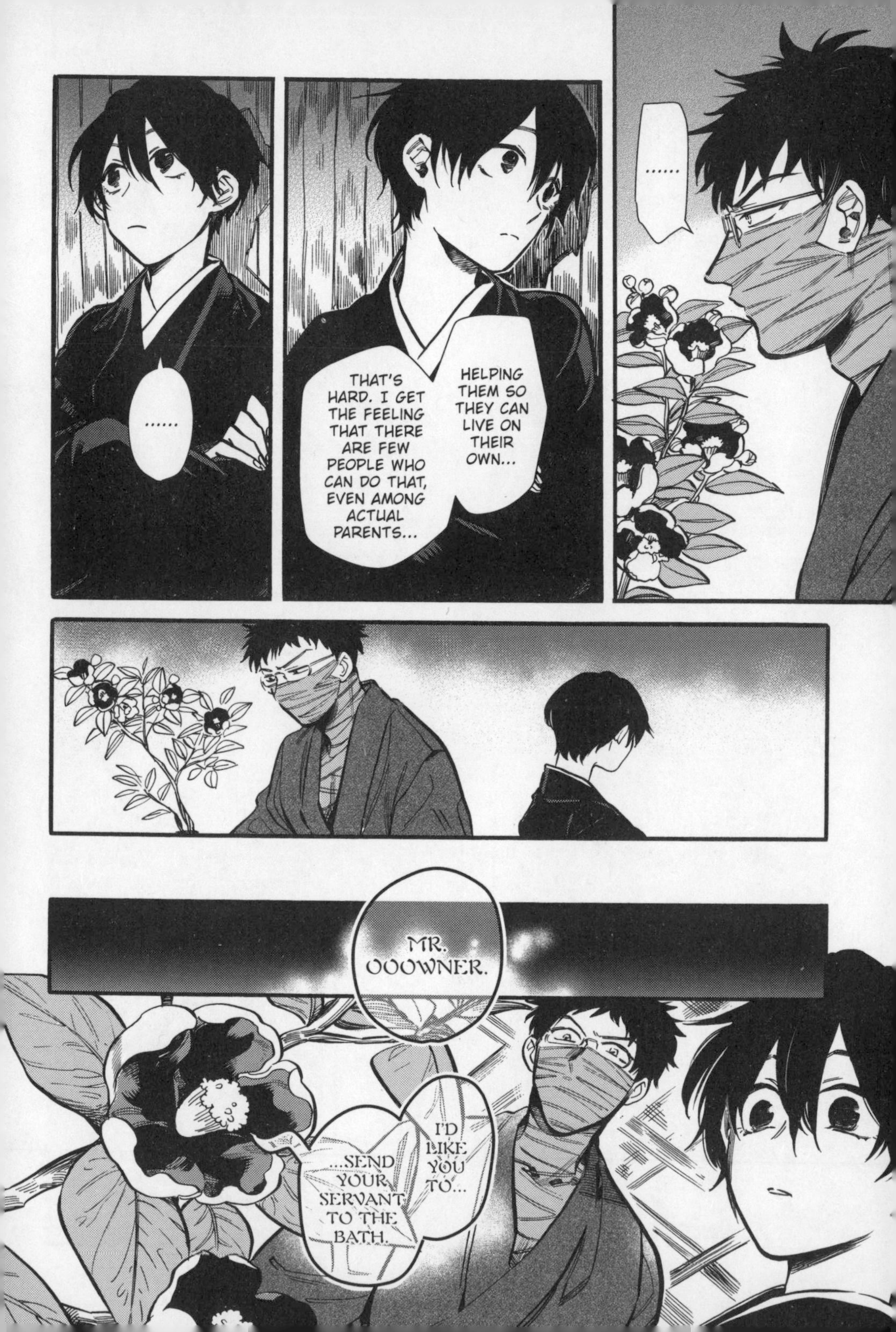
......
HELPING THEM SO THEY CAN LIVE ON THEIR OWN...
THAT'S HARD. I GET THE FEELING THAT THERE ARE FEW PEOPLE WHO CAN DO THAT, EVEN AMONG ACTUAL PARENTS...
......
MR. OOOWNER.
I'D LIKE YOU TO...
...SEND YOUR SERVANT TO THE BATH.

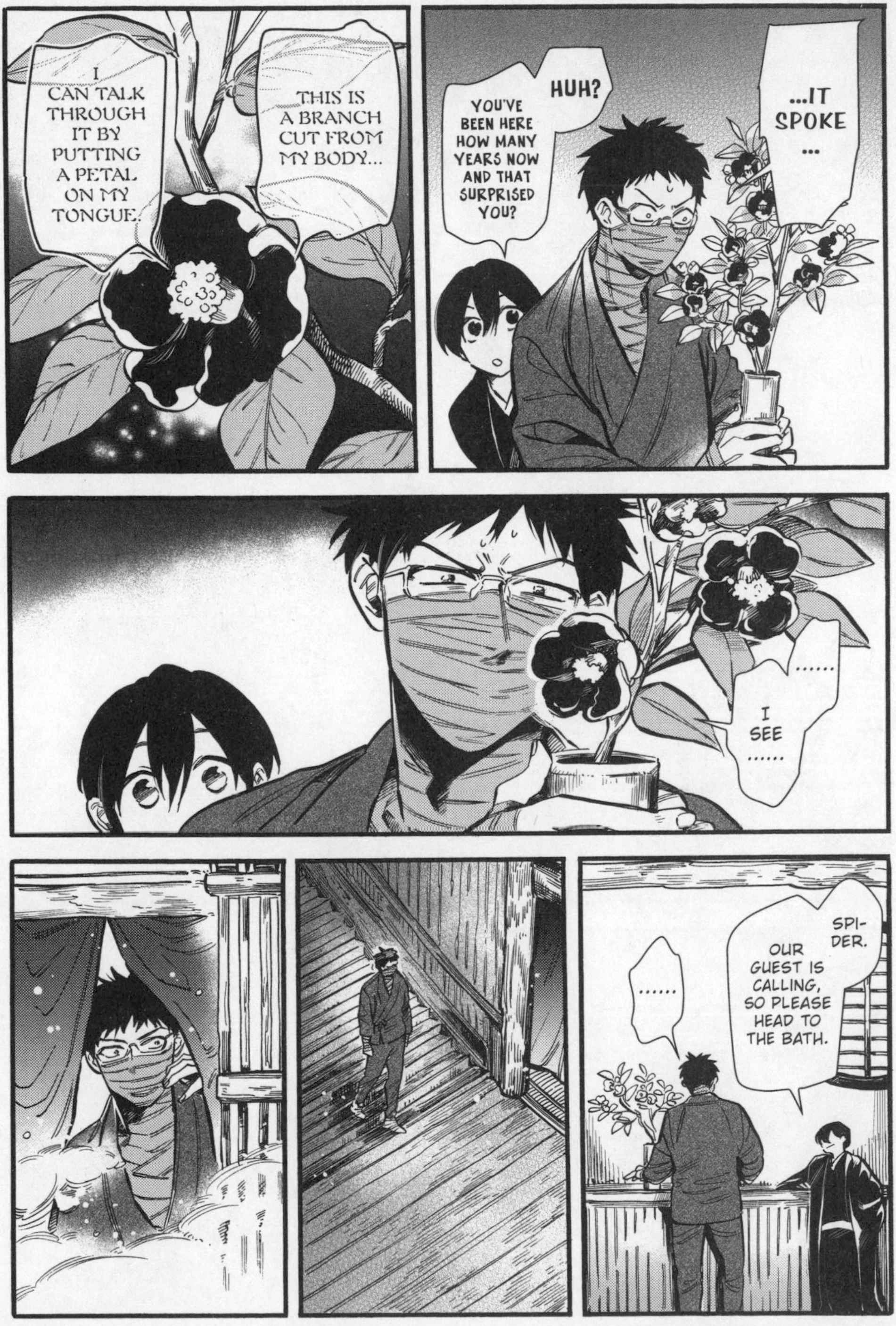
...IT SPOKE ...
HUH?
YOU'VE BEEN HERE HOW MANY YEARS NOW AND THAT SURPRISED YOU?
THIS IS A BRANCH CUT FROM MY BODY...
I CAN TALK THROUGH IT BY PUTTING A PETAL ON MY TONGUE.
...... I SEE ......
SPIDER. OUR GUEST IS CALLING, SO PLEASE HEAD TO THE BATH.
......

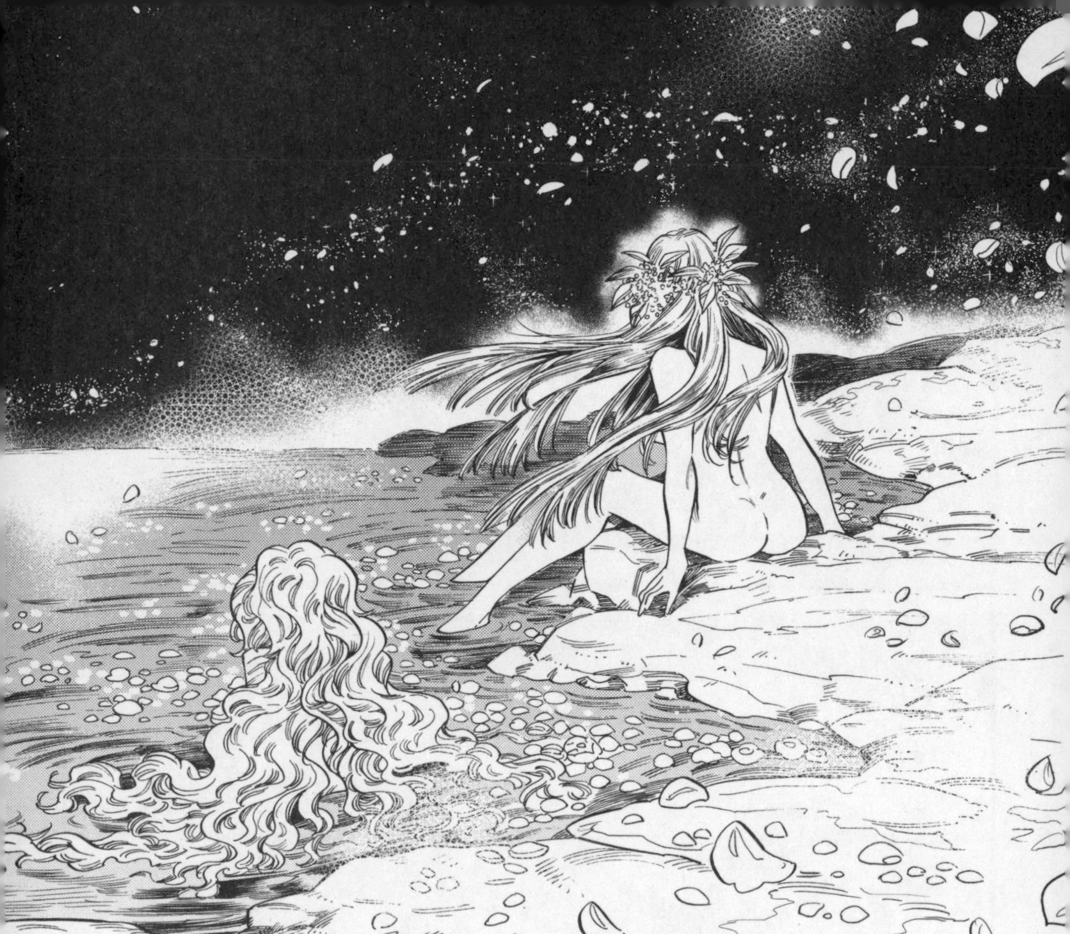

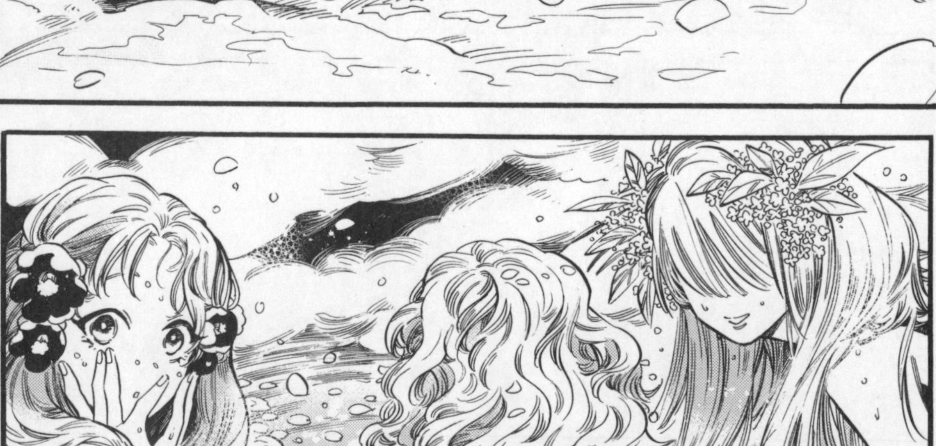

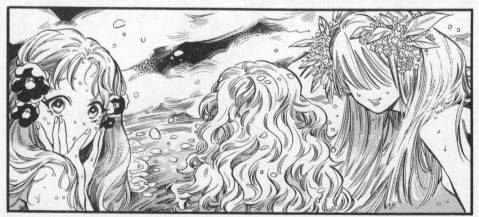

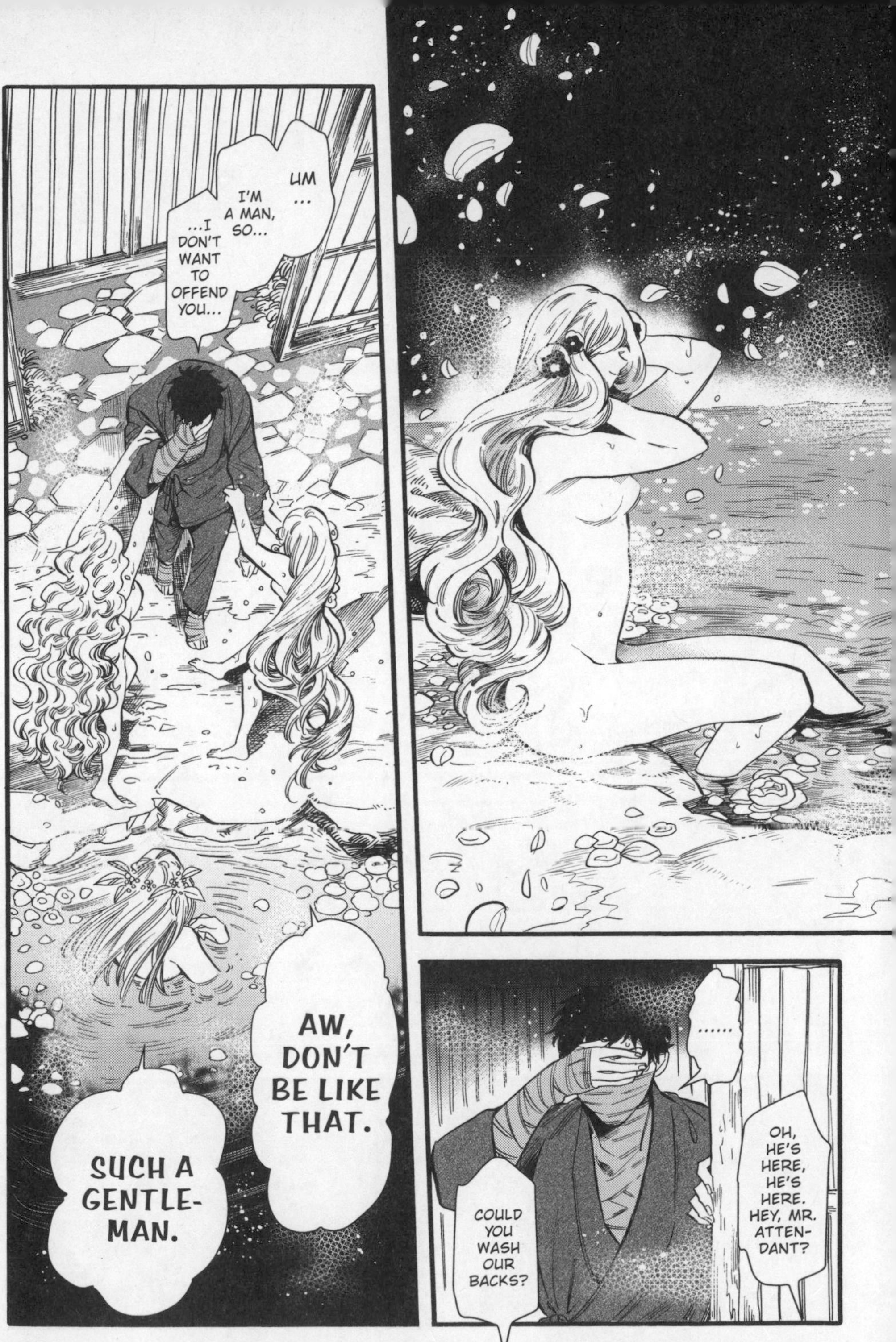
......
OH, HE'S HERE, HE'S HERE. HEY, MR. ATTENDANT?
COULD YOU WASH OUR BACKS?
UM ...
I'M A MAN, SO...
...I DON'T WANT TO OFFEND YOU...
AW, DON'T BE LIKE THAT.
SUCH A GENTLE-MAN.

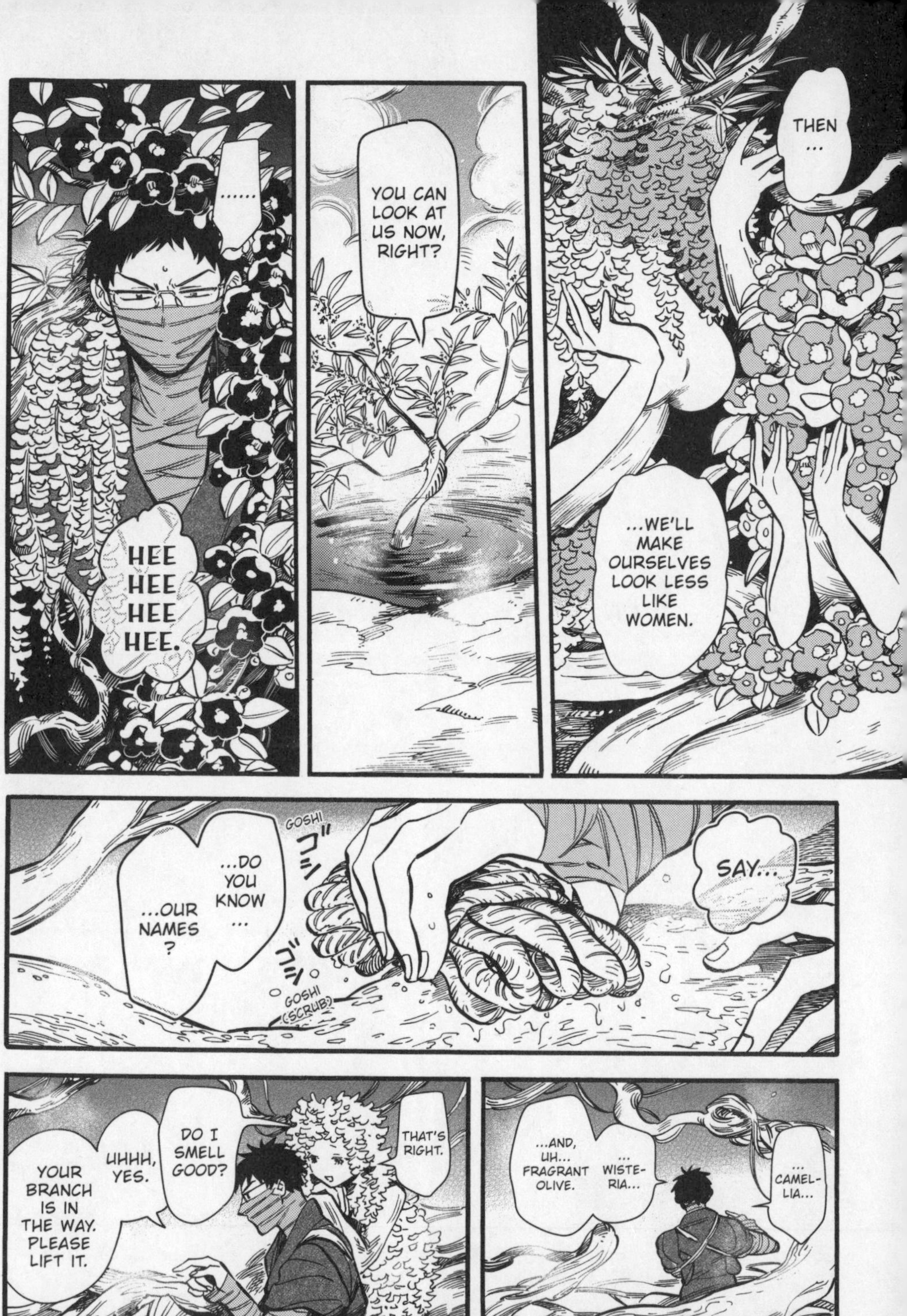
THEN ...
...WE'LL MAKE OURSELVES LOOK LESS LIKE WOMEN.
YOU CAN LOOK AT US NOW, RIGHT?
......
HEE HEE HEE HEE.
SAY...
ゴシ
GOSHI
...DO YOU KNOW ...
...OUR NAMES ?
ゴシ
GOSHI (SCRUB)
... CAMEL-LIA...
... WISTE-RIA...
...AND, UH... FRAGRANT OLIVE.
THAT'S RIGHT.
DO I SMELL GOOD?
UHHH, YES.
YOUR BRANCH IS IN THE WAY. PLEASE LIFT IT.

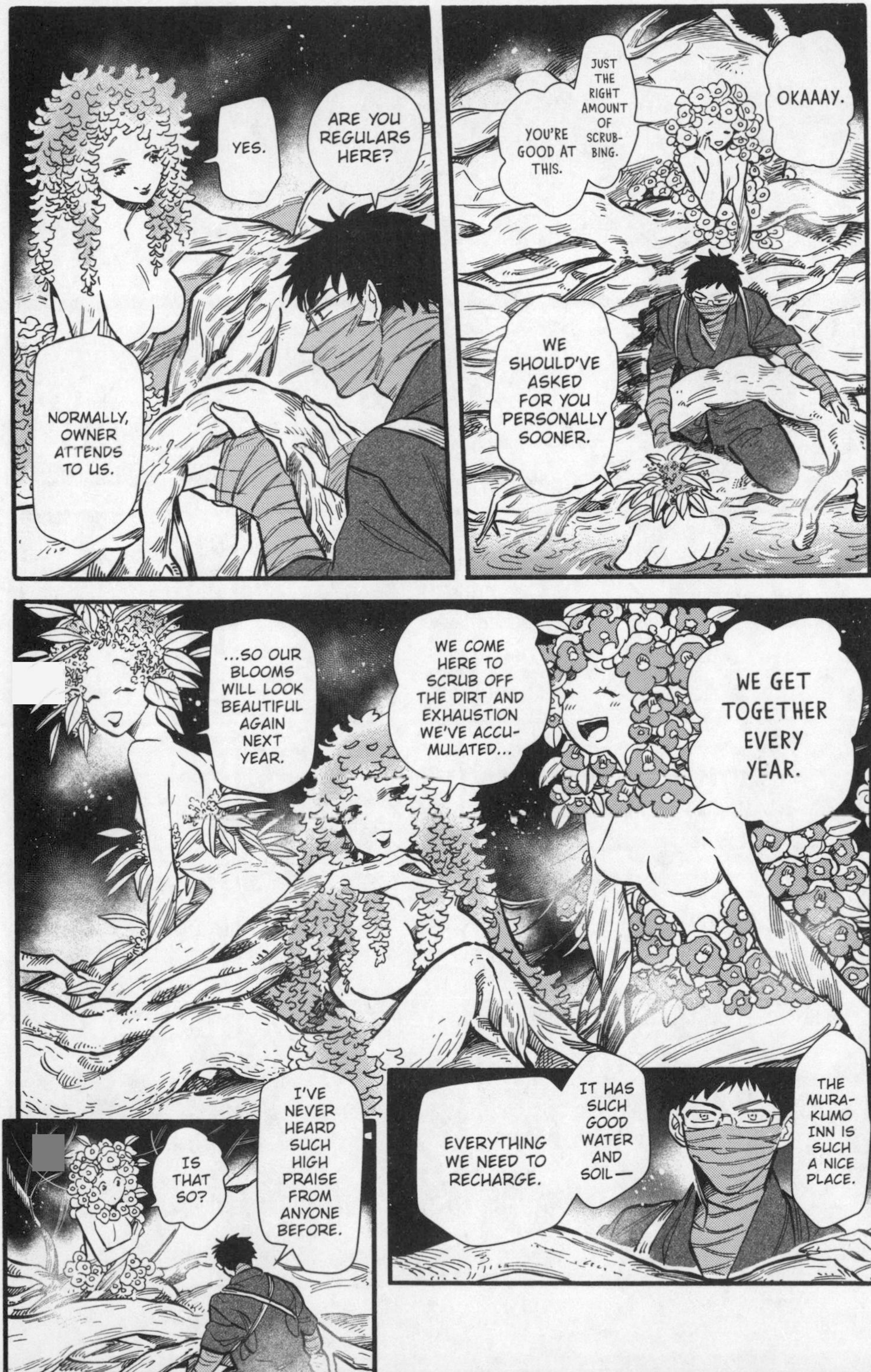
OKAAAY.
JUST THE RIGHT AMOUNT OF SCRUB-BING.
YOU'RE GOOD AT THIS.
WE SHOULD'VE ASKED FOR YOU PERSONALLY SOONER.
ARE YOU REGULARS HERE?
YES.
NORMALLY, OWNER ATTENDS TO US.
WE GET TOGETHER EVERY YEAR.
WE COME HERE TO SCRUB OFF THE DIRT AND EXHAUSTION WE'VE ACCU-MULATED...
...SO OUR BLOOMS WILL LOOK BEAUTIFUL AGAIN NEXT YEAR.
THE MURA-KUMO INN IS SUCH A NICE PLACE.
IT HAS SUCH GOOD WATER AND SOIL—
EVERYTHING WE NEED TO RECHARGE.
I'VE NEVER HEARD SUCH HIGH PRAISE FROM ANYONE BEFORE.
IS THAT SO?

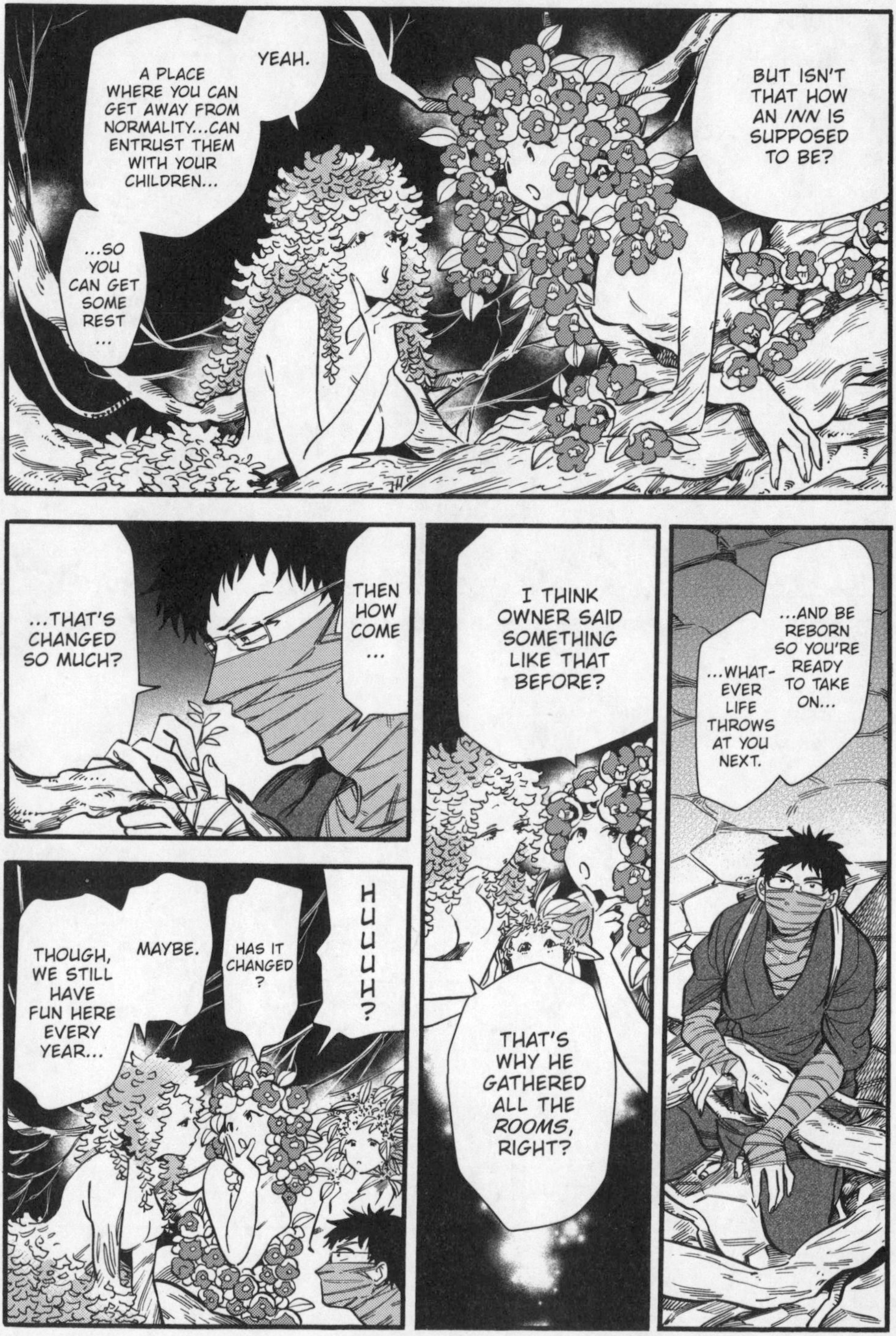
BUT ISN'T THAT HOW AN *INN* IS SUPPOSED TO BE?
YEAH.
A PLACE WHERE YOU CAN GET AWAY FROM NORMALITY...CAN ENTRUST THEM WITH YOUR CHILDREN...
...SO YOU CAN GET SOME REST...
...AND BE REBORN SO YOU'RE READY TO TAKE ON...
...WHAT-EVER LIFE THROWS AT YOU NEXT.
I THINK OWNER SAID SOMETHING LIKE THAT BEFORE?
THAT'S WHY HE GATHERED ALL THE *ROOMS*, RIGHT?
THEN HOW COME...
...THAT'S CHANGED SO MUCH?
HUUUUH?
HAS IT CHANGED?
MAYBE.
THOUGH, WE STILL HAVE FUN HERE EVERY YEAR...

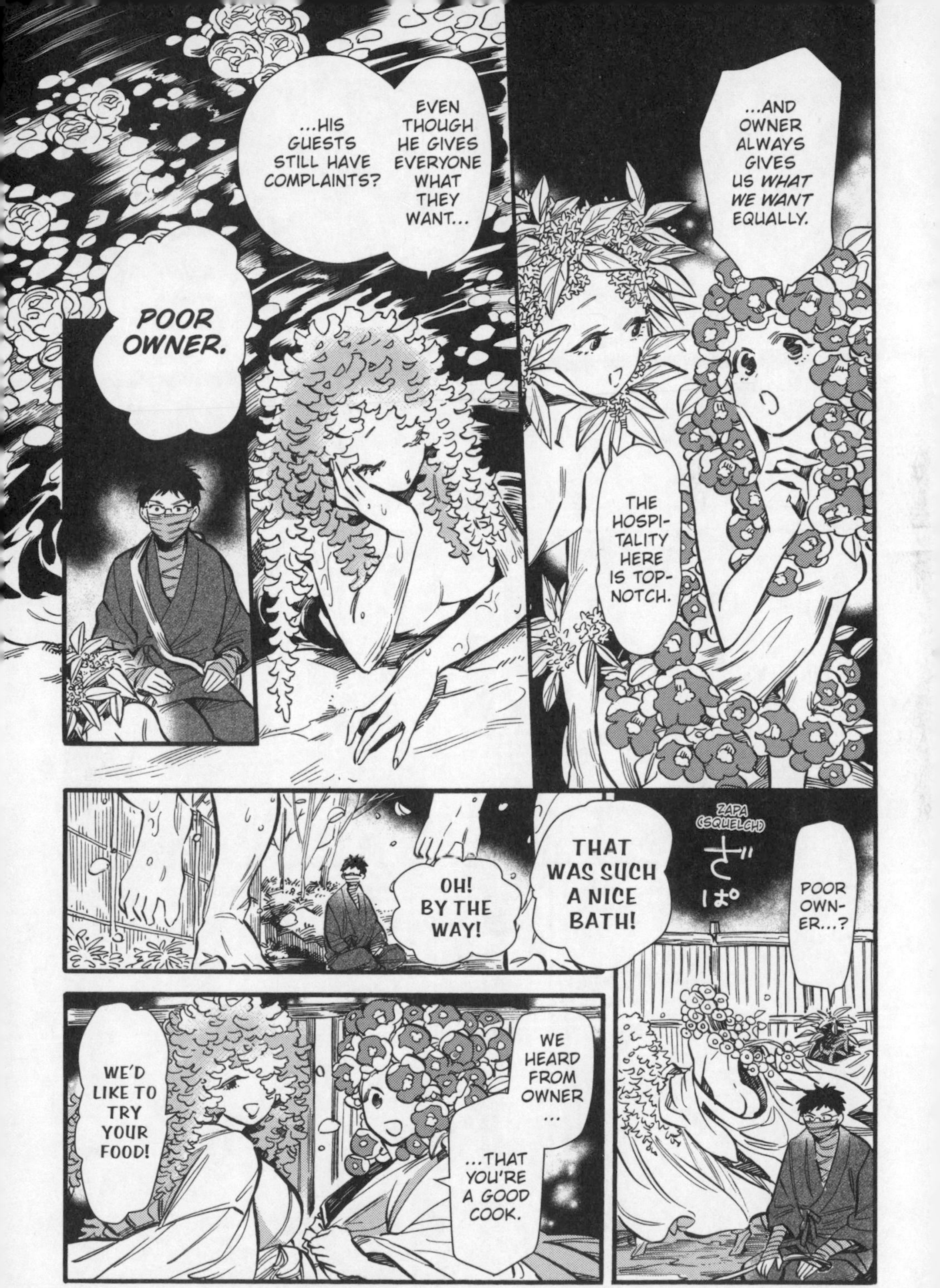
...AND OWNER ALWAYS GIVES US *WHAT WE WANT* EQUALLY.
THE HOSPITALITY HERE IS TOP-NOTCH.
EVEN THOUGH HE GIVES EVERYONE WHAT THEY WANT...
...HIS GUESTS STILL HAVE COMPLAINTS?
POOR OWNER.
ZAPA (SQUELCH)
ざぱ
POOR OWNER...?
THAT WAS SUCH A NICE BATH!
OH! BY THE WAY!
WE HEARD FROM OWNER...
...THAT YOU'RE A GOOD COOK.
WE'D LIKE TO TRY YOUR FOOD!

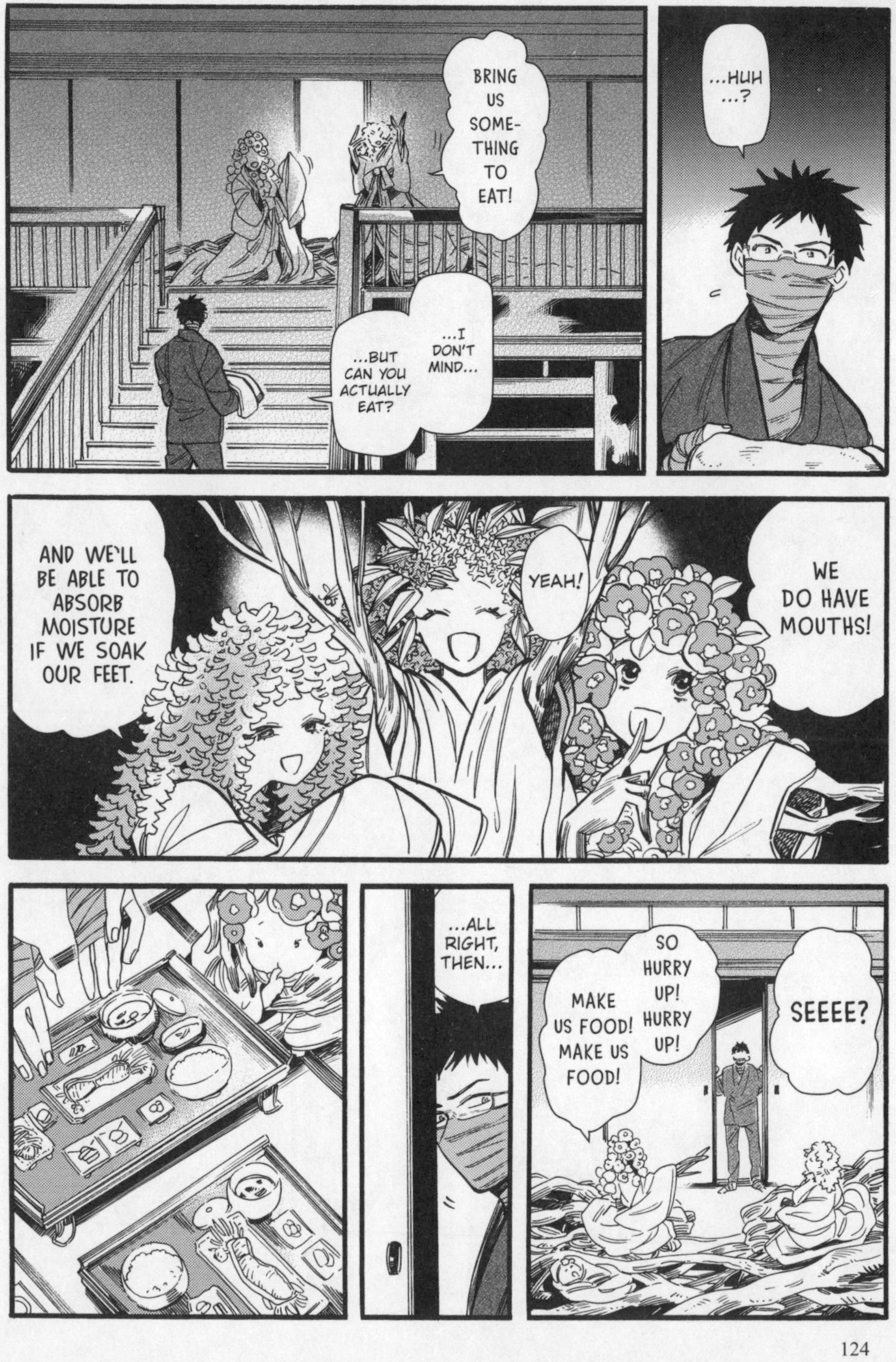
...HUH ...?
BRING US SOME-THING TO EAT!
...I DON'T MIND...
...BUT CAN YOU ACTUALLY EAT?
WE DO HAVE MOUTHS!
YEAH!
AND WE'LL BE ABLE TO ABSORB MOISTURE IF WE SOAK OUR FEET.
SEEEE?
SO HURRY UP! HURRY UP!
MAKE US FOOD! MAKE US FOOD!
...ALL RIGHT, THEN...

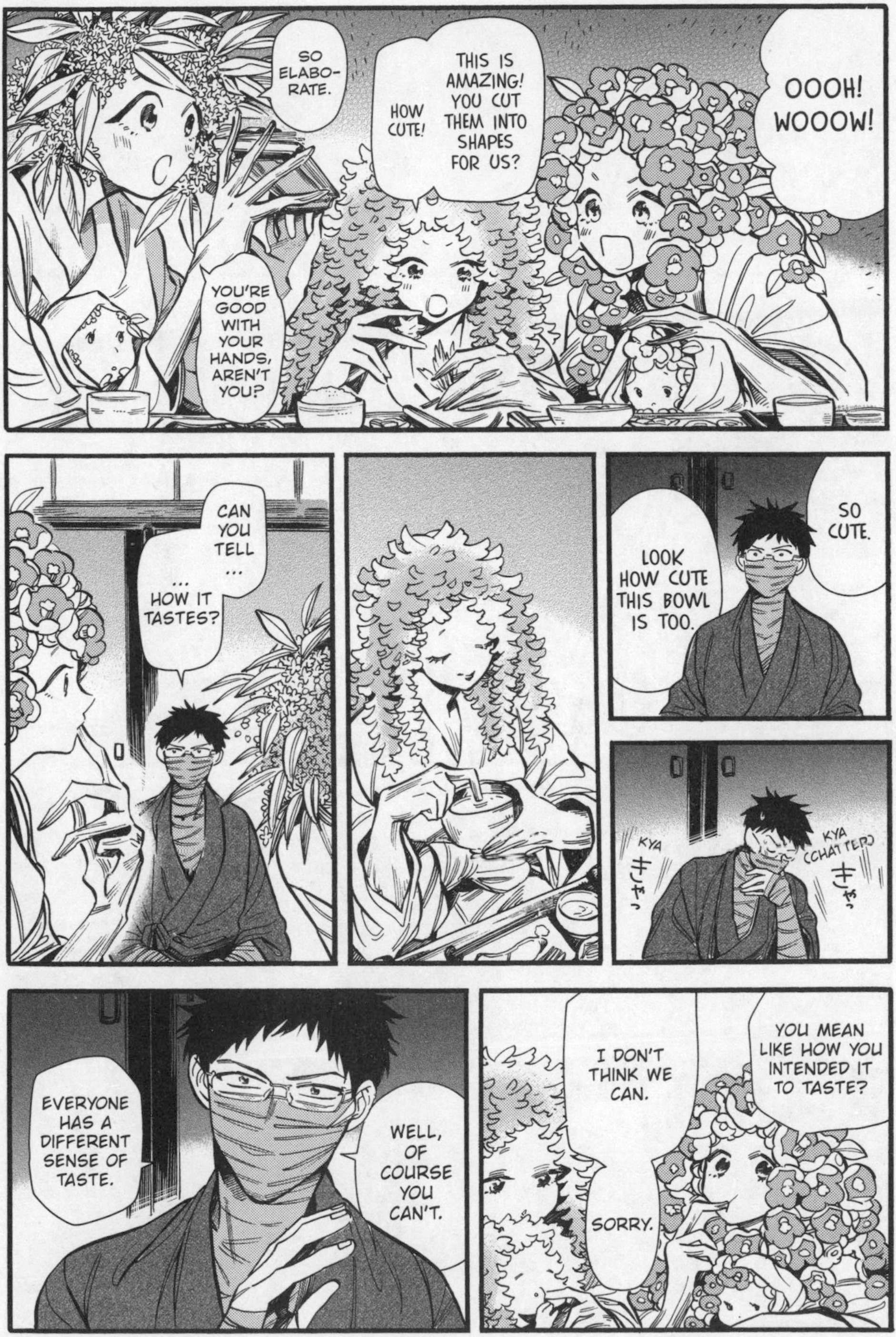
OOOH! WOOOW!
THIS IS AMAZING! YOU CUT THEM INTO SHAPES FOR US?
HOW CUTE!
SO ELABORATE.
YOU'RE GOOD WITH YOUR HANDS, AREN'T YOU?
SO CUTE.
LOOK HOW CUTE THIS BOWL IS TOO.
KYA (CHATTER)
きゃっ
KYA
きゃっ
CAN YOU TELL ...
... HOW IT TASTES?
YOU MEAN LIKE HOW YOU INTENDED IT TO TASTE?
I DON'T THINK WE CAN.
SORRY.
WELL, OF COURSE YOU CAN'T.
EVERYONE HAS A DIFFERENT SENSE OF TASTE.

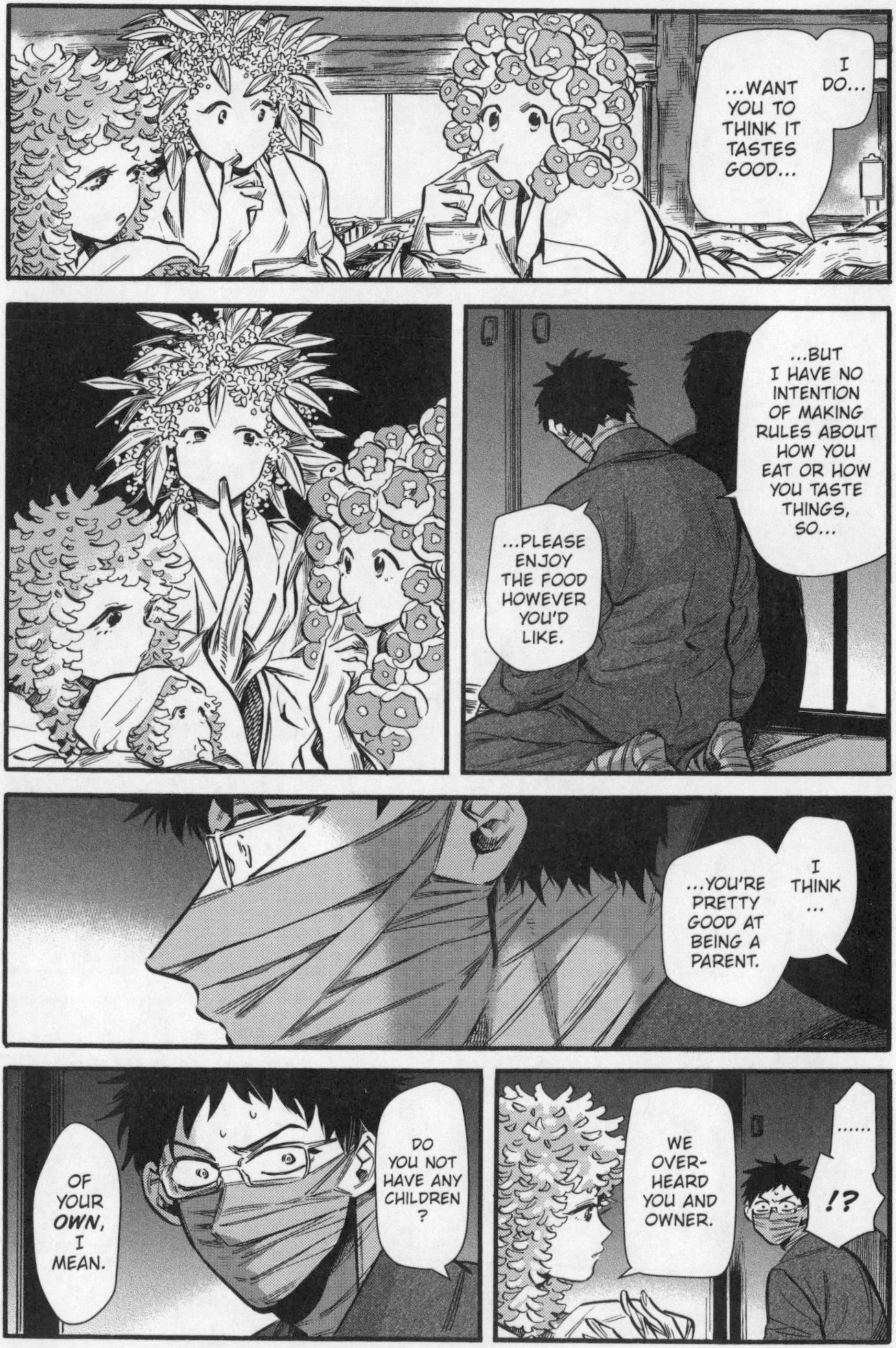
I DO...
...WANT YOU TO THINK IT TASTES GOOD...
...BUT I HAVE NO INTENTION OF MAKING RULES ABOUT HOW YOU EAT OR HOW YOU TASTE THINGS, SO...
...PLEASE ENJOY THE FOOD HOWEVER YOU'D LIKE.
I THINK...
...YOU'RE PRETTY GOOD AT BEING A PARENT.
......
!?
WE OVER-HEARD YOU AND OWNER.
DO YOU NOT HAVE ANY CHILDREN?
OF YOUR *OWN*, I MEAN.

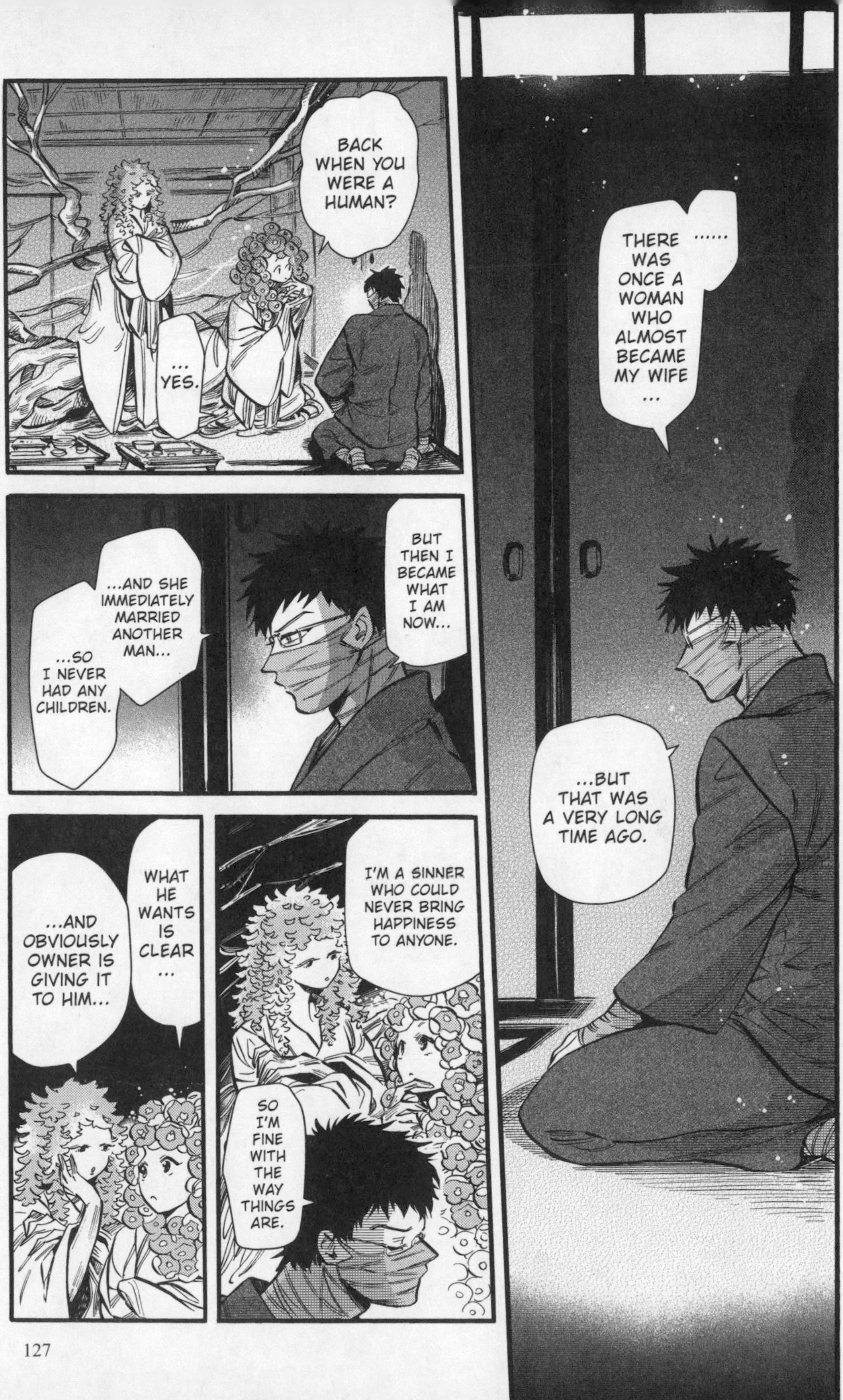

...... THERE WAS ONCE A WOMAN WHO ALMOST BECAME MY WIFE ...
...BUT THAT WAS A VERY LONG TIME AGO.
BACK WHEN YOU WERE A HUMAN?
... YES.
BUT THEN I BECAME WHAT I AM NOW...
...AND SHE IMMEDIATELY MARRIED ANOTHER MAN...
...SO I NEVER HAD ANY CHILDREN.
I'M A SINNER WHO COULD NEVER BRING HAPPINESS TO ANYONE.
SO I'M FINE WITH THE WAY THINGS ARE.
WHAT HE WANTS IS CLEAR ...
...AND OBVIOUSLY OWNER IS GIVING IT TO HIM...

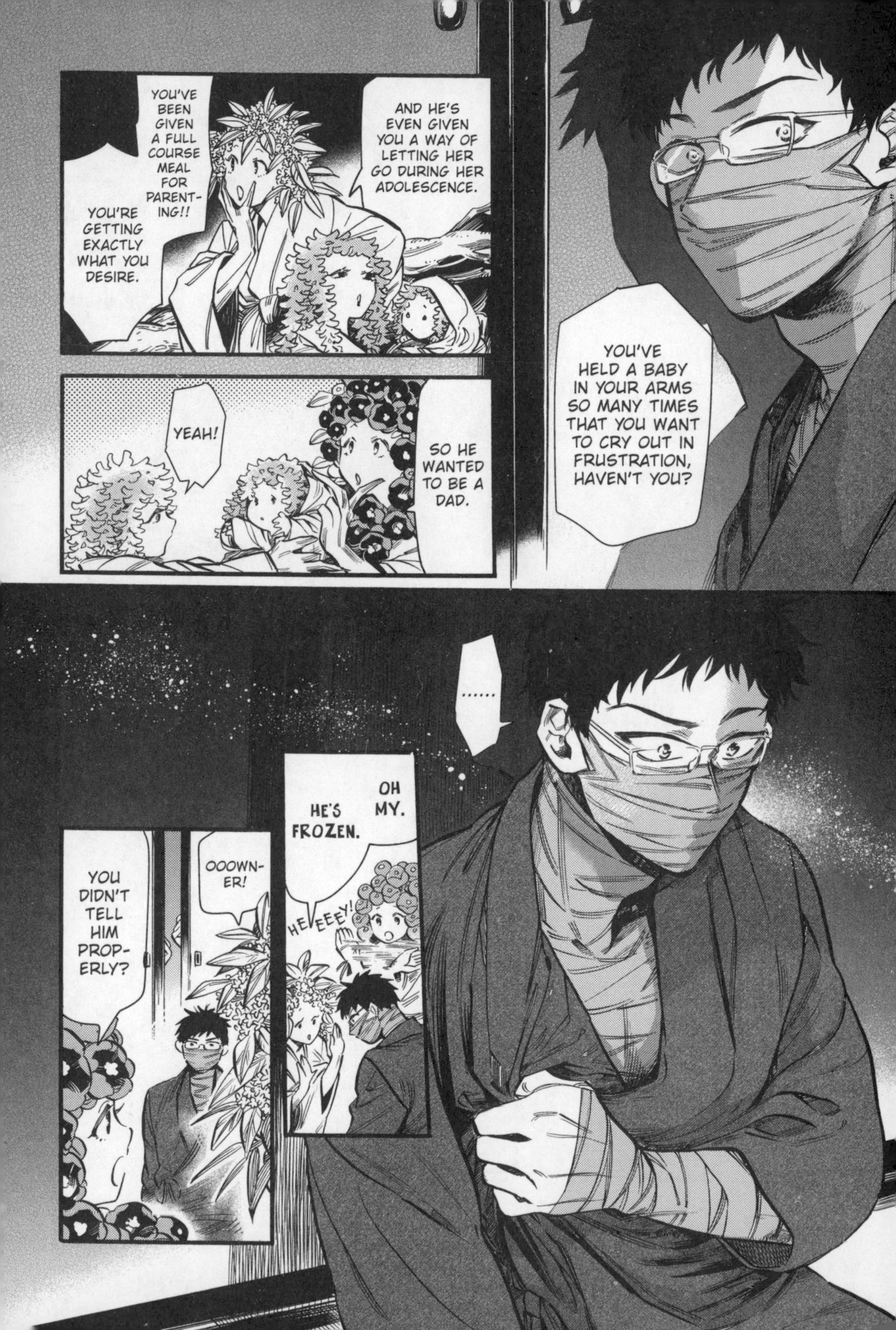
YOU'VE HELD A BABY IN YOUR ARMS SO MANY TIMES THAT YOU WANT TO CRY OUT IN FRUSTRATION, HAVEN'T YOU?
AND HE'S EVEN GIVEN YOU A WAY OF LETTING HER GO DURING HER ADOLESCENCE.
YOU'VE BEEN GIVEN A FULL COURSE MEAL FOR PARENT-ING!!
YOU'RE GETTING EXACTLY WHAT YOU DESIRE.
SO HE WANTED TO BE A DAD.
YEAH!
......
OH MY. HE'S FROZEN.
HEEEEY!
OOOWN-ER!
YOU DIDN'T TELL HIM PROP-ERLY?

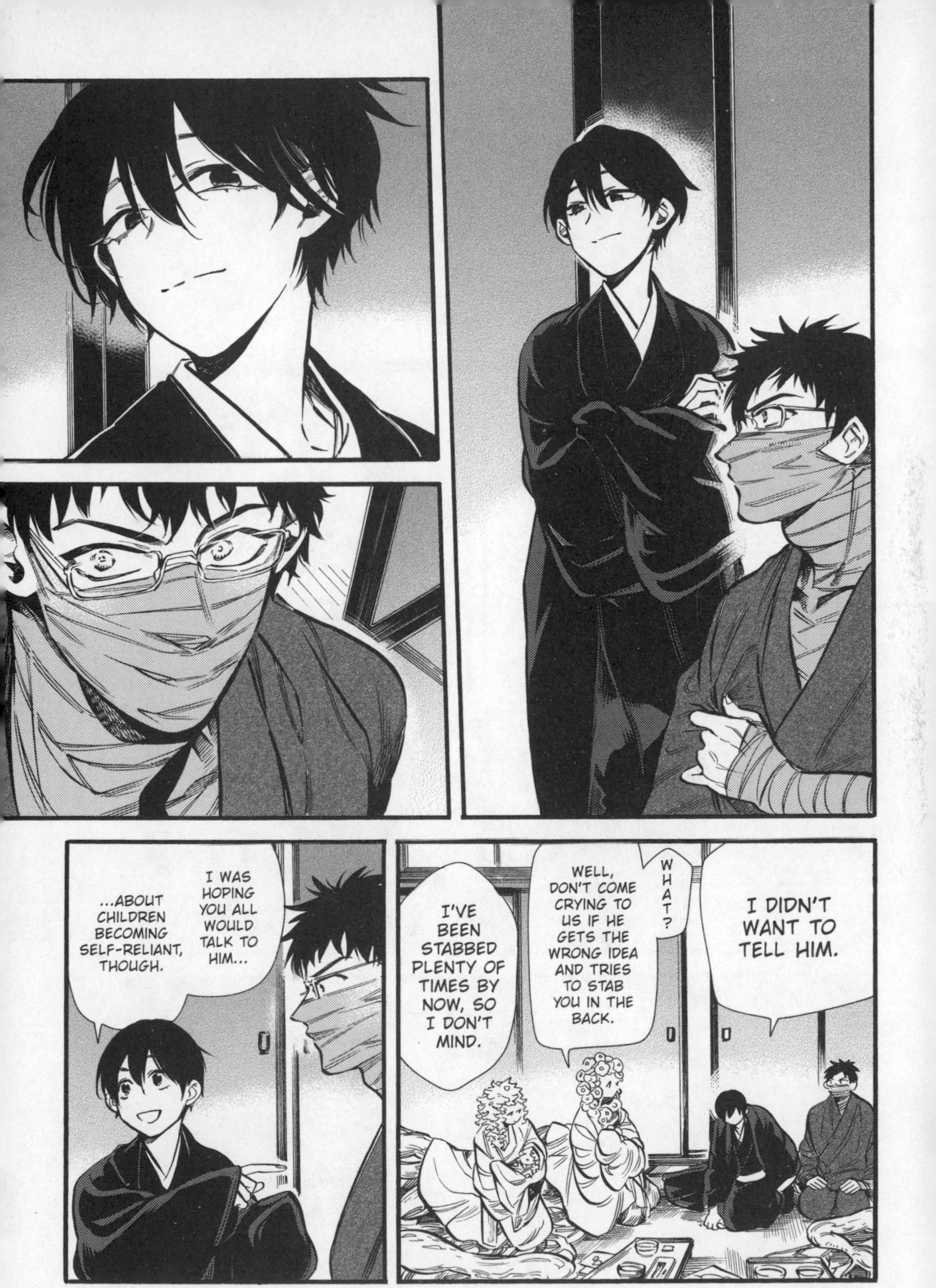

I DIDN'T WANT TO TELL HIM.
WHAT?
WELL, DON'T COME CRYING TO US IF HE GETS THE WRONG IDEA AND TRIES TO STAB YOU IN THE BACK.
I'VE BEEN STABBED PLENTY OF TIMES BY NOW, SO I DON'T MIND.
I WAS HOPING YOU ALL WOULD TALK TO HIM...
...ABOUT CHILDREN BECOMING SELF-RELIANT, THOUGH.

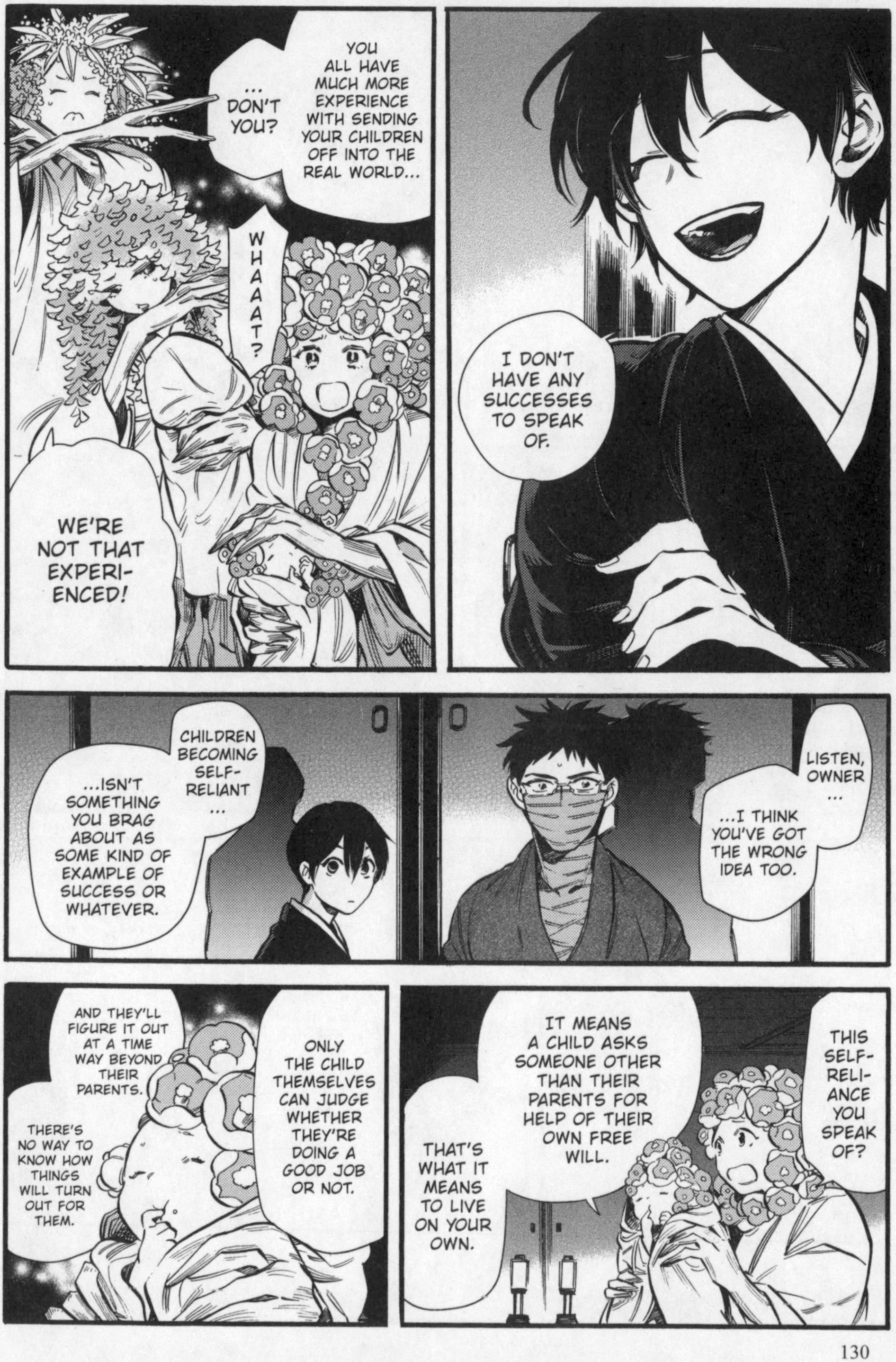
I DON'T HAVE ANY SUCCESSES TO SPEAK OF.
YOU ALL HAVE MUCH MORE EXPERIENCE WITH SENDING YOUR CHILDREN OFF INTO THE REAL WORLD...
...DON'T YOU?
WHAAAAT?
WE'RE NOT THAT EXPERI-ENCED!
LISTEN, OWNER...
...I THINK YOU'VE GOT THE WRONG IDEA TOO.
CHILDREN BECOMING SELF-RELIANT...
...ISN'T SOMETHING YOU BRAG ABOUT AS SOME KIND OF EXAMPLE OF SUCCESS OR WHATEVER.
THIS SELF-RELI-ANCE YOU SPEAK OF?
IT MEANS A CHILD ASKS SOMEONE OTHER THAN THEIR PARENTS FOR HELP OF THEIR OWN FREE WILL.
THAT'S WHAT IT MEANS TO LIVE ON YOUR OWN.
ONLY THE CHILD THEMSELVES CAN JUDGE WHETHER THEY'RE DOING A GOOD JOB OR NOT.
AND THEY'LL FIGURE IT OUT AT A TIME WAY BEYOND THEIR PARENTS.
THERE'S NO WAY TO KNOW HOW THINGS WILL TURN OUT FOR THEM.

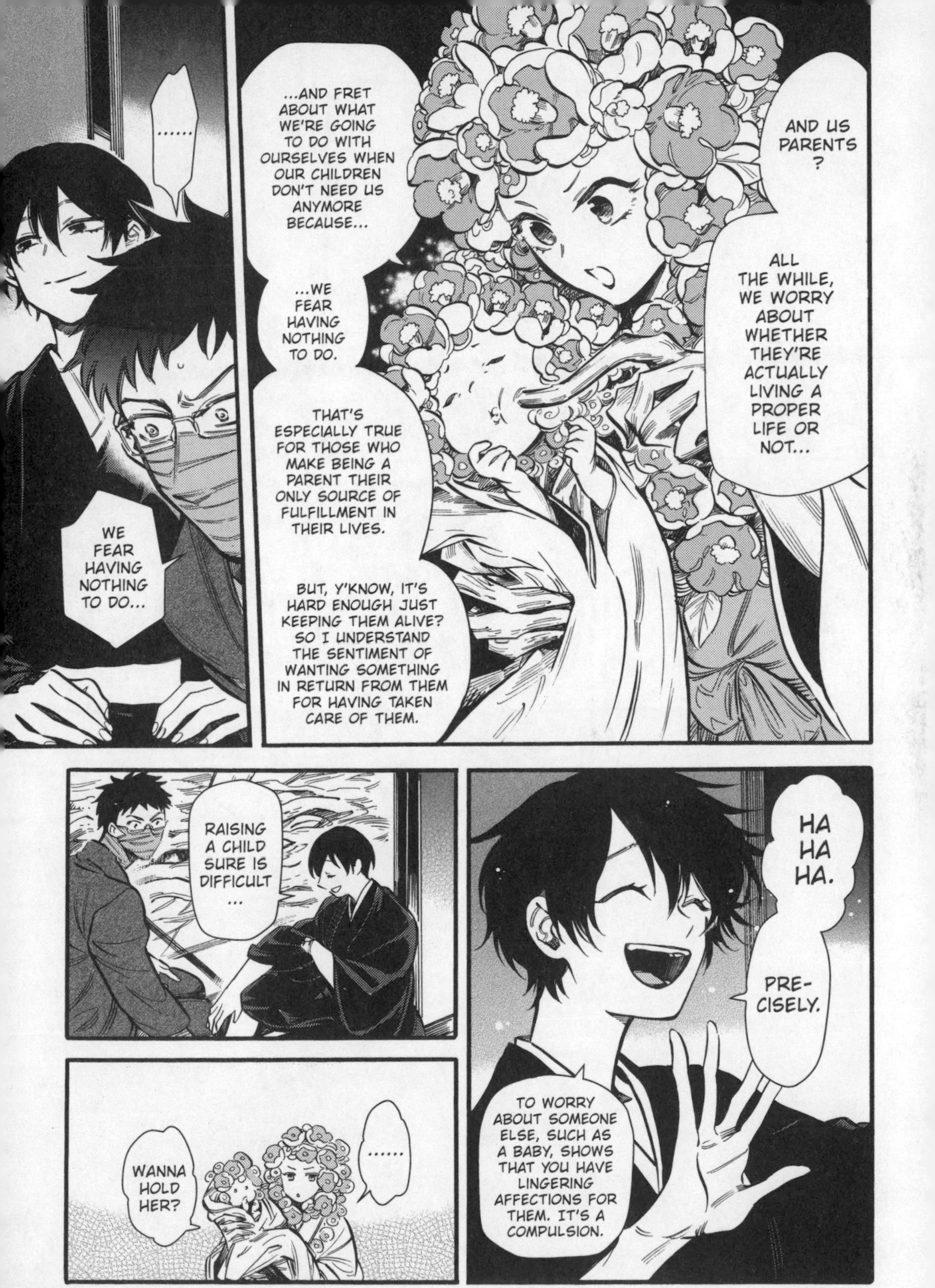
AND US PARENTS ?
ALL THE WHILE, WE WORRY ABOUT WHETHER THEY'RE ACTUALLY LIVING A PROPER LIFE OR NOT...
...AND FRET ABOUT WHAT WE'RE GOING TO DO WITH OURSELVES WHEN OUR CHILDREN DON'T NEED US ANYMORE BECAUSE...
...WE FEAR HAVING NOTHING TO DO.
THAT'S ESPECIALLY TRUE FOR THOSE WHO MAKE BEING A PARENT THEIR ONLY SOURCE OF FULFILLMENT IN THEIR LIVES.
BUT, Y'KNOW, IT'S HARD ENOUGH JUST KEEPING THEM ALIVE? SO I UNDERSTAND THE SENTIMENT OF WANTING SOMETHING IN RETURN FROM THEM FOR HAVING TAKEN CARE OF THEM.
......
WE FEAR HAVING NOTHING TO DO...
HA HA HA.
PRE-CISELY.
TO WORRY ABOUT SOMEONE ELSE, SUCH AS A BABY, SHOWS THAT YOU HAVE LINGERING AFFECTIONS FOR THEM. IT'S A COMPULSION.
RAISING A CHILD SURE IS DIFFICULT ...
......
WANNA HOLD HER?

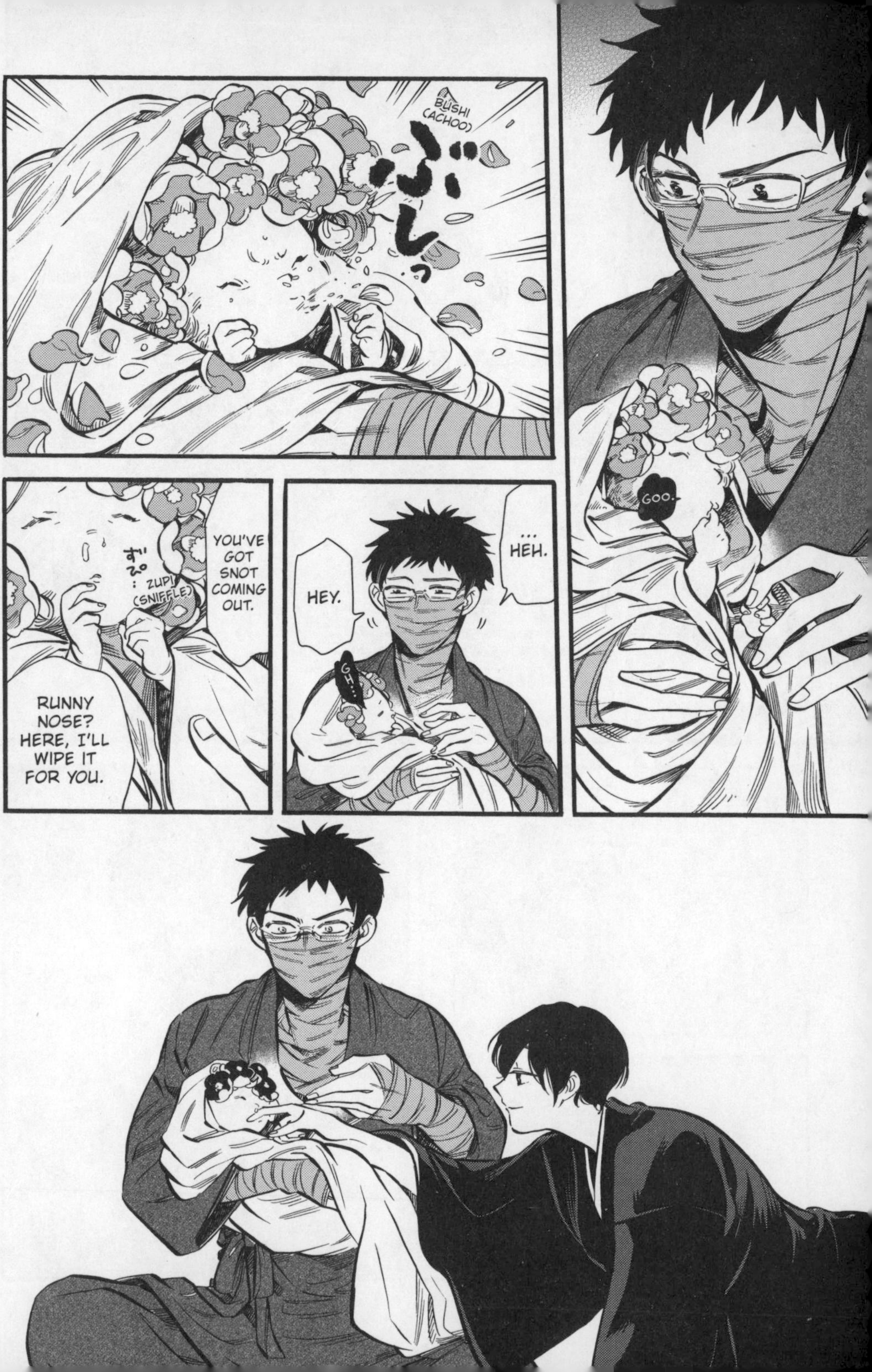
GOO.
BUSHI (ACHOO)
ぶしっ
...HEH.
HEY.
GH...
YOU'VE GOT SNOT COMING OUT.
ずぴ
ZUPI (SNIFFLE)
RUNNY NOSE? HERE, I'LL WIPE IT FOR YOU.

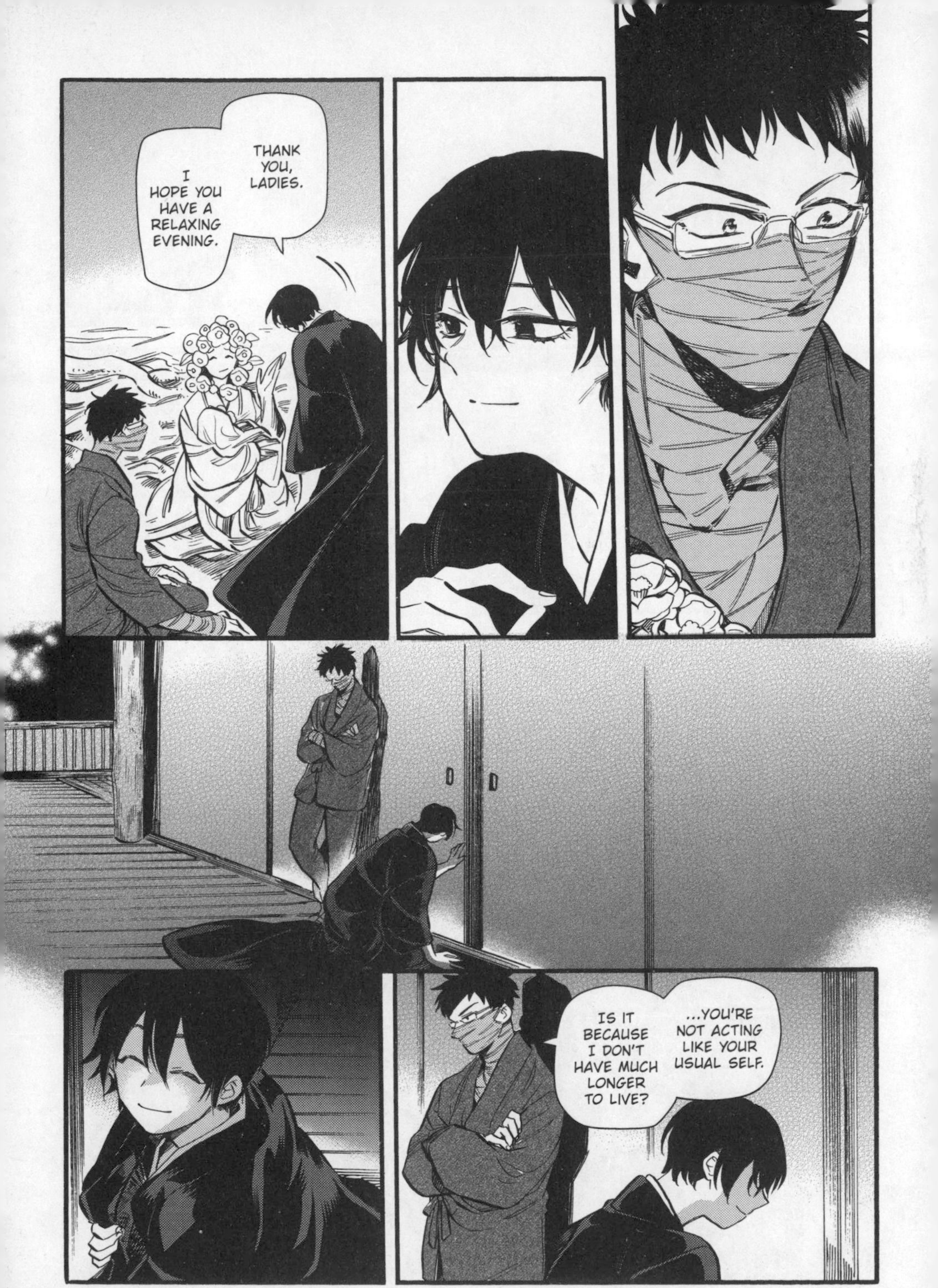
THANK YOU, LADIES.
I HOPE YOU HAVE A RELAXING EVENING.
...YOU'RE NOT ACTING LIKE YOUR USUAL SELF.
IS IT BECAUSE I DON'T HAVE MUCH LONGER TO LIVE?

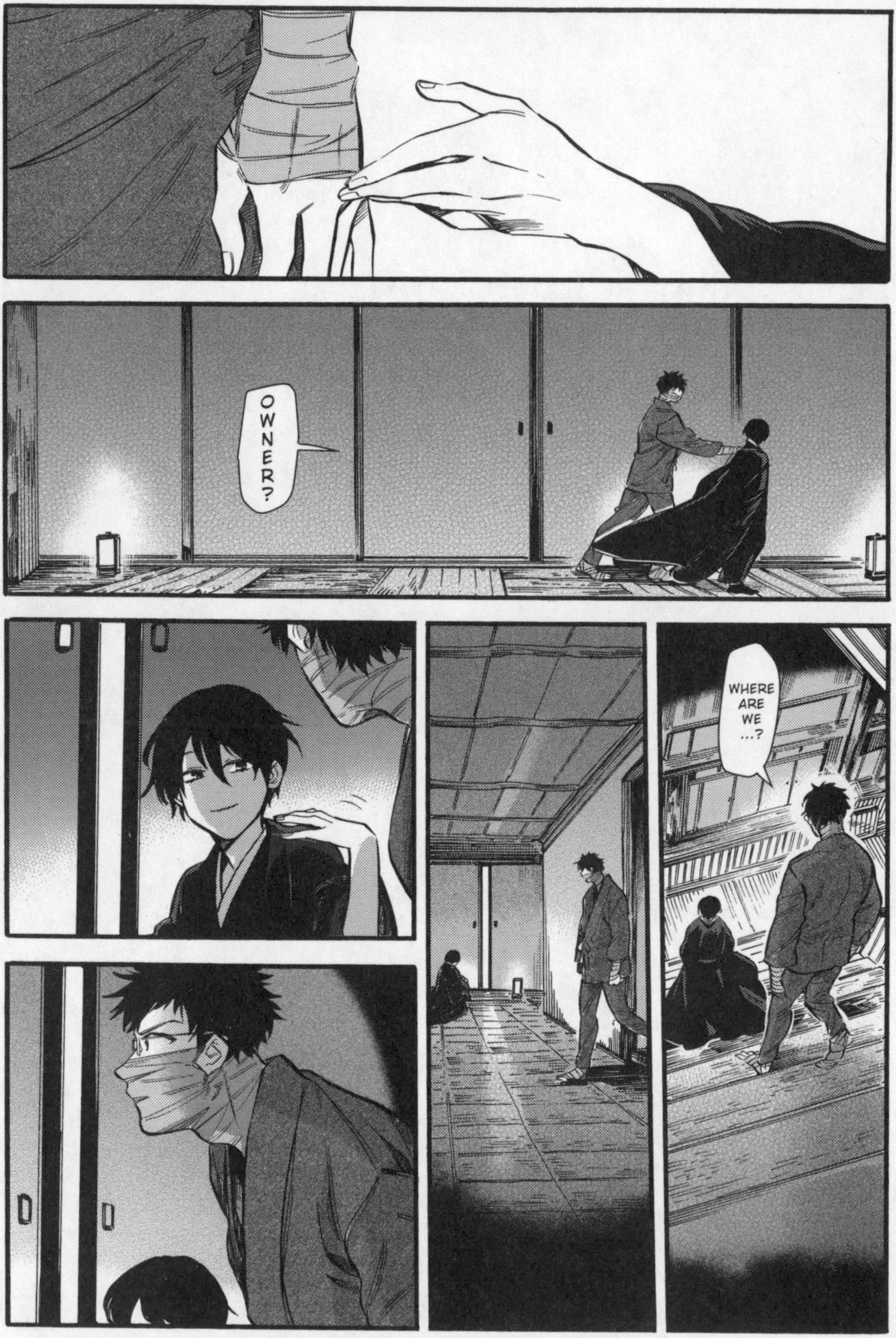
OWNER?
WHERE ARE WE ...?

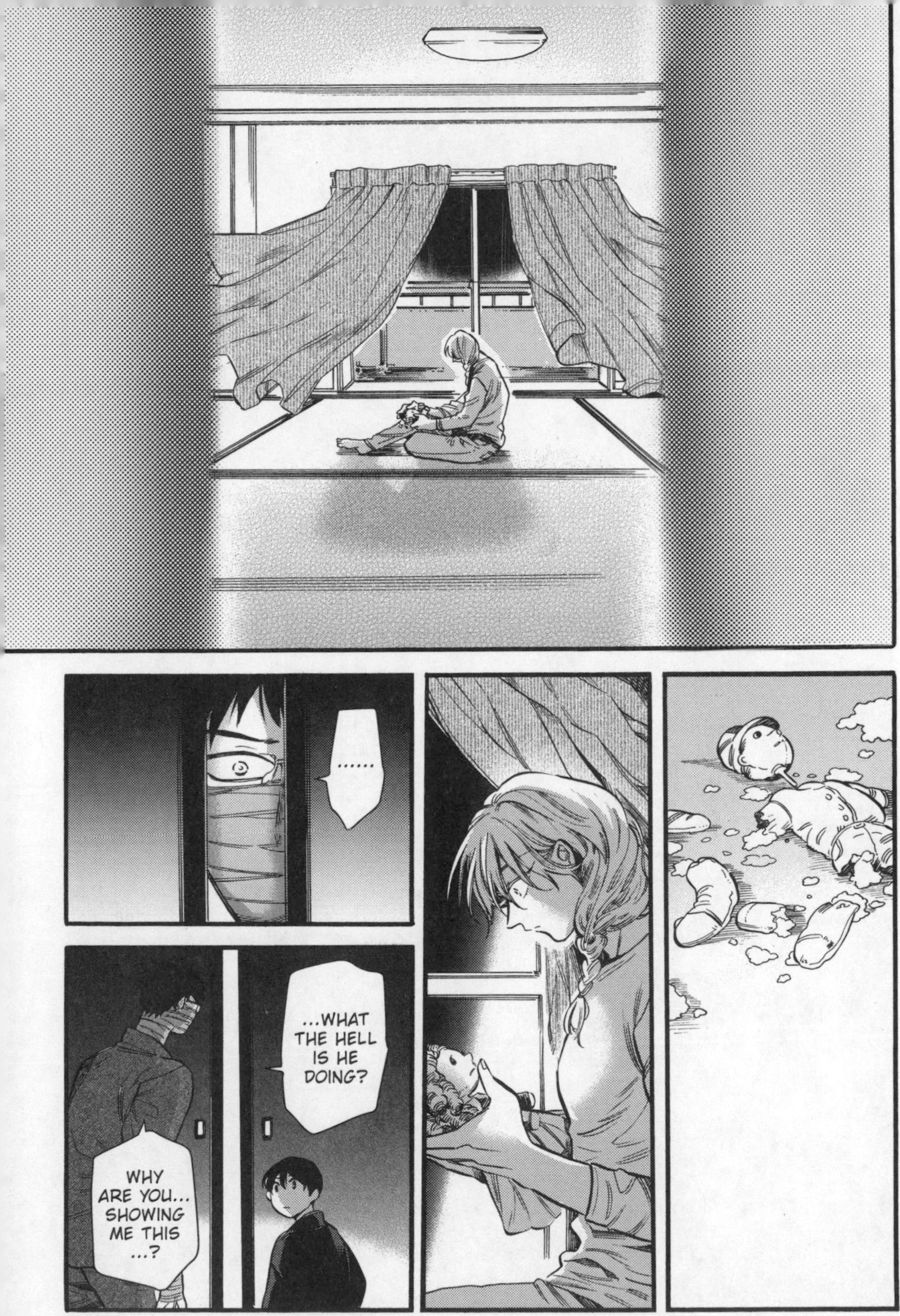
......
...WHAT THE HELL IS HE DOING?
WHY ARE YOU... SHOWING ME THIS ...?

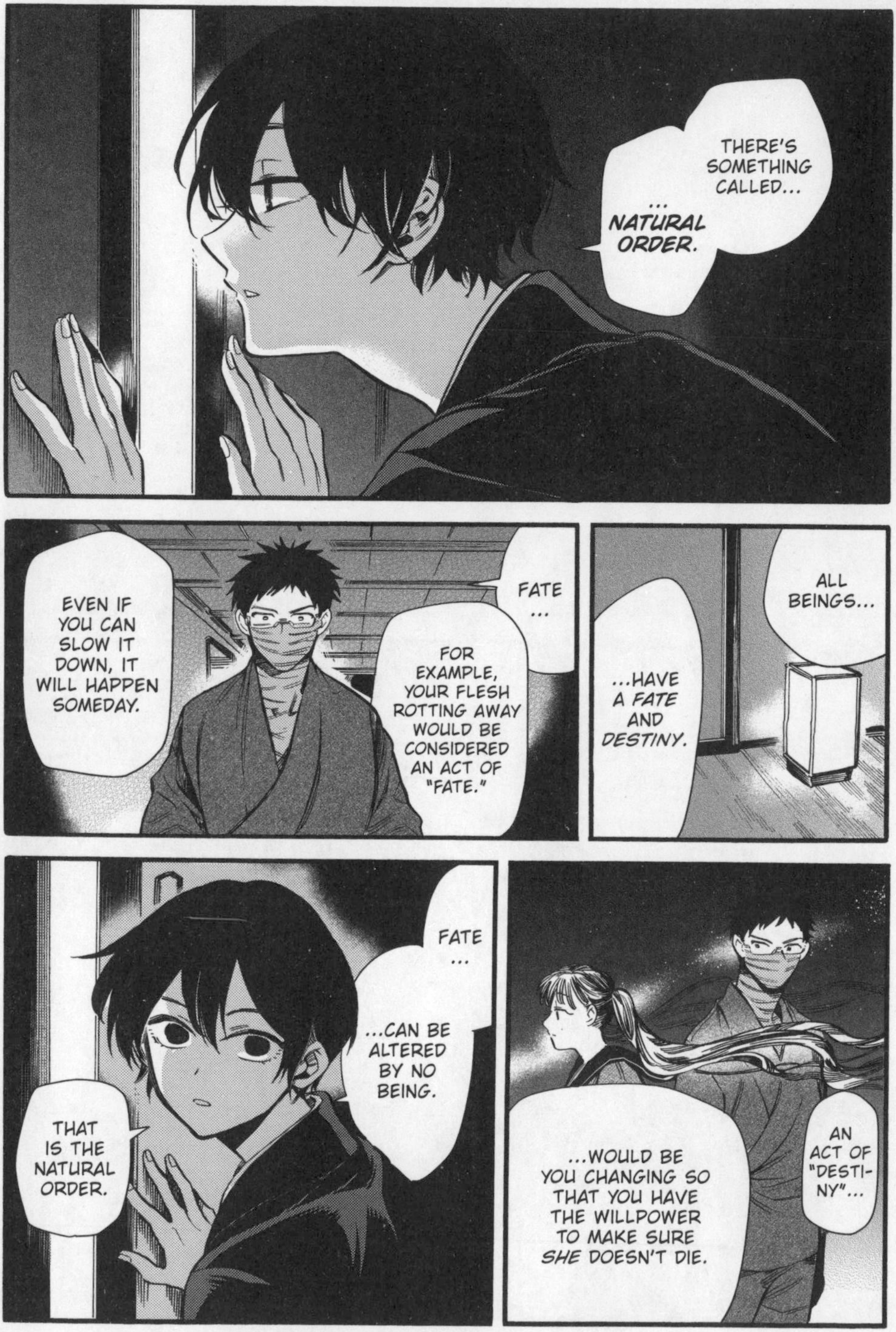
THERE'S SOMETHING CALLED...
... *NATURAL ORDER.*
ALL BEINGS...
...HAVE A *FATE* AND *DESTINY.*
FATE ...
FOR EXAMPLE, YOUR FLESH ROTTING AWAY WOULD BE CONSIDERED AN ACT OF "FATE."
EVEN IF YOU CAN SLOW IT DOWN, IT WILL HAPPEN SOMEDAY.
AN ACT OF "DESTI-NY"...
...WOULD BE YOU CHANGING SO THAT YOU HAVE THE WILLPOWER TO MAKE SURE *SHE* DOESN'T DIE.
FATE ...
...CAN BE ALTERED BY NO BEING.
THAT IS THE NATURAL ORDER.

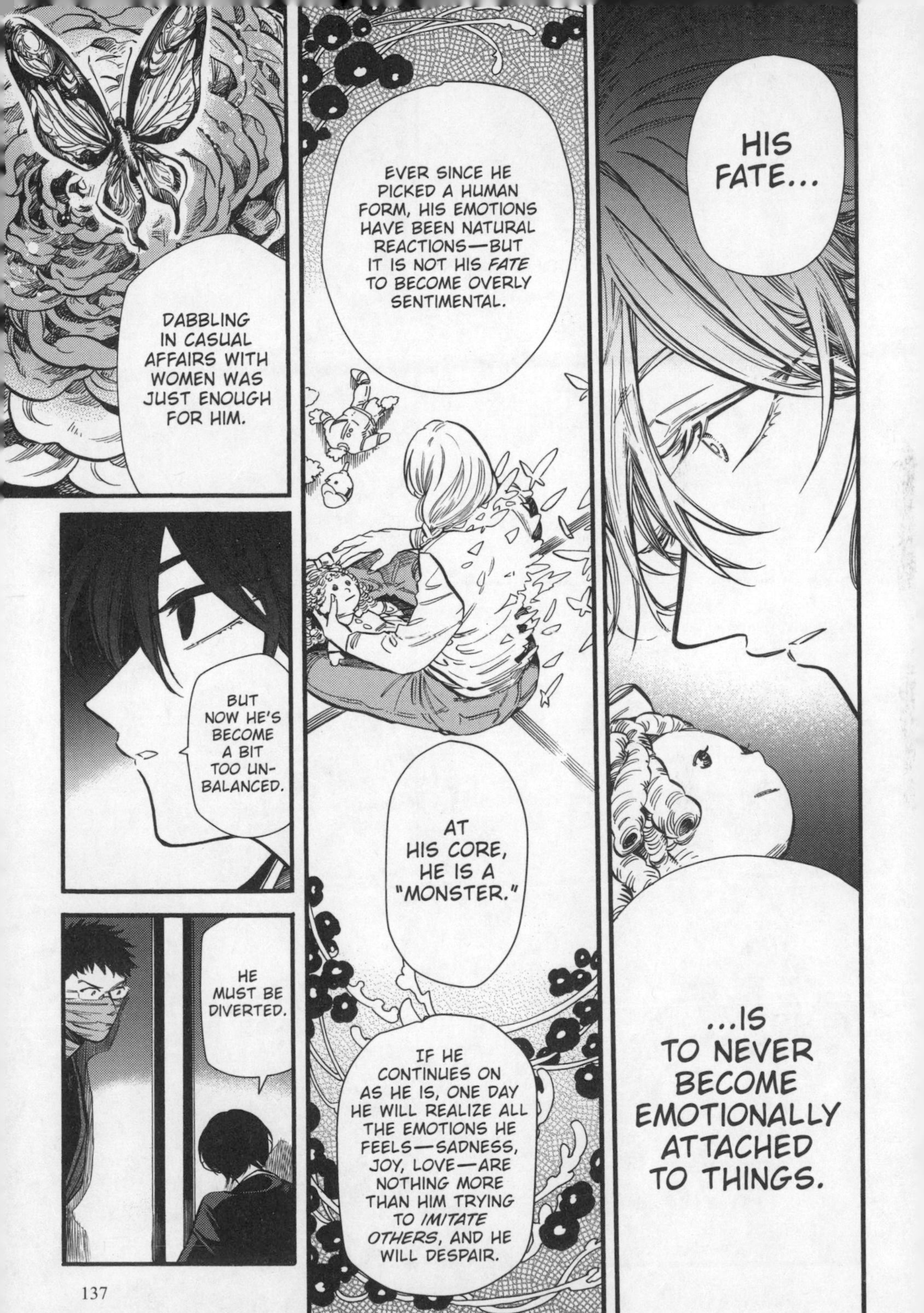
HIS FATE...
...IS TO NEVER BECOME EMOTIONALLY ATTACHED TO THINGS.
EVER SINCE HE PICKED A HUMAN FORM, HIS EMOTIONS HAVE BEEN NATURAL REACTIONS—BUT IT IS NOT HIS *FATE* TO BECOME OVERLY SENTIMENTAL.
AT HIS CORE, HE IS A "MONSTER."
IF HE CONTINUES ON AS HE IS, ONE DAY HE WILL REALIZE ALL THE EMOTIONS HE FEELS—SADNESS, JOY, LOVE—ARE NOTHING MORE THAN HIM TRYING TO *IMITATE OTHERS*, AND HE WILL DESPAIR.
DABBLING IN CASUAL AFFAIRS WITH WOMEN WAS JUST ENOUGH FOR HIM.
BUT NOW HE'S BECOME A BIT TOO UN-BALANCED.
HE MUST BE DIVERTED.

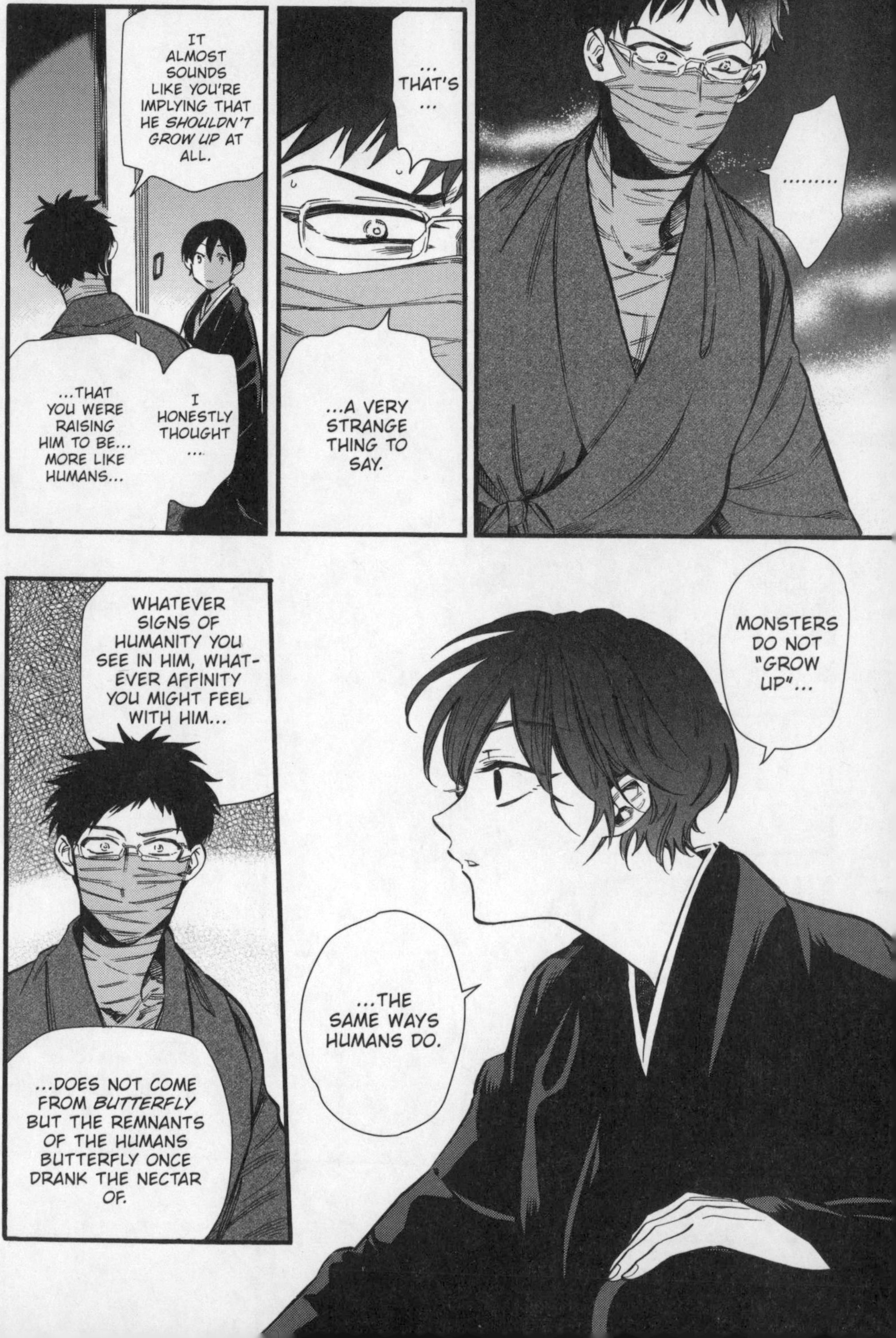
....
...THAT'S...
...A VERY STRANGE THING TO SAY.
IT ALMOST SOUNDS LIKE YOU'RE IMPLYING THAT HE *SHOULDN'T GROW UP* AT ALL.
I HONESTLY THOUGHT...
...THAT YOU WERE RAISING HIM TO BE... MORE LIKE HUMANS...
MONSTERS DO NOT "GROW UP"...
...THE SAME WAYS HUMANS DO.
WHATEVER SIGNS OF HUMANITY YOU SEE IN HIM, WHATEVER AFFINITY YOU MIGHT FEEL WITH HIM...
...DOES NOT COME FROM *BUTTERFLY* BUT THE REMNANTS OF THE HUMANS BUTTERFLY ONCE DRANK THE NECTAR OF.

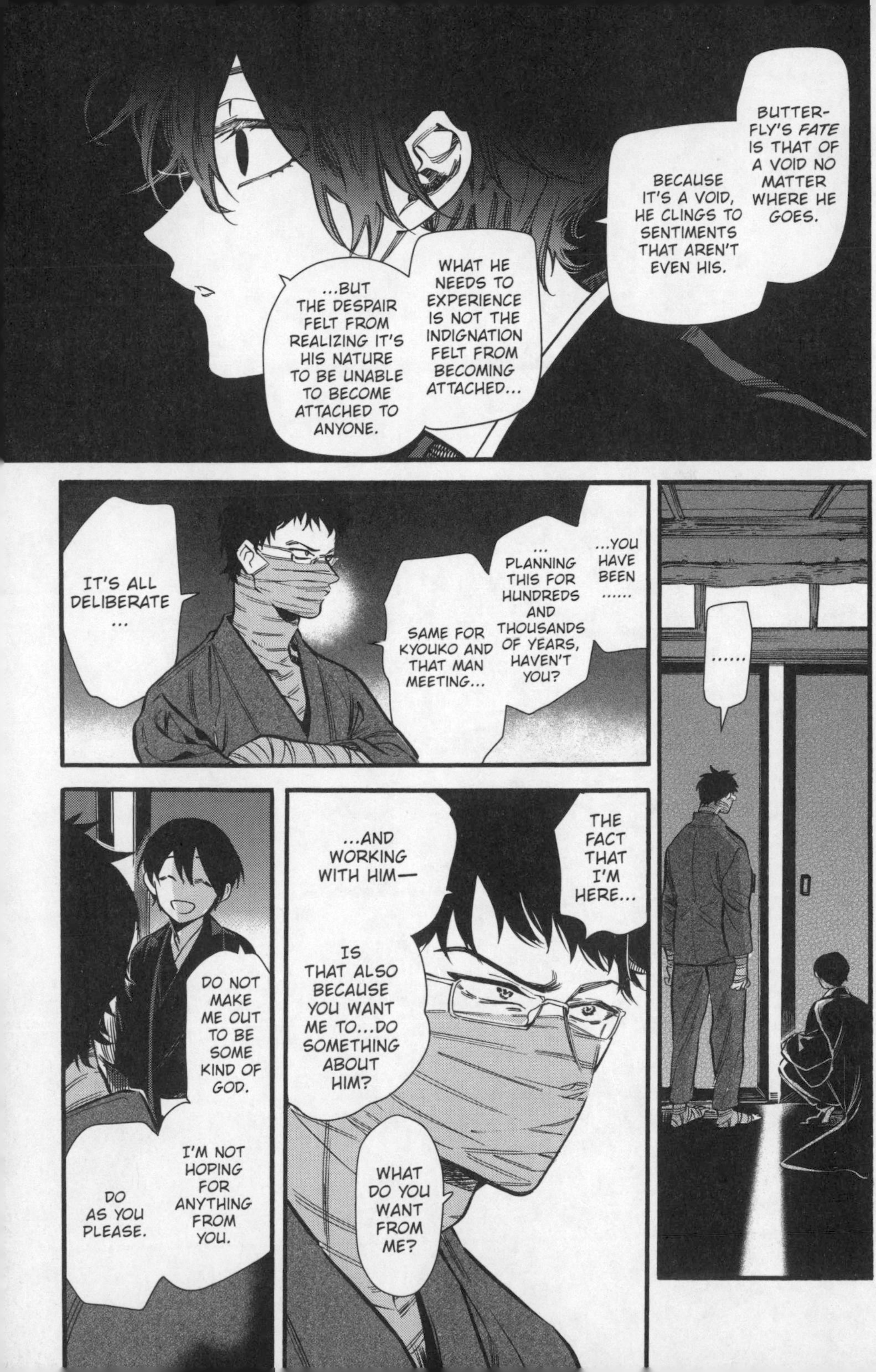
BUTTERFLY'S *FATE* IS THAT OF A VOID NO MATTER WHERE HE GOES.
BECAUSE IT'S A VOID, HE CLINGS TO SENTIMENTS THAT AREN'T EVEN HIS.
WHAT HE NEEDS TO EXPERIENCE IS NOT THE INDIGNATION FELT FROM BECOMING ATTACHED...
...BUT THE DESPAIR FELT FROM REALIZING IT'S HIS NATURE TO BE UNABLE TO BECOME ATTACHED TO ANYONE.
......
...YOU HAVE BEEN ......
... PLANNING THIS FOR HUNDREDS AND THOUSANDS OF YEARS, HAVEN'T YOU?
SAME FOR KYOUKO AND THAT MAN MEETING...
IT'S ALL DELIBERATE ...
THE FACT THAT I'M HERE...
...AND WORKING WITH HIM—
IS THAT ALSO BECAUSE YOU WANT ME TO...DO SOMETHING ABOUT HIM?
WHAT DO YOU WANT FROM ME?
DO NOT MAKE ME OUT TO BE SOME KIND OF GOD.
I'M NOT HOPING FOR ANYTHING FROM YOU.
DO AS YOU PLEASE.

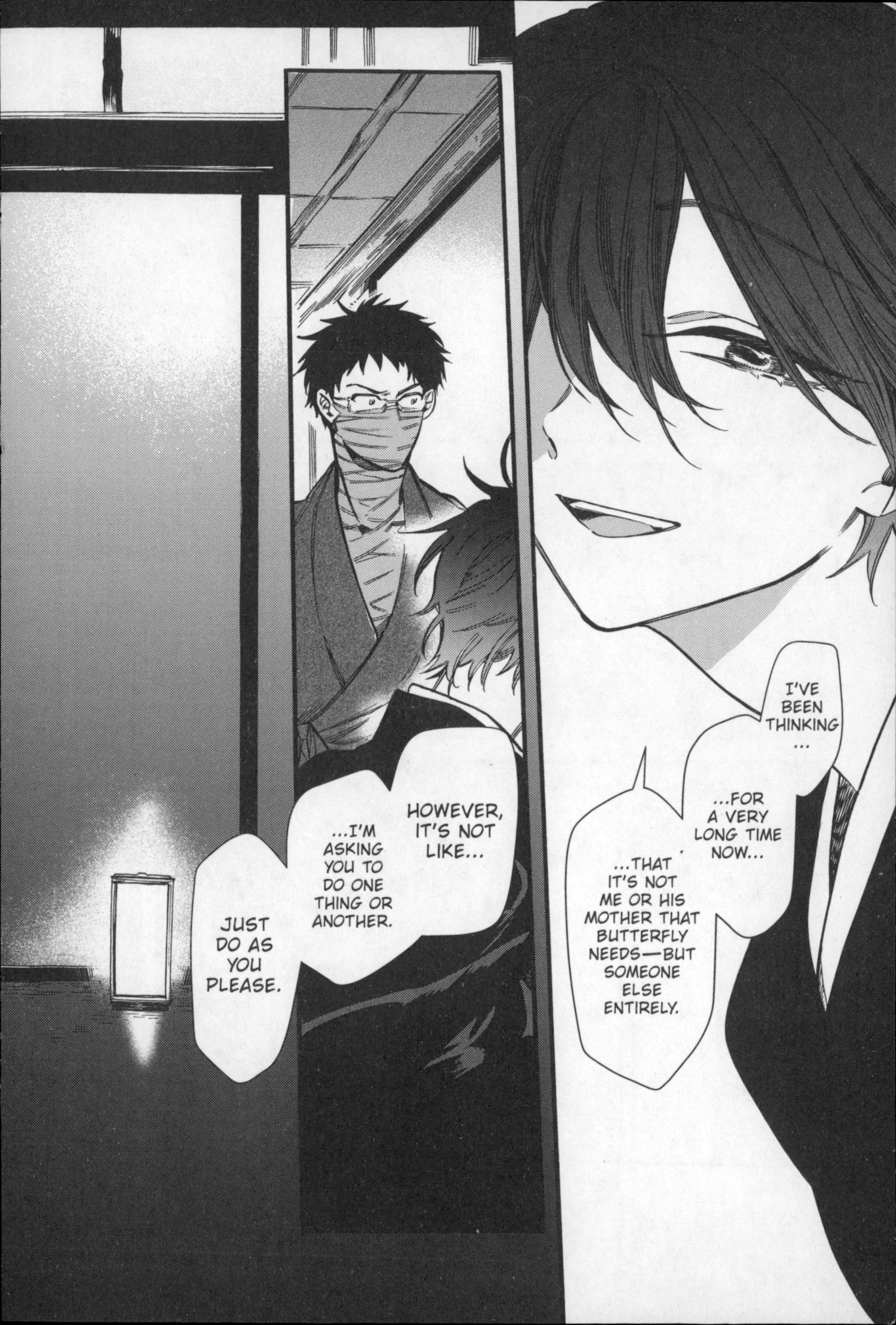
I'VE BEEN THINKING...
...FOR A VERY LONG TIME NOW...
...THAT IT'S NOT ME OR HIS MOTHER THAT BUTTERFLY NEEDS—BUT SOMEONE ELSE ENTIRELY.
HOWEVER, IT'S NOT LIKE...
...I'M ASKING YOU TO DO ONE THING OR ANOTHER.
JUST DO AS YOU PLEASE.

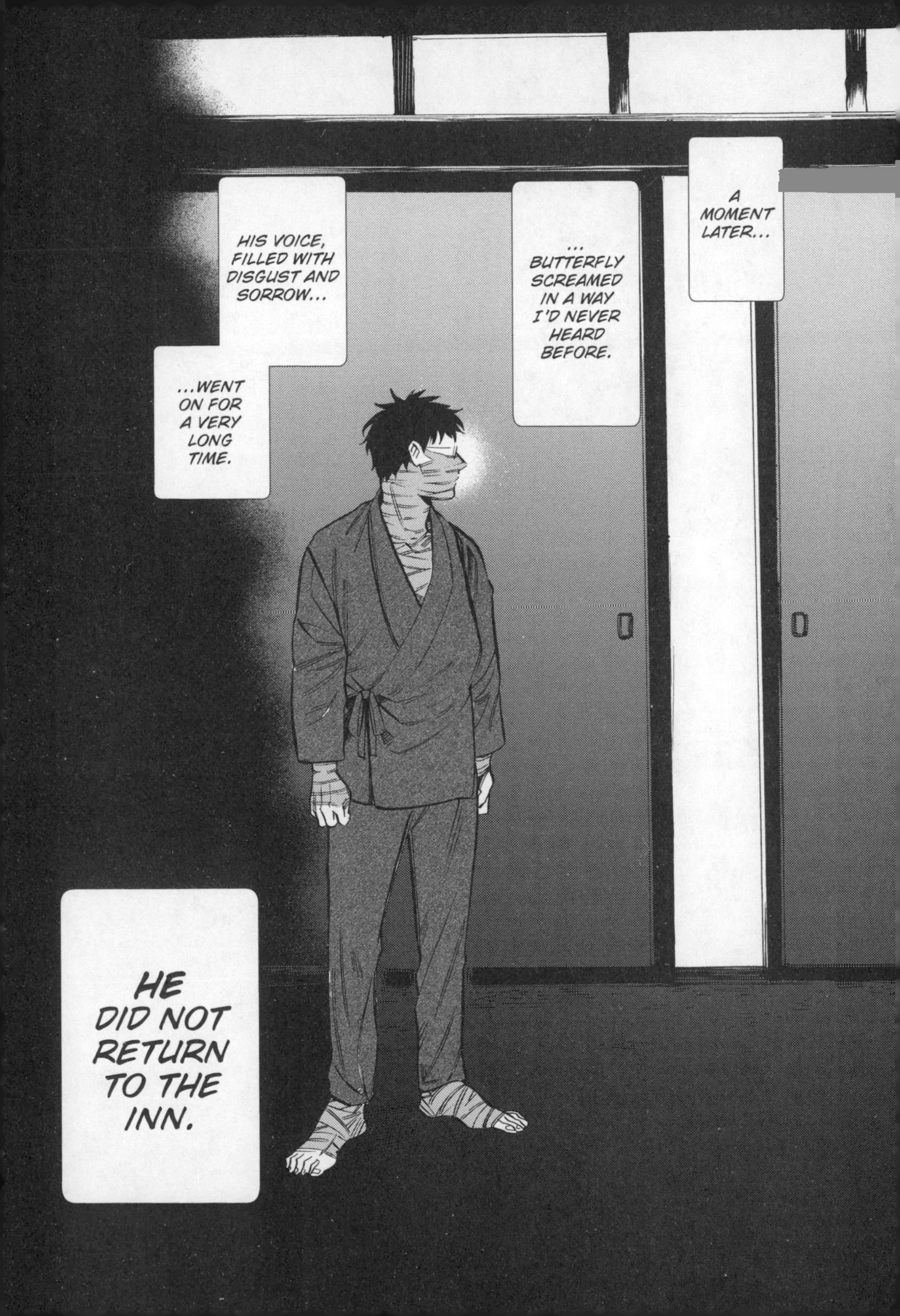
A MOMENT LATER...
...BUTTERFLY SCREAMED IN A WAY I'D NEVER HEARD BEFORE.
HIS VOICE, FILLED WITH DISGUST AND SORROW...
...WENT ON FOR A VERY LONG TIME.
HE DID NOT RETURN TO THE INN.

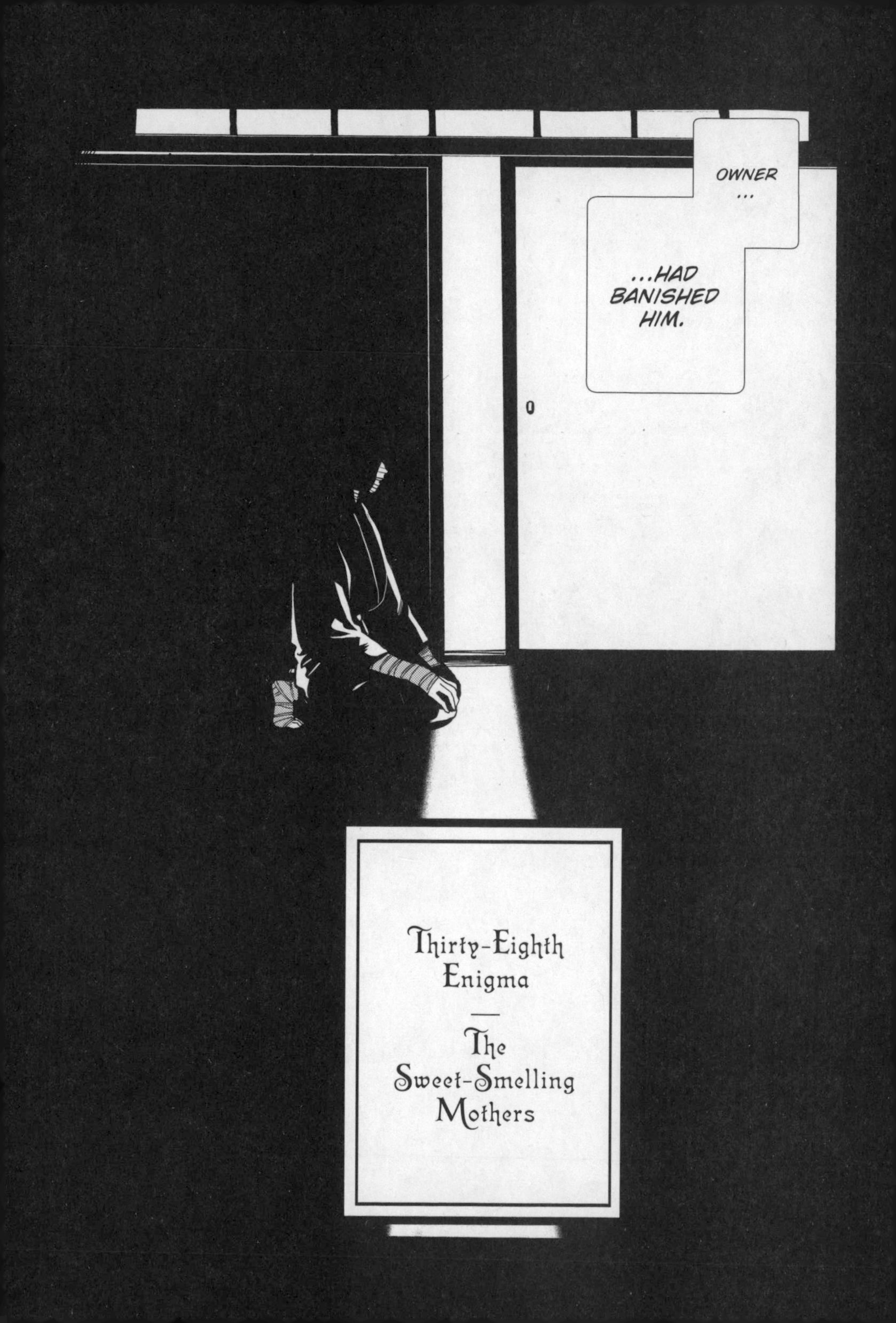
OWNER ...
...HAD BANISHED HIM.

Thirty-Eighth Enigma — The Sweet-Smelling Mothers

Phantom Tales of the Night

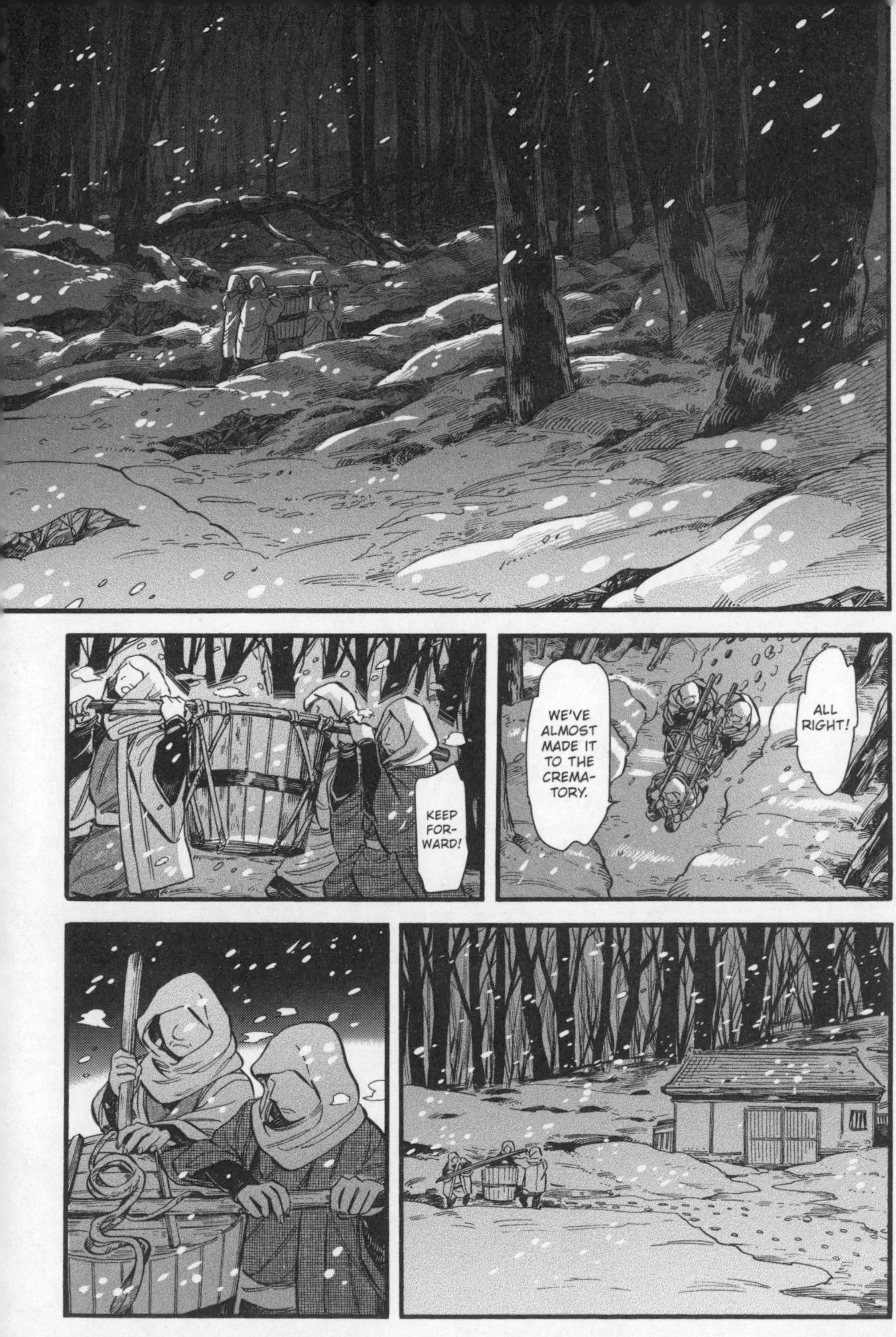
ALL RIGHT!
WE'VE ALMOST MADE IT TO THE CREMATORY.
KEEP FOR-WARD!

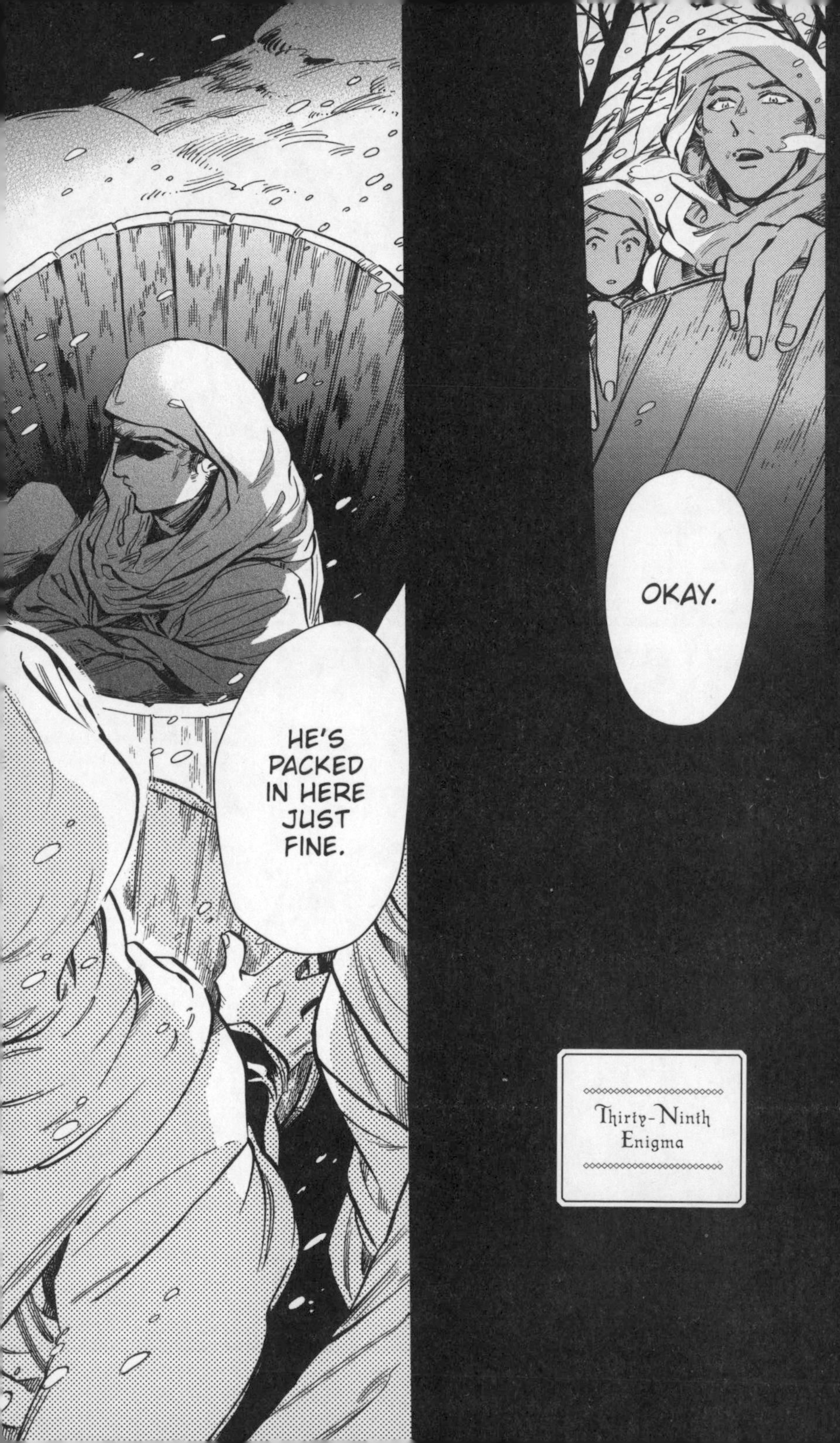
OKAY.
Thirty-Ninth Enigma
HE'S PACKED IN HERE JUST FINE.

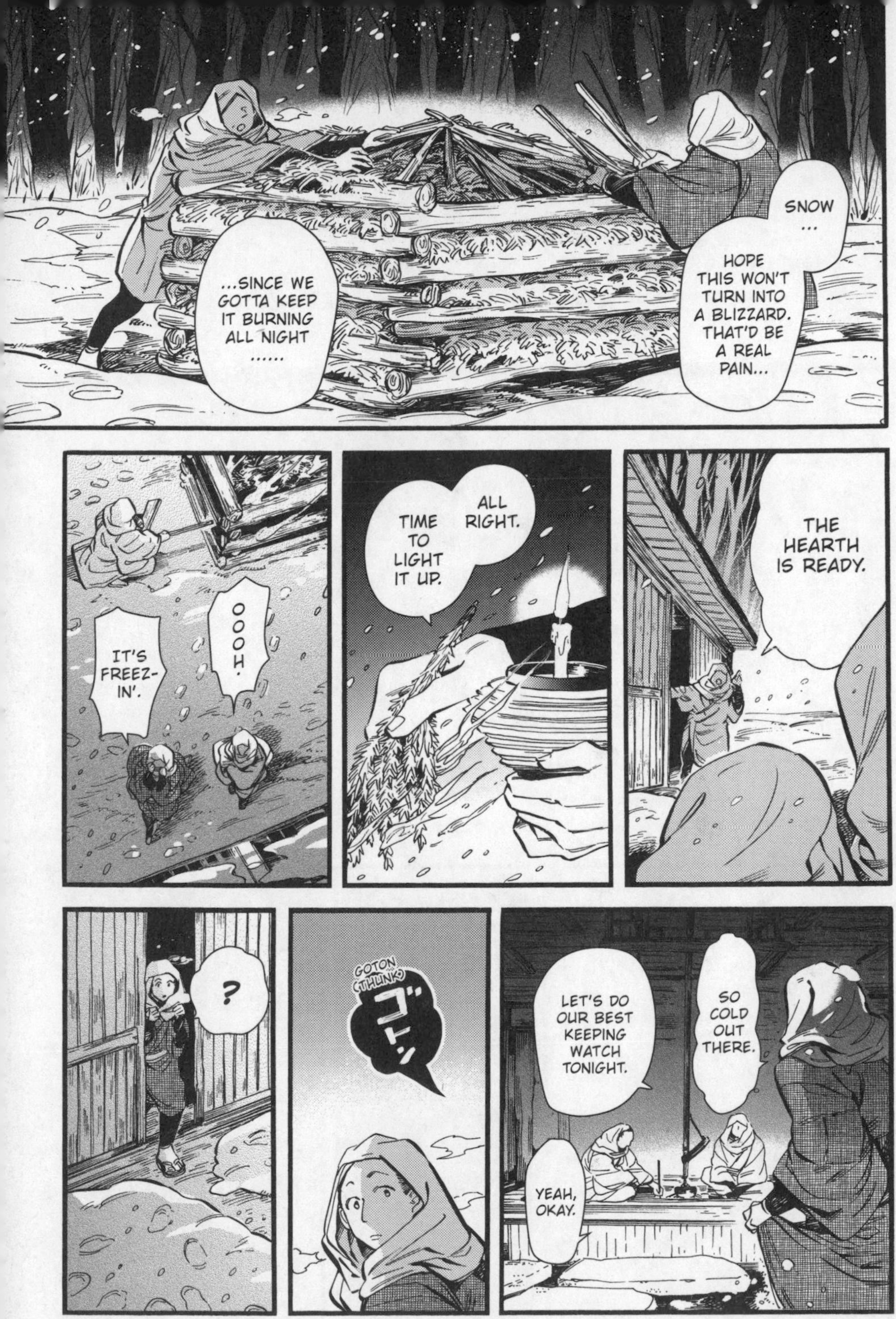
SNOW ...
HOPE THIS WON'T TURN INTO A BLIZZARD. THAT'D BE A REAL PAIN...
...SINCE WE GOTTA KEEP IT BURNING ALL NIGHT ......
THE HEARTH IS READY.
ALL RIGHT.
TIME TO LIGHT IT UP.
OOOH.
IT'S FREEZ-IN'.
SO COLD OUT THERE.
LET'S DO OUR BEST KEEPING WATCH TONIGHT.
YEAH, OKAY.
GOTON (THUNK)
ゴトン
?

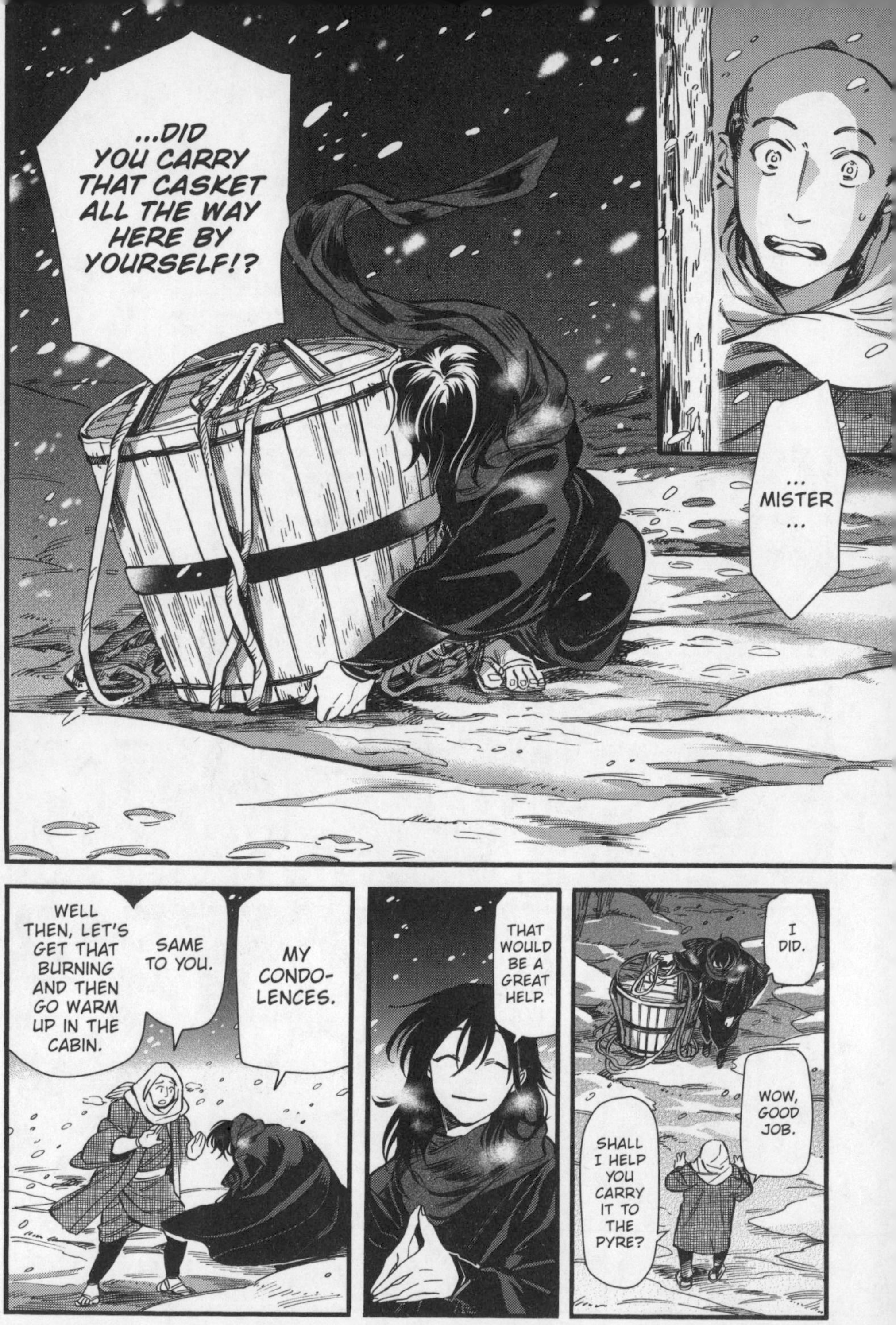
... MISTER ...
...DID YOU CARRY THAT CASKET ALL THE WAY HERE BY YOURSELF!?
I DID.
WOW, GOOD JOB.
SHALL I HELP YOU CARRY IT TO THE PYRE?
THAT WOULD BE A GREAT HELP.
MY CONDOLENCES.
SAME TO YOU.
WELL THEN, LET'S GET THAT BURNING AND THEN GO WARM UP IN THE CABIN.

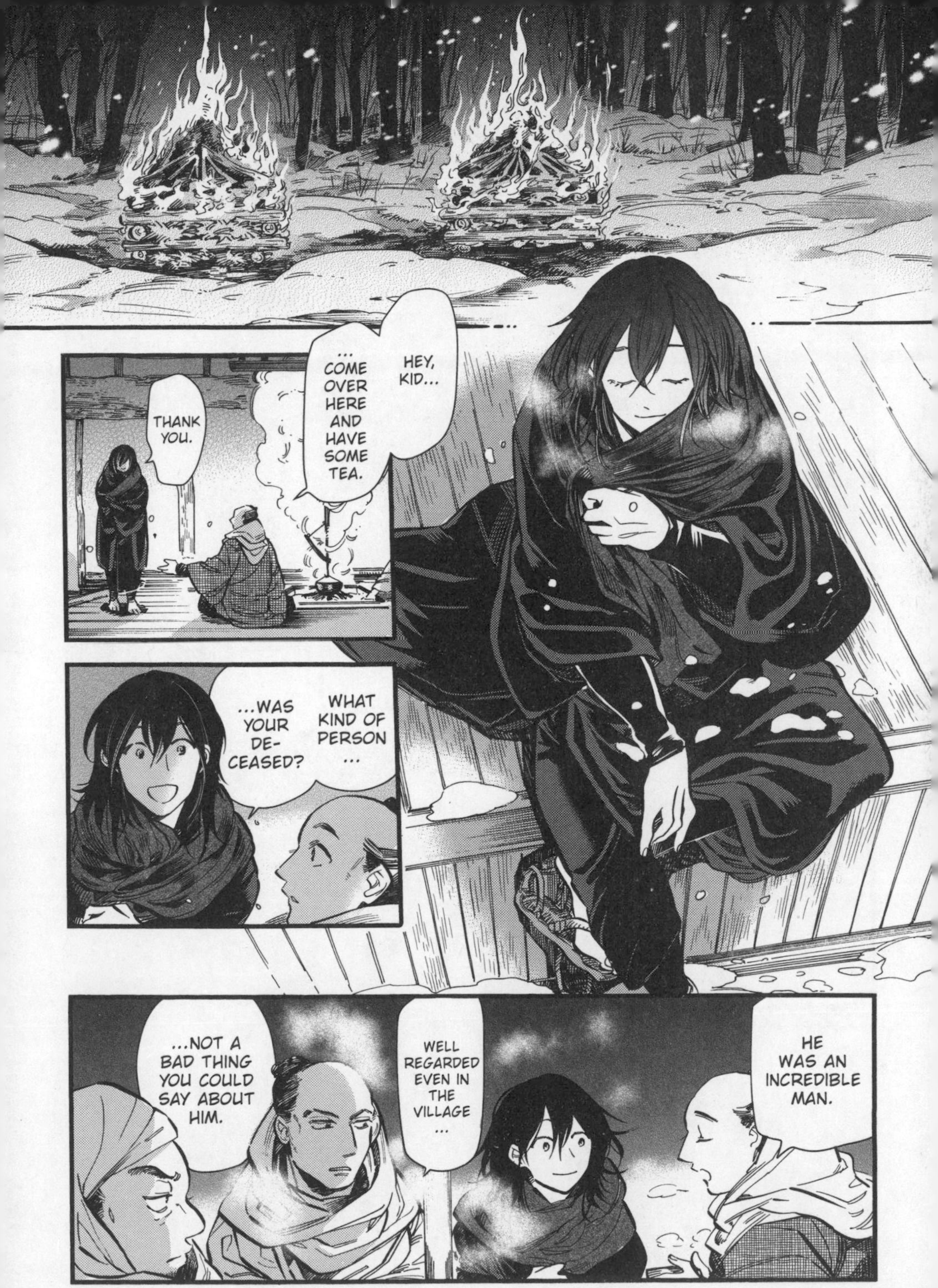
HEY, KID... ...COME OVER HERE AND HAVE SOME TEA.
THANK YOU.
WHAT KIND OF PERSON... ...WAS YOUR DE-CEASED?
HE WAS AN INCREDIBLE MAN.
WELL REGARDED EVEN IN THE VILLAGE...
...NOT A BAD THING YOU COULD SAY ABOUT HIM.

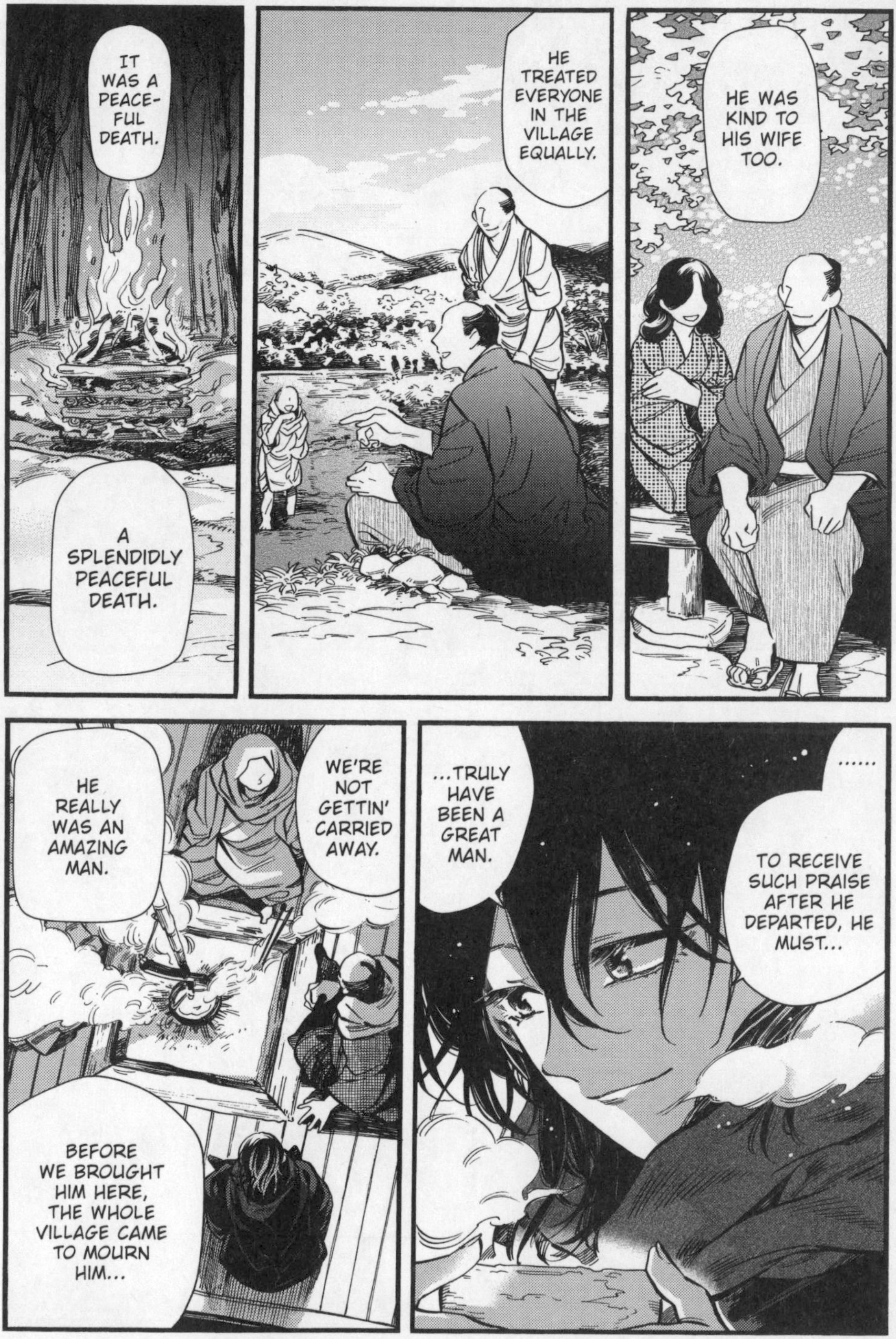
HE WAS KIND TO HIS WIFE TOO.
HE TREATED EVERYONE IN THE VILLAGE EQUALLY.
IT WAS A PEACE-FUL DEATH.
A SPLENDIDLY PEACEFUL DEATH.
......
TO RECEIVE SUCH PRAISE AFTER HE DEPARTED, HE MUST...
...TRULY HAVE BEEN A GREAT MAN.
WE'RE NOT GETTIN' CARRIED AWAY.
HE REALLY WAS AN AMAZING MAN.
BEFORE WE BROUGHT HIM HERE, THE WHOLE VILLAGE CAME TO MOURN HIM...

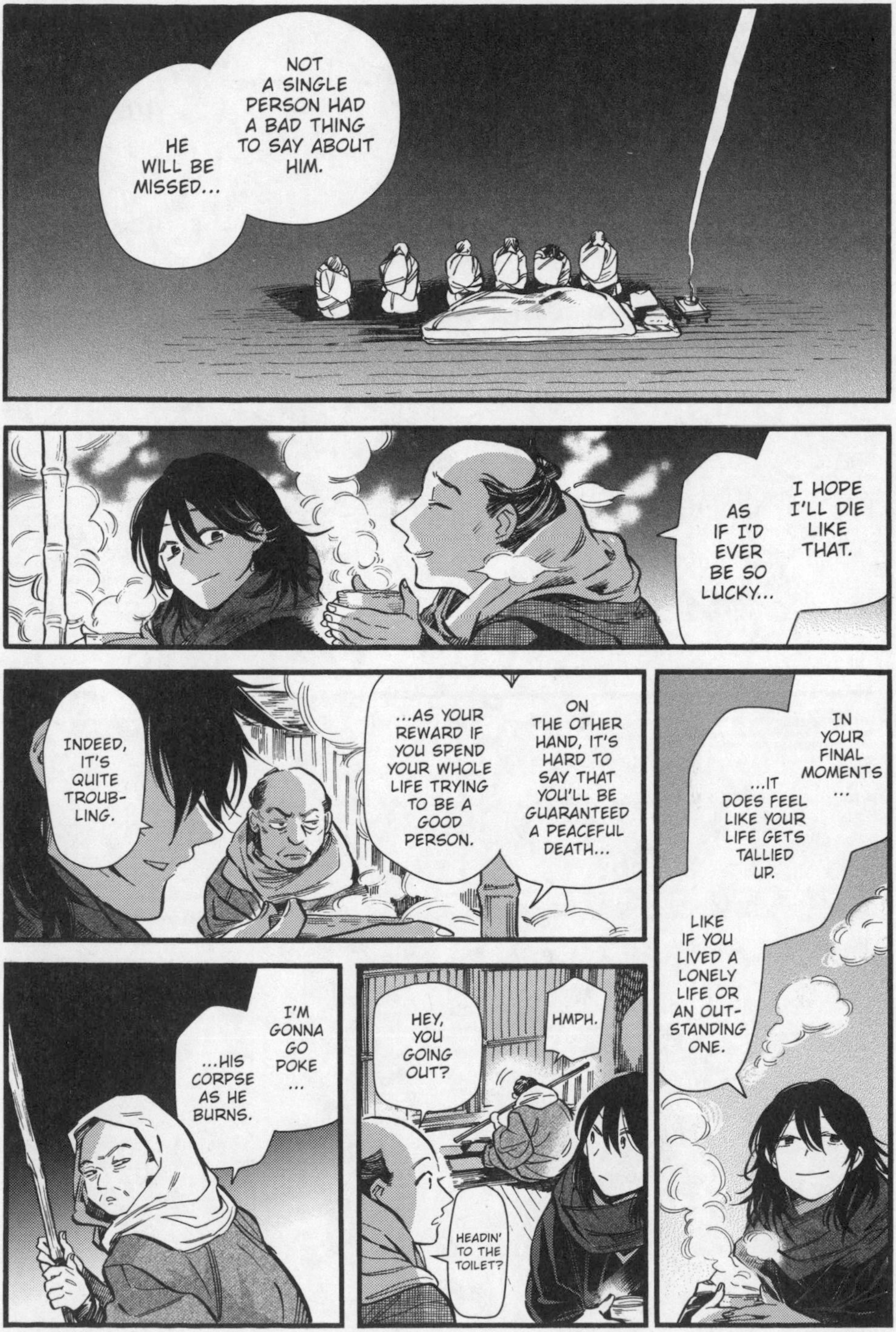
NOT A SINGLE PERSON HAD A BAD THING TO SAY ABOUT HIM.
HE WILL BE MISSED...
I HOPE I'LL DIE LIKE THAT.
AS IF I'D EVER BE SO LUCKY...
IN YOUR FINAL MOMENTS...
...IT DOES FEEL LIKE YOUR LIFE GETS TALLIED UP.
LIKE IF YOU LIVED A LONELY LIFE OR AN OUT-STANDING ONE.
ON THE OTHER HAND, IT'S HARD TO SAY THAT YOU'LL BE GUARANTEED A PEACEFUL DEATH...
...AS YOUR REWARD IF YOU SPEND YOUR WHOLE LIFE TRYING TO BE A GOOD PERSON.
INDEED, IT'S QUITE TROUB-LING.
HMPH.
HEY, YOU GOING OUT?
HEADIN' TO THE TOILET?
I'M GONNA GO POKE...
...HIS CORPSE AS HE BURNS.

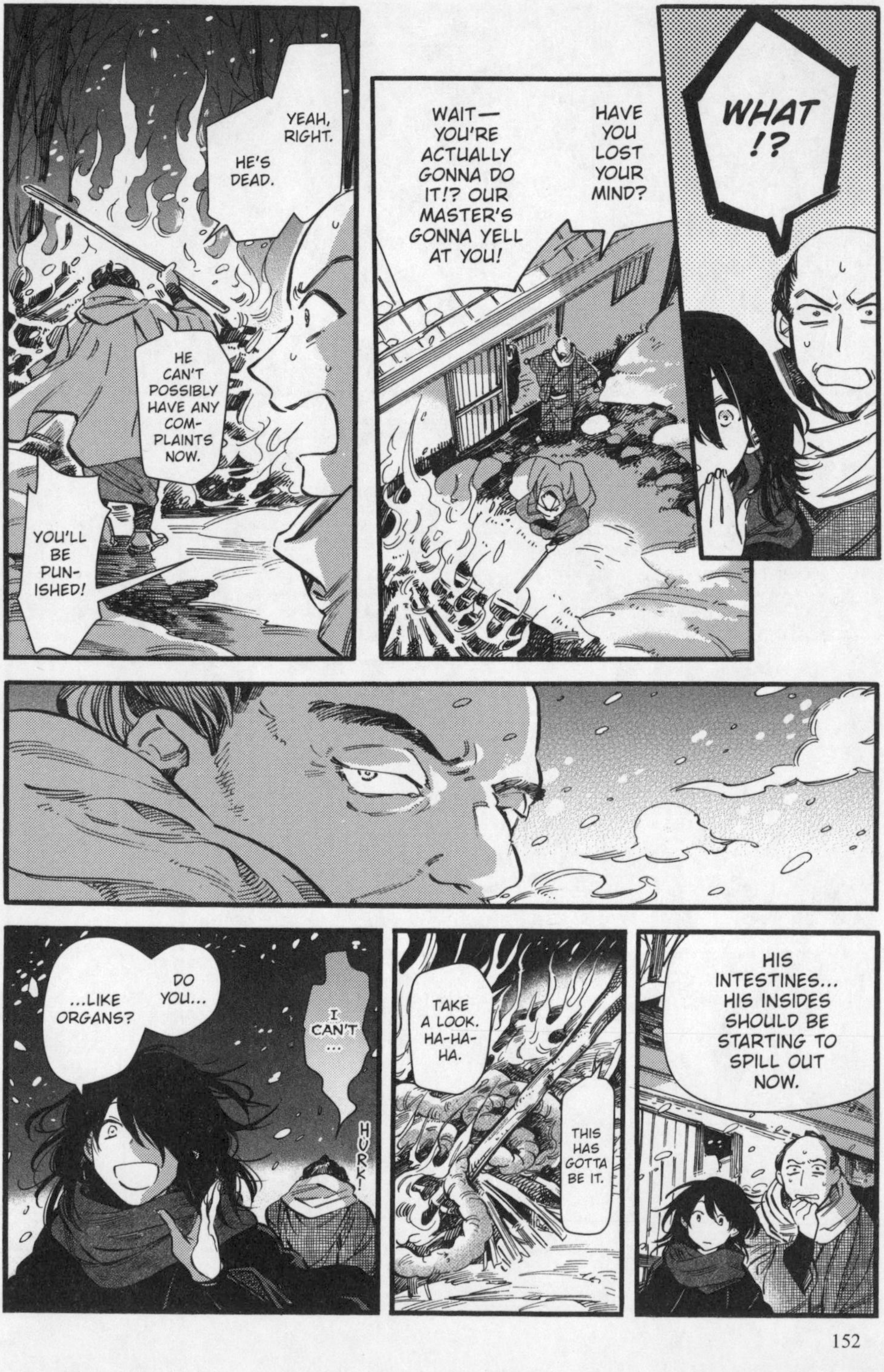
WHAT!?
HAVE YOU LOST YOUR MIND?
WAIT— YOU'RE ACTUALLY GONNA DO IT!? OUR MASTER'S GONNA YELL AT YOU!
YEAH, RIGHT.
HE'S DEAD.
HE CAN'T POSSIBLY HAVE ANY COMPLAINTS NOW.
YOU'LL BE PUNISHED!
HIS INTESTINES... HIS INSIDES SHOULD BE STARTING TO SPILL OUT NOW.
TAKE A LOOK. HA-HA-HA.
THIS HAS GOTTA BE IT.
I CAN'T ...
HURK!
DO YOU...
...LIKE ORGANS?

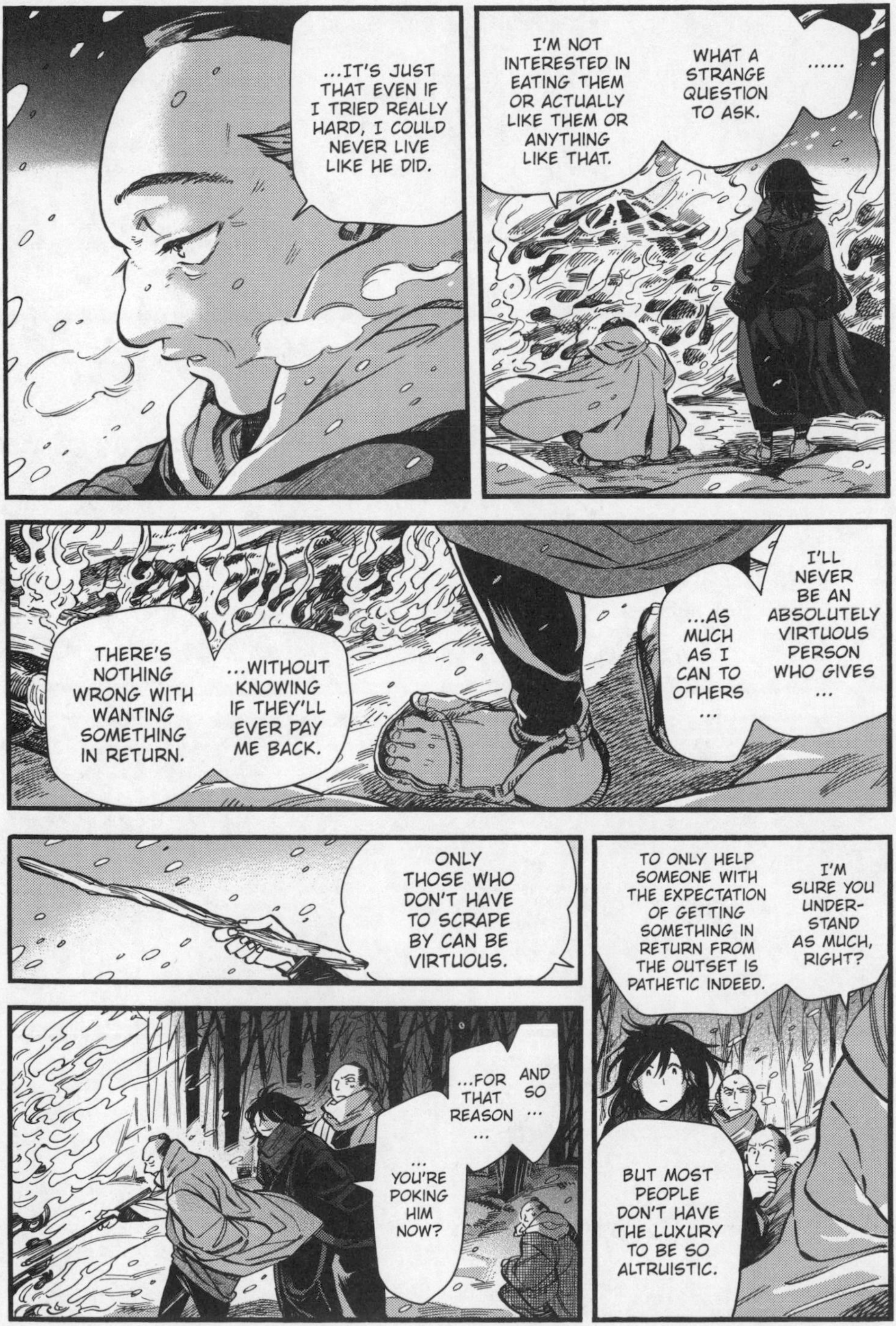
......
WHAT A STRANGE QUESTION TO ASK.
I'M NOT INTERESTED IN EATING THEM OR ACTUALLY LIKE THEM OR ANYTHING LIKE THAT.
...IT'S JUST THAT EVEN IF I TRIED REALLY HARD, I COULD NEVER LIVE LIKE HE DID.
I'LL NEVER BE AN ABSOLUTELY VIRTUOUS PERSON WHO GIVES ...
...AS MUCH AS I CAN TO OTHERS ...
...WITHOUT KNOWING IF THEY'LL EVER PAY ME BACK.
THERE'S NOTHING WRONG WITH WANTING SOMETHING IN RETURN.
I'M SURE YOU UNDERSTAND AS MUCH, RIGHT?
TO ONLY HELP SOMEONE WITH THE EXPECTATION OF GETTING SOMETHING IN RETURN FROM THE OUTSET IS PATHETIC INDEED.
BUT MOST PEOPLE DON'T HAVE THE LUXURY TO BE SO ALTRUISTIC.
ONLY THOSE WHO DON'T HAVE TO SCRAPE BY CAN BE VIRTUOUS.
AND SO ...
...FOR THAT REASON ...
... YOU'RE POKING HIM NOW?

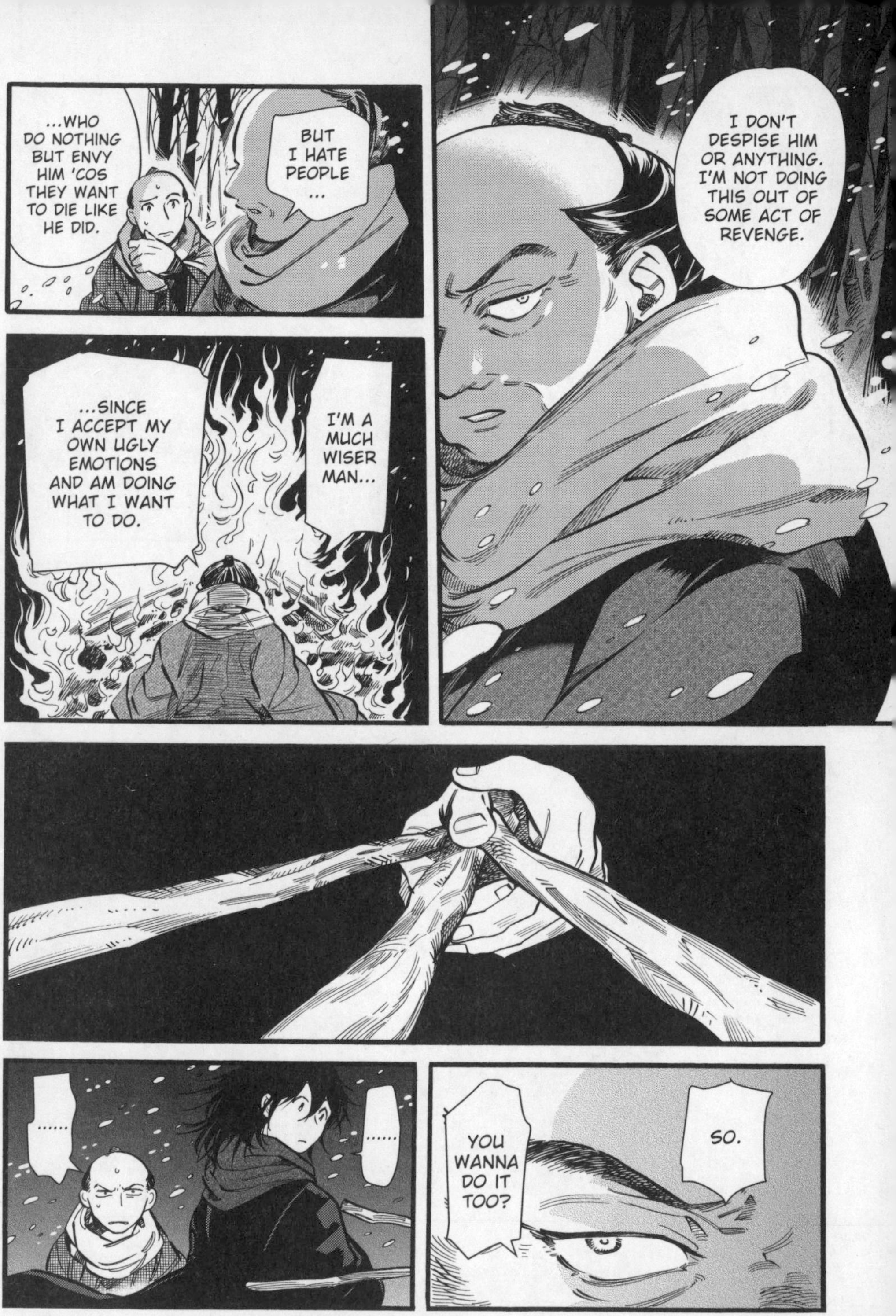
I DON'T DESPISE HIM OR ANYTHING. I'M NOT DOING THIS OUT OF SOME ACT OF REVENGE.
BUT I HATE PEOPLE ...
...WHO DO NOTHING BUT ENVY HIM 'COS THEY WANT TO DIE LIKE HE DID.
I'M A MUCH WISER MAN...
...SINCE I ACCEPT MY OWN UGLY EMOTIONS AND AM DOING WHAT I WANT TO DO.
SO.
YOU WANNA DO IT TOO?
......
......

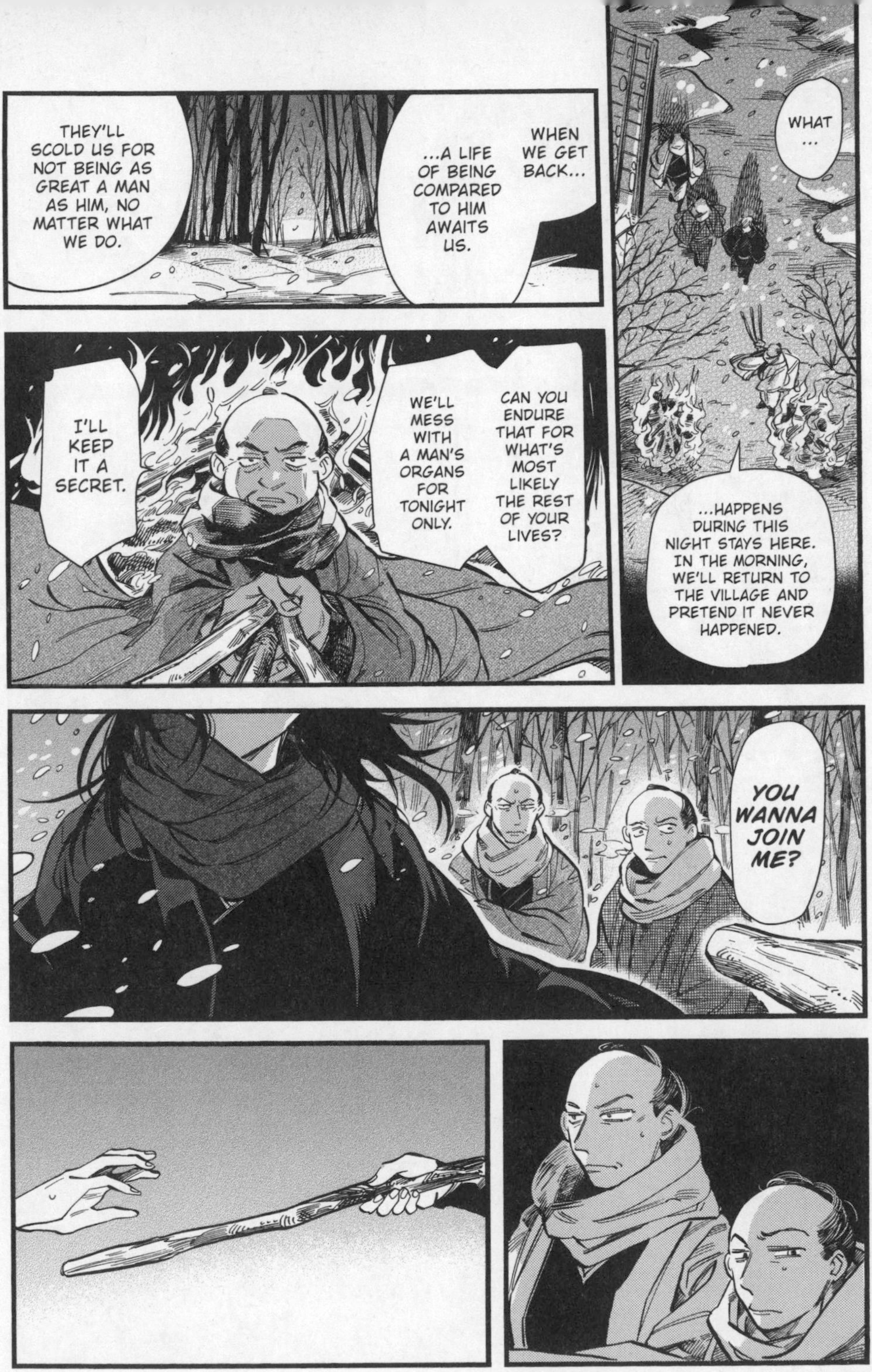
WHAT ...
...HAPPENS DURING THIS NIGHT STAYS HERE. IN THE MORNING, WE'LL RETURN TO THE VILLAGE AND PRETEND IT NEVER HAPPENED.
WHEN WE GET BACK...
...A LIFE OF BEING COMPARED TO HIM AWAITS US.
THEY'LL SCOLD US FOR NOT BEING AS GREAT A MAN AS HIM, NO MATTER WHAT WE DO.
CAN YOU ENDURE THAT FOR WHAT'S MOST LIKELY THE REST OF YOUR LIVES?
WE'LL MESS WITH A MAN'S ORGANS FOR TONIGHT ONLY.
I'LL KEEP IT A SECRET.
YOU WANNA JOIN ME?

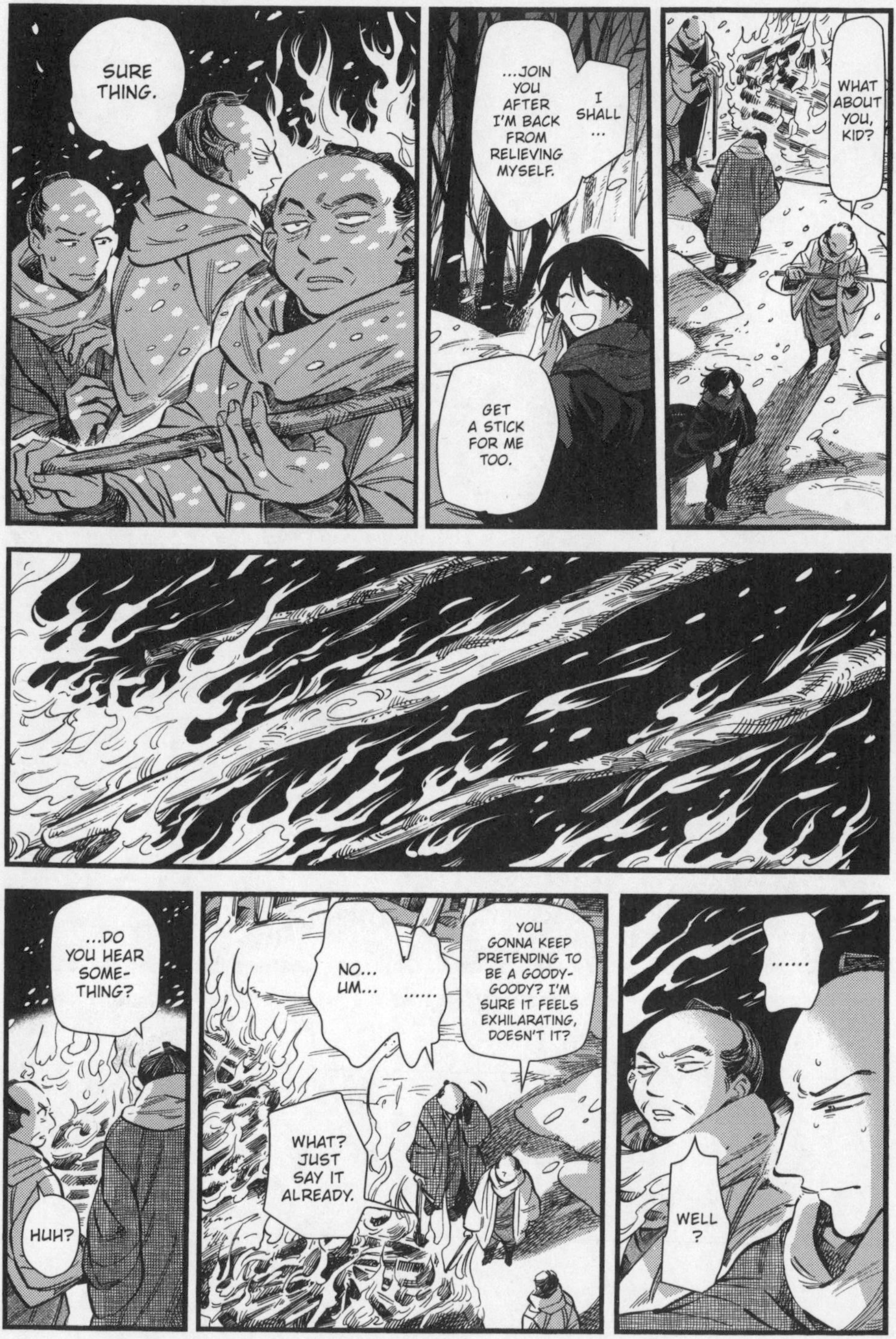
WHAT ABOUT YOU, KID?
I SHALL ...
...JOIN YOU AFTER I'M BACK FROM RELIEVING MYSELF.
GET A STICK FOR ME TOO.
SURE THING.
......
WELL ?
YOU GONNA KEEP PRETENDING TO BE A GOODY-GOODY? I'M SURE IT FEELS EXHILARATING, DOESN'T IT?
......
NO... UM...
WHAT? JUST SAY IT ALREADY.
...DO YOU HEAR SOME-THING?
HUH?

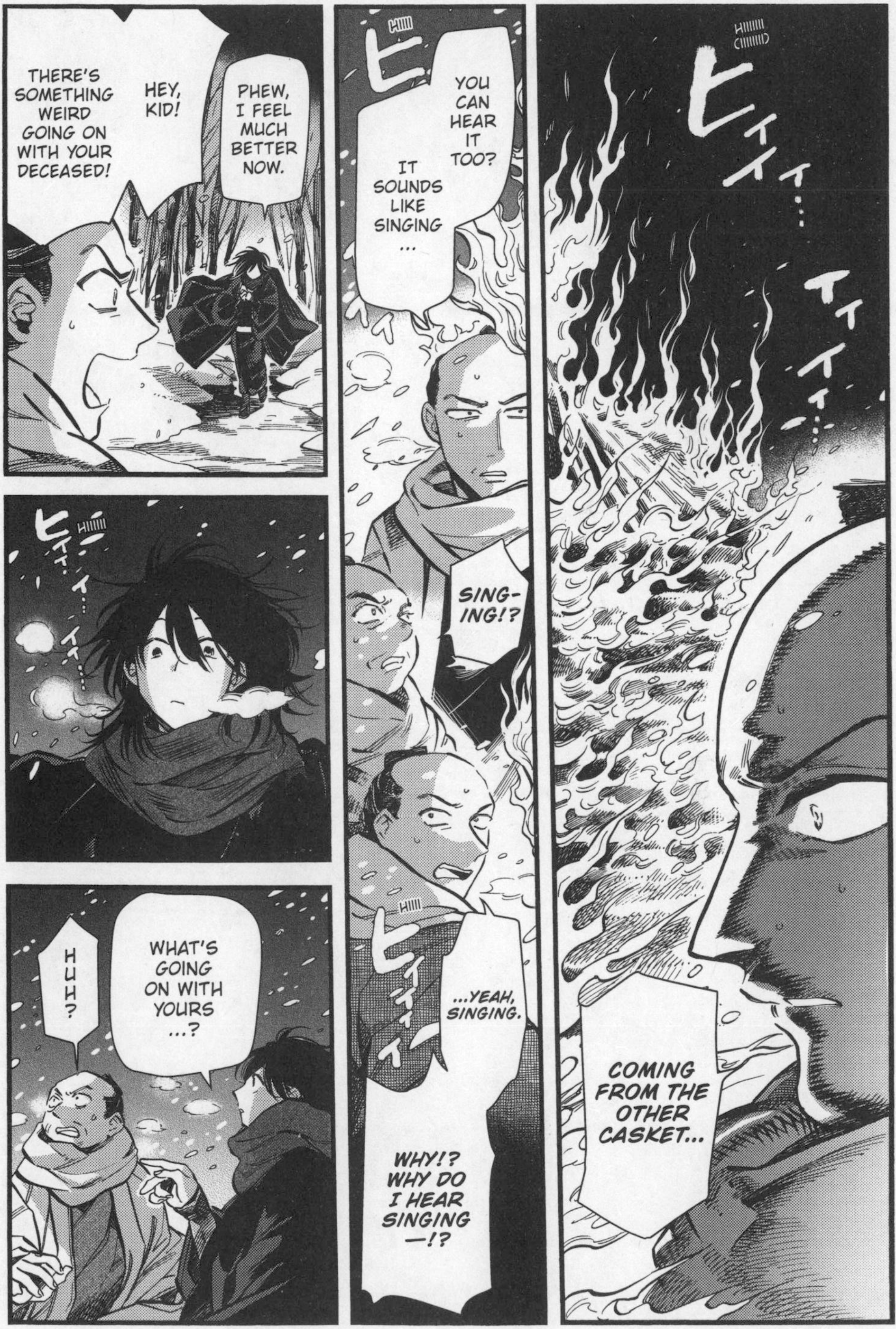
HIIIIII
COMING FROM THE OTHER CASKET...
HIIII
YOU CAN HEAR IT TOO?
IT SOUNDS LIKE SINGING...
SINGING!?
HIIII
...YEAH, SINGING.
WHY!? WHY DO I HEAR SINGING—!?
PHEW, I FEEL MUCH BETTER NOW.
HEY, KID!
THERE'S SOMETHING WEIRD GOING ON WITH YOUR DECEASED!
HIIIIII
WHAT'S GOING ON WITH YOURS...?
HUH?

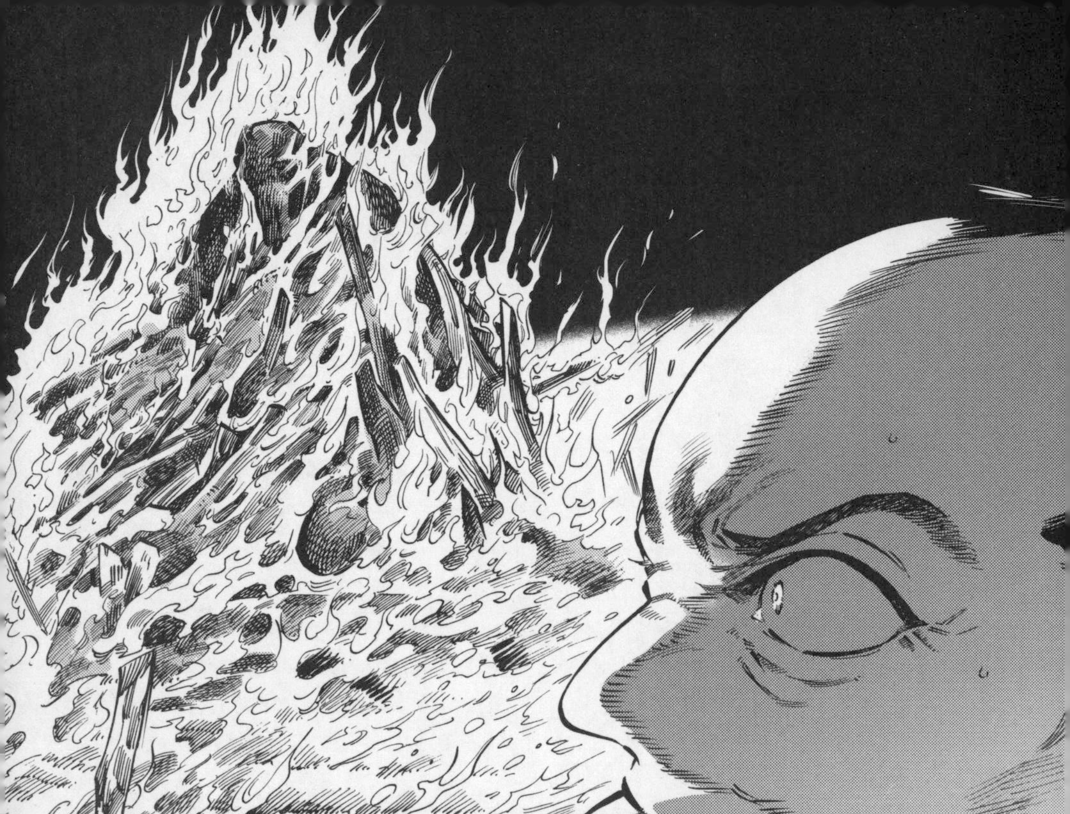
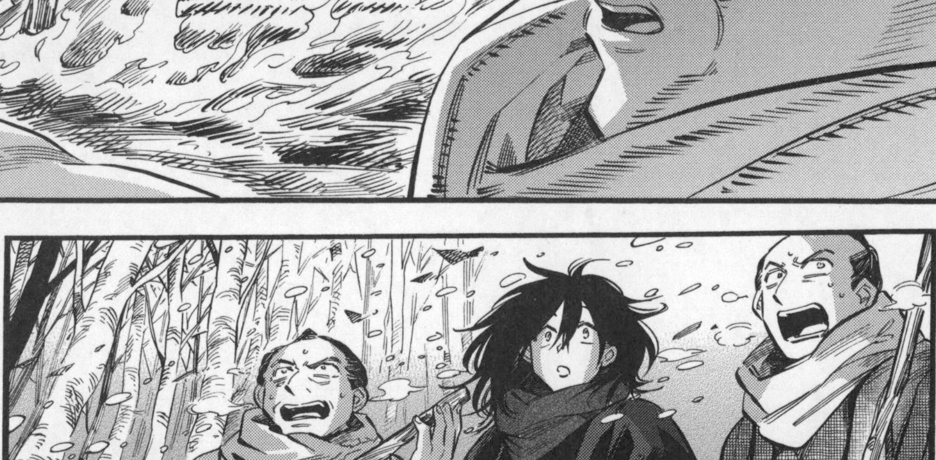

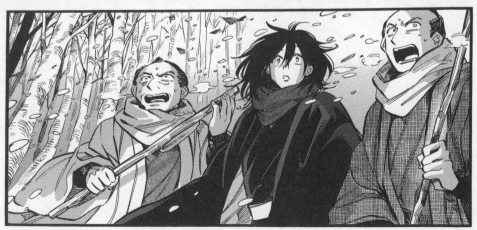

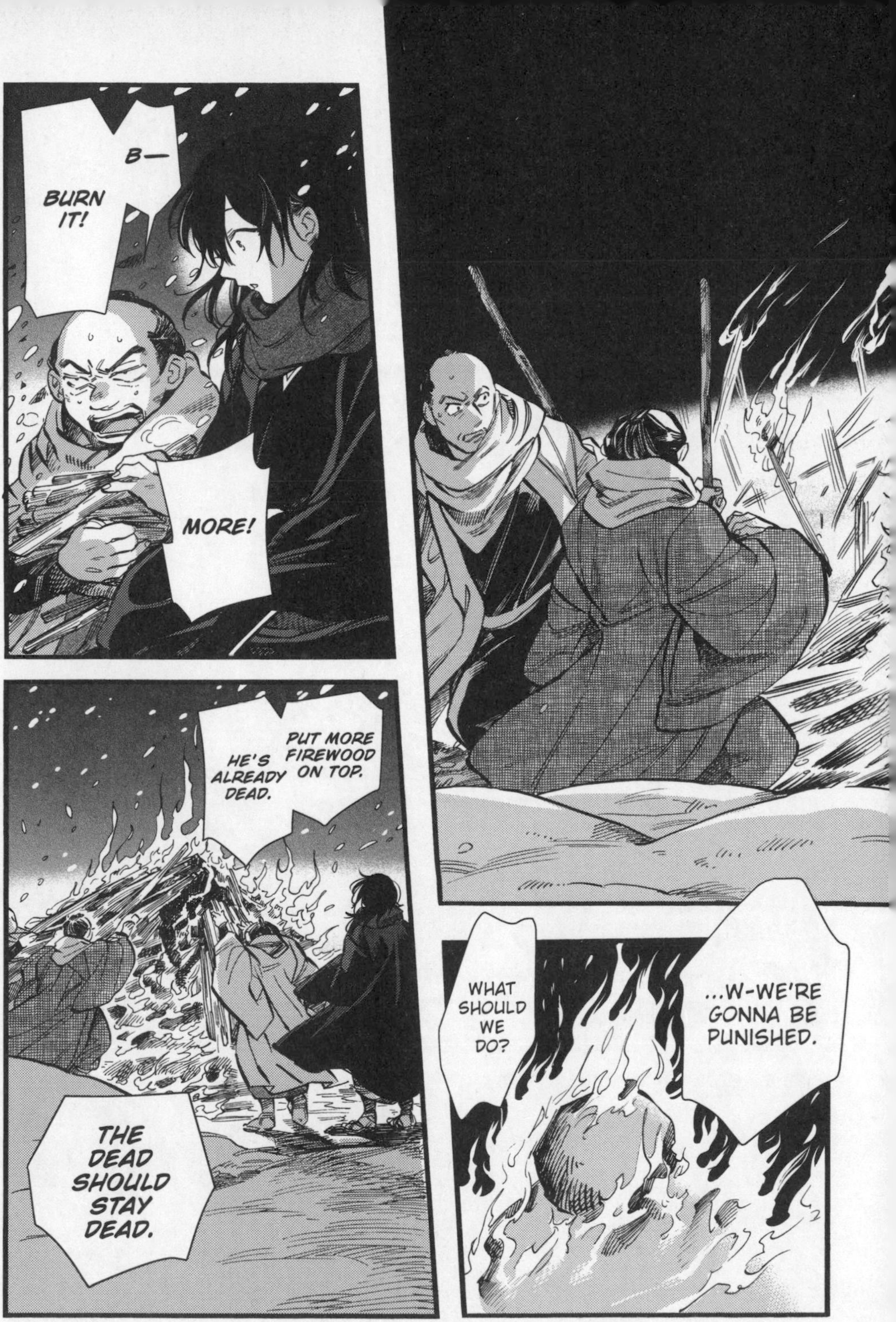
B—
BURN IT!
MORE!
PUT MORE FIREWOOD ON TOP.
HE'S ALREADY DEAD.
THE DEAD SHOULD STAY DEAD.
...W-WE'RE GONNA BE PUNISHED.
WHAT SHOULD WE DO?

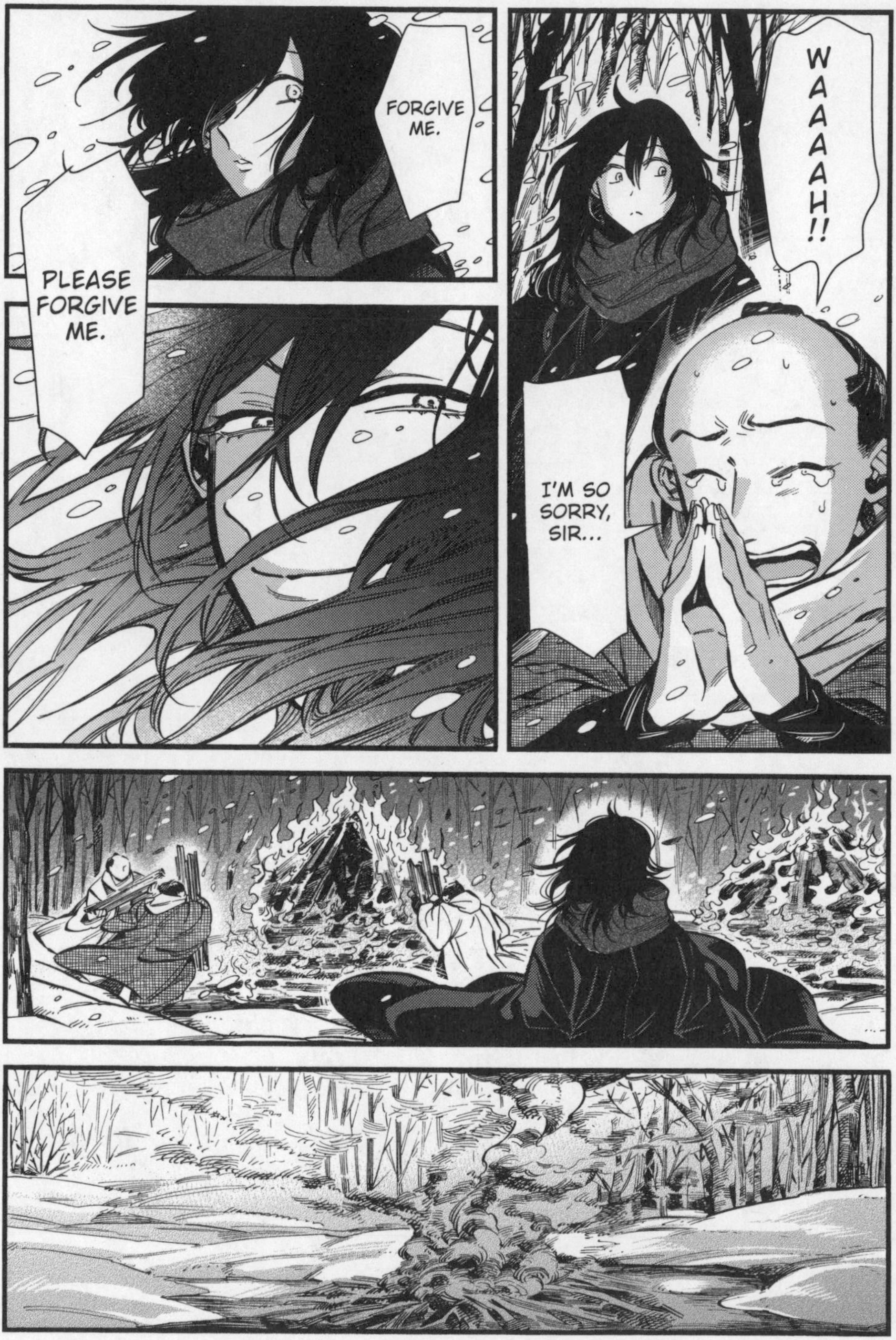
WAAAAAH!!
I'M SO SORRY, SIR...
FORGIVE ME.
PLEASE FORGIVE ME.

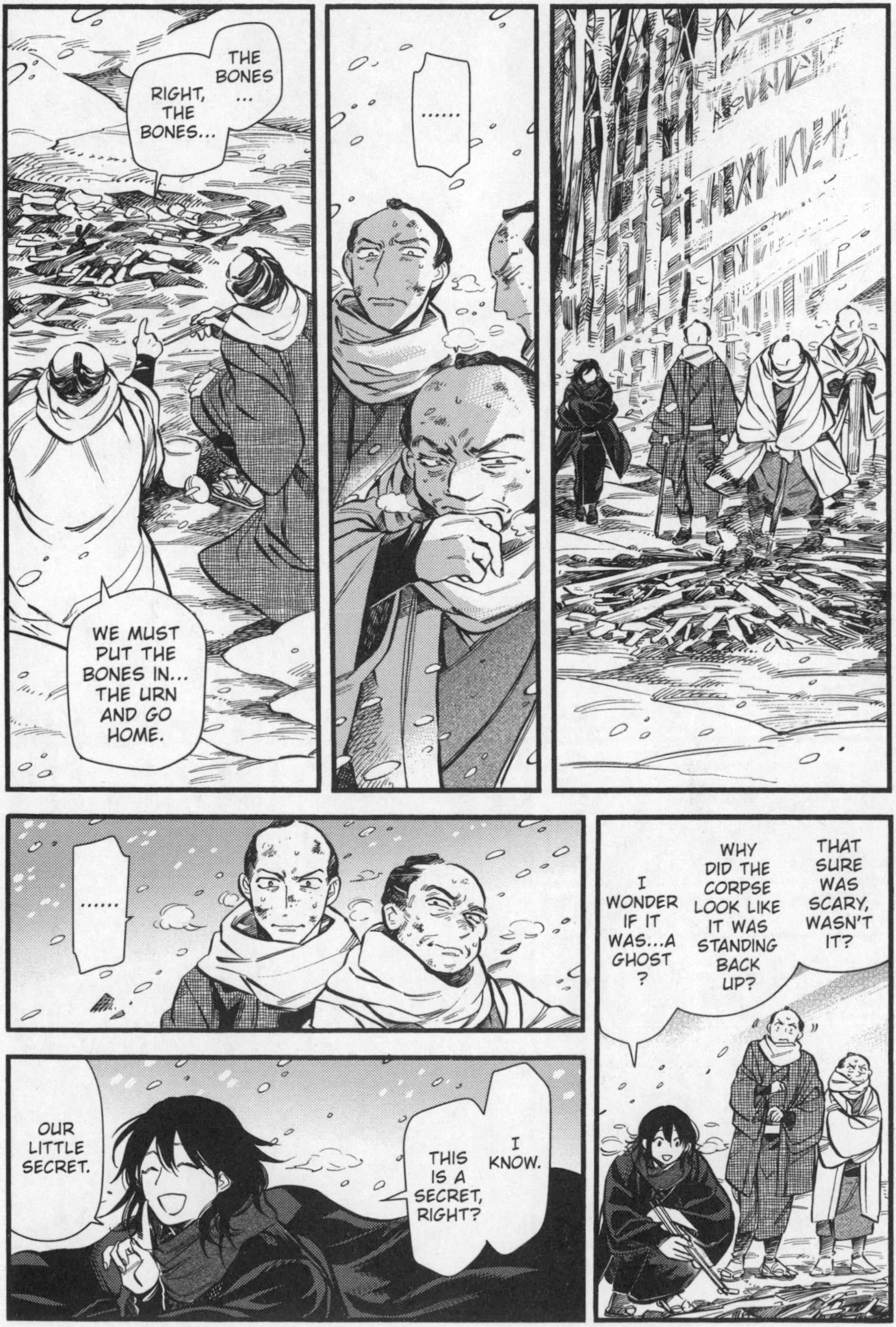
......
THE BONES... RIGHT, THE BONES...
WE MUST PUT THE BONES IN... THE URN AND GO HOME.
THAT SURE WAS SCARY, WASN'T IT?
WHY DID THE CORPSE LOOK LIKE IT WAS STANDING BACK UP?
I WONDER IF IT WAS...A GHOST?
......
I KNOW.
THIS IS A SECRET, RIGHT?
OUR LITTLE SECRET.

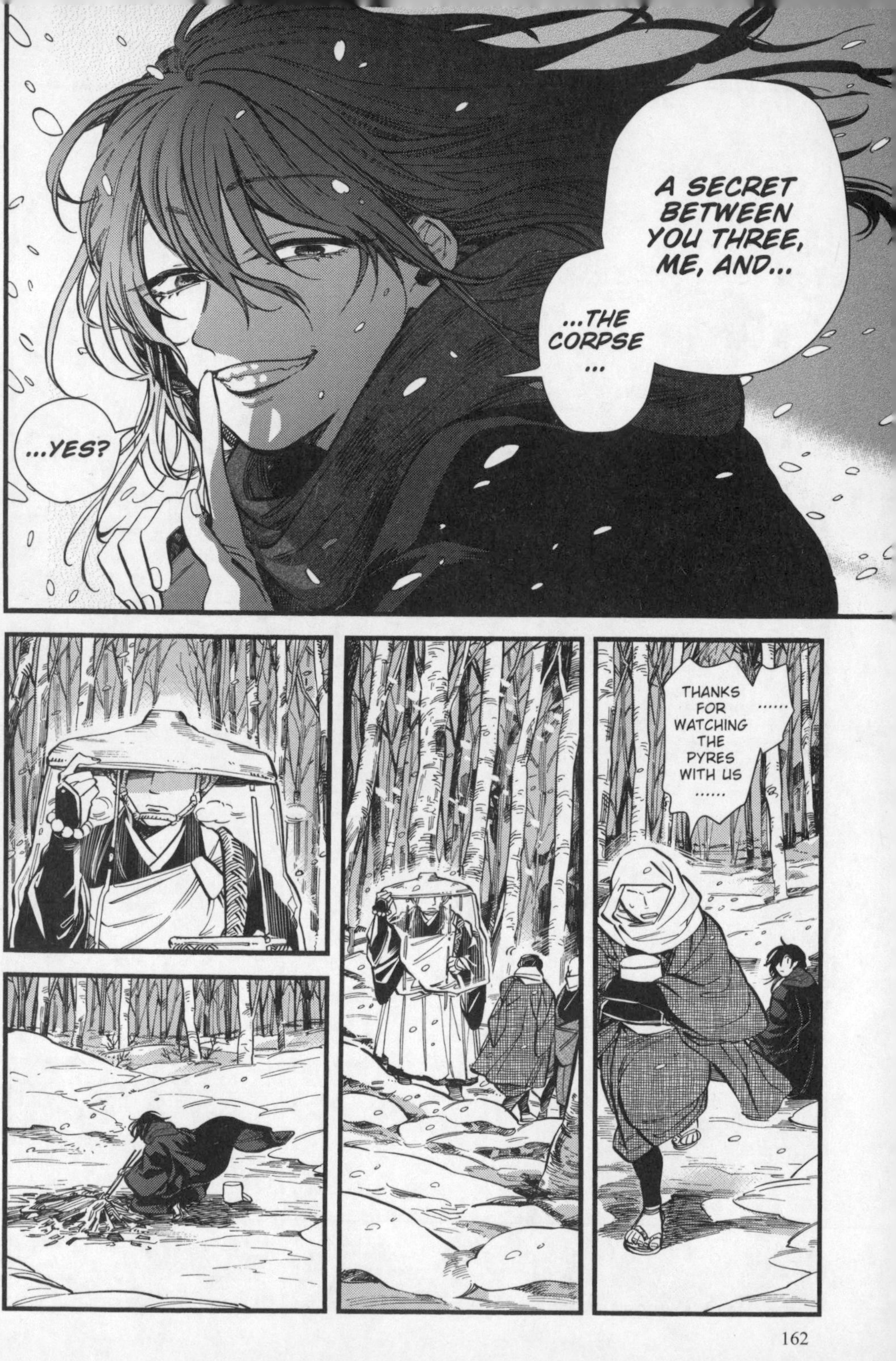
A SECRET BETWEEN YOU THREE, ME, AND...
...THE CORPSE ...
...YES?
......
THANKS FOR WATCHING THE PYRES WITH US ......

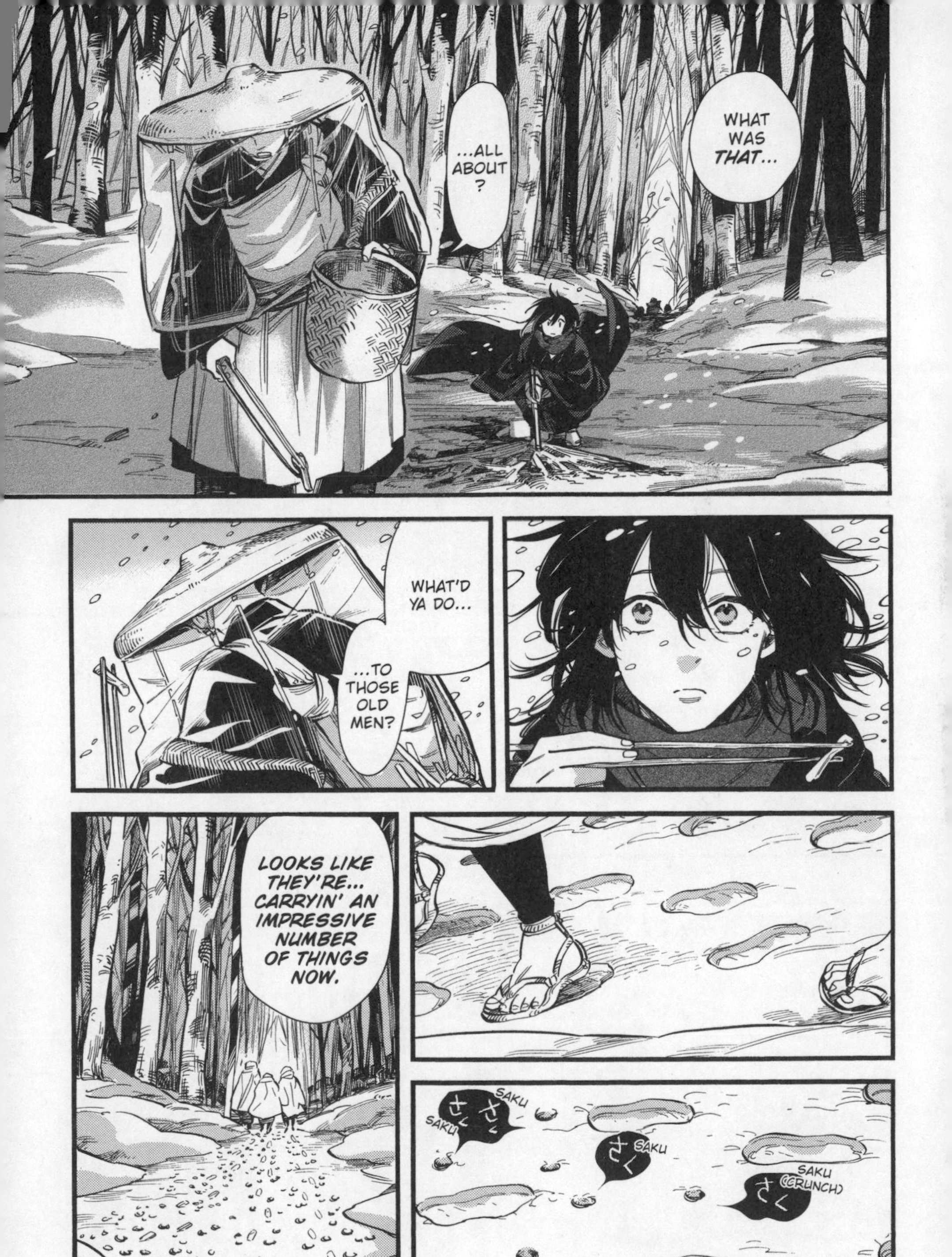
WHAT WAS THAT...
...ALL ABOUT?
WHAT'D YA DO...
...TO THOSE OLD MEN?
さく SAKU (CRUNCH)
さく SAKU
さく SAKU
さく SAKU
LOOKS LIKE THEY'RE... CARRYIN' AN IMPRESSIVE NUMBER OF THINGS NOW.

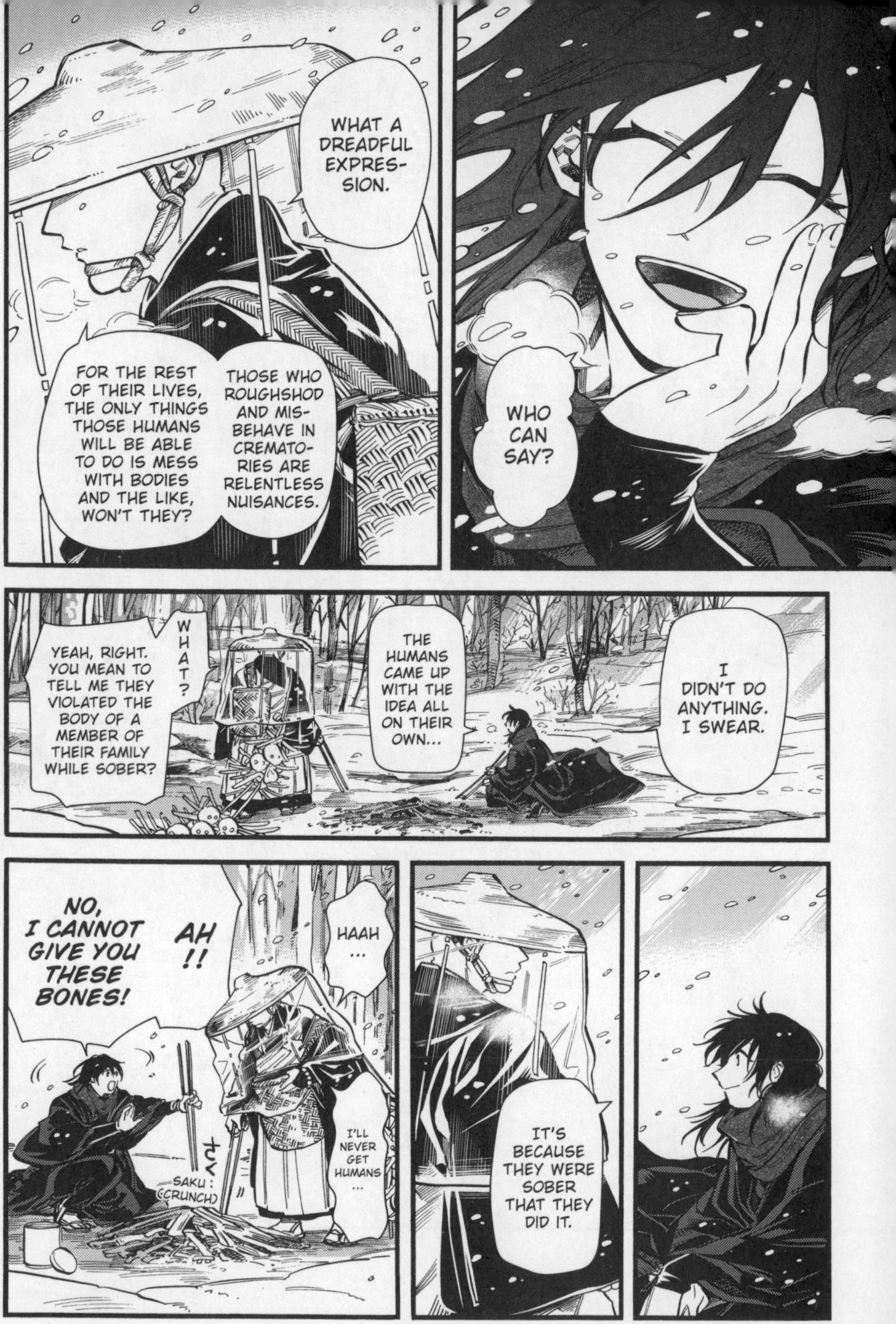
WHO CAN SAY?
WHAT A DREADFUL EXPRESSION.
THOSE WHO ROUGHSHOD AND MISBEHAVE IN CREMATORIES ARE RELENTLESS NUISANCES.
FOR THE REST OF THEIR LIVES, THE ONLY THINGS THOSE HUMANS WILL BE ABLE TO DO IS MESS WITH BODIES AND THE LIKE, WON'T THEY?
I DIDN'T DO ANYTHING. I SWEAR.
THE HUMANS CAME UP WITH THE IDEA ALL ON THEIR OWN...
WHAT?
YEAH, RIGHT. YOU MEAN TO TELL ME THEY VIOLATED THE BODY OF A MEMBER OF THEIR FAMILY WHILE SOBER?
IT'S BECAUSE THEY WERE SOBER THAT THEY DID IT.
HAAH ...
AH !!
NO, I CANNOT GIVE YOU THESE BONES!
I'LL NEVER GET HUMANS ...
サク
SAKU: (CRUNCH)

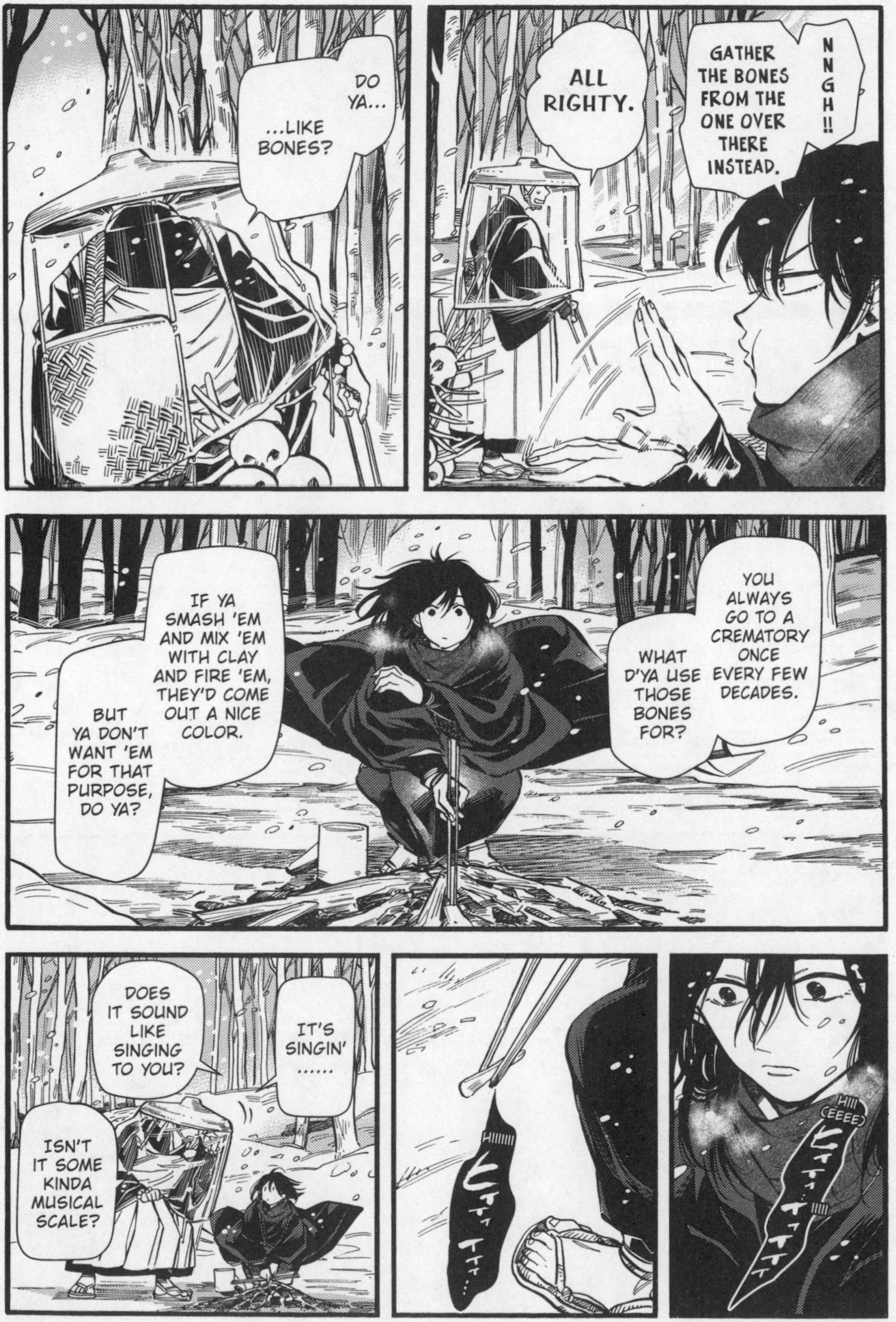

NNGH!!
GATHER THE BONES FROM THE ONE OVER THERE INSTEAD.
ALL RIGHTY.
DO YA...
...LIKE BONES?
YOU ALWAYS GO TO A CREMATORY ONCE EVERY FEW DECADES.
WHAT D'YA USE THOSE BONES FOR?
IF YA SMASH 'EM AND MIX 'EM WITH CLAY AND FIRE 'EM, THEY'D COME OUT A NICE COLOR.
BUT YA DON'T WANT 'EM FOR THAT PURPOSE, DO YA?
HIII (EEEE)
HIIIIII
IT'S SINGIN' ......
DOES IT SOUND LIKE SINGING TO YOU?
ISN'T IT SOME KINDA MUSICAL SCALE?

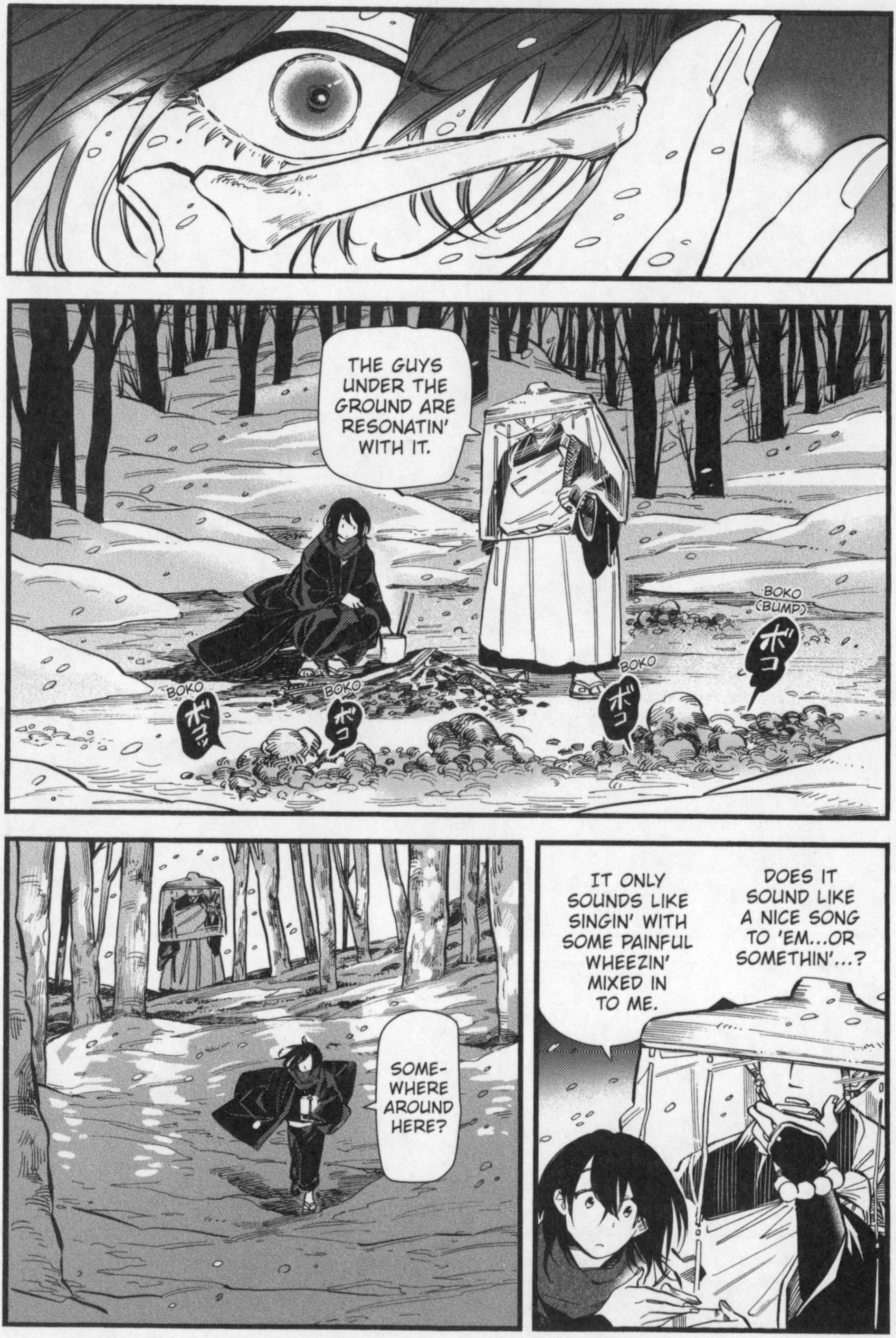
THE GUYS UNDER THE GROUND ARE RESONATIN' WITH IT.
BOKO (BUMP)
ボコ
BOKO
ボコ
BOKO
ボコ
BOKO
ボコッ
DOES IT SOUND LIKE A NICE SONG TO 'EM...OR SOMETHIN'...?
IT ONLY SOUNDS LIKE SINGIN' WITH SOME PAINFUL WHEEZIN' MIXED IN TO ME.
SOME-WHERE AROUND HERE?

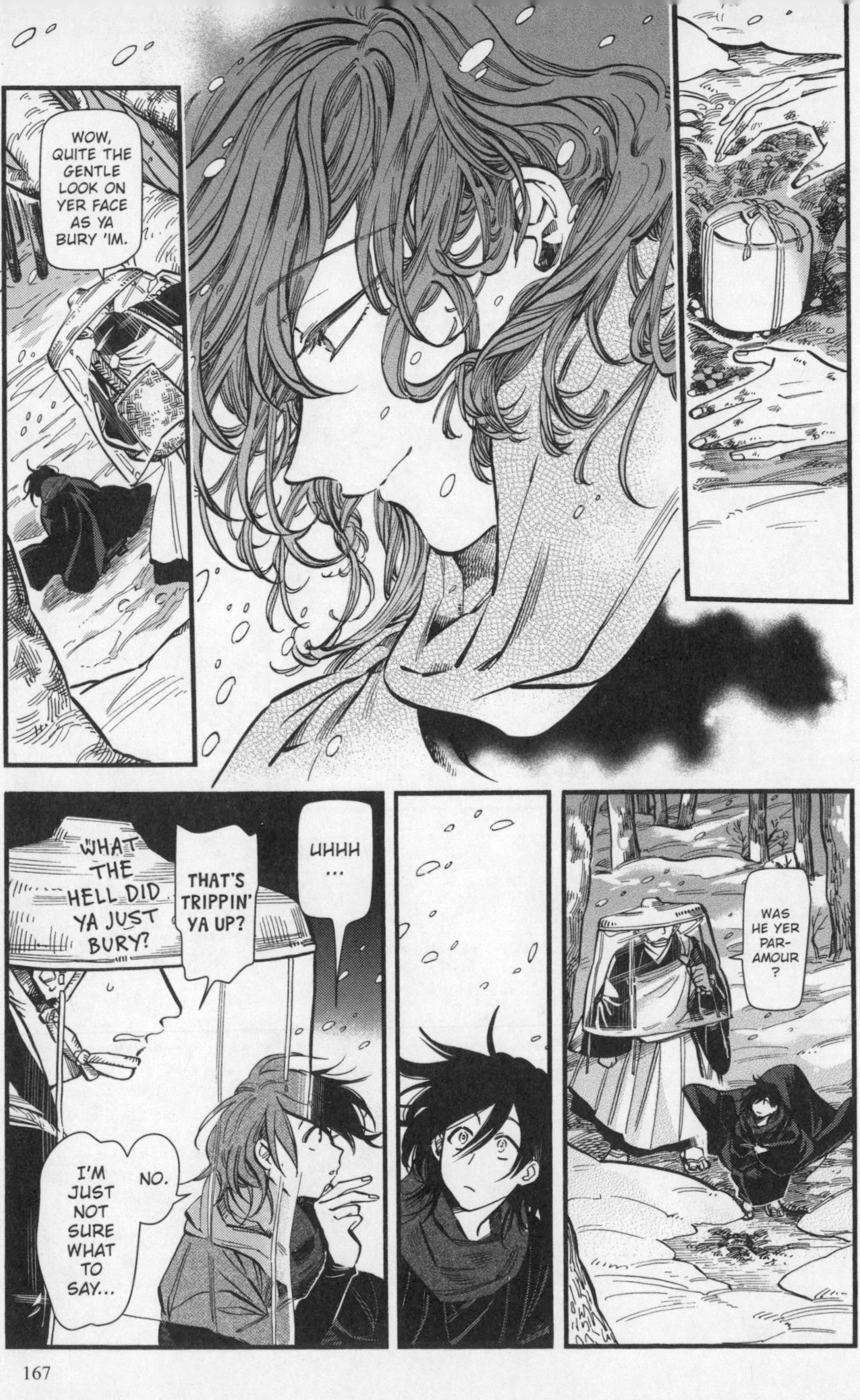
WOW, QUITE THE GENTLE LOOK ON YER FACE AS YA BURY 'IM.
WAS HE YER PAR-AMOUR?
UHHH...
THAT'S TRIPPIN' YA UP?
WHAT THE HELL DID YA JUST BURY?
NO.
I'M JUST NOT SURE WHAT TO SAY...

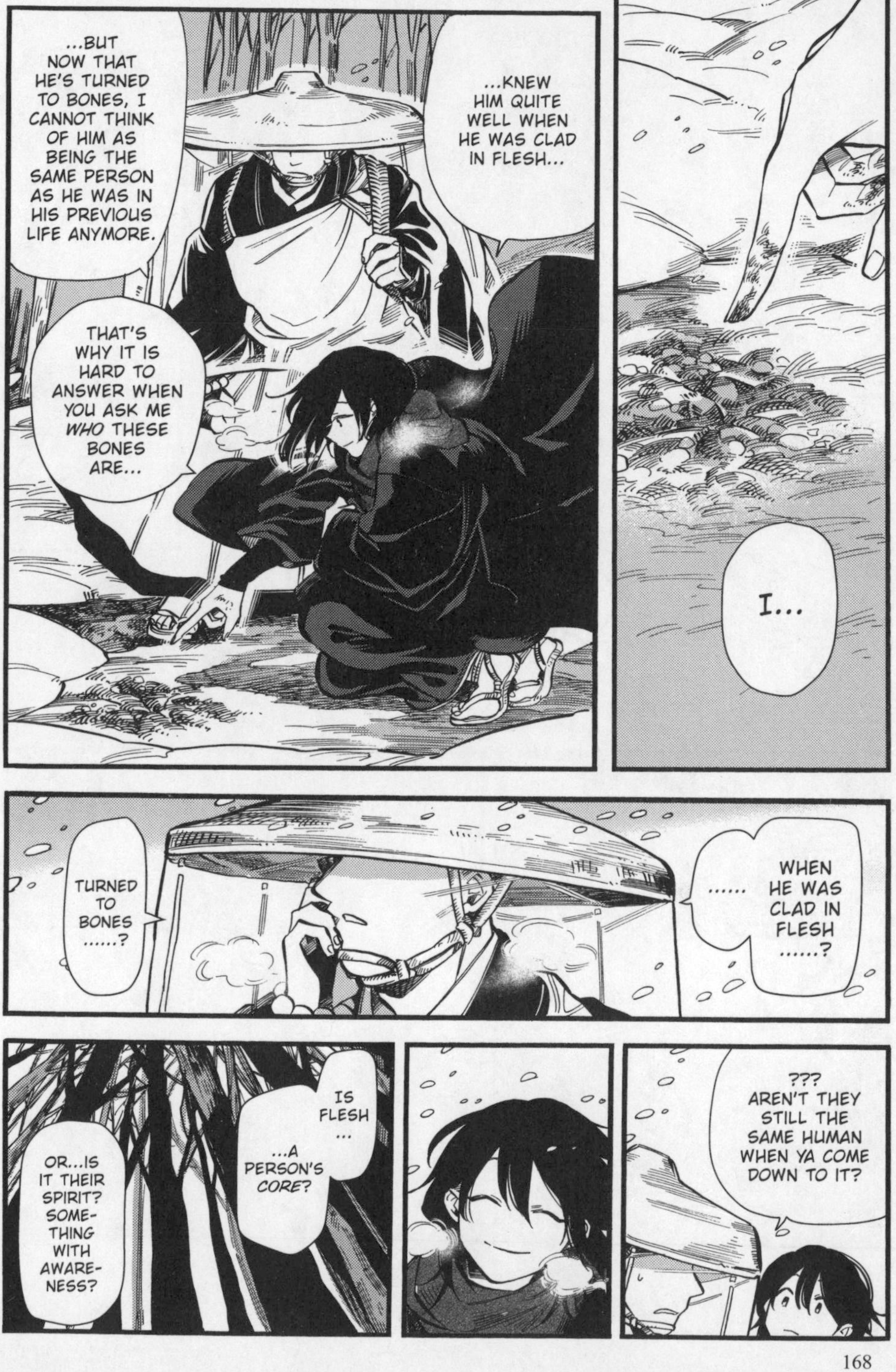
I...
...KNEW HIM QUITE WELL WHEN HE WAS CLAD IN FLESH...
...BUT NOW THAT HE'S TURNED TO BONES, I CANNOT THINK OF HIM AS BEING THE SAME PERSON AS HE WAS IN HIS PREVIOUS LIFE ANYMORE.
THAT'S WHY IT IS HARD TO ANSWER WHEN YOU ASK ME *WHO* THESE BONES ARE...
...... WHEN HE WAS CLAD IN FLESH ......?
TURNED TO BONES ......?
??? AREN'T THEY STILL THE SAME HUMAN WHEN YA COME DOWN TO IT?
IS FLESH ... ...A PERSON'S CORE?
OR...IS IT THEIR SPIRIT? SOMETHING WITH AWARENESS?

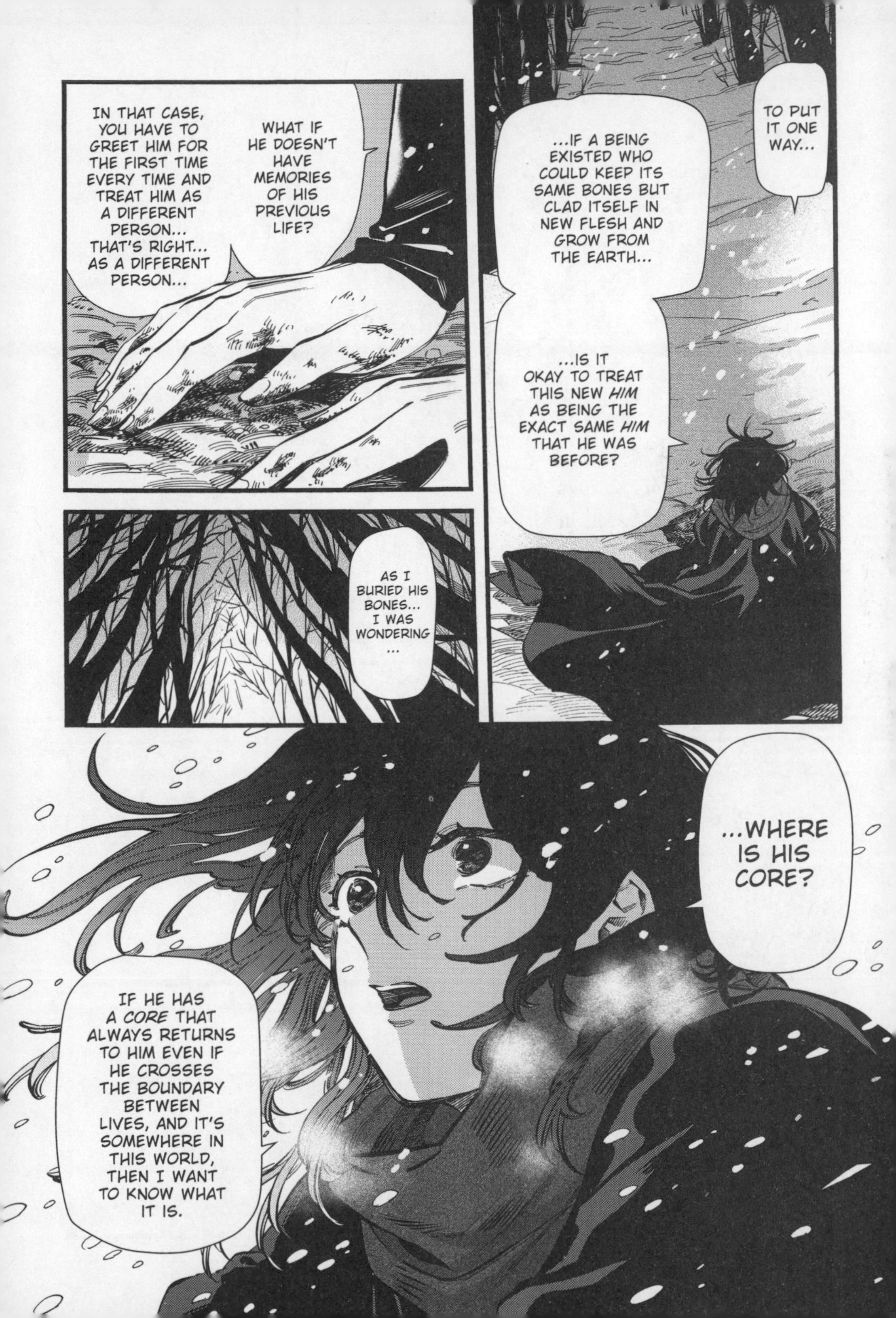
TO PUT IT ONE WAY...
...IF A BEING EXISTED WHO COULD KEEP ITS SAME BONES BUT CLAD ITSELF IN NEW FLESH AND GROW FROM THE EARTH...
...IS IT OKAY TO TREAT THIS NEW *HIM* AS BEING THE EXACT SAME *HIM* THAT HE WAS BEFORE?
WHAT IF HE DOESN'T HAVE MEMORIES OF HIS PREVIOUS LIFE?
IN THAT CASE, YOU HAVE TO GREET HIM FOR THE FIRST TIME EVERY TIME AND TREAT HIM AS A DIFFERENT PERSON... THAT'S RIGHT... AS A DIFFERENT PERSON...
AS I BURIED HIS BONES... I WAS WONDERING...
...WHERE IS HIS CORE?
IF HE HAS A *CORE* THAT ALWAYS RETURNS TO HIM EVEN IF HE CROSSES THE BOUNDARY BETWEEN LIVES, AND IT'S SOMEWHERE IN THIS WORLD, THEN I WANT TO KNOW WHAT IT IS.

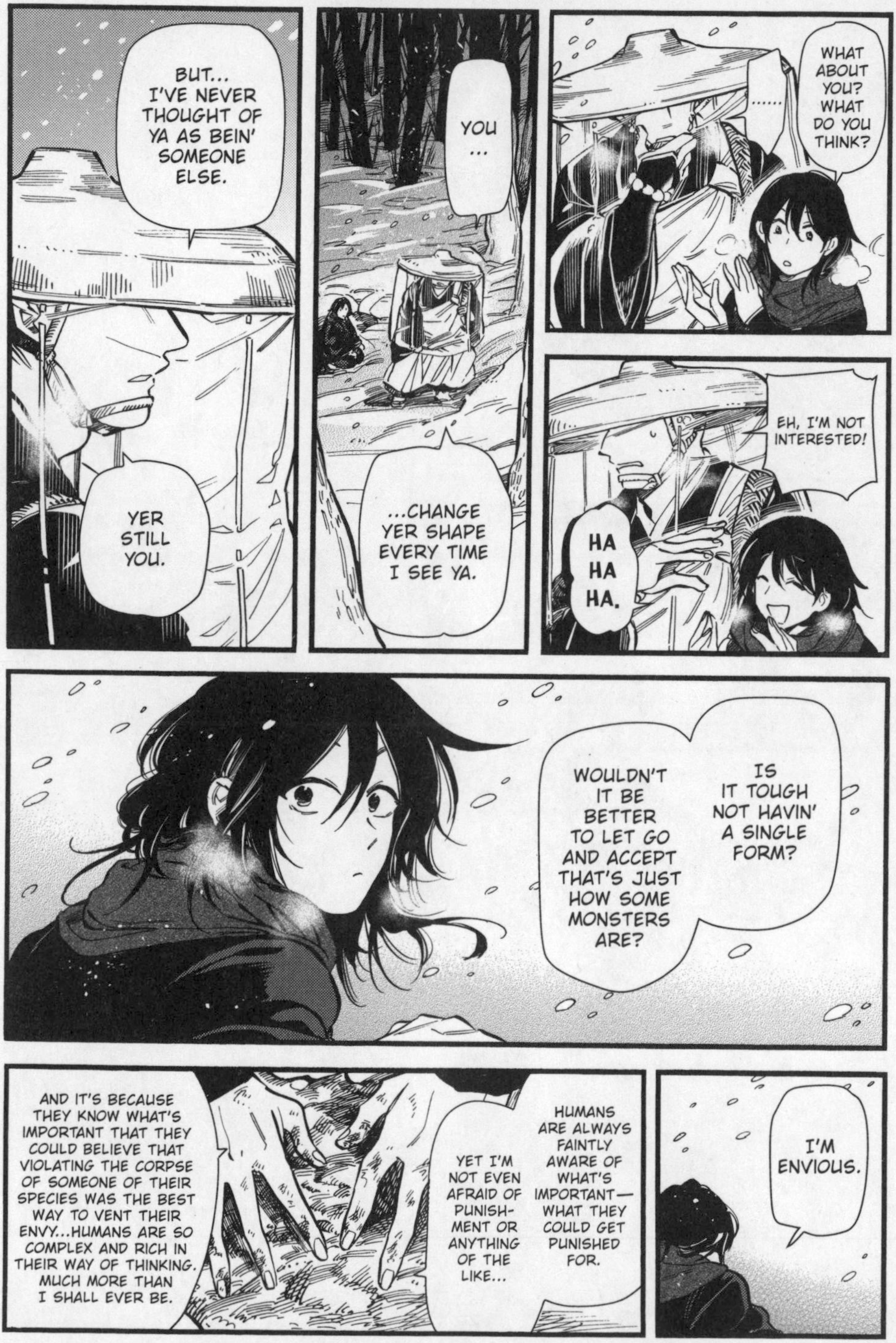
WHAT ABOUT YOU? WHAT DO YOU THINK?
......
EH, I'M NOT INTERESTED!
HA HA HA.
YOU ...
...CHANGE YER SHAPE EVERY TIME I SEE YA.
BUT... I'VE NEVER THOUGHT OF YA AS BEIN' SOMEONE ELSE.
YER STILL YOU.
IS IT TOUGH NOT HAVIN' A SINGLE FORM?
WOULDN'T IT BE BETTER TO LET GO AND ACCEPT THAT'S JUST HOW SOME MONSTERS ARE?
I'M ENVIOUS.
HUMANS ARE ALWAYS FAINTLY AWARE OF WHAT'S IMPORTANT—WHAT THEY COULD GET PUNISHED FOR.
YET I'M NOT EVEN AFRAID OF PUNISH-MENT OR ANYTHING OF THE LIKE...
AND IT'S BECAUSE THEY KNOW WHAT'S IMPORTANT THAT THEY COULD BELIEVE THAT VIOLATING THE CORPSE OF SOMEONE OF THEIR SPECIES WAS THE BEST WAY TO VENT THEIR ENVY...HUMANS ARE SO COMPLEX AND RICH IN THEIR WAY OF THINKING. MUCH MORE THAN I SHALL EVER BE.

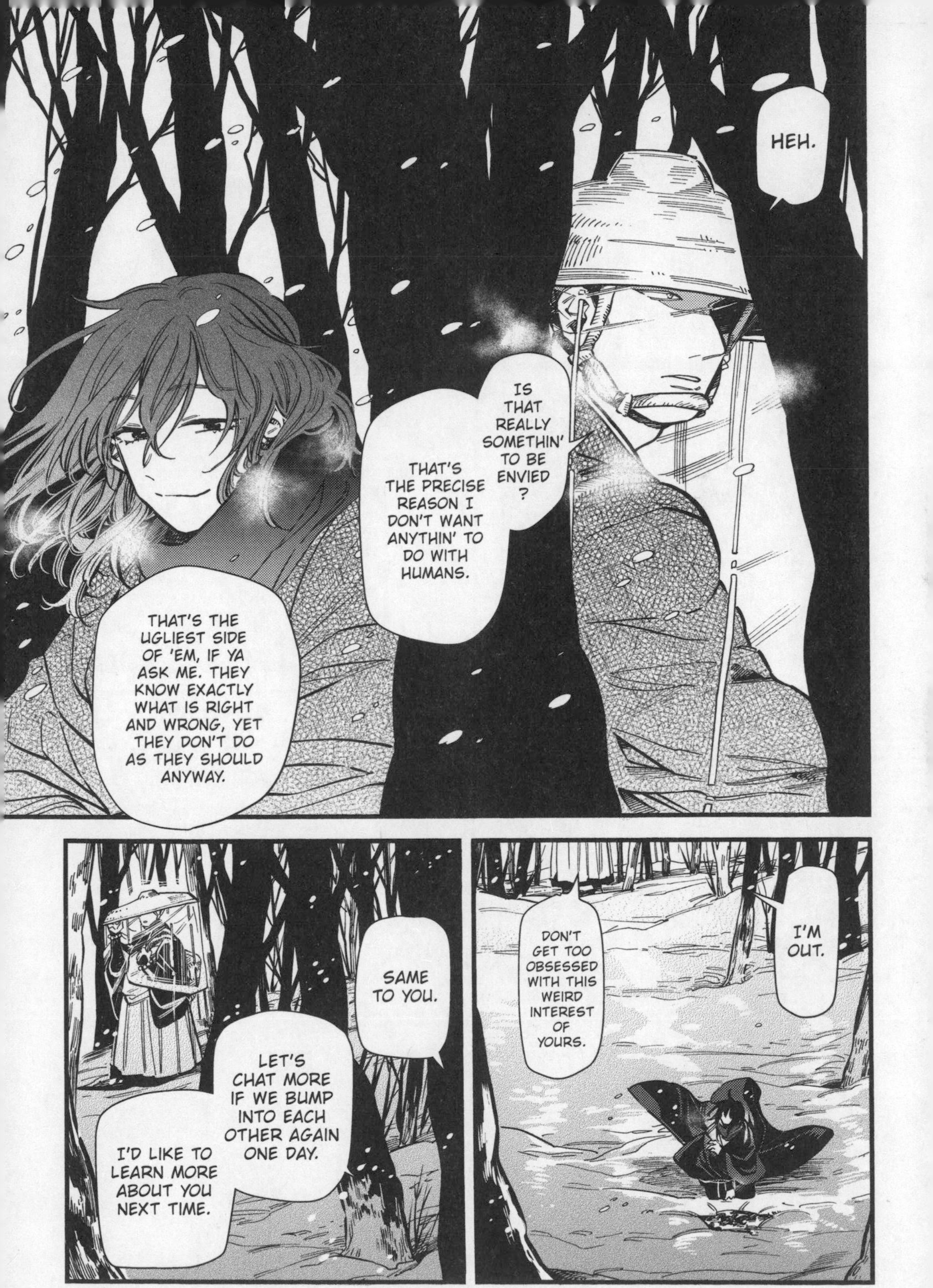
HEH.
IS THAT REALLY SOMETHIN' TO BE ENVIED?
THAT'S THE PRECISE REASON I DON'T WANT ANYTHIN' TO DO WITH HUMANS.
THAT'S THE UGLIEST SIDE OF 'EM, IF YA ASK ME. THEY KNOW EXACTLY WHAT IS RIGHT AND WRONG, YET THEY DON'T DO AS THEY SHOULD ANYWAY.
I'M OUT.
DON'T GET TOO OBSESSED WITH THIS WEIRD INTEREST OF YOURS.
SAME TO YOU.
LET'S CHAT MORE IF WE BUMP INTO EACH OTHER AGAIN ONE DAY.
I'D LIKE TO LEARN MORE ABOUT YOU NEXT TIME.

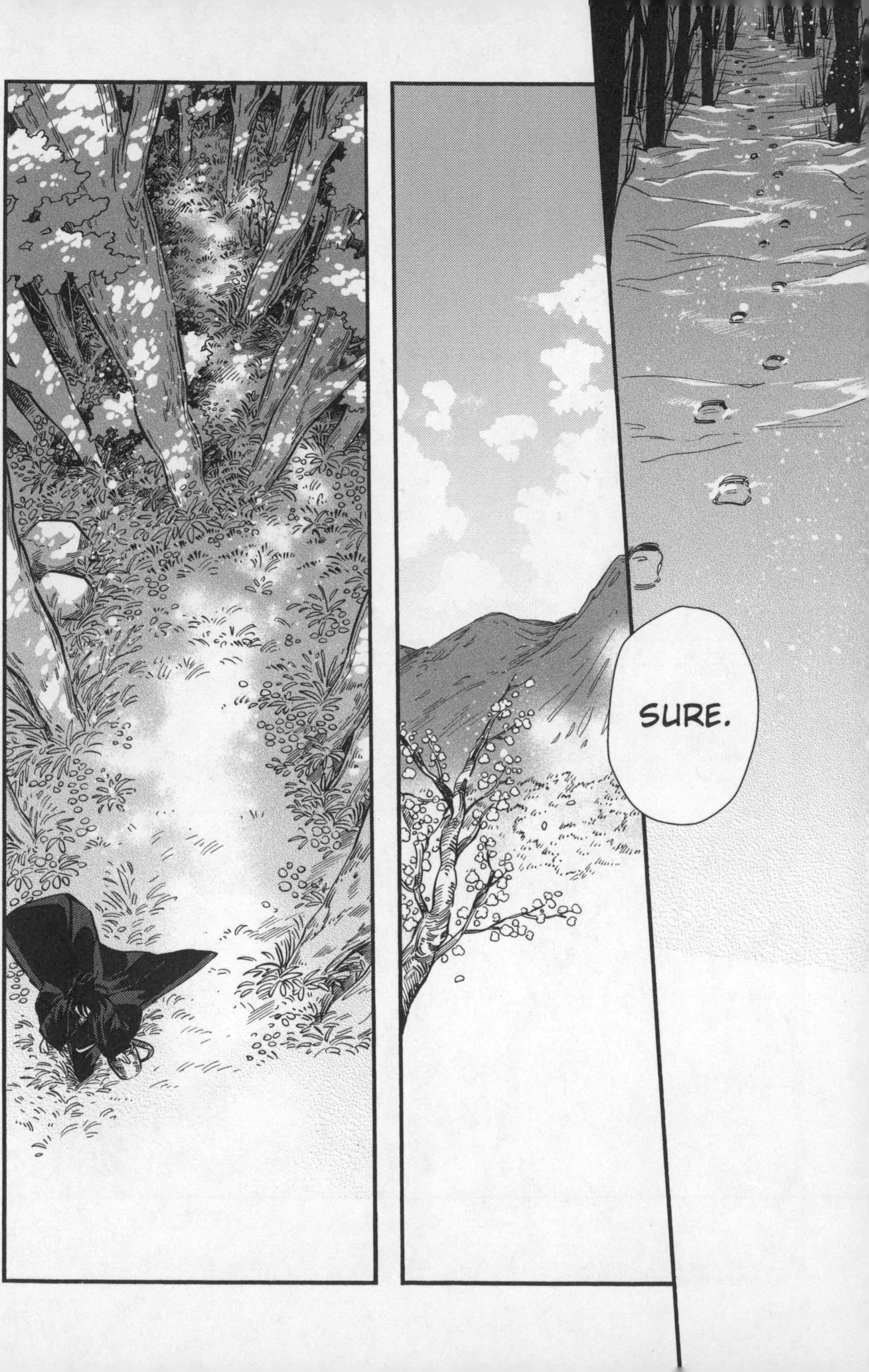
SURE.

ARE YOU ABOUT READY NOW?

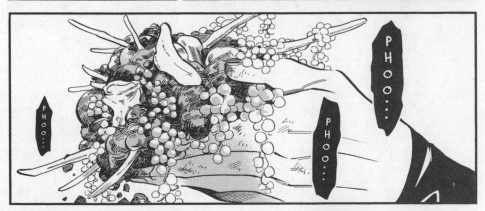

PHOO....

PHOO....

PHOO....

THERE WE ARE.

BOTO (THUNK)

173

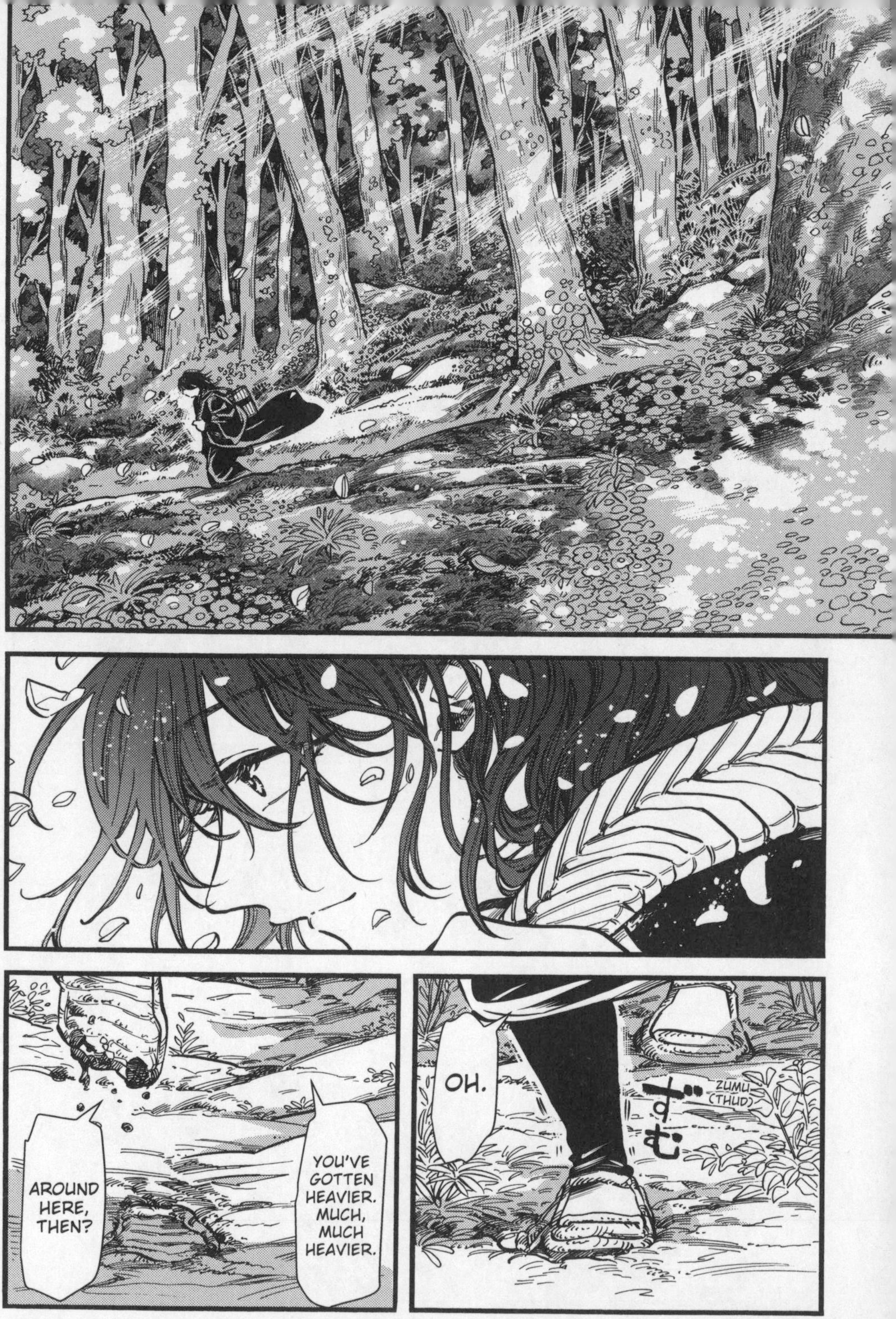
OH.
ずむ
ZUMU (THUD)
YOU'VE GOTTEN HEAVIER. MUCH, MUCH HEAVIER.
AROUND HERE, THEN?

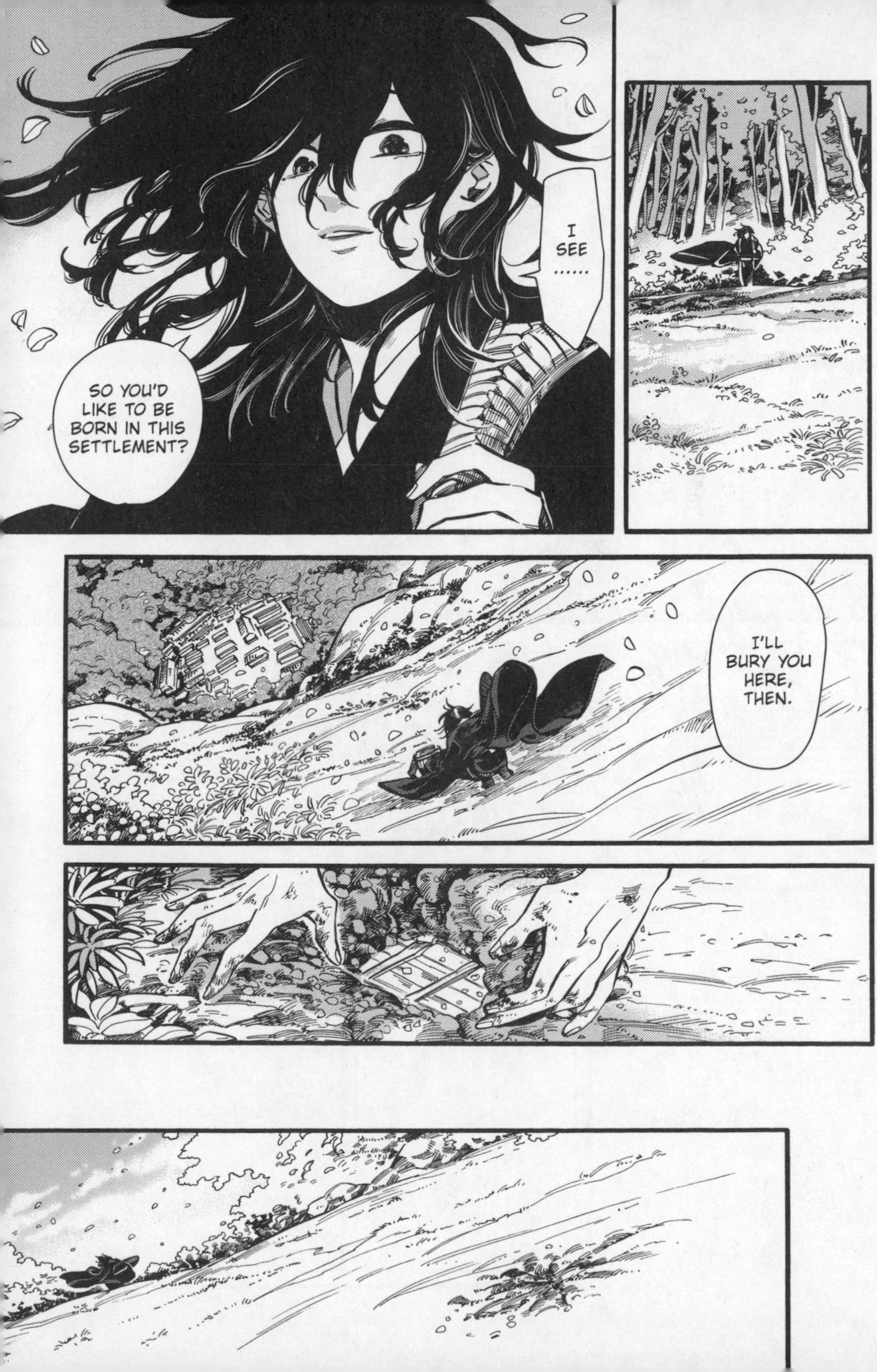
I SEE ......
SO YOU'D LIKE TO BE BORN IN THIS SETTLEMENT?
I'LL BURY YOU HERE, THEN.

Thirty-Ninth
Enigma
—
Singing
Bones

To be continued in Volume 9

Translation Notes

Common Honorifics

no honorific: Indicates familiarity or closeness; if used without permission or reason, addressing someone in this manner would constitute an insult.

***-san*:** The Japanese equivalent of Mr./Mrs./Miss. If a situation calls for politeness, this is the fail-safe honorific.

***-kun*:** Used most often when referring to boys, this indicates affection or familiarity. Occasionally used by older men among their peers, but it may also be used by anyone referring to a person of lower standing.

***-chan*:** An affectionate honorific indicating familiarity used mostly in reference to girls; also used in reference to cute persons or animals of either gender.

***-sensei*:** A respectful term for teachers, artists, or high-level professionals.

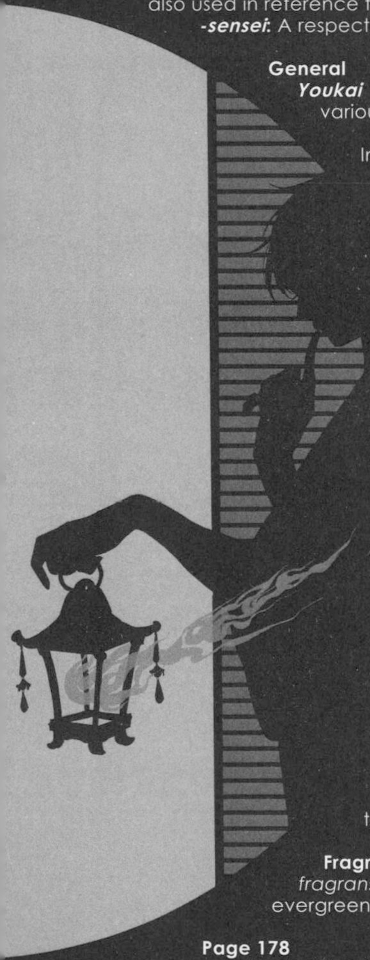

General

Youkai are a class of Japanese supernatural being, translated variously in English as "ghosts," "demons," "monsters," etc.

In Japanese, **Owner** is called *Taishou*, a term used to refer to the owners of traditional Japanese restaurants and inns. It generally means "boss" or "chief."

Spider in Japanese is *kumo*, and the character is referred to as such in Japanese. His full name, **Earth Spider**, is a translation of *tsuchigumo*, a *youkai* spider grown to gigantic size.

Butterfly in Japanese is *chou*, which is also the character's name in Japanese. His full name, **Incarnate Butterflies**, is a translation of *chou keshin*, a *youkai* consisting of butterflies merged with human souls.

Page 25

The **Special Higher Police** was a police unit established in 1911 and ultimately abolished in 1945 for controlling political thought and expression. They had branches in every prefecture, and their focus was to suppress what they considered dangerous ideologies, such as communism and socialism. The scope of their work also included censorship of works such as published literature.

Page 120

Camellia is the most common English name for *tsubaki*, which is a tree or shrub that can be used to make tea.

Fuji is the name for **wisteria**. Wisteria is a twining vine plant that usually appears in a purple color.

Fragrant olive is the common name of the plant *osmanthus fragrans aurantiacus*. This Japanese plant generally appears as an evergreen shrub or a tree with orange flowers.

Page 178

In Japan, the first food given to a baby is usually very watered-down rice porridge that is slowly made thicker as the baby gets used to eating solid food.

"**The Tale of Genji**" or *Genji Monogatari* was written by the lady-in-waiting Murasaki Shikibu in the eleventh century. It follows the story of Prince Genji and the members of his court during the Heian period (794-1185 CE). Since it was written using an archaic script and poetic verse that is not commonly used today, reading the original version of "The Tale of Genji" requires specialized study.

BONUS MANGA STARTS HERE!

BABY FOOD OR FERTILIZER

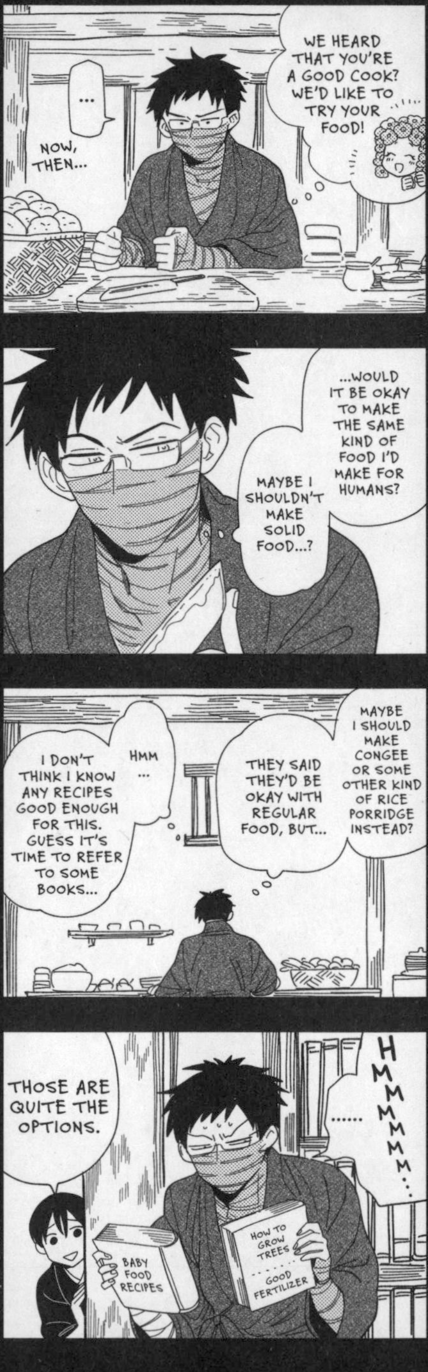
WE HEARD THAT YOU'RE A GOOD COOK? WE'D LIKE TO TRY YOUR FOOD!
...
NOW, THEN...
...WOULD IT BE OKAY TO MAKE THE SAME KIND OF FOOD I'D MAKE FOR HUMANS?
MAYBE I SHOULDN'T MAKE SOLID FOOD...?
MAYBE I SHOULD MAKE CONGEE OR SOME OTHER KIND OF RICE PORRIDGE INSTEAD?
THEY SAID THEY'D BE OKAY WITH REGULAR FOOD, BUT...
HMM...
I DON'T THINK I KNOW ANY RECIPES GOOD ENOUGH FOR THIS. GUESS IT'S TIME TO REFER TO SOME BOOKS...
HMMMMMM...
......
THOSE ARE QUITE THE OPTIONS.
HOW TO GROW TREES
GOOD FERTILIZER
BABY FOOD RECIPES

OTAKU

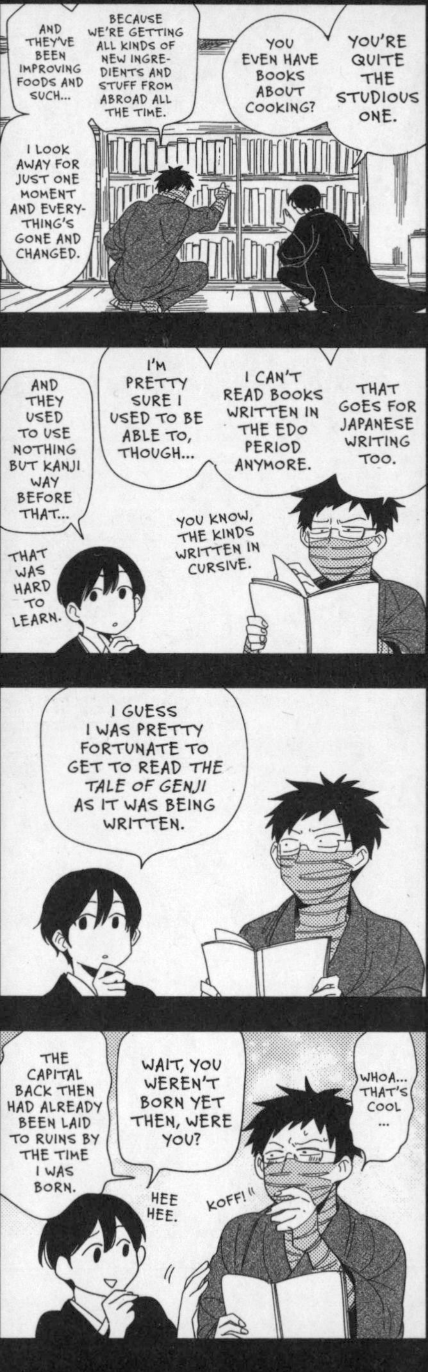
YOU'RE QUITE THE STUDIOUS ONE.
YOU EVEN HAVE BOOKS ABOUT COOKING?
BECAUSE WE'RE GETTING ALL KINDS OF NEW INGREDIENTS AND STUFF FROM ABROAD ALL THE TIME.
AND THEY'VE BEEN IMPROVING FOODS AND SUCH...
I LOOK AWAY FOR JUST ONE MOMENT AND EVERYTHING'S GONE AND CHANGED.
THAT GOES FOR JAPANESE WRITING TOO.
I CAN'T READ BOOKS WRITTEN IN THE EDO PERIOD ANYMORE.
I'M PRETTY SURE I USED TO BE ABLE TO, THOUGH...
YOU KNOW, THE KINDS WRITTEN IN CURSIVE.
AND THEY USED TO USE NOTHING BUT KANJI WAY BEFORE THAT...
THAT WAS HARD TO LEARN.
I GUESS I WAS PRETTY FORTUNATE TO GET TO READ THE TALE OF GENJI AS IT WAS BEING WRITTEN.
WHOA... THAT'S COOL...
KOFF!
WAIT, YOU WEREN'T BORN YET THEN, WERE YOU?
HEE HEE.
THE CAPITAL BACK THEN HAD ALREADY BEEN LAID TO RUINS BY THE TIME I WAS BORN.

NOT IN FOCUS

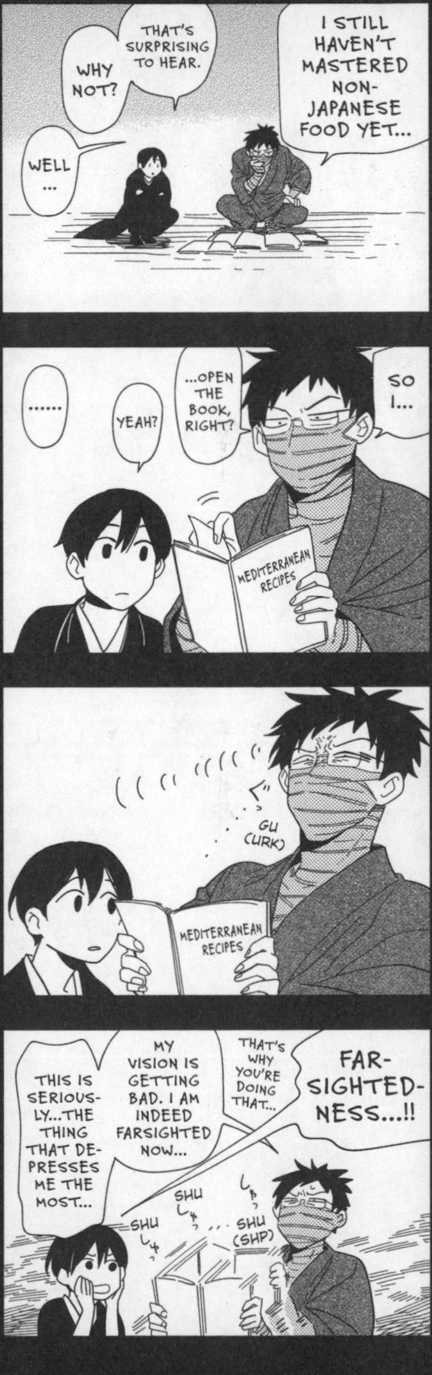
I STILL HAVEN'T MASTERED NON-JAPANESE FOOD YET...
THAT'S SURPRISING TO HEAR.
WHY NOT?
WELL ...
SO I...
...OPEN THE BOOK, RIGHT?
YEAH?
......
MEDITERRANEAN RECIPES
ぐ
GU (URK)
MEDITERRANEAN RECIPES
FAR-SIGHTED-NESS...!!
THAT'S WHY YOU'RE DOING THAT...
MY VISION IS GETTING BAD. I AM INDEED FARSIGHTED NOW...
THIS IS SERIOUSLY...THE THING THAT DEPRESSES ME THE MOST...
しゅ
SHU (SHP)
SHU しゅっ
SHU しゅっ

YOUKAI THAT WHISPER RECIPES EVERY NIGHT BY YOUR BEDSIDE PROBABLY DON'T EXIST

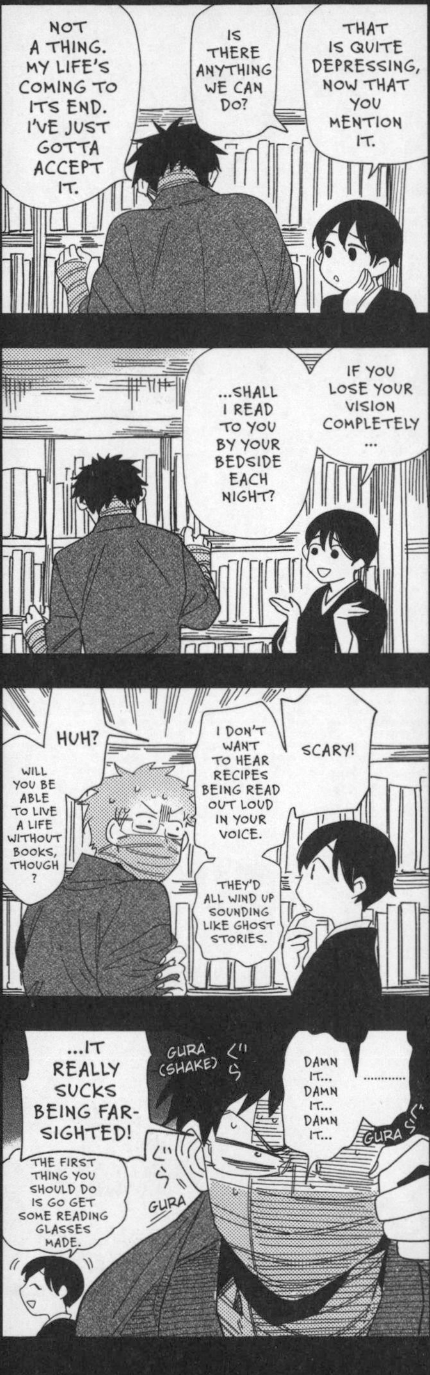
THAT IS QUITE DEPRESSING, NOW THAT YOU MENTION IT.
IS THERE ANYTHING WE CAN DO?
NOT A THING. MY LIFE'S COMING TO ITS END. I'VE JUST GOTTA ACCEPT IT.
IF YOU LOSE YOUR VISION COMPLETELY ...
...SHALL I READ TO YOU BY YOUR BEDSIDE EACH NIGHT?
SCARY!
I DON'T WANT TO HEAR RECIPES BEING READ OUT LOUD IN YOUR VOICE.
THEY'D ALL WIND UP SOUNDING LIKE GHOST STORIES.
HUH?
WILL YOU BE ABLE TO LIVE A LIFE WITHOUT BOOKS, THOUGH?
GURA
....
DAMN IT... DAMN IT... DAMN IT...
GURA (SHAKE)
...IT REALLY SUCKS BEING FAR-SIGHTED!
GURA
THE FIRST THING YOU SHOULD DO IS GO GET SOME READING GLASSES MADE.

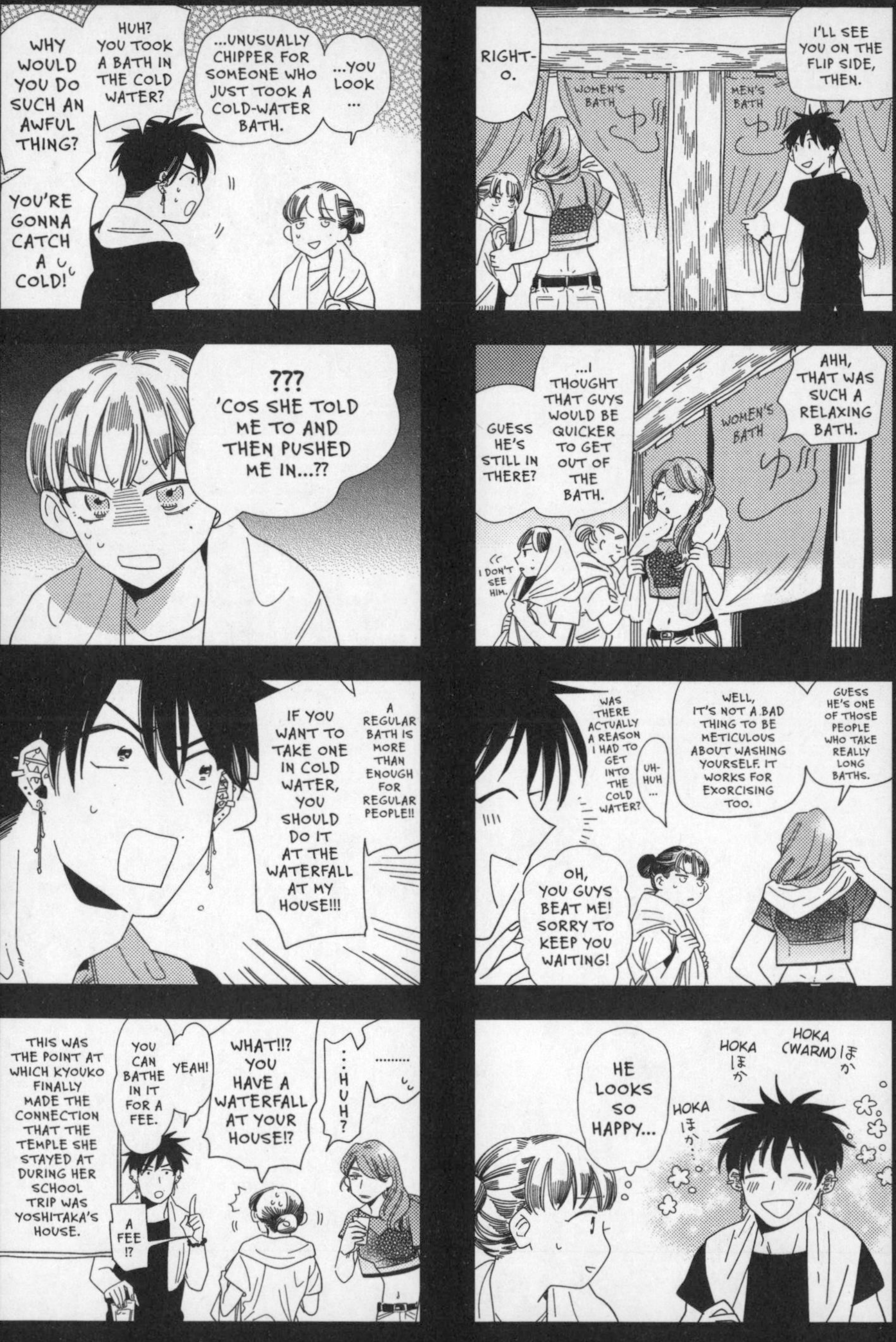
I'LL SEE YOU ON THE FLIP SIDE, THEN.
RIGHT-O.
MEN'S BATH
WOMEN'S BATH
AHH, THAT WAS SUCH A RELAXING BATH.
...I THOUGHT THAT GUYS WOULD BE QUICKER TO GET OUT OF THE BATH.
WOMEN'S BATH
GUESS HE'S STILL IN THERE?
I DON'T SEE HIM.
GUESS HE'S ONE OF THOSE PEOPLE WHO TAKE REALLY LONG BATHS.
WELL, IT'S NOT A BAD THING TO BE METICULOUS ABOUT WASHING YOURSELF. IT WORKS FOR EXORCISING TOO.
UH-HUH...
WAS THERE ACTUALLY A REASON I HAD TO GET INTO THE COLD WATER?
OH, YOU GUYS BEAT ME! SORRY TO KEEP YOU WAITING!
HOKA (WARM) ほか
HOKA ほか
HE LOOKS SO HAPPY...
HOKA ほか...
...YOU LOOK ...
...UNUSUALLY CHIPPER FOR SOMEONE WHO JUST TOOK A COLD-WATER BATH.
HUH? YOU TOOK A BATH IN THE COLD WATER?
WHY WOULD YOU DO SUCH AN AWFUL THING?
YOU'RE GONNA CATCH A COLD!
??? 'COS SHE TOLD ME TO AND THEN PUSHED ME IN...??
A REGULAR BATH IS MORE THAN ENOUGH FOR REGULAR PEOPLE!!
IF YOU WANT TO TAKE ONE IN COLD WATER, YOU SHOULD DO IT AT THE WATERFALL AT MY HOUSE!!!
....
...HUH?
WHAT!!? YOU HAVE A WATERFALL AT YOUR HOUSE!?
YEAH!
YOU CAN BATHE IN IT FOR A FEE.
THIS WAS THE POINT AT WHICH KYOUKO FINALLY MADE THE CONNECTION THAT THE TEMPLE SHE STAYED AT DURING HER SCHOOL TRIP WAS YOSHITAKA'S HOUSE.
A FEE!?

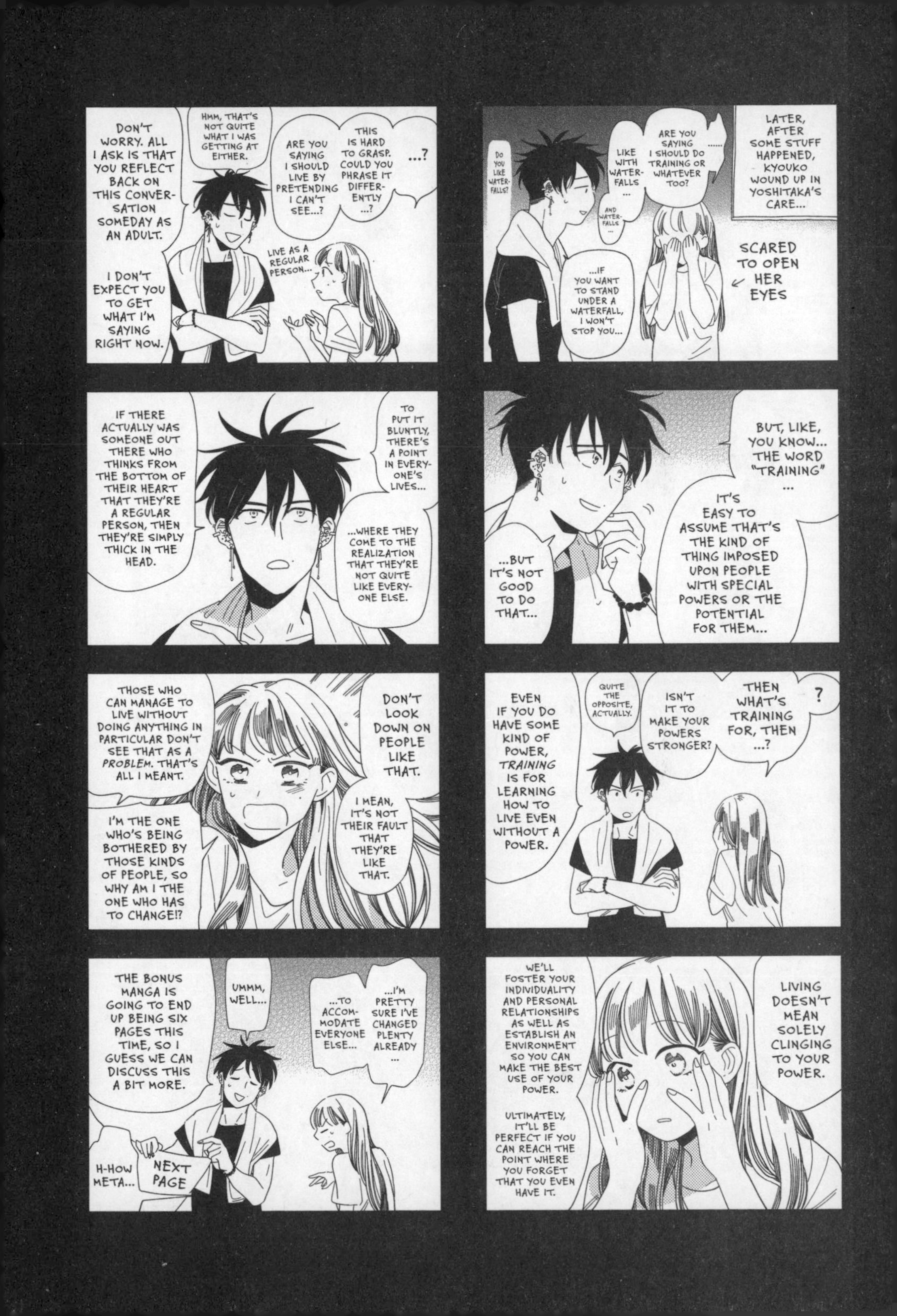
LATER, AFTER SOME STUFF HAPPENED, KYOUKO WOUND UP IN YOSHITAKA'S CARE...
......
ARE YOU SAYING I SHOULD DO TRAINING OR WHATEVER TOO?
LIKE WITH WATERFALLS...
AND WATERFALLS...
DO YOU LIKE WATERFALLS?
SCARED TO OPEN HER EYES
...IF YOU WANT TO STAND UNDER A WATERFALL, I WON'T STOP YOU...
BUT, LIKE, YOU KNOW... THE WORD "TRAINING"...
IT'S EASY TO ASSUME THAT'S THE KIND OF THING IMPOSED UPON PEOPLE WITH SPECIAL POWERS OR THE POTENTIAL FOR THEM...
...BUT IT'S NOT GOOD TO DO THAT...
?
THEN WHAT'S TRAINING FOR, THEN ...?
ISN'T IT TO MAKE YOUR POWERS STRONGER?
QUITE THE OPPOSITE, ACTUALLY.
EVEN IF YOU DO HAVE SOME KIND OF POWER, *TRAINING* IS FOR LEARNING HOW TO LIVE EVEN WITHOUT A POWER.
LIVING DOESN'T MEAN SOLELY CLINGING TO YOUR POWER.
WE'LL FOSTER YOUR INDIVIDUALITY AND PERSONAL RELATIONSHIPS AS WELL AS ESTABLISH AN ENVIRONMENT SO YOU CAN MAKE THE BEST USE OF YOUR POWER.
ULTIMATELY, IT'LL BE PERFECT IF YOU CAN REACH THE POINT WHERE YOU FORGET THAT YOU EVEN HAVE IT.
...?
THIS IS HARD TO GRASP. COULD YOU PHRASE IT DIFFERENTLY...?
ARE YOU SAYING I SHOULD LIVE BY PRETENDING I CAN'T SEE...?
HMM, THAT'S NOT QUITE WHAT I WAS GETTING AT EITHER.
DON'T WORRY. ALL I ASK IS THAT YOU REFLECT BACK ON THIS CONVERSATION SOMEDAY AS AN ADULT.
LIVE AS A REGULAR PERSON...
I DON'T EXPECT YOU TO GET WHAT I'M SAYING RIGHT NOW.
TO PUT IT BLUNTLY, THERE'S A POINT IN EVERYONE'S LIVES...
...WHERE THEY COME TO THE REALIZATION THAT THEY'RE NOT QUITE LIKE EVERYONE ELSE.
IF THERE ACTUALLY WAS SOMEONE OUT THERE WHO THINKS FROM THE BOTTOM OF THEIR HEART THAT THEY'RE A REGULAR PERSON, THEN THEY'RE SIMPLY THICK IN THE HEAD.
DON'T LOOK DOWN ON PEOPLE LIKE THAT.
I MEAN, IT'S NOT THEIR FAULT THAT THEY'RE LIKE THAT.
THOSE WHO CAN MANAGE TO LIVE WITHOUT DOING ANYTHING IN PARTICULAR DON'T SEE THAT AS A *PROBLEM*. THAT'S ALL I MEANT.
I'M THE ONE WHO'S BEING BOTHERED BY THOSE KINDS OF PEOPLE, SO WHY AM I THE ONE WHO HAS TO CHANGE!?
...I'M PRETTY SURE I'VE CHANGED PLENTY ALREADY...
...TO ACCOMMODATE EVERYONE ELSE...
UMMM, WELL...
THE BONUS MANGA IS GOING TO END UP BEING SIX PAGES THIS TIME, SO I GUESS WE CAN DISCUSS THIS A BIT MORE.
NEXT PAGE
H-HOW META...

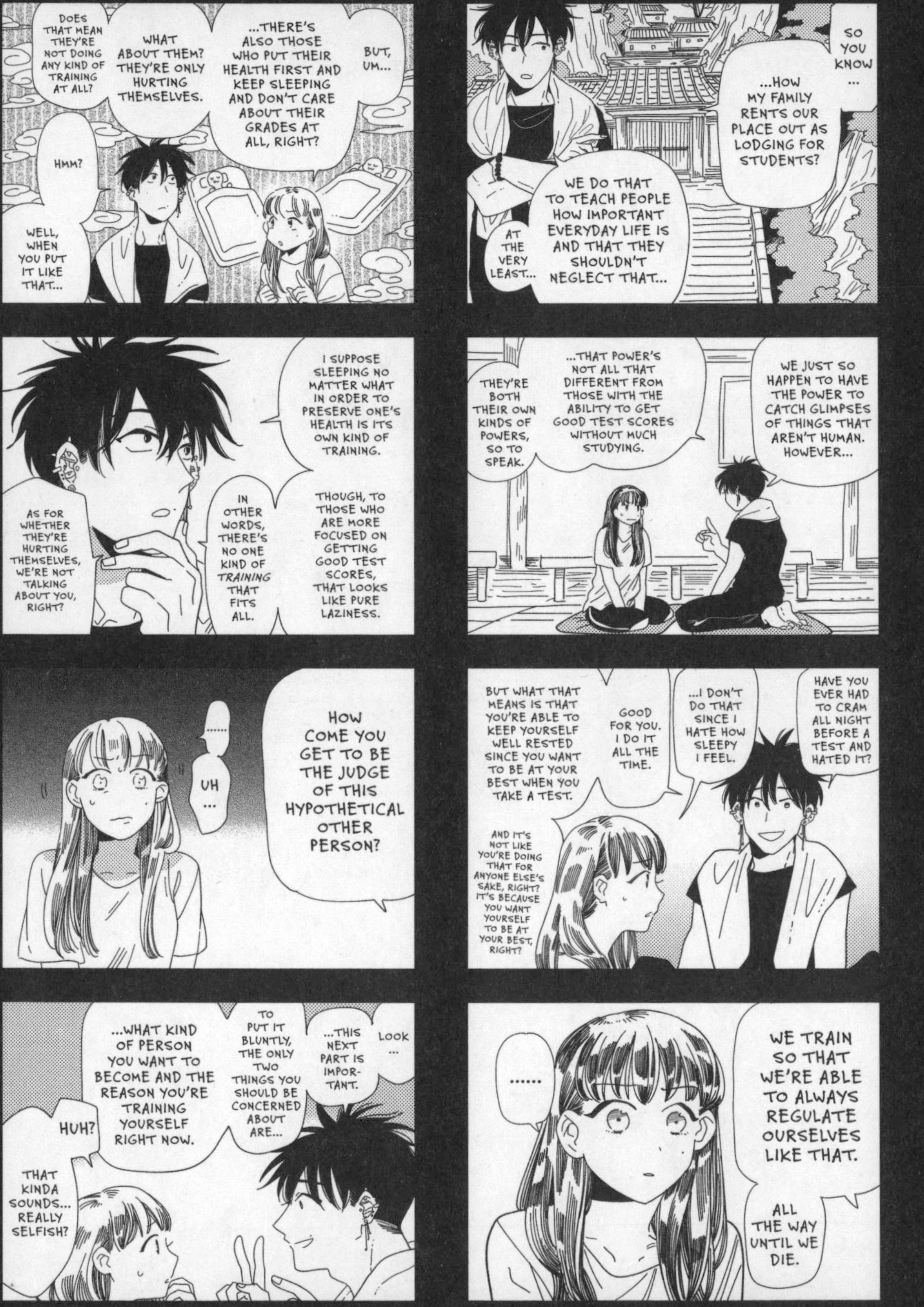
SO YOU KNOW ...
...HOW MY FAMILY RENTS OUR PLACE OUT AS LODGING FOR STUDENTS?
WE DO THAT TO TEACH PEOPLE HOW IMPORTANT EVERYDAY LIFE IS AND THAT THEY SHOULDN'T NEGLECT THAT...
AT THE VERY LEAST...
BUT, UM...
...THERE'S ALSO THOSE WHO PUT THEIR HEALTH FIRST AND KEEP SLEEPING AND DON'T CARE ABOUT THEIR GRADES AT ALL, RIGHT?
WHAT ABOUT THEM? THEY'RE ONLY HURTING THEMSELVES.
DOES THAT MEAN THEY'RE NOT DOING ANY KIND OF TRAINING AT ALL?
HMM?
WELL, WHEN YOU PUT IT LIKE THAT...
WE JUST SO HAPPEN TO HAVE THE POWER TO CATCH GLIMPSES OF THINGS THAT AREN'T HUMAN. HOWEVER...
...THAT POWER'S NOT ALL THAT DIFFERENT FROM THOSE WITH THE ABILITY TO GET GOOD TEST SCORES WITHOUT MUCH STUDYING.
THEY'RE BOTH THEIR OWN KINDS OF POWERS, SO TO SPEAK.
I SUPPOSE SLEEPING NO MATTER WHAT IN ORDER TO PRESERVE ONE'S HEALTH IS ITS OWN KIND OF TRAINING.
THOUGH, TO THOSE WHO ARE MORE FOCUSED ON GETTING GOOD TEST SCORES, THAT LOOKS LIKE PURE LAZINESS.
IN OTHER WORDS, THERE'S NO ONE KIND OF *TRAINING* THAT FITS ALL.
AS FOR WHETHER THEY'RE HURTING THEMSELVES, WE'RE NOT TALKING ABOUT YOU, RIGHT?
HAVE YOU EVER HAD TO CRAM ALL NIGHT BEFORE A TEST AND HATED IT?
...I DON'T DO THAT SINCE I HATE HOW SLEEPY I FEEL.
GOOD FOR YOU. I DO IT ALL THE TIME.
BUT WHAT THAT MEANS IS THAT YOU'RE ABLE TO KEEP YOURSELF WELL RESTED SINCE YOU WANT TO BE AT YOUR BEST WHEN YOU TAKE A TEST.
AND IT'S NOT LIKE YOU'RE DOING THAT FOR ANYONE ELSE'S SAKE, RIGHT? IT'S BECAUSE YOU WANT YOURSELF TO BE AT YOUR BEST, RIGHT?
HOW COME YOU GET TO BE THE JUDGE OF THIS HYPOTHETICAL OTHER PERSON?
......
UH ...
WE TRAIN SO THAT WE'RE ABLE TO ALWAYS REGULATE OURSELVES LIKE THAT.
......
ALL THE WAY UNTIL WE DIE.
LOOK ...
...THIS NEXT PART IS IMPOR-TANT.
TO PUT IT BLUNTLY, THE ONLY TWO THINGS YOU SHOULD BE CONCERNED ABOUT ARE...
...WHAT KIND OF PERSON YOU WANT TO BECOME AND THE REASON YOU'RE TRAINING YOURSELF RIGHT NOW.
HUH?
THAT KINDA SOUNDS... REALLY SELFISH?

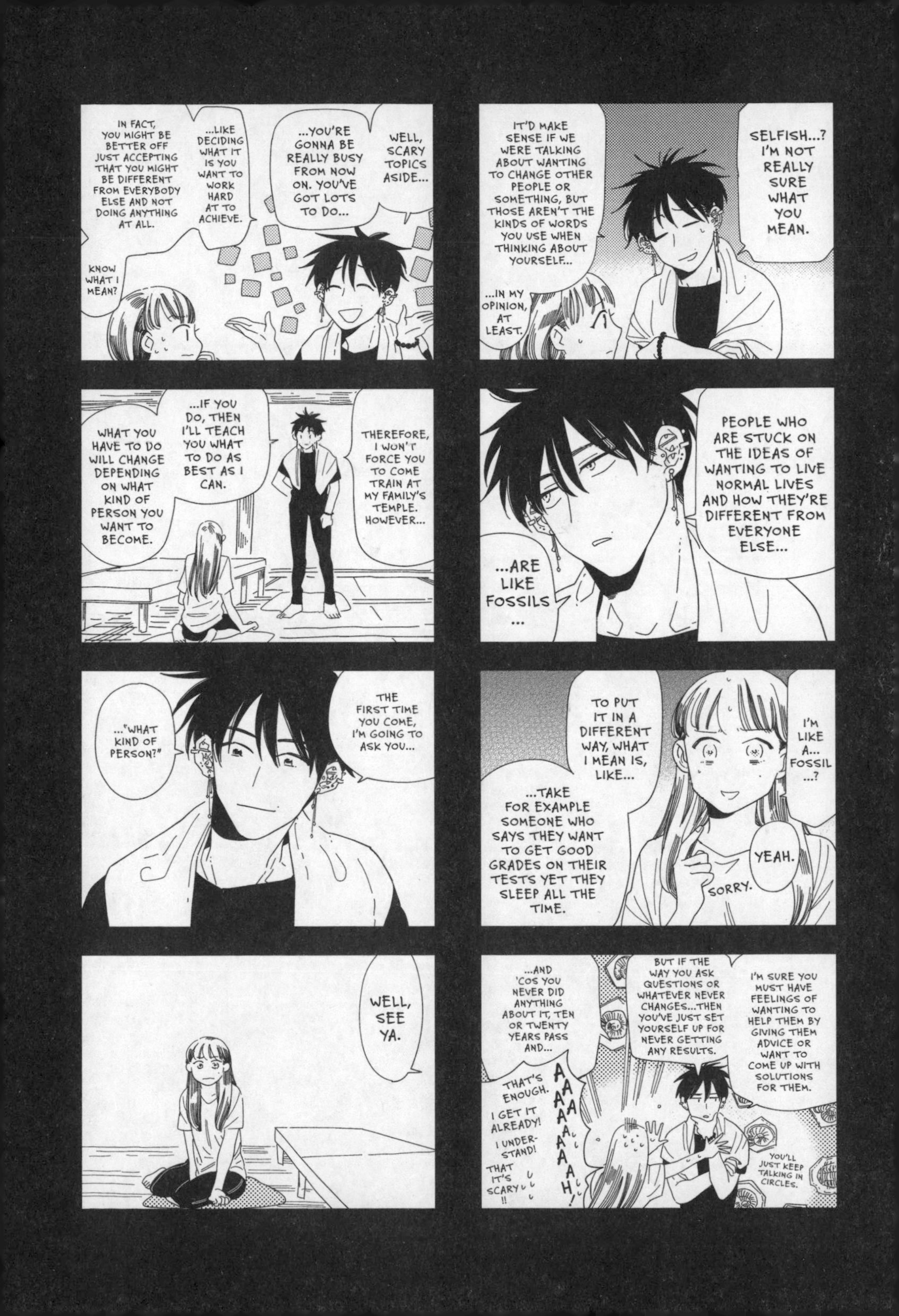
SELFISH...? I'M NOT REALLY SURE WHAT YOU MEAN.
IT'D MAKE SENSE IF WE WERE TALKING ABOUT WANTING TO CHANGE OTHER PEOPLE OR SOMETHING, BUT THOSE AREN'T THE KINDS OF WORDS YOU USE WHEN THINKING ABOUT YOURSELF...
...IN MY OPINION, AT LEAST.
PEOPLE WHO ARE STUCK ON THE IDEAS OF WANTING TO LIVE NORMAL LIVES AND HOW THEY'RE DIFFERENT FROM EVERYONE ELSE...
...ARE LIKE FOSSILS ...
I'M LIKE A... FOSSIL ...?
TO PUT IT IN A DIFFERENT WAY, WHAT I MEAN IS, LIKE...
...TAKE FOR EXAMPLE SOMEONE WHO SAYS THEY WANT TO GET GOOD GRADES ON THEIR TESTS YET THEY SLEEP ALL THE TIME.
YEAH.
SORRY.
I'M SURE YOU MUST HAVE FEELINGS OF WANTING TO HELP THEM BY GIVING THEM ADVICE OR WANT TO COME UP WITH SOLUTIONS FOR THEM.
BUT IF THE WAY YOU ASK QUESTIONS OR WHATEVER NEVER CHANGES...THEN YOU'VE JUST SET YOURSELF UP FOR NEVER GETTING ANY RESULTS.
...AND 'COS YOU NEVER DID ANYTHING ABOUT IT, TEN OR TWENTY YEARS PASS AND...
YOU'LL JUST KEEP TALKING IN CIRCLES.
THAT'S ENOUGH.
I GET IT ALREADY!
I UNDER-STAND!
THAT IT'S SCARY!!
AAAAAAAAH!
WELL, SCARY TOPICS ASIDE...
...YOU'RE GONNA BE REALLY BUSY FROM NOW ON. YOU'VE GOT LOTS TO DO...
...LIKE DECIDING WHAT IT IS YOU WANT TO WORK HARD AT TO ACHIEVE.
IN FACT, YOU MIGHT BE BETTER OFF JUST ACCEPTING THAT YOU MIGHT BE DIFFERENT FROM EVERYBODY ELSE AND NOT DOING ANYTHING AT ALL.
KNOW WHAT I MEAN?
THEREFORE, I WON'T FORCE YOU TO COME TRAIN AT MY FAMILY'S TEMPLE. HOWEVER...
...IF YOU DO, THEN I'LL TEACH YOU WHAT TO DO AS BEST AS I CAN.
WHAT YOU HAVE TO DO WILL CHANGE DEPENDING ON WHAT KIND OF PERSON YOU WANT TO BECOME.
THE FIRST TIME YOU COME, I'M GOING TO ASK YOU...
..."WHAT KIND OF PERSON?"
WELL, SEE YA.

Phantom Tales of the Night 8

Matsuri

Translation: Julie Goniwich
Lettering: Chiho Christie

This book is a work of fiction. Names, characters, places, and incidents are the product of the author's imagination or are used fictitiously. Any resemblance to actual events, locales, or persons, living or dead, is coincidental.

BAKEMONO YAWA ZUKUSHI vol. 8
©Matsuri 2021
First published in Japan in 2021 by KADOKAWA CORPORATION, Tokyo. English translation rights arranged with KADOKAWA CORPORATION, Tokyo through TUTTLE-MORI AGENCY, INC., Tokyo.

English translation © 2022 by Yen Press, LLC

Yen Press
150 West 30th Street, 19th Floor
New York, NY 10001

Visit us at yenpress.com
facebook.com/yenpress
twitter.com/yenpress
yenpress.tumblr.com
instagram.com/yenpress

First Yen Press Edition: March 2022

Yen Press is an imprint of Yen Press, LLC.
The Yen Press name and logo are trademarks of Yen Press, LLC.

The publisher is not responsible for websites (or their content) that are not owned by the publisher.

Library of Congress Control Number: 2019942895

ISBNs: 978-1-9753-3631-8 (paperback)
        978-1-9753-3632-5 (ebook)

10 9 8 7 6 5 4 3 2 1

WOR

Printed in the United States of America

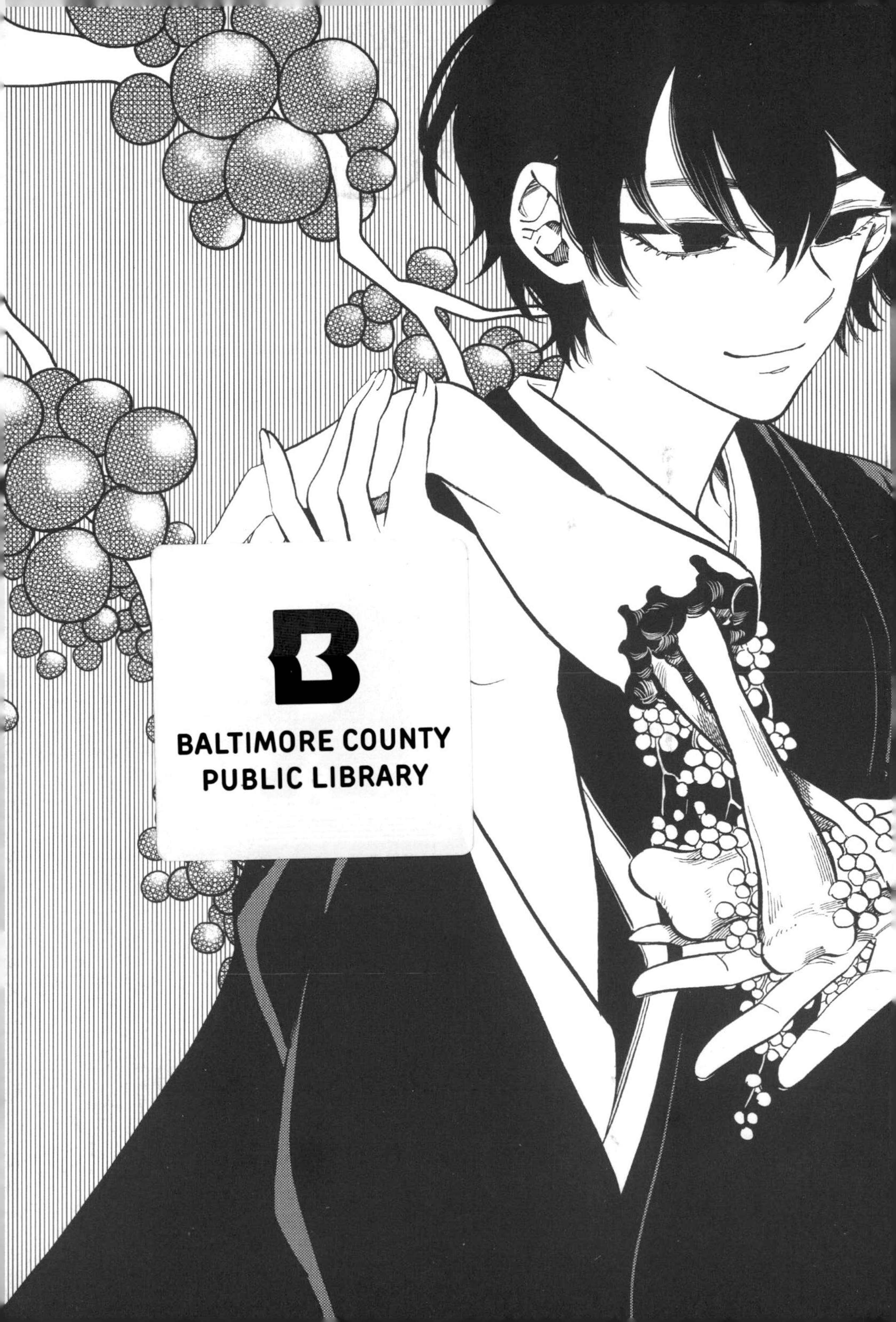

US $15.00 CAN $19.50
ISBN 978-1-9753-3631-8
EAN
9 781975 336318

OLDER TEEN OT LNV

Yen Press

Follow us on
or at yenpress.com

“The secret of your flame is quite beautiful, don’t you think?”

Murakumo Inn always welcomes the troubled masses, human or otherwise. However, payment takes one form only—your most enigmatic secrets. Tonight’s account encompasses the subject of the transmigration of souls.

Perhaps a glimpse of the final destination may be revealed in the dead of night…

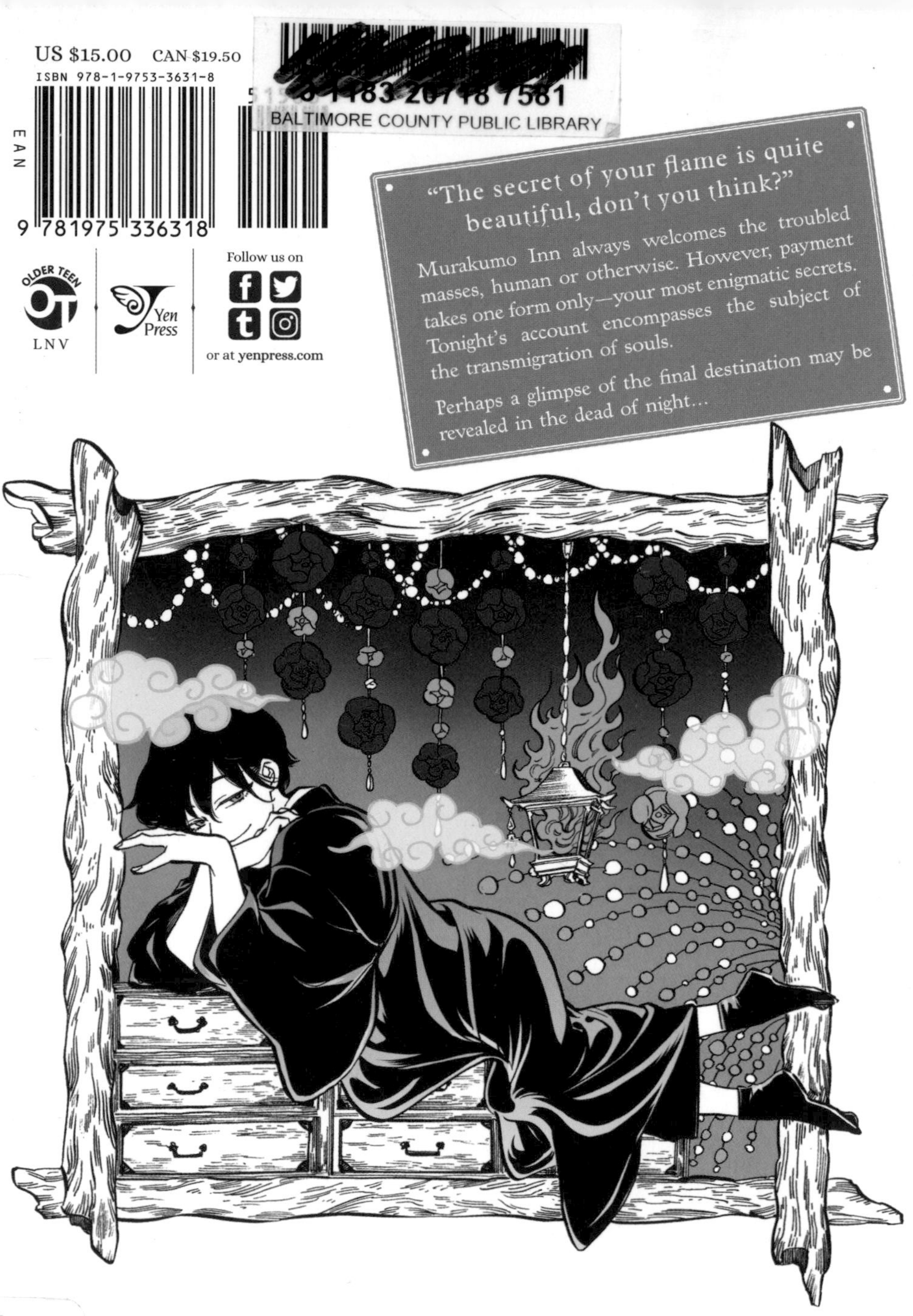